Who Is This Book For?

Visual Studio 2012 Express is available for download **completely free of charge** from Microsoft's web site. You won't need to invest in any other software in order to follow all of the exercises in this book. All you will need is a computer with Microsoft Windows 7 or Windows 8 (recommended).

This book isn't for absolute beginners. If you're just starting out you should buy our *Essential Skills* book to learn the most important features of ASP.NET, C# and Visual Studio. But if you already know the essentials of ASP.NET, C# and Visual Studio and want to take your skills to true Expert level, you've found the right book.

Having spent over 10 years developing applications with Visual Studio and managing teams of professional programmers, I can assert that completing this course will raise your skills well above those of the average professional software developer.

This book will teach you to create cutting-edge ASP.NET websites with the very latest technologies. You'll also learn advanced C# programming techniques and how to get the most out of Visual Studio. The express version of Visual Studio is used in this book. This can be downloaded **completely free of charge** from Microsoft's web site.

The book begins by introducing Visual Studio 2012's advanced features. You'll then move on to learning advanced C# programming and object-oriented programming techniques. Skills are taught in the context of web application development but can also be applied to stand-alone and other types of applications.

An entire session is dedicated to AJAX and web services, as these are some of the most important new technologies in web development today. When you have finished this session you will fully understand how AJAX works.

In the final session of the book, you'll use your skills to implement some of the most useful advanced features in use on the web today. These include running external programs, sending files from a database to a user's browser and creating 'captcha' images.

The emphasis throughout this book is on solid, professional coding practices and techniques. Instead of simple code snippets the book takes you through the process of developing high-quality, sophisticated web applications. By the end of the course you will have several working and complete applications that can be used as the basis for your own real-world commercial projects.

This book is for users who:

- Are already comfortable with the essentials of ASP.NET, C# and Visual Studio (ideally by completing our *Essential Skills* course)

- Want to take their skills to expert level

- Want to learn AJAX and web service techniques

- Want to learn about regular expressions

- Want to create advanced ASP.NET websites with cutting-edge features

Use of this book as courseware

This book is also the official courseware for The Smart Method's ASP.NET Expert Skills course.

The book is also suitable for use by other training organizations, teachers, schools and colleges to provide structured, objective-led, and highly effective classroom courses.

Learn ASP.NET 4.5, C# and Visual Studio 2012 Expert Skills with The Smart Method

Simon Smart

Published by:

The Smart Method Ltd
Burleigh Manor
Peel Road
Douglas, IOM,
Great Britain
IM1 5EP

Tel: +44 (0)845 458 3282 Fax: +44 (0)845 458 3281

E-mail: sales@ASPNETCentral.com
Web: www.ASPNETCentral.com (this book's dedicated web site)

FIRST EDITION

International Standard Book Number (ISBN13): 978-1-909253-05-6

1 2 4 6 8 10 9 7 5 4

About the Author

Simon Smart has spent the last 10 years working in almost every aspect of software development, from accounting systems to manufacturing machinery programming. Over the course of his career he has seen software move away from desktop machines and towards web-based applications like the ones covered in this book.

Starting with the earliest versions of ASP he experienced its growth into ASP.NET 4.5, spending many long hours finding out what works and what doesn't.

Simon always found books and documentation about ASP.NET to be of limited use, even to the experienced. In 2011 he set out to write a series of two books (*Essential Skills* and *Expert Skills*), hoping to pass on the knowledge gained in his years working as a programmer. To date, his books represent over 3 years of full-time work.

In his spare time, Simon can usually be found in the outdoors, roaming the forests and hills looking for new places to explore. His dad finds this amusing, particularly when it's raining.

Author's Acknowledgements

The level of our success is limited only by our imagination and no act of kindness, however small, is ever wasted.

Aesop, Greek Author (620BC – 560BC)

As with my previous books, special thanks are due to my father Mike Smart, who founded The Smart Method. Without his encouragement and support these books would never have been written.

As always, special thanks are due to everyone who helped to proofread this book and to all readers who sent in useful feedback.

Finally, I would like to thank the readers of this book. I wrote this book with the aim of giving its readers the skills they need to become experts in ASP.NET, C# and Visual Studio. I truly hope that this book will bring many people great success in their programming careers.

Contents

Appendix A: Skills Covered in the Essential Skills Course   365

Index   371

Introduction

Welcome to *Learn ASP.NET 4.5, C# and Visual Studio 2012 Expert Skills with The Smart Method.* This book has been designed to enable students to master ASP.NET by self-study. The book is equally useful as courseware for teachers who need to deliver structured, objective-based classroom courses.

Smart Method publications are continually evolving as we discover better ways of explaining or teaching the concepts presented.

Feedback

At The Smart Method we love feedback – be it positive or negative. If you have any suggestions for improvements to future versions of this book, or if you find content or typographical errors, the author would always love to hear from you via e-mail to:

feedback@ASPNETCentral.com

Future editions will always incorporate your feedback so that there are never any known errors at time of publication.

If you have any difficulty understanding or completing a lesson, or if you feel that anything could have been more clearly explained, we'd also love to hear from you. We've made hundreds of detail improvements to our books based upon reader's feedback and continue to chase the impossible goal of 100% perfection!

Downloading the sample files

In order to use this book it is sometimes necessary to download sample files from the Internet. The sample files are available from:

http://www.ASPNETCentral.com

Type the above URL into your web browser and you'll see the link to the sample files at the top of the home page.

Problem resolution

If you encounter any problem downloading or using the sample files please send an e-mail to:

feedback@ASPNETCentral.com

We'll do everything possible to quickly resolve the problem.

Typographical Conventions Used In This Book

This guide consistently uses typographical conventions to differentiate parts of the text.

When you see this	Here's what it means
Right-click on *My Project* in the Solution Explorer and then click *Build* from the shortcut menu.	Italics are used to refer to text that appears in a menu, a dialog, or elsewhere within the Visual Studio application. At times, italics may also be used for emphasis or distinction.
Click File→New Project.... ![File menu: New Project... Ctrl+Shift+N; New Web Site... Shift+Alt+N; New File... Ctrl+N]	Click on the *File* menu and choose *New Project...* from the drop-down menu.
Click Edit→Outlining→ Collapse To Definitions. ![Outlining sub-menu: Toggle Outlining Expansion Ctrl+M, Ctrl+M; Toggle All Outlining Ctrl+M, Ctrl+L; Stop Outlining Ctrl+M, Ctrl+P; Stop Hiding Current Ctrl+M, Ctrl+U; Collapse to Definitions Ctrl+M, Ctrl+O]	Click on the *Edit* menu and look for the *Outlining* sub-menu. Click the *Outlining* menu and then click on *Collapse to Definitions*.
Click Tools→Options...→Formatting→ Server tag→Assembly definition. 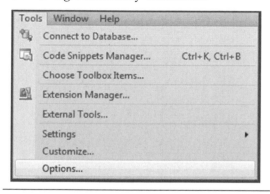	This is a more involved example. 1. Click the *Tools* menu, and then click the *Options...* button. A new dialog pops up. 2. Click on the *Formatting* group in the *Options* dialog. 3. Drop down the *Server Tag* list and click *Assembly definition*.
Type **int X;** on the next line.	Whenever you are asked to actually type something on the keyboard it is shown in bold faced text.
Press **\<Ctrl\> + \<Z\>**.	You should hold down the **Ctrl** key and then press the **Z** key.

Toolbox

When a lesson tells you to click a button, an image of the relevant button will often be shown either in the page margin or within the text itself.

note

If you switch to *Design* view and click on the properties of an object in the *Properties* window, you'll notice a short description of the property…

If you want to read through the book as quickly as possible, notes which usually expand a little on the lesson text, may be ignored.

important

Do not click the Delete button at this point as to do so would erase the entire table.

Whenever something can easily go wrong, or when the subject text is particularly important, you will see the *important* sidebar.

You should always read important sidebars.

tip

Moving between tabs using the keyboard

You can also use <Ctrl>+<Tab> on the keyboard to cycle through all of the tabs you have open.

Tips add to the lesson text by showing you shortcuts or time-saving techniques relevant to the lesson.

The bold text at the top of the tip box enables you to establish whether the tip is appropriate to your needs without reading all of the text.

In this example you may not be interested in keyboard shortcuts so you do not need to read further.

anecdote

I worked on an ASP.NET project for a gaming company a couple of years ago…

Sometimes I add an anecdote gathered over the years from my work or from other areas of my experience.

If you simply want to learn ASP.NET as quickly as possible, ignore anecdotes.

trivia

The Mosaic browser

Before 1993, the Internet was very different to the way it is today…

Sometimes I indulge myself by adding a little piece of trivia in the context of the skill being taught.

Just like my anecdotes you can ignore these if you want to. They won't help you to learn ASP.NET any better!

If you are not completing the course incrementally use the sample file: **Lesson 5-1** to begin this lesson.

When there is a sample file (or files) to accompany a session, the file name will be shown in a folder icon.

You can download the lesson or file from: *www.ASPNETCentral.com.*

Putting the Smart Method to Work

Visual Studio version and service pack

This edition was written using *Visual Web Developer 2012 Express* running under the *Microsoft Windows 8* operating system. Installing Visual Studio and checking your version is covered in Session 1 of the *Essential Skills* course in this series.

If you are using a different operating system (such as Windows 7) this book will be equally relevant, but you may notice small differences in the appearance of some of the screen grabs in the book. This will only occur when describing an operating system (rather than a Visual Studio) feature.

This book is written purely for Visual Studio 2012 Express and, due to changes in this version, some features may not be available in earlier or later versions (such as 2008 and 2010).

Sessions and lessons

The book is arranged into Sessions and Lessons. In a *Smart Method* course a Session would generally last for between forty-five and ninety minutes. Each Session would represent a continuous period of interactive instruction followed by a coffee break of ten or fifteen minutes.

When this book is used for self-instruction I recommend that you do the same. You'll learn better if you lock yourself away, switch off your telephone and complete the whole session without interruption. The memory process is associative, and each lesson within each session is very closely coupled (contextually) with the others. By learning the whole session in one sitting, you'll store all of that information in the same part of your memory and should find it easier to recall later.

The experience of being able to remember all of the words of a song as soon as somebody has got you "started" with the first line is an example of the memory's associative system of data storage.

It is highly recommend that you do take a break between sessions and spend it relaxing rather than catching up on your e-mails. This gives your brain a little idle time to do some data sorting and storage.

Read the book from beginning to end

Many books consist of disassociated self-contained chapters, often all written by different authors. This approach works well for pure reference books (such as encyclopedias). The problem with this approach is that there's no concept of building knowledge upon assumed prior knowledge, so the text is either confusing or unduly verbose as instructions for the same skill are repeated in many parts of the book.

This book is more effective as a learning tool because it takes a holistic approach. You will learn ASP.NET 4.5 in the same way you would be taught during one of our *Smart Method* courses.

In our classroom courses it's often the case that a delegate turns up late. One golden rule is that we can't begin until everybody is present, as each hands-on lesson builds upon skills taught in the previous lesson.

I strongly recommend that you read the book from beginning to end in the order in which it is written. Because of the unique presentational style, you'll hardly waste any time reading about things that you already know and even the most advanced ASP.NET developer will find some nugget of extremely useful information in every session.

How this book avoids wasting your time

> Nobody has things just as he would like them. The thing to do is to make a success with what material I have.
>
> *Dr. Frank Crane (1861–1928), American clergyman and journalist*

The only material available to me in teaching you ASP.NET is the written word and sample files. I'd rather have you sitting next to me in a classroom, but Frank Crane would have told me to stop complaining and use the tools I have in the most effective way.

Over the years I have read many hundreds of computer text books. Most of my time was wasted. The main problem with most books is having to wade through thousands of words just to learn one important technique. Not reading everything could mean missing that one essential insight.

This book utilizes some of the tried and tested techniques developed after teaching vast numbers of people during many years of delivering *Smart Method* classroom courses.

As you'll see in this section, many presentational methods are used to help you to avoid reading about things you already know, or things that are of little interest.

Why our classroom courses work so well

In our classroom courses we don't waste time teaching skills that the delegates already know. If it is clear that the delegate already understands a skill no time is wasted explaining it, but if the delegate has difficulty, more information is given until success is demonstrated.

Another key to learning effectively is to teach only the best way to accomplish a task. For example, you can comment code by typing two forward slashes or you can click the shortcut buttons on the toolbar. Because typing forward slashes is the easiest, fastest and most intuitive method, only this is practiced in the classroom. In the book we do mention the alternatives, but only in a sidebar.

How this book mimics our classroom technique

Here's a lesson step:

---

tip

Comment shortcuts using the toolbar

You can quickly comment and uncomment code using the comment buttons on the toolbar:

1   Add a basic comment.

   1.   Add a new line before:

       return RoundNumber(FirstNumber + SecondNumber);

   2.   Add a comment with the code:

       //Add FirstNumber and SecondNumber

       You'll see that the comment is shown in green.

If you already know how to add a comment, read only the line: *Add a basic comment* and just do it. Don't waste your time reading anything else.

Read the smaller print only when the information is new to you.

If you're in a hurry to learn only the essentials, as fast as possible, don't bother with the sidebars unless they are labeled **important**.

Read the sidebars only when you want to know everything and have the time and interest.

Avoiding repetition

2	Open the code-behind file of *default.aspx*.
	You learned how to do this in: *Lesson 1 7: Manage a project with the Solution Explorer.*

A goal of this book (and in our classroom courses) is not to waste your time by explaining any skill twice.

In a classroom course, a delegate will sometimes forget something that has already been covered that day. The instructor must then try to get the student to remember and drop little hints reminding them about how they completed the task earlier.

This isn't possible in a book, so I've made extensive use of cross references in the text pointing you back to the lesson in which the relevant skill was learned. The cross references also help when you use this book as a reference work but have forgotten the more basic skills needed to complete each step.

Use of American English

American English (rather than British English) spelling has been used throughout. This is because the help system and screen elements all use American English spelling, making the use of British English confusing.

Examples of differences are the British English spelling: *Colour* and *Dialogue* as opposed to the American English spelling: *Color* and *Dialog*.

Because this book is available worldwide, much care has been taken to avoid any country-specific terminology. For example, in most of the English speaking world, apart from North America, the symbol # is referred to as the **hash sign**, so the term *hash* is used throughout this book.

First page of a session

1/ The first page begins with a quotation, often from an era before the age of the computer, that is particularly pertinent to the session material. As well as being fun, this helps us to remember that all of the real-world problems we solve with technology have been around for a long time.

3/ The session objectives *formally* state the precise skills that you will learn in the session.

At the end of the session you should re-visit the objectives and not progress to the next session until you can honestly agree that you have achieved them.

In a *Smart Method* course we never progress to the next session until all delegates are completely confident that they have achieved the previous session's objectives.

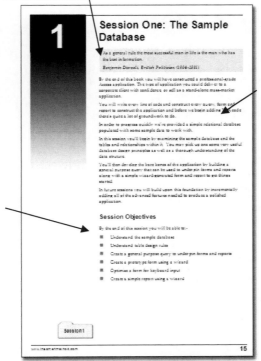

2/ In the next few paragraphs we *informally* summarise why the session is important and the benefits that can be gained.

This is important because without motivation adults do not learn. For adults, learning is a means to an end and not an end in itself.

The aim of the introduction is to motivate your retention of the skills that will be taught in the following session by allowing you to preview the relevance of the material that will be presented. This may subconsciously put your brain into "must remember this" mode—assuming, of course, that the introduction convinces you that the skills will be useful to you!

Every lesson is presented on two facing pages

> Pray this day, on one side of one sheet of paper, explain how the Royal Navy is prepared to meet the coming conflict.
> *Winston Churchill, Letter to the Admiralty, Sep 1, 1939*

Winston Churchill was well aware of the power of brevity. The discipline of condensing thoughts into one side of a single sheet of A4 paper resulted in the efficient transfer of information.

A tenet of our teaching system is that every lesson is presented on *two* facing sheets of A4. We've had to double Churchill's rule as they didn't have to contend with screen grabs in 1939!

If we can't teach an essential concept in two pages of A4 we know that the subject matter needs to be broken into two smaller lessons.

Tips, important information and notes appear in sidebars.

Each step is numbered and begins with the thing you need to do in bold type. Sometimes this is all you need to read to accomplish the task.

Step notes sometimes provide precise instructions on how to progress if the one-line description is inadequate. Notes often also include interesting information about the current task.

If you are not working through the course sequentially, a file is available on our web site that contains the starting point for every lesson. The file name you need to download is stated in the file icon at bottom left of every lesson page.

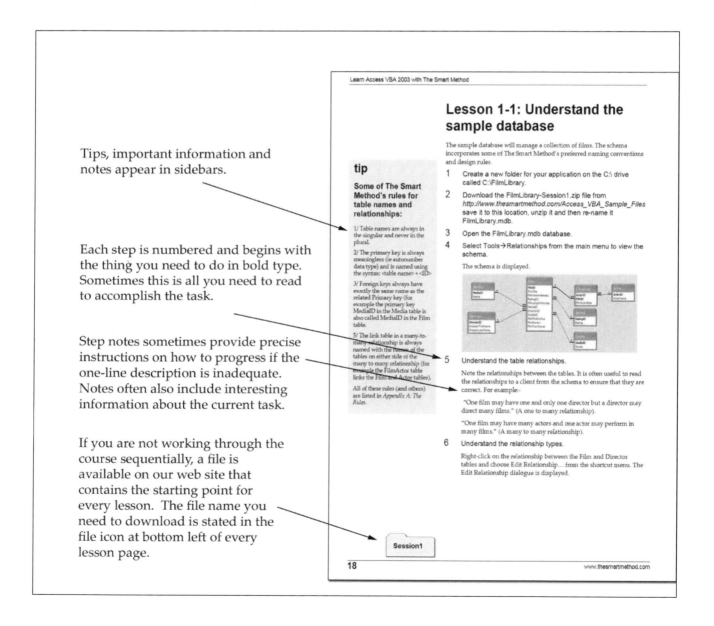

Learning by participation

Tell me, and I will forget. Show me, and I may remember. Involve me, and I will understand.

Confucius (551-479 BC)

Confucius would probably have agreed that the best way to teach IT skills is hands-on (actively) and not hands-off (passively). This is another of the principal tenets of the *Smart Method* teaching system. Research has backed up the assertion that you will learn more material, learn more quickly, and understand more of what you learn, if you learn using active, rather than passive methods.

For this reason pure theory pages are kept to an absolute minimum with most theory woven into the hands-on sessions either within the text or in sidebars. This echoes the teaching method in Smart Method courses, where snippets of pertinent theory are woven into the lessons themselves so that interest and attention is maintained by hands-on involvement, but all necessary theory is still covered.

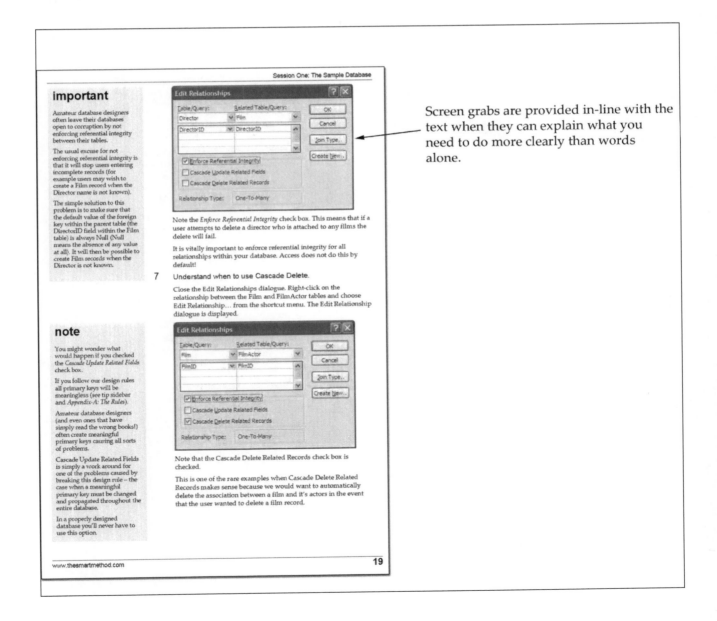

Screen grabs are provided in-line with the text when they can explain what you need to do more clearly than words alone.

Session One: Advanced Visual Studio features

Any sufficiently advanced technology is indistinguishable from magic.

Arthur C. Clarke, English physicist & science fiction author (born 1917)

The most important features of Visual Studio were covered in the *Essential Skills* course in this series, but Visual Studio contains a host of more advanced features that can make working with ASP.NET a lot easier.

In this session you'll discover Visual Studio's advanced code editing tools and how to use them to speed up writing and working with C# code.

This session also shows you how to work with advanced settings to change how Visual Studio compiles your project.

Session Objectives

By the end of this session you will be able to:

- Convert a Web Site project into a Web Forms Application project
- Add references to a project
- Use the Debug and Release profiles
- Build, Rebuild and Clean a project
- Change Build options
- Change Web options
- Change the version of ASP.NET that is used by the project
- Create an XML documentation file
- Use the Error List window
- Understand the Output window
- Use the Immediate window
- Use Code Snippets
- Use Surround With
- Use the Extract Method refactoring utility
- Use the Rename refactoring utility
- Understand NuGet packages

Lesson 1-1: Convert a Web Site project into a Web Forms Application project

In Session 1 of the *Essential Skills* course in this series, you learned how to create and open Web Site and Web Forms Application projects and learned about the differences between them.

Web Forms Application projects are generally a better option than Web Site projects (see sidebar), but you might have to work on a Web Site project that was created by another developer. In this case it is useful to convert it into a Web Forms Application project.

1 Open the *JoesBar* project from your sample files folder.

This is a Web Site project. Web Forms Application projects are preferred, so you're going to convert it.

Before you can convert a Web Site project into a Web Forms Application project, you will need a Project (.csproj) file. Web Site projects don't have their own Project file, so you will have to create a new project in order to do this.

2 Add a new project to the solution.

1. Click File→Add→New Project.

   The *Add New Project* dialog appears.

2. Expand *Visual C#* in the left-hand pane and click *Web*.

3. Click *ASP.NET Empty Web Application* in the central pane.

4. Type **JoesBarWebApplication** into the *Name* box.

5. Click *Browse* and navigate to your sample files folder.

   If you have installed your sample files to the recommended location, this will be: **C:\Practice\ASP.NET45 Expert**

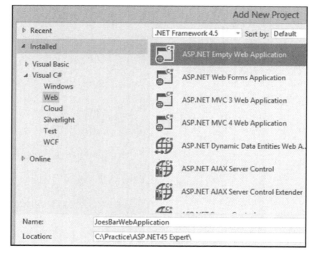

6. Click *Select Folder* and then click *OK*.

The new project is added to the solution.

3 Copy the files from the *JoesBar* project into the new *JoesBarWebApplication* project.

1. In the *Solution Explorer,* select all of the files and folders for the *JoesBar* project.

   To do this, click the *Images* folder, then hold down **<SHIFT>** and click the first *Web.config* file.

2. Right-click on the selected files and click *Copy* from the shortcut menu.

3. Right-click on the *JoesBarWebApplication* project and click *Paste* from the shortcut menu.

   A dialog appears, prompting you to overwrite the *Web.config* file in the new project.

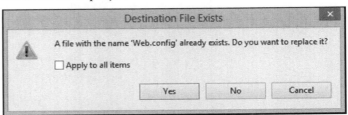

4. Tick *Apply to all items* and click *Yes*.

All of the files from the *JoesBar* project are copied into the *JoesBarWebApplication* project.

4 Convert the files from the Web Site project so that they will work within the new Web Application project.

1. Right-click *JoesBarWebApplication* in the *Solution Explorer* and click *Convert to Web Application* from the shortcut menu.

   It would be logical to expect to be able to simply do this with the original *JoesBar* project but Visual Studio doesn't allow you to do this. You have to use the technique taught in this lesson.

2. Click *Yes* to confirm that you want to convert the project.

   After a short delay, the files are all converted to work in the new Web Application project.

   You must do this when copying files from a Web Site project into a Web Forms Application project or certain aspects of the project will not work properly.

5 Test your new Web Forms Application project.

1. Click the *JoesBarWebApplication* project in the *Solution Explorer*.

2. Click Debug→Start Debugging.

The site is displayed in your web browser, proving that the conversion worked correctly.

Problems when converting Web Site projects into Web Forms Application projects

The Web Site project that you convert in this example is very simple and is unlikely to cause any problems. Very large projects, however, can experience some issues when converting between project types.

The most likely problem is that your new project doesn't have the same references as the original. Add any missing references to your new project and the problem will disappear.

You'll learn about adding references in: *Lesson 1-2: Add references to a project.*

Sometimes there can also be issues converting files in the *App_Code* folder of a Web Site project if they are copied along with all of the other files in the project. To work around this, first copy the *App_Code* folder and run the *Convert to Web Application* option and then repeat the process for the rest of the files in the project.

Lesson 1-2: Add references to a project

The *using* keyword allows you to access a vast array of features from the .NET framework, but you're only able to access classes that your project has a *reference* to.

The *using* keyword is covered in Session 6 of the *Essential Skills* course.

In this lesson you'll learn how to add new references to your projects, enabling you to work with custom class libraries and components.

1   Close Visual Studio if it is open.

2   Open *JoesBarWebApplication.csproj* from your sample files folder.

note

I can't open the project!

Some users have reported problems opening the *JoesBarWebApplication* project.

If you're unable to open the project by double-clicking *JoesBarWebApplication.csproj,* try the following steps:

1. Close any Visual Studio windows.

2. Right-click *JoesBarWebApplication.csproj* and click:
Open With→Microsoft Visual Studio Express 2012 for Web

The project will open successfully and will open normally from now on.

There's a common glitch in Visual Studio that can prevent it from opening a .csproj file the first time you try. See sidebar for a work-around if the file will not open.

You may have noticed that the *Joe's Bar* site needs to be able to send e-mail messages. You're going to add a reference to a class library called *MailModule*, which you'll then use to send an e-mail.

3   Expand *References* in the *Solution Explorer*.

You can now see all of the references that are currently added to the project. These are all parts of the .NET framework, but this isn't a complete list of the class libraries that the .NET framework has to offer.

4   Open the *Add Reference* dialog.

Right-click *References* in the *Solution Explorer* and click *Add Reference* from the shortcut menu.

5   Examine the *Framework* options.

Expand *Assemblies* and click *Framework* (if it isn't selected already).

Reference Manager	
▲ Assemblies	Targeting: .NET Framework 4.5
Framework	Name
Extensions	☐ Accessibility
	CustomMarshalers

You can now see a list showing all of the class libraries within the .NET framework. It is possible to add a reference to any of these libraries by ticking the boxes and clicking *OK*.

6   Expand the *COM* group and examine the options.

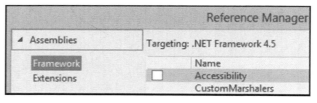

If you are not completing the course incrementally use the sample file: **Lesson 1-2** to begin this lesson.

Sample files with the starting point for each lesson are also provided for all of the other lessons in this session.

COM stands for Component Object Model. Before the .NET framework was introduced, COM components were the only way to add external components to a project. This often caused problems, because the COM components had to be installed on any machine that ran the software.

The .NET framework has mostly replaced COM components and it is unusual to need one, but there may be obscure features that are still only available as COM components. You can access these here, but it isn't likely that you'll ever need to.

7   Add a reference to *MailModule.dll*.

1.   Click the *Browse* button at the bottom of the window.

2.   Browse to your sample files folder.

3.   Click *MailModule.dll*.

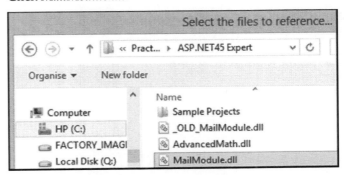

This is a very simple class library that I've created and only contains one method. You'll learn how to create class libraries of your own in: *Lesson 4-4: Create a class library.*

4.   Click *Add* and click *OK*.

The reference is added and appears in the *References* list.

8   Examine the components of the new *MailModule* reference.

1.   Open the code-behind file of *Default.aspx*.

2.   Add the following code to the end of the *ButtonSignUpEmail_Click* event handler:

MailModule.MailModule.SendEmail(

The IntelliSense menu appears, displaying the arguments of the *SendEmail* method from the *MailModule* class library.

```
MailModule.MailModule.SendEmail(
  bool MailModule.SendEmail(string From, string To, string Subject, string Message)
  Basic email method. Returns true if mail is sent successful, false if there is a problem.
  From: Email sender.
```

3.   Delete the code that you typed.

You're going to revisit the *MailModule* class library later. For the moment, remove the code you've added.

Lesson 1-3: Use the Debug and Release profiles

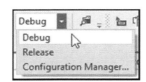

You might have noticed a drop-down menu on the top toolbar of Visual Studio which has the options *Debug* and *Release*. These are called *build profiles*.

1   Open *JoesBarWebApplication.sln* from your sample files folder (if it isn't open already).

2   Build the project.

Right-click on *JoesBarWebApplication* in the *Solution Explorer* and click *Build* from the shortcut menu.

You can also do this by clicking Build→Build JoesBarWebApplication.

Building a project compiles all of its C# code into a DLL (Dynamic Link Library) file.

3   View the compiled code in Windows Explorer.

1. Navigate to your sample files folder using Windows Explorer.

2. Open the *JoesBarWebApplication* folder.

3. Open the *obj* folder.

4. Open the *Debug* folder.

This folder contains all of the compiled *DLL* files used by the project, along with some other files created by the compiler.

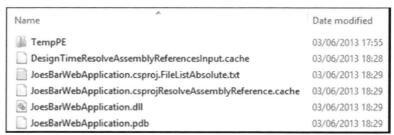

The *JoesBarWebApplication.dll* file contains all of the project's C# code in a compiled form that can be used by a web server.

4   Switch to the *Release* build profile.

1. Return to Visual Studio.

2. Click the drop-down menu on the top toolbar.

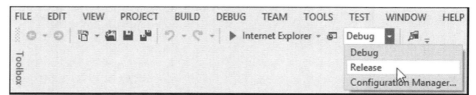

If your toolbars look different, you may need to reset your Visual Studio layout. This was covered in: *Lesson 1-1: Convert a Web Site project into a Web Forms Application* project *(sidebar)*.

3. Select *Release* from the drop-down menu.

5   Build the project again.

Right-click *JoesBarWebApplication* in the *Solution Explorer* and click *Build* from the shortcut menu.

6   View the new compiled code in Windows Explorer.

Using Windows Explorer, navigate back to the *obj* folder inside the *JoesBarWebApplication* folder.

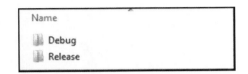

A new *Release* folder has appeared. This folder contains another compiled version of the *JoesBarWebApplication* project.

The *Release* profile's settings are optimized for the final release of a project, while the *Debug* profile's settings are optimized to be easy to work with during the development process.

By using the two profiles, you can keep a compiled *Release* version while still being able to work with your *Debug* version.

7   Create a custom build profile called: **MyProfile**

1. Return to Visual Studio.

2. Click the build profiles drop-down menu on the top toolbar and click *Configuration Manager...*

   The *Configuration Manager* dialog appears.

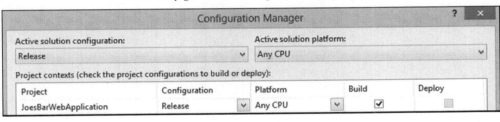

3. Click the *Active solution configuration:* drop-down menu and choose *<New...>*.

4. Type **MyProfile** into the *Name* box.

5. Select *Debug* from the *Copy settings from:* drop-down menu.

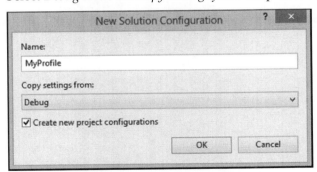

6. Click *OK*.

7. Click *Close*.

8. Click the build profiles drop-down menu on the top toolbar.

   MyProfile appears in the list. This profile is currently identical to the *Debug* profile.

   You'll learn how to customize build profiles in: *Lesson 1-5: Change Build options*.

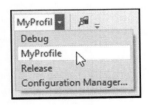

Lesson 1-4: Build, Rebuild and Clean a project

When you built the project in: *Lesson 1-3: Use the Debug and Release profiles,* you might have noticed the *Clean* and *Rebuild* options in the shortcut menu.

You'll learn how to use *Clean* and *Rebuild* in this lesson.

1 Open the *JoesBarWebApplication* folder in Windows Explorer.

You'll find it in your sample files folder.

2 Open the *bin* folder and examine its contents.

Whenever you build the project, a copy of its compiled code is placed into this folder (as well as the original compiled code in the *obj* folder) regardless of which build profile you use.

The *bin* folder is only used by Visual Studio's debugger. These are the files that are used by the virtual web server when you run a project in debug mode.

3 Open *JoesBarWebApplication.sln* in Visual Studio.

Don't close Windows Explorer as you'll return to the *bin* folder in a moment.

4 Build the project.

Right-click *JoesBarWebApplication* in the *Solution Explorer* and click *Build* from the shortcut menu.

Building the project compiles its code into a DLL file, but a new DLL file will only be created if the code has changed.

Note that the project is automatically built every time you start debugging.

5 Examine the contents of the *bin* folder again.

If you examine the *Date modified* fields, you can see that building the project has not changed the *dll* files. The code hasn't changed since the project was last built, so Visual Studio didn't bother to rebuild the files.

Note that the *MailModule.dll* and *MailModule.xml* files are never updated when you build this project. This is because *MailModule.dll* is not created by this project's C# code.

You added *MailModule.dll* to this project in: *Lesson 1-2: Add references to a project.*

6 Clean the project.

1. Return to Visual Studio.

2. Right-click *JoesBarWebApplication* in the *Solution Explorer* and click *Clean* from the shortcut menu.

7 Examine the contents of the *bin* folder again.

The *bin* folder is now completely empty. Cleaning the project removes all of the compiled files from the *bin* folder.

This folder is empty.

Cleaning also removes the compiled files (the *dll* files and other compiled files) from the *obj* folder for the selected build profile (See: *Lesson 1-3: Use the Debug and Release profiles*).

8 Build the project again.

1. Return to Visual Studio.

2. Right-click *JoesBarWebApplication* in the *Solution Explorer* and click *Build* from the shortcut menu.

9 Examine the *bin* folder again.

The compiled files have reappeared, but if you look at the *Date modified* field you can see that *JoesBarWebApplication.dll* has actually been recreated (recompiled) this time.

The *MailModule* files have also been copied from the location pointed to by the project's references.

Name	Date modified	Type
JoesBarWebApplication.dll	03/06/2013 18:44	Application extens...
JoesBarWebApplication.pdb	03/06/2013 18:44	PDB File
MailModule.dll	03/06/2013 13:32	Application extens...
MailModule.xml	03/06/2013 13:32	XML Document

This is a more complete way of rebuilding your project, but it's a little inconvenient to both *Clean* and *Build* every time you want to do this. This is why the *Rebuild* option exists.

10 Rebuild the project.

1. Return to Visual Studio.

2. Right-click *JoesBarWebApplication* in the *Solution Explorer* and click *Rebuild* from the shortcut menu.

This is exactly the same as first cleaning and then building your project.

11 Examine the *bin* folder again.

The *Date modified* fields show that the files have been completely recreated, even though the code has not changed.

Name	Date modified	Type
JoesBarWebApplication.dll	03/06/2013 18:45	Application extens...
JoesBarWebApplication.pdb	03/06/2013 18:45	PDB File
MailModule.dll	03/06/2013 13:32	Application extens...
MailModule.xml	03/06/2013 13:32	XML Document

note

When should I use Clean and Rebuild?

Since your project automatically builds whenever you publish it or run it in Debug mode, you rarely need to build it manually.

On rare occasions Visual Studio will not recognize changes to your project and they will not be visible in Debug mode. If this happens you should use the *Rebuild* option to force Visual Studio to completely recompile the code.

There is really never any reason to use the *Clean* option followed by *Build* as using *Rebuild* does both in one operation.

Lesson 1-5: Change Build options

You learned about build profiles in: *Lesson 1-3: Use the Debug and Release profiles*. In this lesson you'll learn how to change the settings of build profiles.

1   Open *JoesBarWebApplication.sln* from your sample files folder.

2   View the properties of the project.

Right-click on *JoesBarWebApplication* in the *Solution Explorer* and click *Properties* from the shortcut menu.

Your project's settings appear in the main Visual Studio window.

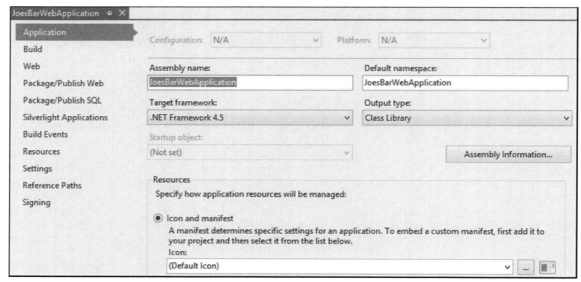

3   Examine the *Build* properties for the *Debug* profile.

1. Click the *Build* tab on the left if it isn't selected already.

This page shows the settings of the currently selected build profile.

2. Choose the *Debug* profile from the drop-down menu on the top toolbar.

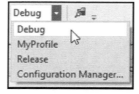

You learned how to do this in: *Lesson 1-3: Use the Debug and Release profiles*.

The properties for the *Debug* profile are now visible in the main window. The most important properties for the moment are those in the *General* group.

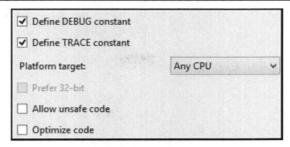

4   Examine the *Build* properties for the *Release* profile.

Just as you did earlier, switch to the *Release* profile using the drop-down menu on the top toolbar.

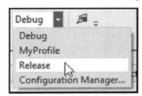

The settings for the *Release* profile are displayed.

You can see that the *General* settings are different for the *Release* profile.

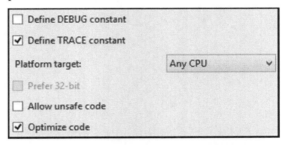

The most important difference here is the *Optimize code* setting. When *Optimize code* is selected, all kinds of optimizations will be added to your code when it is compiled.

These optimizations can greatly improve the performance of your applications but they can also cause problems when debugging. For this reason, *Optimize code* is disabled in the *Debug* profile.

You'll learn about the DEBUG and TRACE constants in: *Lesson 6-2: Use the #if directive to selectively compile code.*

Allow unsafe code is an option that you're unlikely to need to use as it is impossible to write unsafe code in C#. Unsafe code will only become an issue if you are referencing a class library that was written in another programming language (see sidebar).

You're unlikely to need to use any of the other options in the *Build* tab, except for the *XML documentation file* option. You'll use this option in: *Lesson 1-8: Create an XML documentation file.*

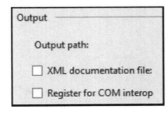

Lesson 1-6: Change Web options

In this lesson you'll work with the options in the *Web* category of your project's properties.

1   Open *JoesBarWebApplication* from your sample files folder.

2   View the properties of the project.

Right-click on *JoesBarWebApplication* in the *Solution Explorer* and click *Properties* from the shortcut menu.

Your project's settings appear in the main Visual Studio window.

3   Examine the properties in the Web tab.

Click the *Web* tab on the left.

The *Web* options for your project appear. First let's look at the *Start Action* settings.

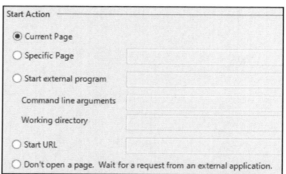

note

Start Action options

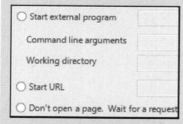

Start external program allows you to start an entirely different program when you start debugging. The virtual server will still start, but no pages will be displayed.

Start URL allows you to open an entirely different web site when you start debugging. This is sometimes used to test web services.

Don't open a page simply starts the virtual web server without taking any other action.

4   Set the Start Page of your project to *Default.aspx*.

1.   Right-click *Default.aspx* in the *Solution Explorer* and click *Set as Start Page* from the shortcut menu.

Although the start page has been changed, it isn't immediately reflected in the *Web* options.

2.   Close the project properties window by clicking the *X* next to its tab.

3.   Reopen the properties window by right-clicking *JoesBarWebApplication* in the *Solution Explorer* and clicking *Properties*.

You can now see that *Default.aspx* is the *Start Page*.

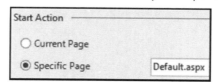

This means that *Default.aspx* will always be opened first when you run your project in Debug mode.

5   Set the *Start Action* back to the default.

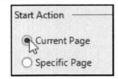

Click the *Current Page* option under *Start Action*.

Visual Studio will now open whichever file is currently open whenever you start your project in Debug mode. This is the default and is usually the preferred way of working.

The other *Start Action* options are rarely used. See sidebar on the previous page for more information.

6 Examine the options in the *Servers* group.

The *Servers* options control the virtual web server that Visual Studio uses when you debug a project.

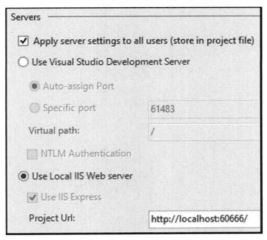

note

What are ports?

Ports can be thought of as 'channels' for web traffic. Some ports are reserved for specific purposes. For example, port 25 is used for e-mail traffic.

Web pages are usually sent through port 80. If you set the *Project Url* to **http://localhost** without specifying a port, it would default to port 80.

Visual Studio assigns a random port to the virtual web server by default. The virtual web server can run more than one web application at the same time by assigning them to different ports.

By default, Visual Studio 2012 uses the new *IIS Express* virtual web server for debugging. Visual Studio 2010 used the *Visual Studio Development Server* option.

IIS Express offers more customization than the older *Visual Studio Development Server* system, but both options are identical for most purposes. You should usually leave this setting at the default.

7 Change the virtual path used by the virtual web server.

1. Click Debug→Start Debugging.

2. Examine the path in the address bar of your web browser.

    The address is *http://localhost:* followed by a number which indicates the the *port* (see sidebar).

3. Close your web browser and return to Visual Studio.

4. Add the following to the end of the address in the *Project Url* box: **/JoesBar/**

note

Why use a different project URL?

In this example you use the *Project Url* option to simulate a site hosted in a sub-folder of a domain. For example:

http://www.learnasp4.com/JoesBar

This is very useful if your application will be hosted in a sub-folder, as it allows you to simulate the live environment.

Hosting in a subfolder can cause problems, particularly when working with files. By setting the *Project Url* option correctly, you will ensure that you catch these problems before publishing your site to the web.

5. Click Debug→Start Debugging and click *Yes* if prompted.

6. Examine the path in the address bar of your browser again.

    Notice that the home page is now shown in the */JoesBar/* folder. This is a useful simulation of hosting the site in a subfolder of a domain (see sidebar).

Lesson 1-7: Change the version of ASP.NET that is used by a project

This book is about ASP.NET 4.5, but many web hosts still have yet to upgrade their systems to be compatible with the latest version. In these cases it's useful to be able to configure your projects to use an earlier version of ASP.NET.

You can also use the skills that you'll learn in this lesson to upgrade an older project to the newest version of ASP.NET.

1   Open *JoesBarWebApplication.sln* from your sample files folder.

2   Open the *Web.config* file from the *Solution Explorer*.

There's very little code in this file, as the project is currently using the latest version of ASP.NET. In earlier versions of ASP.NET, a lot more code was needed in the *Web.config* file.

```
Web.config ✕
    <?xml version="1.0"?>
    <!--
        For more information on how to configure your ASP.NET
        http://go.microsoft.com/fwlink/?LinkId=169433
    -->
    <configuration>
        <system.web>
            <compilation debug="true" targetFramework="4.5"/>
            <httpRuntime targetFramework="4.5"/>
        </system.web>
    </configuration>
```

3   View the properties of the project.

Right-click *JoesBarWebApplication* in the *Solution Explorer* and click *Properties* from the shortcut menu.

Your project's settings appear in the main Visual Studio window.

4   Examine the *Application* properties of your project.

Click the *Application* tab on the left.

The *Application* options for your project appear. The only option that's really important in this window is the *Target framework* drop-down menu (see sidebar for information about the other options).

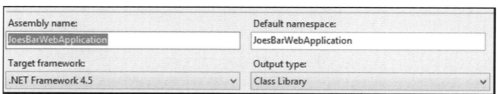

5   Change the project to use *.NET Framework version 3.5*.

1. Click the *Target framework* drop-down menu and select *.NET Framework 3.5*.

2. When prompted to confirm, click *Yes*.

note

Other Application options

Assembly name:
JoesBarWebApplication

Assembly name is the name of the application's base class. By default it is the same as the name of the project. There's no need to ever change this in a Web Forms Application project.

Default namespace:
JoesBarWebApplication

Default namespace is similar to *Assembly name*, but it controls the name of the application's default namespace. By default this is always the same as the *Assembly name*.

Resources
Specify how application

The *Resources* options are intended for Windows desktop applications. There's no reason that you would ever use these options in a Web Forms Application project.

note

Problems when upgrading projects to ASP.NET 4.5

ASP.NET 4.5 introduces several new features that require supporting files to be present in each project. Errors may occur if you upgrade an older project to ASP.NET 4.5 because these files are missing in the older project.

Specifically, ASP.NET 4.5 requires *JQuery* and a number of other javascript files. If these files are missing, validation and AJAX controls may not work. You'll learn more about these files in: *Lesson 9-3: Create ScriptManager and UpdatePanel controls (sidebar).*

Additionally, some of the new features of ASP.NET 4.5 will only be available if the required NuGet package has been added to the project. This includes *FriendlyUrls* and *Web Optimization,* which were covered in Session 12 of the Essential Skills course in this series.

To avoid problems when upgrading older projects, I recommend creating a new ASP.NET 4.5 Web Forms Application project and then copying the required files from your older project into the new project. This will ensure that all of the required resources are available.

After a short delay, the project is converted to use ASP.NET version 3.5. This version should be supported by every ASP.NET web host on the internet.

6 Open the *Web.config* file from the *Solution Explorer.*

There's now an enormous amount of code in the *Web.config* file. All of this is required for ASP.NET version 3.5 to work correctly.

```
<?xml version="1.0"?>
<!--
  For more information on how to configure your ASP.NET application,
  http://go.microsoft.com/fwlink/?LinkId=169433
  -->
<configuration>
  <configSections>
    <sectionGroup name="system.web.extensions" type="System.Web.Conf
      <sectionGroup name="scripting" type="System.Web.Configuration.
        <section name="scriptResourceHandler" type="System.Web.Confi
        <sectionGroup name="webServices" type="System.Web.Configurat
          <section name="jsonSerialization" type="System.Web.Configu
          <section name="profileService" type="System.Web.Configurat
          <section name="authenticationService" type="System.Web.Con
          <section name="roleService" type="System.Web.Configuration
        </sectionGroup>
```

7 Siwtch back to *.NET Framework version 4.5.*

1. Re-open the project properties window by right-clicking *JoesBarWebApplication* in the *Solution Explorer* and clicking *Properties* from the shortcut menu.

2. Click the *Application* tab if it isn't selected already.

3. Click the *Target framework* drop-down menu and set it back to *.NET Framework 4.5.*

```
Target framework:
.NET Framework 4.5                    ∨
```

4. Click *Yes* when prompted.

8 Re-open *Web.config.*

The huge amount of supporting code required by ASP.NET version 3.5 has been removed from *Web.config,* but one line has appeared that wasn't there previously.

```
<configuration>
  ...
  <system.web>
    <compilation debug="true" targetFramework="4.5"/>
    <httpRuntime/>
    <pages controlRenderingCompatibilityVersion="3.5" clientIDMode="AutoID"/>
  </system.web>
</configuration>
```

Because you converted the project from version 3.5 to 4.5, a *<pages>* tag with *controlRenderCompatibilityVersion="3.5"* has appeared. This line is intended to improve compatibility for older form controls. Because this project was actually created with the latest version of ASP.NET, you could remove this line without causing any problems.

note

What is XML?

XML isn't actually a specific programming language; it's really a standard for storing information. For example, HTML code is a form of XML.

XML always works as a series of nested tags enclosed in < and > symbols, which open and close in the same way HTML tags do.

XML documentation files use different tags to HTML, but basically work in the same way.

Because XML can be used to store any kind of data in a hierarchy, it's an extremely versatile way to store data.

XML is covered in greater depth in Session 3 of the *Essential Skills* course in this series.

You'll learn how to use C# code to manipulate XML data in: *Lesson 10-9: Write data to an XML file.*

Lesson 1-8: Create an XML documentation file

You added a reference to the *MailModule.dll* class library in: *Lesson 1-2: Add references to a project.* You then saw that the IntelliSense menu provides useful information about the methods and properties of the class library.

This was only possible was because I created an XML documentation file to accompany the *MailModule* class library, but this doesn't happen by default. Without an XML documentation file, none of the XML summary information would have been displayed in the IntelliSense menu.

When you create a class library you should always include summary information for each property and method, along with an accompanying XML documentation file. This will make the class easier to work with by programmers that use the library. (Summary information was covered in depth in Session 7 of the *Essential Skills* book in this series).

You will create a class library of your own in: *Lesson 4-4: Create a class library.*

You'll rarely find it useful to manually inspect the contents of an XML documentation file, but you'll manually examine one in this lesson to understand how it works.

1   Open *JoesBarWebApplication* from your sample files folder.

2   View the properties of the project.

Right-click *JoesBarWebApplication* in the *Solution Explorer* and click *Properties* from the shortcut menu.

Your project's settings appear in the main Visual Studio window.

3   Change the *Build* options to generate an XML documentation file.

1. Click the *Build* tab on the left of the project properties dialog.

2. Check the *XML documentation file* box in the *Output* group.

Whenever the project is built, an XML documentation file will now be created in the *bin* folder.

4   Build the project.

Right-click *JoesBarWebApplication* in the *Solution Explorer* and click *Build* from the shortcut menu.

5   View the XML documentation file.

1. Click File→Open File…

2. Navigate to your sample files folder.

3. Open the *JoesBarWebApplication* folder.

4. Open the *bin* folder.

5. Click *JoesBarWebApplication.XML* and click *Open*.

The XML documentation file opens in Visual Studio. Many other programs are capable of opening XML files, but opening the file with Visual Studio will ensure that you see the same thing that is shown in this book.

6   **Understand the XML file.**

First you'll see a tag called *<assembly>*, which contains the name of the project's base class. The base class is the class that contains all of the other classes in a project.

```
<assembly>
    <name>JoesBarWebApplication</name>
</assembly>
```

Next you'll see a *<members>* tag. This tag contains separate *<member>* tags for each class, property and method in the project including any ASP.NET controls.

One of the *<member>* tags contains the *TextBoxEmailAddress* control on the *Default.aspx* page.

```
<member name="F:_Default.TextBoxEmailAddress">
    <summary>
    TextBoxEmailAddress control.
    </summary>
    <remarks>
    Auto-generated field.
    To modify move field declaration from designer file to code-behind
    </remarks>
</member>
```

You can tell that this control is on the *Default.aspx* page by looking at the *name* property. The full 'path' to the control is: *_Default.TextBoxEmailAddress*

In the *Essential Skills* course in this series, you learned that each ASPX page has an underlying class. Visual Studio's compiler sees the *Default.aspx* page as the *_Default* class.

Note that if you rename a page without renaming its underlying class, the page's class name may no longer match its file name. For this reason it is best to avoid renaming ASPX pages if possible.

7   **Open the *MailModule.xml* file.**

1. Click File→Open File.

2. Click *MailModule.xml* and click *Open*.

This XML documentation file provides the IntelliSense information for the *MailModule* class library. You examined this information in: *Lesson 1-2: Add references to a project.*

```
<summary>
Basic email method. Returns true if mail is s
</summary>
<param name="From">Email sender.</param>
<param name="To">Email recipient.</param>
<param name="Subject">Email subject.</param>
<param name="Message">Email message.</param>
<returns>True if sending successful, false if
```

Lesson 1-9: Use the Error List window

If you've been working with Visual Studio for some time, you've almost certainly encountered the *Error List* window at least once.

In this lesson you'll use the *Error List* window to quickly find and fix errors.

1   Open *AdvancedMath.sln* from your sample files folder.

This is a *Class Library* project, similar to the project that created the *MailModule.dll* file that you added to a project in: *Lesson 1-2: Add references to a project.*

2   Build the project.

Right-click *AdvancedMath* in the *Solution Explorer* and click *Build* from the shortcut menu.

Three errors appear in the *Error List* window at the bottom of the screen. Building a project causes the *Error List* window to display any errors that prevent the project from compiling.

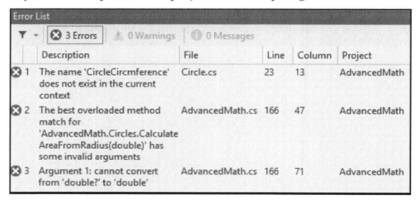

	Description	File	Line	Column	Project
⊗ 1	The name 'CircleCircmference' does not exist in the current context	Circle.cs	23	13	AdvancedMath
⊗ 2	The best overloaded method match for 'AdvancedMath.Circles.Calculate AreaFromRadius(double)' has some invalid arguments	AdvancedMath.cs	166	47	AdvancedMath
⊗ 3	Argument 1: cannot convert from 'double?' to 'double'	AdvancedMath.cs	166	71	AdvancedMath

3   Examine the first error in the *Error List* window.

	Description	File	Line	Column	Project
⊗ 1	The name 'CircleCircmference' does not exist in the current context	Circle.cs	23	13	AdvancedMath

The *Description* field tells you the description of the error. The error mentions a *CircleCircmference* name, which is an obvious misspelling.

The *File* field in the *Error List* window tells you that the error is contained in the *Circle.cs* file.

The *Line* and *Column* fields tell you where the error is located within the file. In this case the error is on line 22 at column 13.

The *Project* field tells you which project contains the error. The *AdvancedMath* project is the only project in this solution.

4   Quickly view the first error.

It wouldn't be difficult to manually find the error, but the *Error List* window is even more helpful.

Simply double-click the first error in the *Error List* window.

Circle.cs is automatically opened with the error highlighted.

```
public Circle(double? Radius, double? Diameter, double? Circumference,
{
    CircleRadius = Radius;
    CircleDiameter = Diameter;
    CircleCircmference = Circumference;
    CircleArea = Area;
}
```

5   Fix the first error.

Change *CircleCircmference* to **CircleCircumference** to fix the problem.

```
public Circle(double? Radius, double? Diameter, double? Circumference,
{
    CircleRadius = Radius;
    CircleDiameter = Diameter;
    CircleCircumference = Circumference;
    CircleArea = Area;
}
```

The error disappears from the *Error List* window.

6   View help for an error.

The *Error List* window allows you to quickly search Microsoft's help files for information about an error.

Right-click the first error in the *Error List* window and click *Show Error Help* from the shortcut menu (see sidebar if the *Error List* window isn't visible).

A web browser window is opened, showing information about the error.

Compiler Error CS1502

Visual Studio 2012 | Other Versions ▾ |

7   Fix the remaining errors.

1. Close your web browser and return to Visual Studio.

2. Double-click the second error in the *Error List* window (*cannot convert from 'double?' to 'double'*).

    This error is the root cause of the other error, so fixing it will fix both problems.

3. Change the underlined code:

    CalculateAreaFromRadius(CircleToPopulate.CircleRadius);

    ...to:

    *CalculateAreaFromRadius(**(double)**CircleToPopulate. CircleRadius);*

    ```
    CircleToPopulate.CircleArea =
    CalculateAreaFromRadius((double)CircleToPopulate.CircleRadius);
    ```

8   Build the project.

This time the project builds successfully and all errors disappear from the *Error List* window.

---

note

If the Error List window doesn't appear

If the Error List window disappears from view, you can easily bring it back by clicking the *Error List* icon in the bottom-left corner of the screen.

Error List   Output

---

note

The cast conversion method

You fix an error in this lesson by using the *cast* conversion method to make C# recognize a value as a *double* type instead of a nullable *double?* type.

The *cast* conversion method is covered in Session 5 of the Essential Skills course in this series.

Lesson 1-10: Understand the Output window

You've probably noticed the *Output* window at the bottom of the Visual Studio screen when you build a project or run one in Debug mode.

In this lesson you'll examine the *Output* window and understand the information it provides.

1 Open *JoesBarWebApplication.sln* from your sample files folder.

2 Build the project.

Right-click *JoesBarWebApplication* in the *Solution Explorer* and click *Build* from the shortcut menu.

The *Output* window appears at the bottom of the screen (see sidebar if it doesn't).

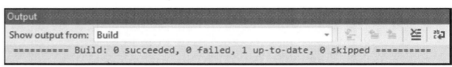

The *Output* window shows the messages that are generated by the compiler as it builds your project.

3 Understand the compiler messages in the *Output* window.

The *Output* window displays the text:

Build: 0 succeeded, 0 failed, 1 up-to-date, 0 skipped

This text means that the compiler found 1 project in the solution and found that it had not changed since it was last built, so the compiler didn't bother to rebuild it.

4 View the *Output* window while debugging.

1. Run the project in Debug mode by clicking Debug→Start Debugging.

   A web browser window opens, displaying the site.

2. Return to Visual Studio without closing your web browser.

   The virtual web server will be stopped if you close your web browser, so it's important to keep it open.

3. Click the *Output* tab at the bottom of the Visual Studio screen to display the *Output* window (if it isn't already displayed).

   The *Output* window appears, showing an enormous number of messages (see sidebar if the window is blank). These messages were generated by the virtual web server.

   The messages list all of the components that the virtual web server has loaded for your web application to use.

note

If the Output window doesn't appear

If the *Output* window isn't visible, you need to reset Visual Studio's window layout.

To do this, click Window→ Reset Window Layout and click *Yes* when prompted to confirm.

If the *Output* window is still not displayed, you can manually display it by clicking Debug→Windows→Output.

note

If there aren't any messages in the Output window

If you don't see any messages in the *Output* window, it's possible that you simply need to scroll up using the window's scroll bar.

If you still don't see any messages, you're seeing a bug in Visual Studio that sometimes prevents the virtual web server from displaying messages.

Simply stop debugging and start debugging again. The correct messages will then be displayed.

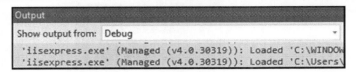

4. Click the drop-down menu at the top of the *Output* window and click *Build* from the shortcut menu.

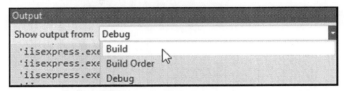

The project is automatically built whenever you start debugging. In *Build* mode, the *Output* window will display any messages generated by the compiler when it built the project.

Since the project has not changed since it was last built, Visual Studio will not recompile it. This means that the *Output* window will be blank in *Build* mode.

You'll also notice the *Build Order* option. This option is only useful when your solution contains multiple projects. The *Build Order* option sorts its messages so that it is easier to see which project each message pertains to. When there is only one project in the solution, *Build Order* is identical to *Build*.

5 View the *Output* window after debugging.

1. Close the web browser window.

2. Return to Visual Studio.

3. Click the *Output* button at the bottom of the window to display the *Output* window (if it isn't already visible).

4. Click the drop-down menu at the top of the *Output* window and switch back to *Debug*.

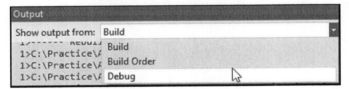

5. Scroll down to the last messages in the *Output* window.

    Here you can see the messages reporting that Internet Explorer (*iexplore.exe*) and the virtual web server (*iisexpress.exe*) have been closed.

```
The program '[1136] iisexpress.exe: Managed (v4.0.30319)' has exited with code 0 (0x0).
The program '[8568] iexplore.exe' has exited with code -1 (0xffffffff).
```

You'll learn how to send your own messages to the *Output* window using compiler directives and the *System.Diagnostics* classes in: *Lesson 6-8: Use System.Diagnostics to write Debug messages.*

Lesson 1-11: Use the Immediate Window

If you've been very observant while debugging your projects, you might have noticed the *Immediate Window* option at the bottom of the Visual Studio window. The *Immediate Window* allows you to execute various commands while the project is running.

1 Open *JoesBarWebApplication* from your sample files folder.

2 Place a breakpoint at the end of the *ButtonSignUpEmail_Click* event handler.

   1. Open the code-behind file of *Default.aspx*.

   2. Add a breakpoint to the following line of code:

   Response.Write(EmailEntered);

```
    protected void ButtonSignUpEmail_Click(object sender,
    {
        string EmailEntered = TextBoxEmailAddress.Text;
        Response.Write(EmailEntered);
    }
}
```

Breakpoints are covered in Session 3 of the *Essential Skills* course in this series.

3 Run the project in Debug mode.

Click Debug→Start Debugging.

note

I don't see the Immediate Window

If the *Immediate Window* isn't visible, you need to reset Visual Studio's window layout.

To do this, click Window→ Reset Window Layout and click *Yes* when prompted to confirm.

If the *Immediate Window* is still not displayed, you can manually display it by clicking Debug→Windows→ Immediate.

4 Open the *Immediate Window*.

   1. Enter a valid email address into the text box on the web page.

   2. Click *Give Me Free Beer!*

You are returned to Visual Studio and the project is paused at the breakpoint.

If you're not automatically returned to Visual Studio, return to it manually without closing your web browser.

   3. Click the *Immediate Window* button at the bottom of the screen.

The *Immediate Window* appears. It's empty at first, waiting for you to enter a command.

5 Get the values of a variable using the *Immediate Window*.

   1. Click in the *Immediate Window* and type the following command:

   >Debug.Print EmailEntered;

When you press the **<Enter>** key, the command is executed and the value of the *EmailEntered* variable is displayed.

2. There's a much quicker way of running the *Debug.Print* command. Type the following to do exactly the same thing:

?EmailEntered

The *?* is a shortcut to the *Debug.Print* command.

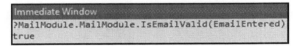

6 Execute commands using the *Immediate Window*.

1. Type the following command into the *Immediate Window*:

?150+12

The result of *162* is displayed when you press the **<Enter>** key. The *Immediate Window* is capable of executing commands, not just displaying information.

2. Now type this command:

?MailModule.MailModule.IsEmailValid(EmailEntered)

This command actually runs a method from the *MailModule* class library that you added a reference to in: *Lesson 1-2: Add references to a project.*

When you press the **<Enter>** key the method returns *true* for the email address, indicating that it is valid.

7 Change the values of variables using the *Immediate Window*.

The *Immediate Window* is also able to change the values of variables while debugging.

1. Enter the following command:

EmailEntered = "not@valid"

When you press the **<Enter>** key, the value of the *EmailEntered* variable is changed to: *not@valid*

2. Check if the email address is valid using the following command:

?MailModule.MailModule.IsEmailValid(EmailEntered)

When you press the **<Enter>** key this time the method returns *false*, because the new value of *EmailEntered* is not a valid e-mail address.

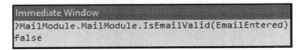

It's worth mentioning that you could also do all of this using the *Watch* window. The *Watch* window is covered in Session 3 of the *Essential Skills* course in this series.

---

note

The Command window

In the Professional version of Visual Studio, another window is available called the *Command* window.

The *Command* window is very similar to the *Immediate* window. In fact, the only difference is that it automatically inserts a > symbol before each command.

If you insert a > before your commands in the *Immediate* window, you will replicate the functionality of the *Command* window.

Lesson 1-12: Use Code Snippets

Code snippets are a great way to speed up writing C# code. With code snippets you can quickly insert common code structures, massively reducing the amount of typing that is needed.

1 Open *AdvancedMath* from your sample files folder.

2 Add a new class to the project, named: **Matrix.cs**

Adding classes is covered in Session 6 of the *Essential Skills* course.

You're going to use code snippets to populate the new class with useful code.

3 Add a new property to the class using a code snippet.

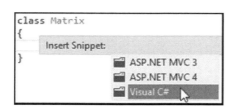

1. Right-click in the empty area between the { } marks.

2. Click *Insert Snippet* from the shortcut menu.

3. Double-click *Visual C#*.

A list of all of the possible code snippets is displayed. Their names aren't very descriptive, but see the sidebar for a list of some of the most useful snippets.

4. Find *prop* in the list and double-click it

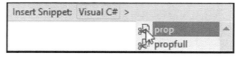

Alternatively, type *prop* and press **<Enter>**.

The code snippet is inserted and its return value is highlighted, ready for you to change it from the default of *int*.

```
class Matrix
{
    public int MyProperty { get; set; }
}
```

5. Type: **List<double>** and press the **<Tab>** key to change the property's data type to a *List* collection. *List* collections are covered in Session 8 of the *Essential Skills* course in this series.

Now the name of the property is highlighted, ready for you to change it.

6. Type: **Numbers**

Your new property is complete.

```
class Matrix
{
    public List<double> Numbers { get; set; }
}
```

4 Add a constructor method to the class using a code snippet.

Constructor methods are covered in session 6 of the *Essential Skills* course in this series.

1. Add a new line after your property.

2. Right-click on the new line, click *Insert Snippet* from the shortcut menu and open the list of *Visual C#* snippets.

3. This time double-click the *ctor* snippet

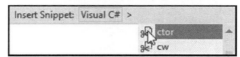

```
public List<double> Numbers { get; set; }
public Matrix()
{
    Numbers = new List<double>();
}
```

The code for a constructor method is automatically inserted.

4. Add the following code to the new constructor method:

Numbers = new List<double>();

5 Create a *for* loop using a code snippet.

The *for* loop is covered in Session 8 of the *Essential Skills* course in this series.

1. Add a new method after your constructor using the following code:

public void AddToNumbers(double Value)
{
}

```
public void AddToNumbers(double Value)
{

}
```

There isn't a code snippet for ordinary methods, so you have to add this code manually.

2. Add a new line inside the new method and open the list of code snippets, as you have done previously in this lesson.

3. This time choose the *for* snippet.

The *for* loop is one of the most complicated C# structures to type, so this code snippet is particularly useful.

```
public void AddToNumbers(double Value)
{
    for (int i = 0; i < length; i++)
    {

    }
}
```

Notice that the first *i* is highlighted, ready for you to change the name of the iteration variable.

4. Type **Counter** and press **<Tab>**.

All three instances of the iteration variable name are automatically changed and *length* is highlighted.

```
for (int Counter = 0; Counter < length; Counter++)
{

}
```

5. Type: **Numbers.Count**

6. Add the following code inside the *for* loop.

Numbers[Counter] += Value;

```
for (int Counter = 0; Counter < Numbers.Count; Counter++)
{
    Numbers[Counter] += Value;
}
```

Your *for* loop is complete. When the *AddToNumbers* method is called, it will add a value to every number in the *Numbers* collection.

Lesson 1-13: Use Surround With

Surround With is a very similar feature to Code Snippets, which you learned about in: *Lesson 1-12: Use Code Snippets*. By using Surround With, you can quickly insert common code structures, removing the need to type large amounts of code manually.

In this lesson you'll use Surround With to add some useful code.

1   Open *AdvancedMath* from your sample files folder.

2   Open the *Matrix.cs* class.

3   Quickly add error handling code using Surround With.

1. Click and drag to highlight all of the code within the *AddToNumbers* method.

```
public void AddToNumbers(double Value)
{
    for (int Counter = 0; Counter < Numbers.Count; Counter++)
    {
        Numbers[Counter] += Value;
    }
}
```

2. Right-click the selected code and click *Surround With…* from the shortcut menu.

A list appears that is very similar to the list of code snippets that you saw in: *Lesson 1-12: Use Code Snippets*. Every item in this list is also available as a code snippet.

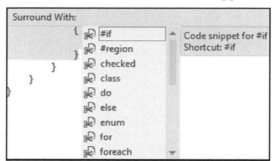

3. Find *try* in the list and double-click it.

The code that you selected is surrounded with a *try* statement, and a *catch* statement is automatically added below it.

```
try
{
    for (int Counter = 0; Counter < Numbers.Count; Counter++)
    {
        Numbers[Counter] += Value;
    }
}
catch (Exception)
{

    throw;
}
```

The *try* and *catch* statements are covered in Session 7 of the *Essential Skills* course in this series.

4 Quickly create a *foreach* loop using *Surround With*.

1. Add a new method to the class using the following code:

public double GetSum()
{
 double Sum = 0;
 Sum += Number;
 return Sum;
}

```
public double GetSum()
{
    double Sum = 0;
    Sum += Number;
    return Sum;
}
```

This code is marked with an error to start with, but you'll fix it using *Surround With*.

2. Click and drag to highlight the code: *Sum += Number*.

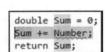

3. Right-click the highlighted code and click *Surround With* from the shortcut menu.

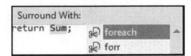

4. Find *foreach* in the list and double-click it.

The line of code is surrounded with a *foreach* statement. Just like code snippets, the important parts of the statement are automatically highlighted for easy editing.

```
double Sum = 0;
foreach (var item in collection)
{
    Sum += Number;
}
```

5. Type: **double** and press the **<Tab>** key.

double is the data type of the values that are held in the *Numbers* collection.

Pressing <Tab> automatically highlights the next element of the code snippet.

6. Type: **Number** and press the **<Tab>** key.

Number is the name of the iteration variable.

7. Type: **Numbers**

Numbers is the name of the collection that the *foreach* statement will iterate through.

Your *foreach* statement is now complete.

```
double Sum = 0;
foreach (double Number in Numbers)
{
    Sum += Number;
}
return Sum;
```

foreach statements are covered in Session 8 of the *Essential Skills* course in this series.

Lesson 1-14: Use the Extract Method refactoring utility

When writing C# code you'll always be trying to make it as efficient as possible, but you can't always predict how the code might need to change in the future.

Rewriting existing code is known as *refactoring*. Visual Studio has refactoring tools that are designed to make it easier to rewrite existing code. One of these tools is *Extract Method.* You'll use it in this lesson.

1 Open *StableBase* from your sample files folder.

2 Examine the project.

1. Run the project in Debug mode.

2. Explore the application and try out some of the pages.

    This is a web-based database system for a stable manager. It's similar to some of the projects created in the *Essential Skills* course in this series.

3. Close your web browser.

3 Fix code repetition using the *Extract Method* refactoring utility.

One of the most common problems that can arise from extended development of applications is the repetition of pieces of code.

It's best practice to avoid repeating code where possible, as repetitive code is much harder to maintain.

1. Open the code-behind file of *ScheduleAdmin.aspx.*

    This page needs to retrieve a task schedule from the project's database in three different places. This is done with the same code each time. The repeated code is marked with comments.

```
//TODO: Fix code repetition
//********************************************************
using (StableBaseDataContext Data = new StableBaseDataContext())
{
    List<TaskRow> TableRows = new List<TaskRow>();
    var HorseTasks = Data.HorseTasks.OrderBy(HorseTask => HorseT
    foreach (HorseTask HorseTask in HorseTasks)
```

This code would be much easier to work with if there was no repetition of the same code.

2. Click and drag to highlight all of the code in the *Page_Load* event handler that is between the comment markers.

3. Right-click the selected code and click Refactor→ Extract Method… from the shortcut menu.

    The *Extract Method* dialog appears.

    This dialog allows you to extract all of the selected code and move it into a new method.

4. Enter **GetData** into the *New method name* box and click *OK*.

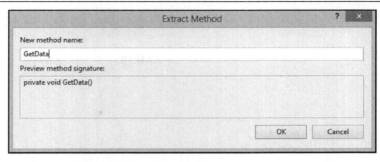

A new *GetData* method is created and the selected code is automatically replaced with code to call the new method.

```
private void GetData()
{
    using (StableBaseDataContext Data = new StableBaseDataContext())
    {
        List<TaskRow> TableRows = new List<TaskRow>();
```

```
//TODO: Fix code repetition
//***************************************************************
GetData();
//***************************************************************
```

5. Find the next *Fix code repetition* comment.

6. Select all code between the comment markers.

7. Delete the code and replace it with: **GetData();**

8. Repeat the process once more for the last *Fix code repetition* comment.

4   Remove the obsolete comments.

Now that the repeated code has been removed, you can remove the comment markers.

```
protected void Page_Load(object sender, EventArgs e)
{
    if (!IsPostBack)
    {
        GetData();
    }
}
```

Now that all of the data access code is contained in a single method it is much easier to modify and maintain this page.

5   View *ScheduleAdmin.aspx* in your web browser.

Everything still works properly, but the page's code is now much easier to work with.

Lesson 1-15: Use the Rename refactoring utility

A common issue when refactoring code is renaming methods and properties that are used in many places throughout a project.

If you simply rename a method, you will need to manually find every piece of code that references the method and change it to match the new method name.

You can make Visual Studio do this automatically by using the *Rename* refactoring utility.

1   Open *StableBase* from your sample files folder.

2   Open the code-behind file of *ScheduleAdmin.aspx*.

3   Rename the *GetData* method by using the *Rename…* refactoring utility.

1.   Find the start of the *GetData* method in the code.

You created this method in: *Lesson 1-14: Use the Extract Method refactoring utility*.

```
private void GetData()
{
    using (StableBaseDataContext Data = new StableBaseDataContext())
    {
        List<TaskRow> TableRows = new List<TaskRow>();
        var HorseTasks = Data.HorseTasks.OrderBy(HorseTask => HorseT
        foreach (HorseTask HorseTask in HorseTasks)
        {
            TaskRow TableRow = new TaskRow();
```

2.   Right-click *GetData()* and click Refactor→Rename… from the shortcut menu.

The *Rename* dialog appears.

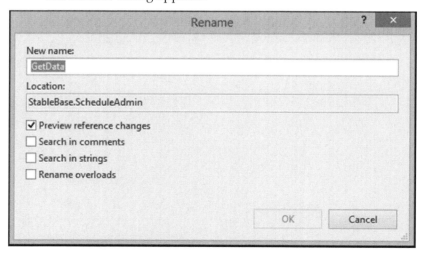

There are a few different options here:

Preview reference changes allows you to preview the changes that this utility will make. You'll see this happen in a moment.

Search in comments tells the *Rename* utility to rename references to the method even if the code referencing it is commented.

Search in strings will replace any mention of *GetData* that is found in a string (ie. in quote marks).

Rename overloads will rename any overloads of the method. You'll learn about overloads in: *Lesson 4-6: Overload a method.*

3. Type **GetSchedule** into the *New name* box and click *OK*.

A dialog appears, previewing all of the changes that the utility will make.

This appeared because you selected *Preview reference changes.*

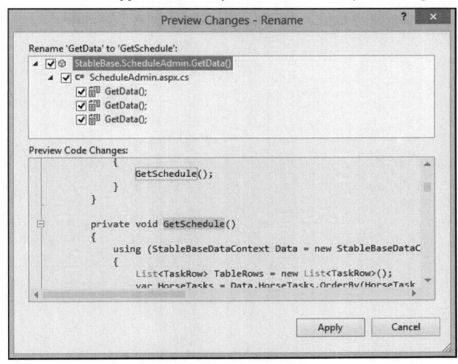

This dialog shows that there are 3 references to the *GetData* method, all held within the *ScheduleAdmin.aspx.cs* file.

You can use the check-boxes to deselect any changes that you don't want to make.

4. Click *Apply* to apply the changes.

If you now examine the code, you'll see that the method has been renamed and all references to it have been automatically updated to use its new name.

```
private void GetSchedule()
{
    using (StableBaseDataContext Data = new StableBaseDataContext())
    {
```

```
protected void Page_Load(object sender, EventArgs e)
{
    if (!IsPostBack)
    {
        GetSchedule();
    }
}
```

Lesson 1-16: Understand NuGet packages

ASP.NET 4.5 introduces several new features to your projects, including the *FriendlyUrls* and *Web Optimization* features. These were covered in the Essential Skills course in this series.

These new features aren't actually part of the .NET framework. Instead, they are included in your project as *'packages'* using a program called *NuGet*. You'll learn about NuGet packages in this lesson.

1   Using Windows Explorer, open the *StableBase* folder from your sample files folder.

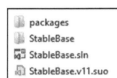

This folder contains a *packages* folder. The *packages* folder is automatically included with all new ASP.NET 4.5 Web Forms Application projects.

2   Open the *packages* folder.

The *packages* folder contains all of the NuGet packages that are used by the project. You'll notice *FriendlyUrls* and *Web Optimization* among them.

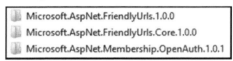

Many of the new features of ASP.NET 4.5 have been included using these packages instead of being included in the .NET framework.

Note that this is not true of all of ASP.NET 4.5's new features. The new multi-threading features, for example, are part of the .NET framework. You'll learn about these in: *Lesson 3-4: Implement multi-threading using the Action and Task classes.*

3   Go back to the *StableBase* folder and open *StableBase.sln* in Visual Studio.

4   Open the *Manage NuGet Packages* window.

Right-click *Solution 'StableBase'* in the *Solution Explorer* window and click *Manage NuGet Packages for Solution…* from the shortcut menu.

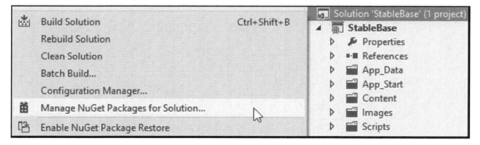

The *Manage NuGet Packages* window appears.

This window allows you to manage the packages that are included in your project and to add new packages from the internet.

The advantage of *NuGet* packages is that they are very easy to update because they come from an online repository. This means, for example, that you can very easily update your project to use the latest version of *jQuery*.

5 Update to the latest version of *jQuery*.

1. Click the *Updates* category in the left pane of the window.

2. Click *jQuery* in the central pane of the window.

   If *jQuery* isn't displayed, you already have the latest version of *jQuery* installed. In this case, try updating one of the other packages instead.

3. Click *Update* next to *jQuery*.

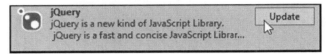

4. Click *OK* when prompted to update the package in the *StableBase* project.

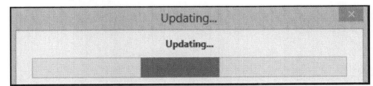

The latest version of *jQuery* is downloaded and installed.

6 Add the Json.NET package to your project.

As well as updating the packages that were automatically included in your project, you can add new packages from the internet.

1. Click the *Online* category in the left pane of the window.

2. Click *Json.NET* in the central pane.

   Json.NET is a package that enables advanced JSON features. You'll learn more about JSON in: *Lesson 9-10: Directly call a web method using JQuery and JSON.*

3. Click *Install* next to *Json.NET*.

4. Click *OK* when prompted to install the package in the *StableBase* project.

   The *Json.NET* package is downloaded and added to your project. All of its features will now be available to your project.

Session 1: Exercise

1   Open *Exercise1* from the *Exercises* folder in your sample files folder.

2   Attempt to build the project. A build error will occur.

3   Use the *Error List* window to find and fix the build error.

4   Switch to the *Release* build profile and build the project.

5   Add a reference to the *AdvancedMath.dll* file from your sample files folder (click *Yes* if prompted to confirm).

6   Enable XML Documentation for the *Release* build profile.

7   Switch back to the Debug profile and completely rebuild the project.

8   The project is currently set to use ASP.NET version 3.5. Change the project's settings so that it uses ASP.NET version 4.5.

9   Open the code-behind file of *Default.aspx*.

10   Use *Surround With* to add a *try, catch* statement around the entire contents of the *ButtonCalculate_Click* event handler.

11   Use the *Extract Method* refactoring utility to extract the code inside the comment markers into a new method named: **AddRowToTable**

12   Set a breakpoint at the start of the *for* loop, start the project in *Debug* mode and click the *Calculate* button.

       Your code is paused at the breakpoint.

13   Use the *Immediate* window to change the value of the *NumberOfYears* variable to: **10**

14   Remove the breakpoint and resume debugging.

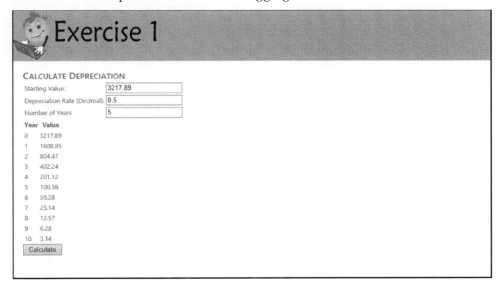

Exercise1 - Start

Exercise1 - End

If you need help slide the page to the left

Session 1: Exercise Answers

These are the four questions that students find the most difficult to answer:

Q 13	Q 11	Q 10	Q 3
1. Click inside the *Immediate* window at the bottom of the Visual Studio screen. 2. Type: **NumberOfYears = 10** 3. Press the **<Enter>** key. This was covered in: *Lesson 1-11: Use the Immediate Window.*	1. Click and drag to highlight all of the code between the comment markers. 2. Right-click the highlighted code and click Refactor→ Extract Method… from the shortcut menu. 3. Type the name: **AddRowToTable** and click *OK*. This was covered in: *Lesson 1-14: Use the Extract Method refactoring utility.*	1. Click and drag to highlight all code inside the *ButtonCalculate_Click* event handler. 2. Right-click the highlighted code and click *Surround With…* from the shortcut menu. 3. Find *try* in the list and double-click it. This was covered in: *Lesson 1-13: Use Surround With.*	1. Double-click the error in the *Error List* window. The code-behind file of *Default.aspx* is opened and the error is highlighted. The problem is that *TextBoxNumberOfYears* has been misspelled. 2. Change *TextBoxNumberOfYear* to **TextBoxNumberOfYears**. This was covered in: *Lesson 1-9: Use the Error List window.*

If you have difficulty with the other questions, here are the lessons that cover the relevant skills:

1 **Refer to: Essential Skills Session 1.**

2 **Refer to: Lesson 1-4: Build, Rebuild and Clean a project.**

4 **Refer to: Lesson 1-3: Use the Debug and Release profiles.**

5 **Refer to: Lesson 1-2: Add references to a project.**

6 **Refer to: Lesson 1-8: Create an XML documentation file.**

7 **Refer to: Lesson 1-3: Use the Debug and Release profiles, Lesson 1-4: Build, Rebuild and Clean a project.**

8 **Refer to: Lesson 1-7: Change the version of ASP.NET that is used by a project.**

9 **Refer to: Essential Skills Session 1.**

12 **Refer to: Essential Skills Session 3.**

14 **Refer to: Essential Skills Session 3.**

Session Two: Advanced .NET classes

> Now this is not the end. It is not even the beginning of the end. But it is, perhaps, the end of the beginning.
>
> *Winston Churchill, British statesman (1874-1965)*

The most common classes of the .NET framework were covered in the *Essential Skills* course in this series. In this session you'll learn about some of the more advanced classes.

The classes covered in this session aren't used as often as those covered in the *Essential Skills* course, but they will be needed to implement some of the advanced techniques you'll learn later on.

Session Objectives

By the end of this session you will be able to:

- Use the Tuple class
- Use the Lazy class
- Use the Stream class
- Use the Byte class
- Use the TimeSpan class
- Create a multidimensional array
- Iterate through a multidimensional array
- Send commands to the Garbage Collector
- Send e-mail messages using the SmtpClient class

Lesson 2-1: Use the Tuple class

The *Tuple* class is a new feature of ASP.NET 4.0 that enables you to very quickly create custom data structures similar to classes. *Tuple* objects can't contain methods; they are only structures for data storage. It's best practice to avoid using Tuples where possible as they don't have the flexibility of 'real' classes and can make your code harder to understand.

1 Open *AdvancedMath* from your sample files folder.

2 Open *Matrix.cs*.

Tuple objects offer an easy way to return multiple values from a method. It's important to note, however, that it's better to do this using either the *out* keyword or, ideally, by returning a custom class. You'll learn about the *out* keyword in: *Lesson 4-8: Use the out keyword to get multiple values from a method.*

You're only using a *Tuple* object as a return value in this lesson to demonstrate how Tuples work, as you may inherit a project that makes use of Tuples.

3 Create a new method that returns a *Tuple* object.

1. Start the method with the following code:

   public Tuple<int, double> GetCountAndSum()
   {
   }

   ```
   public Tuple<int, double> GetCountAndSum()
   {

   }
   ```

   The method is marked with an error because it doesn't yet return a value.

2. Store the values that the method will return by adding the following code to the method:

   int Count = Numbers.Count;
   double Sum = GetSum();

   ```
   public Tuple<int, double> GetCountAndSum()
   {
       int Count = Numbers.Count;
       double Sum = GetSum();
   }
   ```

3. On the next line, create a *Tuple* object from the *Count* and *Sum* values using the following code:

   Tuple<int, double> CountAndSum =
   new Tuple<int, double>(Count, Sum);

   ```
   double Sum = GetSum();
   Tuple<int, double> CountAndSum = Tuple.Create(Count, Sum);
   ```

   You need to set the values of a *Tuple* object's properties when you create it. After the *Tuple* object has been created, its values will be read-only.

If you are not completing the course incrementally use the sample file: **Lesson 2-1** to begin this lesson.

Sample files with the starting point for each lesson are also provided for all of the other lessons in this session.

This code creates a new *Tuple* object containing an *int* property and a *double* property. *Tuple* objects have a limit of 8 properties, but you can 'nest' *Tuple* objects by using *Tuple* as a property type within another *Tuple*.

4. Add the following code to return the *Tuple* object:

return CountAndSum;

Your *Tuple* code is now complete.

```
public Tuple<int, double> GetCountAndSum()
{
    int Count = Numbers.Count;
    double Sum = GetSum();
    Tuple<int, double> CountAndSum =
        new Tuple<int, double>(Count, Sum);
    return CountAndSum;
}
```

4 Examine your *Tuple* object.

Once it is created, a *Tuple* object will behave in exactly the same way as an object with read-only properties.

1. Add a new line before the line:

return CountAndSum;

…and type:

CountAndSum.

The IntelliSense menu for your *Tuple* object appears.

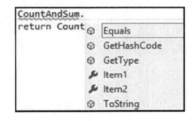

The *Tuple* object's properties are listed as *Item1* and *Item2*. It's impossible to give descriptive names to a *Tuple* object's properties, making them much less useful than classes with descriptive property names.

2. Remove the *CountAndSum.* code.

5 Use an alternative method to create a *Tuple* object.

As well as creating a *Tuple* object using the 'standard' method of instantiating a class, you can use the *Tuple.Create* method.

The only reason to use this method is to cut down on the amount of code that you need to type, as the *Create* method will automatically select the correct data types for the values that you provide.

Replace the code:

Tuple<int, double> CountAndSum =
new Tuple<int, double>(Count, Sum);

…with:

Tuple<int, double> CountAndSum = **Tuple.Create(Count, Sum);**

```
public Tuple<int, double> GetCountAndSum()
{
    int Count = Numbers.Count;
    double Sum = GetSum();
    Tuple<int, double> CountAndSum = Tuple.Create(Count, Sum);
    return CountAndSum;
}
```

note

Tuple objects and the var type

You could make this lesson's code even shorter by using the following code:

var CountAndSum =
Tuple.Create(Count, Sum);

…but I'd recommend against doing this, as it makes the code harder to understand.

The *var* data type is covered in Session 5 of the *Essential Skills* course in this series.

Lesson 2-2: Use the Lazy class

When you create a variable in C# it immediately reserves a space in memory, even if you don't assign a value to it. For example, if you create an *int* variable it immediately reserves 32 bits of memory.

It's very rare for this to be an issue, but there may be cases where you need to work with a class that consumes enormous amounts of memory. In these cases, you can use the *Lazy* class to prevent the object from being loaded into memory until it is needed. This is called 'lazy instantiation'.

If you follow good coding practices it's extremely unlikely that you'll ever need to make use of the *Lazy* class. It's only included in this course as you may see it in use in projects written by other programmers.

An important note when working with *Lazy* objects is that their constructor methods will not run until they are loaded into memory.

1 Open *StableBase* from your sample files folder.

2 Open the code-behind file of *TaskAdmin.aspx*.

```
using (StableBaseDataContext Data =
    new StableBaseDataContext())
{
    Task NewTask = new Task();
```

This code makes use of a LINQ data context object: the *StableBaseDataContext* class. LINQ was covered in Session 10 of the *Essential Skills* course in this series.

LINQ data context objects can take up a lot of memory. For this reason, the code on this page only creates an instance of the class when it is needed. The *using* statement ensures that it is automatically disposed of once it is no longer in use.

This is the best and most efficient coding practice. You're going to re-write this code using the *Lazy* class, even though it will be slightly less efficient.

3 Make the *StableBaseDataContext* object into a public property.

1. Remove the *using* statement, so that the *ButtonAddNewTask_Click* event handler appears as:

   if (TextBoxNewTaskName.Text.Length > 0)
   {
   *   Task NewTask = new Task();*
   *   NewTask.TaskName = TextBoxNewTaskName.Text;*
   *   Data.Tasks.InsertOnSubmit(NewTask);*
   *   Data.SubmitChanges();*
   *   GridViewTask.DataBind();*
   }

   ```
   protected void ButtonAddNewTask_Click(object sender
   {
       if (TextBoxNewTaskName.Text.Length > 0)
       {
           Task NewTask = new Task();
           NewTask.TaskName = TextBoxNewTaskName.Text;
           Data.Tasks.InsertOnSubmit(NewTask);
           Data.SubmitChanges();
           GridViewTask.DataBind();
       }
   }
   ```

   This removes the *Data* object from the method so the two lines that make use of the *Data* object are marked with errors.

2. Add the following line of code outside any event handlers:

**public StableBaseDataContext Data =
new StableBaseDataContext();**

```
public partial class TaskAdmin : System.Web.UI.Page
{
    public StableBaseDataContext Data = new StableBaseDataContext();
```

This declares the *Data* object as a public property. The error markers disappear from the *ButtonAddNewTask_Click* event handler.

The code is now very inefficient, as the *Data* object will be loaded into memory even if it is never used.

4 Use the *Lazy* class to make the *Data* object lazily instantiated.

Change the code:

public StableBaseDataContext Data = new StableBaseDataContext();

...to:

public **Lazy<StableBaseDataContext>** *Data =
new* **Lazy<StableBaseDataContext>();**

```
public Lazy<StableBaseDataContext> Data = new Lazy<StableBaseDataContext>();
```

Now the *Data* object will not be loaded into memory until it is used. However, this has introduced some errors in the *ButtonAddNewTask_Click* event handler.

5 Fix the errors in the *ButtonAddNewTask_Click* event handler.

Because the *Data* object is now wrapped up in the *Lazy* class, you need to access its underlying object by using its *Value* property.

Change the code:

*Data.Tasks.InsertOnSubmit(NewTask);
Data.SubmitChanges();*

...to:

*Data.***Value**.*Tasks.InsertOnSubmit(NewTask);
Data.***Value**.*SubmitChanges();*

All of the errors disappear.

```
Task NewTask = new Task();
NewTask.TaskName = TextBoxNewTaskName.Text;
Data.Value.Tasks.InsertOnSubmit(NewTask);
Data.Value.SubmitChanges();
GridViewTask.DataBind();
```

6 Test the page.

1. View the *TaskAdmin.aspx* page in your web browser.

2. Enter **Poulticing** into the text box and click *Add Task*.

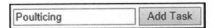

The *Poulticing* task is added to the list successfully.

Lesson 2-3: Use the Stream class

The *Stream* class, and similar classes, are used to handle binary data. You'll often need to use *Stream* objects when reading or writing files.

In this lesson you'll use a *Stream* object to read a file and display its contents on a page.

1   Open *TextLand* from your sample files folder.

2   View *CSV.aspx* in your web browser.

    This page is designed to receive a text file and then display its contents on the page when the user clicks the *Read File* button.

    You're going to read the file using a *Stream* object.

3   Close your web browser and return to Visual Studio.

4   Open the code-behind file of *CSV.aspx*.

5   Add a *using* line for: **System.IO**

    The *Stream* class and related classes are part of the *System.IO* namespace so it's useful to create a 'shortcut' to this namespace by adding *System.IO* to the *using* lines at the top of the code.

    ```
    using System.Web.UI.WebControls;
    using System.IO;
    ```

    using lines are covered in Session 6 of the *Essential Skills* course in this series.

6   Add code to the *ButtonReadFile_Click* event handler to get a *Stream* object from the *FileUpload* control on the page.

    Add the following code to the *ButtonReadFile_Click* event handler:

    Stream CSVStream = FileUploadFileToRead.FileContent;

    ```
    protected void ButtonReadFile_Click(object sender, EventArgs e)
    {
        Stream CSVStream = FileUploadFileToRead.FileContent;
    }
    ```

    This code gets a *Stream* object from the file that the user has chosen to upload. You'll learn more about the *FileUpload* control in: *Lesson 7-3: Use the FileUpload control.*

7   Add code to read text from the *Stream* object.

    The *Stream* object alone isn't particularly helpful in extracting the information you want from the file.

important

The StreamReader class will only work with text files

The *StreamReader* object makes it very easy to read data from a *Stream* object, but it will only work for text files.

Text files include XML, CSV and HTML files.

For binary files such as images, you must manually extract the data from the *Stream* object using a *byte* array. You'll learn how to do this in: *Lesson 12-8: Decompress a file*.

Fortunately, the .NET framework provides the *StreamReader* class which enables you to easily extract text from a *Stream* object.

Add the following code on the next line:

StreamReader Reader = new StreamReader(CSVStream);
while (!Reader.EndOfStream)
{
    string TextFromFile = Reader.ReadLine();
}

```
protected void ButtonReadFile_Click(object sender, EventArgs e)
{
    Stream CSVStream = FileUploadFileToRead.FileContent;
    StreamReader Reader = new StreamReader(CSVStream);
    while (!Reader.EndOfStream)
    {
        string TextFromFile = Reader.ReadLine();
    }
}
```

This code reads each line of text from the file and places it into the *TextFromFile* variable.

8   Add code to display the extracted text on the page.

Add the following code on the next line inside the *while* loop:

LiteralFileContent.Text += TextFromFile;

```
Stream CSVStream = FileUploadFileToRead.FileContent;
StreamReader Reader = new StreamReader(CSVStream);
while (!Reader.EndOfStream)
{
    string TextFromFile = Reader.ReadLine();
    LiteralFileContent.Text += TextFromFile;
}
```

This code displays the text from the file in the *LiteralFileContent* control on the page.

You'll learn how to extract the individual data fields from a CSV (comma separated values) file in: *Lesson 10-8: Read data from a CSV file*. For now you're just extracting the entire contents of the file without doing anything interesting with the data.

9   Test the page.

1. View *CSV.aspx* in your web browser.

2. Click *Browse* and navigate to your sample files folder.

3. Click *RaceResults.csv* and click *Open*.

4. Click *Read File*.

The data is sent to the web page and displayed. This will work efficiently even with large files.

| Browse... | Read File |

"Horse","Date","Position","Jockey","Trainer""Lullaby Debt",01/01/12,1,"E. Long","S. Smart""Gray July",02/01/12,5,"Q. Davis","M. Rizwan""Cut-throat Clash",01/01/12,7,"A. Mitchell","R. Baxendale""Savvy Princess",07/01/12,2,"C. Bannister","D. Caceres""Ebony Bucker",08/01/12,4,"P. Delestre","A. Kennedy""Inverted Piano",09/01/12,3,"L. Ruoff","D. Sylvan""Motionless Rock",07/01/12,6,"K. Jones","L. Bate""Destiny's Streak",08/01/12,1,"E. Long","A. Shoch""Mouse Stamp",09/01/12,4,"H. Ward","R. Elnaghy""Thoughtful Diva",10/01/12,1,"C. Susilraj","E. Gang"

Lesson 2-4: Use the Byte class

You're probably aware that at the most basic level, all information that is processed by a computer is in binary code: a sequence of ones and zeroes.

Each digit of information (ie. each one or zero) is known as a *bit*.

When working with binary data, you rarely access each bit individually. Instead, the bits are placed into groups of eight. A group of eight bits is known as a *byte*. Bytes are usually the most basic element of binary data that you will work with in C#.

In this lesson you'll work with binary data and the *byte* data type.

1 Open *StableBase* from your sample files folder.

The *StableBase* project is able to store pictures in its database. These pictures are stored as binary data.

2 View the *HorsePicture* field in the database.

1. Expand the *App_Data* folder in the *Solution Explorer*.

```
StableBase
  ▷  Properties
  ▷  References
  ▲  App_Data
     ▷  StableBase.mdf
```

2. Double-click *StableBase.mdf*.

The database is opened in the *Database Explorer* window.

3. Expand *Tables*.

4. Right-click *Horse* and click *Show Table Data* from the shortcut menu.

The table's data is displayed. Look at the *HorsePicture* field.

dbo.Horse [Data]		
Max Rows: 1000		
HorseID	HorseName	HorsePicture
1	Sausage	<Binary data>
2	Max	<Binary data>
3	Toffee	<Binary data>
NULL	NULL	NULL

HorsePicture is marked as <Binary data>. You're going to extract this binary data and display it on a page.

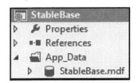

5. Return to the *Solution Explorer* by clicking its tab below the *Database Explorer*.

3 Open the code-behind file of *GetPicture.aspx*.

This page's job is to extract a picture from the database and display it to the user. The code to extract the record from the database is already in place. If you don't understand this code, refer back to Session 10 of the *Essential Skills* course in this series.

```
if (HorseForImage.HorsePicture != null)
{
    //TODO: Add code to display the image.
}
```

4 Examine the *HorsePicture* LINQ field.

1. Type the following code in the space indicated by the *TODO* comment:

   HorseForImage.HorsePicture

   System.Data.Linq.Binary Horse.HorsePicture

   The IntelliSense menu shows you that this field is a *Linq.Binary* object. You will have to convert it into an array of *byte* variables before you will be able to do anything useful with it.

2. Remove the code that you added.

5 Extract the *byte* values from *HorsePicture*.

Add the following code in the space indicated by the *TODO* comment:

byte[] ImageBytes = HorseForImage.HorsePicture.ToArray();

```
if (HorseForImage.HorsePicture != null)
{
    byte[] ImageBytes = HorseForImage.HorsePicture.ToArray();
}
```

This code extracts the binary data from the database into an array of *byte* values. Most of the methods that work with binary data in the .NET framework require *byte[]* arrays like this one.

6 Add code to display the image.

1. Add the following code on the next line:

   Response.ContentType = "image/jpeg";

   This tells the user's web browser that the data it is receiving from the web server should be interpreted as a *jpeg* image.

2. Add the following code on the next line:

   Response.BinaryWrite(ImageBytes);
   Response.End();

```
byte[] ImageBytes = HorseForImage.HorsePicture.ToArray();
Response.ContentType = "image/jpeg";
Response.BinaryWrite(ImageBytes);
Response.End();
```

This code writes the *byte* array into the web server's *Response* to the user's web browser.

7 Test your image extraction code.

1. View *Horses.aspx* in your web browser.

   The *Horses* page makes use of *GetPicture.aspx* to display images for each horse.

2. Click any of the *View Details* links.

   Your code displays the image correctly.

   You'll revisit these skills in more depth in: *Lesson 12-2: Output a file to the user's web browser.* At this stage, you just need to understand that binary data can be stored in a *byte* array.

   In later lessons you'll use *byte* arrays to encrypt, compress and convert binary data.

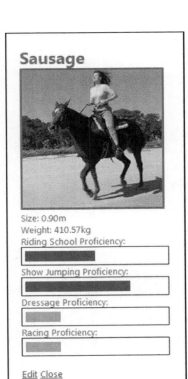

Sausage

Size: 0.90m
Weight: 410.57kg
Riding School Proficiency:

Show Jumping Proficiency:

Dressage Proficiency:

Racing Proficiency:

Edit Close

Lesson 2-5: Use the TimeSpan class

The *TimeSpan* class is used to store lengths of time. You'll use it in this lesson to calculate the length of time between two dates.

The *DateTime* class is used to store and manipulate date and time information, but it isn't capable of measuring a length of time. *DateTime* variables are covered in Session 5 of the *Essential Skills* course.

1   Open *TextLand* from your sample files folder.

2   Open *Dates.aspx* in Design view.

When this page is complete, it will display the length of time between the two dates entered into the text boxes.

3   Open the code-behind file of *Dates.aspx*.

4   Add code to retrieve the dates from the text boxes.

Add the following code to the *ButtonGetDateDifference_Click* event handler:

DateTime Date1 = DateTime.Parse(TextBoxDate1.Text);
DateTime Date2 = DateTime.Parse(TextBoxDate2.Text);

```
protected void ButtonGetDateDifference_Click(object sen
{
    DateTime Date1 = DateTime.Parse(TextBoxDate1.Text);
    DateTime Date2 = DateTime.Parse(TextBoxDate2.Text);
}
```

The *Parse* method of converting *string* data to *DateTime* data is covered in Session 5 of the *Essential Skills* course in this series.

This code would cause an error if the user entered an invalid date into one of the text boxes. You'll learn how to use the *TryParse* method to convert data without causing errors in: *Lesson 4-8: Use the out keyword to get multiple values from a method.*

5   Add code to get the *TimeSpan* between the two *DateTime* values.

Add the following code on the next line:

TimeSpan DateDifference = Date1 - Date2;

```
DateTime Date2 = DateTime.Parse(TextBoxDate2.Text);
TimeSpan DateDifference = Date1 - Date2;
```

This code creates a new *TimeSpan* object that contains the length of time between *Date1* and *Date2*.

note

How the DateTime class works

Underneath all of the *DateTime* class's methods and properties is a single value that drives everything else. If you examine the properties of a *DateTime* object, you'll see this as the *Ticks* property.

The *Ticks* property measures the number of 'ticks' since midnight on the date: 01/01/0001.

A 'tick' is the smallest unit of time that C# is able to measure. A single tick is 100 nanoseconds. There are 10,000,000 ticks in a second.

Finding the difference between two *DateTime* objects is simply a matter of subtracting the number of ticks in each object. You could do this manually if you wanted to, but the *TimeSpan* class provides a lot of useful properties and methods to make lengths of time easier to work with.

Because the number of ticks in a *DateTime* object is limited to the length of a 64-bit integer, there is a maximum limit to the dates it can store. The *DateTime* class is only capable of storing dates up to midnight on the date: 31/12/9999.

The reason that you're able to do this is that underneath all of the *DateTime* object's functionality is a single 64-bit integer that represents the number of 'ticks' since the 1st of January in the year 0001. See sidebar for more on this.

6   Add code to display the difference between the two dates in the *LabelDateDifference* control.

Your *TimeSpan* object now contains the length of time between the two dates. Using the *Days* property of the *TimeSpan* object, it's simple to output the value you want.

Add the following code on the next line:

LabelDateDifference.Text = DateDifference.Days.ToString() + " Days";

```
DateTime Date1 = DateTime.Parse(TextBoxDate1.Text);
DateTime Date2 = DateTime.Parse(TextBoxDate2.Text);
TimeSpan DateDifference = Date1 - Date2;
LabelDateDifference.Text = DateDifference.Days.ToString() + " Days";
```

7   Test the page.

1.   View *Dates.aspx* in your web browser.

2.   Change the dates if you wish and click *Get Difference*.

The number of days between the two dates is displayed.

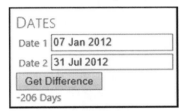

Using the default values, there are *206* days between the two dates.

3.   Close your web browser and return to Visual Studio.

8   Examine the other properties of the *TimeSpan* object.

1.   Add a new line of code at the bottom of your method and type the following:

DateDifference.

The IntelliSense menu appears, displaying the properties and methods of the *TimeSpan* class.

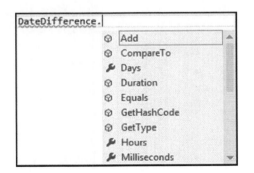

As you can see, the *TimeSpan* class contains properties for the number of *Hours, Minutes, Seconds, Milliseconds* and even *Ticks*.

The *TimeSpan* class has methods that allow you to *Add* and *Subtract* time. You can also compare two *TimeSpan* objects using the *CompareTo* method.

2.   Remove the line of code that you added.

Lesson 2-6: Create a multidimensional array

note

Minesweeper game

Every version of Windows includes the Minesweeper game. You can find it in the Games folder on the Windows Start menu.

The Minesweeper game consists of a grid that contains several hidden 'mines'. The goal of the game is to reveal every unmined cell in the grid without clicking on a cell that contains a mine.

If the player clicks on a cell that does not contain a mine, a number is shown indicating how many mines are present in the surrounding cells. Using these numbers, the player can deduce the positions of the mines.

note

3 dimensions or more

In this lesson you create a 9x9 2-dimensional array. 2-dimensional arrays are probably the most common type of array, but you can easily create an array with as many dimensions as you need.

Here's how you could create a 3-dimensional array of *int* variables:

int[,,] IntCube = new int[9,9,9];

This would create a 9x9x9 array. You would set its values in a very similar way. To set the values of one of the corners of this 'cube' for example, you could use the following code:

IntCube[0,0,0] = 10;

Arrays are only limited by the amount of memory available to the computer but it's very rare to need more than 3 dimensions in an array.

Single-dimensional arrays are covered in Session 8 of the *Essential Skills* course. An array is the most basic collection type available in C#.

As well as arrays, C# offers the *List* collection (this is also covered in *Essential Skills*). The *List* collection is almost always preferred above arrays, as it has many features that arrays lack.

One thing that a *List* collection can't do, however, is store a multidimensional collection. Using arrays, you can create collections that have more than one dimension.

1   Open *Sweep4Mines* from your sample files folder.

This is a very simple remake of the classic "MineSweeper" game (see sidebar if you've never played it). All of the code is already in place except for the code to place the 'mines' in the grid.

Because the game uses a two dimensional grid, you'll need to use a two dimensional array to do this.

2   View *Default.aspx* in Design view.

Here you can see the layout of the page. There are two ASP.NET *Table* controls on this page, overlaid on top of each other.

The JavaScript code on this page checks the *CSSClass* property of the cells in the *TableMask* table in order to determine whether there is a 'mine' in each cell.

3   Open the code-behind file of *Default.aspx*.

4   Add code to create a 2-dimensional array.

Add the following code to the *Page_Load* event handler:

bool[,] MineGrid = new bool[9, 9];

```
protected void Page_Load(object sender, EventArgs e)
{
    bool[,] MineGrid = new bool[9, 9];
}
```

This code creates a two-dimensional 9x9 array of *bool* variables. The default value of the *bool* data type is *false* so all of the values in the array will currently be *false*.

Your two-dimensional array now looks like this:

	0	1	2	3	4	5	6	7	8
0	False	False	False	False	False	False	False	False	False
1	False	False	False	False	False	False	False	False	False
2	False	False	False	False	False	False	False	False	False
3	False	False	False	False	False	False	False	False	False
4	False	False	False	False	False	False	False	False	False
5	False	False	False	False	False	False	False	False	False
6	False	False	False	False	False	False	False	False	False
7	False	False	False	False	False	False	False	False	False
8	False	False	False	False	False	False	False	False	False

5   Add code to place a 'mine' in your array.

Add the following code on the next line to manually set the value of one of the elements in your array to *true*:

MineGrid[3, 5] = true;

```
bool[,] MineGrid = new bool[9, 9];
MineGrid[3, 5] = true;
```

Your array now looks like this:

	0	1	2	3	4	5	6	7	8
0	False	False	False	False	False	False	False	False	False
1	False	False	False	False	False	False	False	False	False
2	False	False	False	False	False	False	False	False	False
3	False	False	False	False	False	False	False	False	False
4	False	False	False	False	False	False	False	False	False
5	False	False	False	**True**	False	False	False	False	False
6	False	False	False	False	False	False	False	False	False
7	False	False	False	False	False	False	False	False	False
8	False	False	False	False	False	False	False	False	False

6   Add code to place 3 more 'mines' in your grid.

Add the following code:

MineGrid[0, 3] = true;
MineGrid[8, 4] = true;
MineGrid[5, 7] = true;

```
bool[,] MineGrid = new bool[9, 9];
MineGrid[3, 5] = true;
MineGrid[0, 3] = true;
MineGrid[8, 4] = true;
MineGrid[5, 7] = true;
```

Your array now looks like this:

	0	1	2	3	4	5	6	7	8
0	False	False	False	False	False	False	False	False	False
1	False	False	False	False	False	False	False	False	False
2	False	False	False	False	False	False	False	False	False
3	**True**	False	False	False	False	False	False	False	False
4	False	False	False	False	False	False	False	False	**True**
5	False	False	False	**True**	False	False	False	False	False
6	False	False	False	False	False	False	False	False	False
7	False	False	False	False	False	**True**	False	False	False
8	False	False	False	False	False	False	False	False	False

Your 4 'mines' are now in place in the array. You'll learn how to iterate through the 2-dimensional array and place the 'mines' onto the page in the next lesson: *Lesson 2-7: Iterate through a multidimensional array.*

tip

Auto-sizing a multidimensional array

In the *Essential Skills* course, you learned that you can create an array that automatically sets its own size.

For example, the following code would create an *int* array with the numbers 1, 2 and 3:

int[] IntArray = new int[]{1,2,3};

You can do the same thing with multidimensional arrays. Here's the code to create and populate a 3x3 *int* array without needing to manually specify its size:

*int[,] IntGrid = new int[,] {
{ 1, 2, 3 }, { 4, 5, 6 }, { 7, 8, 9 } };*

This code would create the following array:

1	2	3
4	5	6
7	8	9

note

Iterating through 3 dimensions

You could easily adapt this lesson's code to iterate through a 3-dimensional array.

Here's how 3-dimensional iteration code would look:

```
for (int X = 0;
X < MineGrid.GetLength(0); X++)
{
  for (int Y = 0;
  Y < MineGrid.GetLength(1);
  Y++)
  {
    for (int Z = 0;
    Z < MineGrid.GetLength(2);
    Z++)
    {
        //Code here
    }
  }
}
```

You could, of course, iterate through more dimensions by adding even more *for* loops.

Lesson 2-7: Iterate through a multidimensional array

In *Lesson 2-6: Create a multidimensional array*, you created a 2-dimensional array of *bool* variables to indicate the positions of 'mines' for a 'minesweeper' game.

In this lesson you'll add code to iterate through each element in your 2-dimensional array and make the web application fully functional.

1   Open *Sweep4Mines* from your sample files folder.

2   Open the code-behind file of *Default.aspx*.

3   Add code to iterate through the first dimension of the array.

Add the following code at the bottom of the *Page_Load* event handler:

for (int X = 0; X < MineGrid.GetLength(0); X++)
{
}

```
bool[,] MineGrid = new bool[9, 9];
MineGrid[3, 5] = true;
MineGrid[0, 3] = true;
MineGrid[8, 4] = true;
MineGrid[5, 7] = true;
for (int X = 0; X < MineGrid.GetLength(0); X++)
{
}
```

This is a simple *for* loop.

The *GetLength* method is used to get the number of elements in a specified dimension of an array. You want the length of the array's first dimension, so you asked the method for dimension *0*.

4   Add code to iterate through the second dimension of the array.

Add the following code inside the *for* loop that you just created:

for (int Y = 0; Y < MineGrid.GetLength(1); Y++)
{
}

```
for (int X = 0; X < MineGrid.GetLength(0); X++)
{
    for (int Y = 0; Y < MineGrid.GetLength(1); Y++)
    {

    }
}
```

Because this *for* loop is nested inside the previous one, it will run each time the first *for* loop cycles. This means that for every address on the 'X axis', the code will iterate through every address on the 'Y axis'.

This technique allows you to iterate through each element of any 2-dimensional array.

note

How this page works

This page uses two Table controls (that will ultimately produce HTML tables on the web page).

The *TableMines* table contains images of mines in the locations specified in the *MineGrid* array along with the numbers applied by the *AddNumbers* method.

The *TableMask* table sits on top of *TableMines*, hiding the mines and numbers from view.

When you set the *CssClass* property of a cell in the *TableMines* table to "*Mine*", an image of a mine is displayed in the *TableMines* table (though it is initially hidden by the *TableMask* table).

The page's JavaScript code runs whenever the user clicks a cell in the *TableMask* HTML table. The JavaScript code examines the *CssClass* property of the cell.

If the JavaScript code finds a *CssClass* of "*MineHere*", it hides the *TableMask* table and displays 'GAME OVER'. Otherwise, it simply reveals the cell that the user clicked.

The page uses *JQuery* to show and hide cells. You'll learn more about *JQuery* in: *Lesson 9-9: Understand JQuery.*

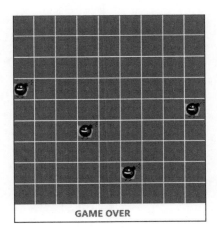

5 Add code to check the value of each element.

Because your *for* loops will search through every element in the array, you can now check each value. You're searching for a *true* value, indicating that a mine is present at that location.

Add the following code inside the second *for* loop:

if (MineGrid[X, Y] == true)
{
}

```
for (int X = 0; X < MineGrid.GetLength(0); X++)
{
    for (int Y = 0; Y < MineGrid.GetLength(1); Y++)
    {
        if (MineGrid[X, Y] == true)
        {

        }
    }
}
```

This code uses the iteration variables from both *for* loops in order to check each item in the array. For example, the first iteration will check:

if (MineGrid[0,0] == true)

…the second will check:

if (MineGrid[0,1] == true)

…and so on.

6 Add code to update the tables.

Add the following code inside the *if* statement:

TableMask.Rows[Y].Cells[X].CssClass = "MineHere";
TableMines.Rows[Y].Cells[X].CssClass = "Mine";

```
if (MineGrid[X, Y] == true)
{
    TableMask.Rows[Y].Cells[X].CssClass = "MineHere";
    TableMines.Rows[Y].Cells[X].CssClass = "Mine";
}
```

This adds information to the page that will be recognized by its JavaScript code. See sidebar for an explanation of how this works.

7 Add code to add numbers to the grid.

Add the following code at the end of the *Page_Load* event handler:

AddNumbers(MineGrid);

I've written a fully commented *AddNumbers* method that uses the skills you've learned in this lesson to add numbers to the grid in compliance with the rules of the minesweeper game. Review the code (you'll find it in *Utilities.cs*) to confirm that you completely understand how it works.

8 Test the page.

View *Default.aspx* in your web browser and try clicking the cells.

Clicking one of the 'mines' will reveal all of the mines and display *GAME OVER*.

Lesson 2-8: Send commands to the Garbage Collector

The Garbage Collector is a special feature of C# that automatically clears objects from memory when they are no longer needed. For example, once a method has finished execution the Garbage Collector removes any variables it used from memory.

Thanks to the Garbage Collector, it's very rare for C# applications to suffer from 'memory leak' issues where the program uses up more and more memory until it overloads the system.

The Garbage Collector will work automatically without you needing to do anything, but you can send commands to it by using the *GC* class. The *GC* class can also provide some useful information about memory usage.

In this lesson you'll use the *GC* class to give commands to the Garbage Collector.

1 Open *StableBase* from your sample files folder.

2 Open the code-behind file of *ScheduleAdmin.aspx*.

The *GetSchedule* method on this page creates a *List* collection of *TaskRow* objects in order to display a schedule on the page.

`List<TaskRow> TableRows`

The Garbage Collector will automatically remove the collection from memory eventually, but you can use the *GC* class to tell the Garbage Collector to remove it as soon as the method is finished.

3 Use the *GC* class to examine memory usage.

1. Add the following code to the *Page_Load* method, just before the code that calls the *GetSchedule()* method:

   Response.Write("Memory usage before GetSchedule method: " + GC.GetTotalMemory(false) + "<br/>");

   ```
   if (!IsPostBack)
   {
       Response.Write("Memory usage before GetSchedule method: "
           + GC.GetTotalMemory(false) + "<br/>");
       GetSchedule();
   ```

2. Add the following code just after the *GetSchedule* method is called:

   Response.Write("Memory usage after GetSchedule method: " + GC.GetTotalMemory(false));

   ```
   Response.Write("Memory usage before GetSchedule method: "
       + GC.GetTotalMemory(false) + "<br/>");
   GetSchedule();
   Response.Write("Memory usage after GetSchedule method: "
       + GC.GetTotalMemory(false));
   ```

3. View *ScheduleAdmin.aspx* in your web browser.

4. Examine the lines at the top of the screen:

This indicates that 13,563,732 bytes of memory were being used before the *GetSchedule* method was called and 14,745,392 bytes were being used afterwards.

These numbers will always be different depending on your computer's current state, so you won't get exactly the same values. You should always find, however, that the second number is higher than the first one.

By subtracting the two numbers, you can see that calling the *GetSchedule* method added 1,181,660 bytes of memory usage to your application (about 1.13Mb).

5. Close your web browser and return to Visual Studio.

4 Manually tell the Garbage Collector to clean up memory.

1. Add the following line of code just after the *GetSchedule* method is called:

    GC.Collect();

    ```
    GetSchedule();
    GC.Collect();
    Response.Write("Memory usage after GetSchedule method: "
    ```

    This tells the Garbage Collector to clean up memory immediately after the *GetSchedule* method is finished.

2. View *ScheduleAdmin.aspx* in your web browser once more.

3. Examine the lines at the top of the screen.

The Garbage Collector cleaned up 22,205,732 bytes of memory when you called its *Collect* method. However, not all of this memory was allocated by the *GetSchedule* method. The Garbage Collector cleaned up some other objects that were added by ASP.NET.

4. Refresh the page by using your web browser's *Refresh* button.

This time the difference is much smaller: only 517,060 bytes. You might find that your application is still using slightly more memory after calling the method than before it, but the difference will be much smaller than it was before.

You might think that telling the Garbage Collector to clean up memory has made a huge improvement to this project's memory efficiency, but it's important to remember that the Garbage Collector would have eventually done this automatically.

It's really never necessary to tell the Garbage Collector to clean up memory, but it is useful to understand how it works and how to use it to monitor memory usage.

---

important

Using the GC class can make your project use more memory!

The Garbage Collector files your objects into one of three categories (or *generations*):

Generation 0 contains objects that will be disposed of quickly, such as variables within methods.

Generation 1 contains objects that are expected to remain in memory for longer. A public property of a class might be a generation 1 object.

Generation 2 contains objects that are expected to remain in memory for a long time, such as static classes.

When the Garbage Collector cleans up memory, it 'promotes' any objects that are still in use to the next generation. Misusing the GC class can lead to objects being promoted to inappropriate generations and remaining in memory for longer than they should.

If in doubt, just don't use the GC class!

Lesson 2-9: Send e-mail messages using the SmtpClient class

It's often necessary for an ASP.NET web application to send e-mail messages. Session 9 of the *Essential Skills* course in this series shows you how to configure e-mail settings for ASP.NET controls that automatically send e-mails.

In this lesson you'll learn how to use the *SmtpClient* class to send e-mail messages using C# code.

1   Open *JoesBarWebApplication* from your sample files folder.

2   Open the code-behind file of *Default.aspx*.

You're going to add code to make the contact form on this page functional.

3   Remove all code from the *ButtonSignUpEmail_Click* event handler.

4   Add code to create an instance of the *SmtpClient* class.

1.   Add *using* lines to the top of the page with the following code:

```
using System.Web.UI.WebControls;
using System.Net;
using System.Net.Mail;
```

using System.Net;
using System.Net.Mail;

The *SmtpClient* class is in the *System.Net.Mail* namespace, so this will make it easier to access.

The *System.Net* namespace contains the *NetworkCredential* class. You'll need this to send a username and password to the SMTP mail server.

2.   Add the following code to the *ButtonSignUpEmail_Click* event handler:

SmtpClient Client = new SmtpClient();

```
protected void ButtonSignUpEmail_Click(object sender, EventArgs e)
{
    SmtpClient Client = new SmtpClient();
}
```

This code creates a new instance of the *SmtpClient* class.

5   Add code to configure the *SmtpClient* object.

The *Host, Port* and *Credentials* properties have to be set manually in order to test the e-mail send facility on your local machine. This isn't always the case when you publish a web site to a web server because if the web server has been configured to allow e-mails to be sent, the SmtpClient object will automatically detect the correct settings.

You may already have access to a working SMTP mail server and know which settings to use. If you don't, but still want to test this fully, you can use google's free e-mail service by signing up for a *GMail* account at: *http://www.gmail.com*

note

Configuring the SmtpClient using Web.config

In this lesson you manually specify the settings for your *SmtpClient* object, but you can avoid doing this entirely if you place e-mail settings in the *Web.config* file.

The easiest way to do this is to configure your application's SMTP settings using the ASP.NET Configuration utility. This was covered in Session 9 of the *Essential Skills* course in this series.

If you've configured your SMTP settings in *Web.config*, you can simply use the *SmtpClient.Send* method without needing to set any properties.

note

Advanced e-mail features

Although this lesson covers the basics, you might want to do more advanced things with e-mail, such as sending attachments.

This can be achieved by using the *MailMessage* class, which has properties and methods for many more advanced features including attachments, encoding and priority.

Once you've created your *MailMessage* object, you can send it by using the *SmtpClient.Send* method that you used in this lesson.

important

If this example doesn't work

If you're sure that you've configured the *SmtpClient* correctly but still receive an error message when testing this code, it is possible that you need to enable SSL (Secure Socket Layer).

To do this, set the *Client.EnableSSL* property to:
true

SSL is used to send e-mail messages securely. Some e-mail services may refuse to send messages without SSL.

From learnasp4@gmail.com
Subject **Discount Sign-Up**
To Me <SimonSmart@ASPNETCentral.com>

Sign up Beer@ASPNETCentral.com

If you are using *GMail*, the following settings were correct in August 2013 (but as with all things on the web they may change):

Client.Host = "smtp.gmail.com";
Client.Port = 587;
Client.Credentials = new NetworkCredential
("*[Your GMail address]*", "*[Your Gmail password]*");

```
SmtpClient Client = new SmtpClient();
Client.Host = "smtp.gmail.com";
Client.Port = 587;
Client.Credentials = new NetworkCredential
    ("[Your GMail address]", "[Your Gmail password]");
```

6   Add code to send the e-mail message.

Add the following code on the next line:

string AddressToSignUp = TextBoxEmailAddress.Text;
Client.Send("SimonSmart@ASPNETCentral.com",
"*[Your e-mail address]*", **"Discount Sign-Up",**
"Sign up " + AddressToSignUp);

```
string AddressToSignUp = TextBoxEmailAddress.Text;
Client.Send("SimonSmart@ASPNETCentral.com", "[Your e-mail address]",
    "Discount Sign-Up", "Sign up " + AddressToSignUp);
```

This code attempts to send an e-mail message from *Simon.Smart@ASPNETCentral.com* to your e-mail address. The message will have the subject *Discount Sign-Up* and the body text *Sign up [the e-mail address that the user has entered on the form]*.

7   Add code to stop the user from clicking again.

In a real project you'd add some kind of confirmation message here, but we'll settle for just disabling the controls on the page.

Add the following code:

ButtonSignUpEmail.Enabled = false;
TextBoxEmailAddress.Enabled = false;

```
    "Discount Sign-Up", "Sign up " + AddressToSignUp);
ButtonSignUpEmail.Enabled = false;
TextBoxEmailAddress.Enabled = false;
```

8   Test the page.

1.   View *Default.aspx* in your web browser.

2.   Enter your e-mail address in the text box.

| Beer@ASPNETCentral.com | Give Me Free Beer! |

3.   Click *Give Me Free Beer!*

The e-mail message is sent and the controls are disabled. If you got an error message it was probably caused by an error in the *Host, Port* or *Credentials* property settings.

See sidebar if you're sure that you have the correct settings.

9   Check your e-mail.

If you correctly configured the *SmtpClient* object and followed this lesson's instructions, you will find the e-mail message in your inbox.

Session 2: Exercise

1   Open *Exercise2* from your sample files folder.

2   Open *MultiMath.aspx* in *Design* view.

This page displays the results of adding, subtracting, multiplying and dividing the numbers entered in the text boxes.

3   Open the code-behind file of *MultiMath.aspx*.

4   Create a new method called *DoAddSubtractMultiplyDivide*. The new method should return a *Tuple* with four *double* properties. It should accept two *double* arguments named *Number1* and *Number2*.

5   Add code to the method to add, subtract, multiply and divide *Number1* and *Number2* and return a *Tuple* containing the results of each calculation.

6   Add code to the *ButtonDoMath_Click* event handler to call the *DoAddSubtractMultipleDivide* method and display the results in the *Label* controls on the page.

RESULTS
Add: 452.2
Subtract: -144.8
Multiply: 45879.45
Divide: 0.514907872696817

7   Open *Upload.aspx* in *Design* view.

This page allows you to upload files, which should then be stored in the database.

8   Open the code-behind file of *Upload.aspx*.

9   Add code to the *ButtonUploadFile_Click* event handler to retrieve a *byte* array from the *FileUploadFileToUpload* control. Note that you can use the *FileBytes* property of the control to do this.

10   Add code to make the *Data* object lazily instantiated.

11   Add code to the *ButtonUploadFile_Click* event handler to set the properties of the *NewFile* object using your *byte* array and the *FileName* property of the *FileUpload* control.

12   Add code to tell the Garbage Collector to clean up memory at the end of the event handler.

13   Open *Grid.aspx* in *Design* view.

This page will populate the *Table* control's cells with random background colors.

14   Open the code-behind file of *Grid.aspx*.

15   Add code to the *ButtonGetColors_Click* event handler to create a 3x3 array of *Color* objects named:
ColorArray

16   Add code to loop through your array and populate each element using the *GetRandomColor* method.

17   Add code to loop through your array and set the *BackColor* property of each cell in the *TableGrid* table with the value from your array. Do this using the following property:
TableGrid.Rows[X].Cells[Y].BackColor

If you need help slide the page to the left

Exercise2 - Start   Exercise2 - End

Session 2: Exercise Answers

These are the four questions that students find the most difficult to answer:

Q 17	Q 10	Q 9	Q 4

Use the following code:
 	
``
for (int X = 0; X < 3; X++)
{
    for (int Y = 0; Y < 3; Y++)
    {
        TableGrid
        .Rows[X].Cells
        [Y].BackColor =
        ColorArray[X, Y];
    }
}
``
 	
This was covered in: *Lesson 2-7: Iterate through a multidimensional array.*
	Use the following code:
	
	``
	Lazy
	<Exercise2Data
	Context>
	Data = new Lazy
	<Exercise2Data
	Context>();
	``
	
	This was covered in: *Lesson 2-2: Use the Lazy class.*
		Use the following code:
		
		``
		byte[] FileBytes =
		FileUploadFileToUpload
		.FileBytes;
		``
		
		This was covered in: *Lesson 2-4: Use the Byte class.*
			Use the following code:
			
			``
			private Tuple
			<double,double,
			double,double>
			DoAddSubtract
			MultiplyDivide
			(double Number1,
			double Number2)
			{
			}
			``
			
			This was covered in: *Lesson 2-1: Use the Tuple class.*

If you have difficulty with the other questions, here are the lessons that cover the relevant skills:

1   **Refer to: Essential Skills Session 1.**

2   **Refer to: Essential Skills Session 1.**

3   **Refer to: Essential Skills Session 1.**

5   **Refer to: Lesson 2-1: Use the Tuple class.**

6   **Refer to: Lesson 2-1: Use the Tuple class.**

7   **Refer to: Essential Skills Session 1.**

8   **Refer to: Essential Skills Session 1.**

11   **Refer to: Essential Skills Session 10 (particularly Lesson 10-8).**

12   **Refer to: Lesson 2-8: Send commands to the Garbage Collector.**

13   **Refer to: Essential Skills Session 1.**

14   **Refer to: Essential Skills Session 1.**

15   **Refer to: Lesson 2-7: Iterate through a multidimensional array.**

16   **Refer to: Lesson 2-7: Iterate through a multidimensional array.**

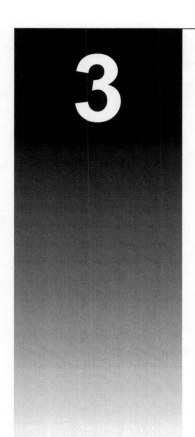

Session Three: Threading and Cryptography

> The only truly secure system is one that is powered off, cast in a block of concrete and sealed in a lead-lined room with armed guards – and even then I have my doubts.
>
> *Gene Spafford, Professor of Computer Science (born 1956)*

Since the dawn of the internet age, privacy has become harder and harder to maintain. Anything that is sent over the internet or stored on a computer can potentially be accessed by unwanted visitors.

One way to mitigate this problem is to encrypt any information that you want to remain a secret. Modern encryption algorithms are capable of producing codes that would take months, years or even centuries for the fastest computers to break. However, as Gene Spafford observes, mankind has not yet developed any encryption system that is truly unbreakable.

In this session you'll learn how to use the features of the System.Security.Cryptography namespace to encrypt and decrypt information.

You'll also learn how to use the Thread class to add multi-threading to your code, enabling you to take advantage of systems with multiple CPU cores.

Session Objectives

By the end of this session you will be able to:

- Understand cryptography and prepare data for encryption
- Encrypt data using the AES standard
- Decrypt data using the AES standard
- Implement multi-threading using the Action and Task classes
- Prevent race conditions when working with the Task class
- Implement multi-threading using the Thread class
- Implement multi-threading using the ThreadPool class
- Use the lock statement to prevent threads from conflicting
- Display a loading indicator using JavaScript
- Implement multi-threading using the Parallel class

Lesson 3-1: Understand cryptography and prepare data for encryption

Cryptography is the science of hiding information using secret codes.

Although there's evidence of cryptography dating back to the ancient Egyptians, the rise of computer technology has led to codes that no human could break without the aid of a computer.

In this lesson you'll learn about how cryptography works in C# and prepare some information to be encrypted. You'll carry out the actual encryption in: *Lesson 3-2: Encrypt data using the AES standard.*

1   Open *TextLand* from your sample files folder.

2   View *Encryption.aspx* in Design view.

The text box on this page contains some military orders from World War 2.

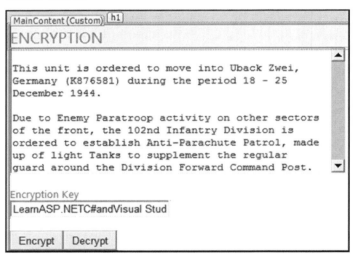

In 1944, the army would have had to encrypt and decrypt these orders by hand, but when this page is complete it will be able to encrypt and decrypt the orders in less than a second.

3   Open the code-behind file of *Encryption.aspx*.

```
using System.Web.UI.WebControls;
using System.Security.Cryptography;
using System.IO;
using System.Text;
```

4   Add *using* lines to speed up access to the important classes.

Add the following *using* lines at the top of the page:

using System.Security.Cryptography;
using System.IO;
using System.Text;

System.Security.Cryptography contains ASP.NET's encryption algorithms.

System.IO contains the *Stream* objects that will be used for encryption.

System.Text contains methods to convert text into binary data.

If you are not completing the course incrementally use the sample file: **Lesson 3-1** to begin this lesson.

Sample files with the starting point for each lesson are also provided for all of the other lessons in this session.

5   Add code to prepare the text for encryption.

note

Encoding

In order to save *string* data as binary data, it must be *encoded*. Different encoding standards will produce different binary data. In this lesson you encode the text with the UTF8 standard.

All encoding standards are capable of handling standard English letters and numbers, as well as most symbols.

The differences between encoding standards appear when working with different languages as some characters will not be supported by all encoding standards.

note

Initialization Vectors

As noted in the lesson, the initialization vector is not unlike a secondary encryption key as its presence makes the encryption harder to crack.

If you use an encryption standard that requires initialization vectors, you will need to keep a record of the initialization vector as it will be needed (along with the encryption key) to decrypt the data.

It's not recommended to reuse initialization vectors.

Someone trying to crack your encryption can detect patterns arising from repeated initialization vectors. This may enable them to break your encryption.

1. Add the following code to the *ButtonEncrypt_Click* event handler:

    byte[] BytesToEncrypt = Encoding.UTF8.GetBytes(TextBoxEncryption.Text);

    ```
    protected void ButtonEncrypt_Click(object sender, EventArgs e)
    {
        byte[] BytesToEncrypt =
            Encoding.UTF8.GetBytes(TextBoxEncryption.Text);
    ```

    This code converts the contents of the *TextBoxEncryption* control into a *byte* array, representing binary data. You learned about byte arrays in: *Lesson 2-4: Use the Byte class.*

    Encryption in C# always works with binary data, so you'll have to convert anything that you need to encrypt into a *byte* array.

    The *Encoding* class is used to convert *string* data into binary data and back again. See sidebar for more on this.

2. Add the following code on the next line:

    string StringEncryptionKey = TextBoxEncryptionKey.Text.PadRight(32);
    byte[] EncryptionKey = Encoding.UTF8.GetBytes(StringEncryptionKey);

    ```
    byte[] BytesToEncrypt = Encoding.UTF8.GetBytes(TextBoxEncryption.Text);
    string StringEncryptionKey = TextBoxEncryptionKey.Text.PadRight(32);
    byte[] EncryptionKey = Encoding.UTF8.GetBytes(StringEncryptionKey);
    ```

    An encryption key is always needed when encrypting data and will be needed in order to decrypt the information again.

    The AES algorithm requires a 32 byte (256 bit) encryption key, so this code uses the *PadRight* method to pad the text if the user has entered a key that is less than 32 characters long.

3. Add the following property by placing its code outside any event handlers:

    byte[] InitializationVector = new byte[]
    { 1, 2, 3, 4, 5, 6, 7, 8, 9, 10, 11, 12, 13, 14, 15, 16 };

    ```
    byte[] InitializationVector = new byte[]
    { 1, 2, 3, 4, 5, 6, 7, 8, 9, 10, 11, 12, 13, 14, 15, 16 };

    protected void ButtonEncrypt_Click(object sender, EventArgs e)
    ```

    The AES standard requires an *initialization vector* as well as an encryption key. This is essentially a secondary encryption key, although reusing the same initialization vector is bad practice (see sidebar).

    The initialization vector that I've used (sequential numbers from 1 to 16) is just about the worst vector you could possibly use in a real-world situation as it can easily be guessed!

You'll use your binary data, encryption key and initialization vector to encrypt the military orders in the next lesson: *Lesson 3-2: Encrypt data using the AES standard.*

note

How secure is AES?

The AES encryption standard is used by the US government to encrypt its secret information.

The security of encryption depends on the length of the encryption key. AES can use encryption keys that are 128, 192 or 256 bits long.

With a 256-bit encryption key, the fastest computer in the world would take thousands of years to crack the encryption.

You're using a 256-bit encryption key in this example.

Lesson 3-2: Encrypt data using the AES standard

The .NET framework has many cryptography classes. You're only going to use the widely-used *Advanced Encryption Standard* (or *AES*) in this course, but you'll be able to apply the skills that you learn to implement any of the other encryption standards supported by C#.

1 Open *TextLand* from your sample files folder.

2 Open the code-behind file of *Encryption.aspx*.

3 Add code to prepare the AES encryption algorithm.

Add the following code at the end of the *ButtonEncrypt_Click* event handler.

Aes AESAlgorithm = Aes.Create();
AESAlgorithm.Key = EncryptionKey;
AESAlgorithm.IV = InitializationVector;

```
byte[] EncryptionKey = Encoding.UTF8.GetBytes(StringEncryptionKey);
Aes AESAlgorithm = Aes.Create();
AESAlgorithm.Key = EncryptionKey;
AESAlgorithm.IV = InitializationVector;
```

This code creates an *Aes* object and sets its encryption key and initialization vector to the values that you prepared in: *Lesson 3-1: Understand cryptography and prepare data for encryption.*

The *Aes* class is in the *System.Security.Cryptography* namespace.

The other encryption algorithms in the *System.Security.Cryptography* namespace behave in a very similar way to the *Aes* class (see sidebar: *Other encryption standards*).

4 Add code to encrypt the binary data.

1. Add the following code on the next line to create a new *MemoryStream* object:

    using (MemoryStream StreamIntoMemory =
    new MemoryStream()) { }

    ```
    AESAlgorithm.IV = InitializationVector;
    using (MemoryStream StreamIntoMemory =
        new MemoryStream())
    {
    }
    ```

    The *MemoryStream* class is very similar to the *Stream* class that you worked with in: *Lesson 2-3: Use the Stream class*. The *MemoryStream* class is specifically designed to work with binary data that is stored in memory (as opposed to binary data that is stored in a file).

    This *MemoryStream* object will be used to receive and store the encrypted binary data from your encryption algorithm.

2. Add the following code inside the *using* statement:

    using (CryptoStream EncryptionStream =
    new CryptoStream(StreamIntoMemory,
    AESAlgorithm.CreateEncryptor(),
    CryptoStreamMode.Write)) { }

    ```
    using (MemoryStream StreamIntoMemory = new M
    {
        using (CryptoStream EncryptionStream =
            new CryptoStream(StreamIntoMemory,
            AESAlgorithm.CreateEncryptor(),
            CryptoStreamMode.Write))
        {
        }
    }
    ```

    The *CryptoStream* class comes from the *System.Security.Cryptography* namespace. It's a special kind of *Stream* object that is used to encrypt and decrypt data.

The first argument tells the *CryptoStream* object to write the encrypted data into the *StreamIntoMemory* object.

The second argument contains the object that provides the encryption algorithm: the *AESAlgorithm* object.

The third argument tells the *CryptoStream* object that it is going to *Write* information into the *StreamIntoMemory* object, rather than *Read* from it.

3. Add the following code inside the *using* statement:

EncryptionStream.Write(BytesToEncrypt, 0, BytesToEncrypt.Length);

```
        CryptoStreamMode.Write))
{
    EncryptionStream.Write(BytesToEncrypt, 0, BytesToEncrypt.Length);
}
```

This code tells your *CryptoStream* object to carry out the encryption and write all of the encrypted data into the *StreamIntoMemory* object.

The *StreamIntoMemory* object will now contain an encrypted version of the data.

5 Add code to extract and display the encrypted data.

1. Add the following code outside the second *using* statement, but still inside the first *using* statement:

byte[] EncryptedBytes = StreamIntoMemory.ToArray();

```
        EncryptionStream.Write(BytesToEncrypt, 0, BytesT
    }
    byte[] EncryptedBytes = StreamIntoMemory.ToArray();
}
```

This code extracts the encrypted data from the *StreamIntoMemory* object and places it into a *byte* array.

2. Add the following code on the next line:

string EncryptedString = Convert.ToBase64String(EncryptedBytes); TextBoxEncryption.Text = EncryptedString;

```
byte[] EncryptedBytes = StreamIntoMemory.ToArray();
string EncryptedString = Convert.ToBase64String(EncryptedBytes);
TextBoxEncryption.Text = EncryptedString;
```

This code converts the encrypted data back into a *string* and displays it on the page (see sidebar for more on the *Convert.ToBase64String* method).

6 Test your encryption code.

1. View *Encryption.aspx* in your web browser.

2. Click *Encrypt*.

The military orders are encrypted into a meaningless series of characters. You could be confident that nobody will be able to decrypt the text without the correct encryption keys.

In the next lesson you'll write code that will enable you to decrypt this data back into its original form.

ENCRYPTION

DrGqS6E2WkuQ4gIIJJR6lxaUna5m3k0/7a3qR+RKoZpTukYGCm
PeSnOUCNVtEMsxzhb/EhQJ6ZSeYO10rqpG3Vw2DnFKCPVFnAuI
c88AtHRg5i204xQQ2CNLgG851dWm8Hz3EXopNATDjQQVknoWul
NA/U7G871NIAP/MEQInjCbhOVziDg+0JJjWlwnFzYRXhi21LKi
YdMsu1QywIveCbquOKhiitQQNvNuFU31qkTuNqGXHfbUHd1OYL
rvb1ouTXLpkwv3Lk204XXTsMPrKkIvt/Puz2ZdCz6T+ugeRDXp
WFb/uNfpAtK/gwaUjncHsQvN7sOmfYdI0T0KmVZx5CEYLKq/+I
9VV+RH279rgYGzVLuQLDX5LncpEyn5letSf+1kf9f2VKYnP8Fu
4CKsp02uK8nGrsH1SjrO72EjbOiPaC1G+OakAcbwrgcDHdOuah
aywd7CP7z5tnVVL4h0Tg==

Lesson 3-3: Decrypt data using the AES standard

You encrypted some data in the previous lesson: *Lesson 3-2: Encrypt data using the AES standard.* In this lesson you're going to write code that will decrypt the data back into its original form.

1   Open *TextLand* from your sample files folder.

2   Open the code-behind file of *Encryption.aspx*.

3   Add code to retrieve the encrypted binary data.

Add the following line of code to the *ButtonDecrypt_Click* event handler:

byte[] BytesToDecrypt = Convert.FromBase64String(TextBoxEncryption.Text);

```
protected void ButtonDecrypt_Click(object sender, EventArgs e)
{
    byte[] BytesToDecrypt = Convert.FromBase64String(TextBoxEncryption.Text);
}
```

This code converts the text from the *TextBoxEncryption* control into a *byte* array. You learned about the *Convert.FromBase64String* method in: *Lesson 3-2: Encrypt data using the AES standard (sidebar).*

4   Add code to prepare the AES encryption algorithm.

Add the following code on the next line:

string StringEncryptionKey = TextBoxEncryptionKey.Text.PadRight(32);
byte[] EncryptionKey = Encoding.UTF8.GetBytes(StringEncryptionKey);
Aes AESAlgorithm = Aes.Create();
AESAlgorithm.Key = EncryptionKey;
AESAlgorithm.IV = InitializationVector;

```
byte[] BytesToDecrypt = Convert.FromBase64String(TextBoxEncryption.Text);
string StringEncryptionKey = TextBoxEncryptionKey.Text.PadRight(32);
byte[] EncryptionKey = Encoding.UTF8.GetBytes(StringEncryptionKey);
Aes AESAlgorithm = Aes.Create();
AESAlgorithm.Key = EncryptionKey;
AESAlgorithm.IV = InitializationVector;
```

This code prepares the classes in the same way as you did in: *Lesson 3-1: Understand cryptography and prepare data for encryption.*

5   Add code to decrypt the binary data.

Add the following code on the next line:

using (MemoryStream StreamIntoMemory = new MemoryStream())
{
    using (CryptoStream DecryptionStream = new CryptoStream(StreamIntoMemory, AESAlgorithm.<u>CreateDecryptor</u>(), CryptoStreamMode.Write))
    {
        DecryptionStream.Write(BytesToDecrypt, 0, BytesToDecrypt.Length);

```
        }
        byte[] DecryptedBytes = StreamIntoMemory.ToArray();
        string DecryptedString =
        Encoding.UTF8.GetString(DecryptedBytes);
        TextBoxEncryption.Text = DecryptedString;
    }
```

This code is exactly the same as the encryption code except for one detail: instead of calling the *CreateEncryptor* method of the *AESAlgorithm* object, you are calling the *CreateDecryptor* method.

```
protected void ButtonDecrypt_Click(object sender, EventArgs e)
{
    byte[] BytesToDecrypt = Convert.FromBase64String(TextBoxEncryption.Text);
    string StringEncryptionKey = TextBoxEncryptionKey.Text.PadRight(32);
    byte[] EncryptionKey = Encoding.UTF8.GetBytes(StringEncryptionKey);
    Aes AESAlgorithm = Aes.Create();
    AESAlgorithm.Key = EncryptionKey;
    AESAlgorithm.IV = InitializationVector;
    using (MemoryStream StreamIntoMemory = new MemoryStream())
    {
        using (CryptoStream DecryptionStream = new CryptoStream(
            StreamIntoMemory,
            AESAlgorithm.CreateDecryptor(),
            CryptoStreamMode.Write))
        {
            DecryptionStream.Write(BytesToDecrypt, 0, BytesToDecrypt.Length);
        }
        byte[] DecryptedBytes = StreamIntoMemory.ToArray();
        string DecryptedString = Encoding.UTF8.GetString(DecryptedBytes);
        TextBoxEncryption.Text = DecryptedString;
    }
}
```

Your decryption code is now complete.

6   Test your decryption code.

1. View *Encryption.aspx* in your web browser.

2. Change the encryption key if you wish.

3. Click *Encrypt*.

    The text is encrypted into a jumble of characters.

    ENCRYPTION

    DrGqS6E2WkuQ4gIIJJR61xaUna5m3k0/7a3qR+RKoZpTukYGCm
    PeSnOUCNVtEMsxzhb/EhQJ6ZSeYO10rqpG3Vw2DnFKCPVFnAuT
    c88AtHRg5i204xQQ2CNLgG851dWm8Hz3EXopNATDjQQVknoWul
    NA/U7G871NIAP/MEQInjCbhOVziDg+0JJjWlwnFzYRXhi21LKi
    YdMsu1QywTveCbquOKhiitQQNvNuFU31qkTuNqGXHfbUHd1OYL
    rvb1ouTXLpkwv3Lk204XXTsMPrKkIvt/Puz2ZdCz6T+ugeRDXp
    WFb/uNfpAtK/gwaUjncHsQvN7sOmfYdI0T0KmVZx5CEYLKq/+I
    9VV+RH279rgYGzVLuQLDX5LncpEynSletSf+1kf9f2VKYnP8Fu
    4CKsp02uK8nGrsH1SjrO72EjbOiPaC1G+OakAcbwrgcDHdOuah
    aywd7CP7z5tnVVL4h0Tg==

4. Click *Decrypt*.

    The data is decrypted back into its original form.

    ENCRYPTION

    This unit is ordered to move into Uback Zwei,
    Germany (K876581) during the period 18 - 25
    December 1944.

    Due to Enemy Paratroop activity on other sectors
    of the front, the 102nd Infantry Division is
    ordered to establish Anti-Parachute Patrol, made
    up of light Tanks to supplement the regular guard
    around the Division Forward Command Post.

Lesson 3-4: Implement multi-threading using the Action and Task classes

note

The Task class in ASP.NET 4.0

An earlier version of the *Task* class existed in ASP.NET 4.0, but it was extremely limited compared to the version that is provided in ASP.NET 4.5.

I would recommend against using the *Task* class in earlier versions of ASP.NET.

When a program runs on a computer, it is assigned to a process (or "thread") which runs on the computer's processor. Until recent years, most computers only contained a single processor, so there was no benefit to having more than one thread running at a time.

Modern computers often contain two, four, or even more processors. By creating multiple threads using the *Action* and *Task* classes, you can divide intensive tasks between the computer's processors, significantly speeding up the task.

The *Action* and *Task* classes are almost completely new in ASP.NET 4.5 (see sidebar). In previous versions, the *Thread* or *ThreadPool* classes would have been used. The *Task* class combines the features of the *Thread* and *ThreadPool* classes, making it the ideal choice for multi-threading.

1   Open *MathLand* from your sample files folder.

2   View *Primes.aspx* in your web browser.

This page calculates prime numbers up to the value specified. It does this by counting backwards and attempting to divide each number by every number below it.

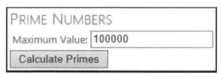

This may not be the best way to calculate prime numbers, but it's a good example of a computationally intensive task.

3   Test *Primes.aspx*.

1.   Click *Calculate Primes* to calculate every prime number up to 100,000.

Depending on your computer's speed, there may now be a long delay. The calculation took 22 seconds on my computer.

The prime numbers are displayed in a *ListBox* control.

2.   Close your web browser and return to Visual Studio.

4   Open the code-behind file of *Primes.aspx*.

5   Examine the existing code.

1.   Examine the *ButtonCalculatePrimes_Click* event handler and find the line:

CalculatePrimes(new int[] {2, MaximumValue});

```
CalculatePrimes(new int[] {2, MaximumValue});
```

This code calls the *CalculatePrimes* method with an *int* array as an argument.

2.   Examine the *CalculatePrimes* method.

This method may look a little strange.

```
public void CalculatePrimes(object ValueFromAndTo)
{
    int[] ValueFromAndToArray = (int[])ValueFromAndTo;
```

Instead of an *int[]* argument, it accepts an *object* argument and then converts it into an *int[]* on the first line.

This is necessary because the *Task* object is only able to work with methods that either have no arguments or have a single *object* argument.

6   Add code to create a new *Action* object.

1.   Add the following *using* line at the top of the code:

using System.Threading.Tasks;

The *Task* class is in the new *System.Threading.Tasks* namespace, so this line will make it easier to access.

2.   In the *ButtonCalculatePrimes_Click* event handler, replace:

CalculatePrimes(new int[] {2, MaximumValue});

…with:

Action<object> CalculatePrimesAction = new Action<object>(CalculatePrimes);

This code creates a new *Action* object that points to the *CalculatePrimes* method.

The *Action* class actually creates a *delegate* for the *CalculatePrimes* method. You'll learn more about delegates in: *Lesson 4-10: Understand delegate methods.*

3.   Add the following code on the next line:

Task Thread1 = Task.Factory.StartNew (CalculatePrimesAction, new int[] { 2, MaximumValue / 2 });

```
Action<object> CalculatePrimesAction = new Action<object>(CalculatePrimes);
Task Thread1 = Task.Factory.StartNew(CalculatePrimesAction, new int[] { 2, MaximumValue / 2 });
```

This code creates and starts a new thread. Because you only want *Task1* to do half of the work, you are telling it to calculate prime numbers from 2 to half of the maximum value.

7   Add code to create a second thread.

Add the following code on the next line:

Task Thread2 = Task.Factory.StartNew(CalculatePrimesAction, new int[] { (MaximumValue / 2) + 1, MaximumValue });

```
Action<object> CalculatePrimesAction = new Action<object>(CalculatePrimes);
Task Thread1 = Task.Factory.StartNew(CalculatePrimesAction, new int[] { 2, MaximumValue / 2 });
Task Thread2 = Task.Factory.StartNew(CalculatePrimesAction, new int[] { (MaximumValue / 2) + 1, MaximumValue });
```

This code creates and starts a second thread, which will calculate the other half of the prime numbers.

You might think that this code is now complete, but this code is vulnerable to a terrible form of error known as a *race condition*.

In the next lesson you'll learn about race conditions and fix this code to prevent one from occurring.

Lesson 3-5: Prevent race conditions when working with the Task class

In *Lesson 3-4: Implement multi-threading using the Action and Task classes*, you learned how to create multiple threads to speed up complex tasks, but the code you added introduced something called a *race condition*.

In this lesson you'll learn about race conditions and fix the code to prevent one from occurring.

1 Open *MathLand* from your sample files folder.

2 View *Primes.aspx* in Debug mode.

1. Open *Primes.aspx*.

2. Click Debug→Start Debugging.

3 See the race condition problem.

1. Enter **100** into the *Maximum Value* box.

2. Click *Calculate Primes*.

The calculation may work without any problems.

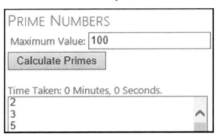

Note that you may also find that no results are returned. This is also related to the race condition problem.

3. Enter **100000** into the *Maximum Value* box.

4. Click *Calculate Primes*.

This time an exception occurs and you are returned to Visual Studio (see sidebar if it doesn't).

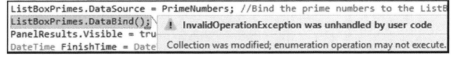

To understand why this error occurs, consider what is happening in the code. First *Thread1* begins and, while it is still running in the background, *Thread2* begins.

Without waiting for *Thread1* and *Thread2* to finish, the code then immediately attempts to populate the *ListBox* control with the results (even though the results are not complete).

When you calculated only 100 numbers, *Thread1* and *Thread2* managed to finish very quickly so the results were already complete before the code populated the *ListBox* control.

This problem is called a race condition because everything works perfectly if *Thread1* and *Thread2* 'win the race'. They must finish before the code tries to display the results in order for the code to work.

Clearly it is necessary to wait until *Thread1* and *Thread2* are finished before populating the *ListBox* control. You'll do this now to correct the error.

4   Stop debugging.

5   Add code to wait until both threads are finished.

Add the following code after the line that begins *Task Thread2:*

Thread1.Wait();
Thread2.Wait();

```
Task Thread2 = Task.Factory.StartNew(

Thread1.Wait();
Thread2.Wait();
```

This very simple code will wait until both *Thread1* and *Thread2* have finished before continuing.

You could also have done this using the *Task.WaitAll* method, with the following code:

Task.WaitAll(new Task[] { Thread1, Thread2 });

Task.WaitAll is useful if you have many *Task* objects that are stored in a collection, as you can easily wait for them all to finish with a single line of code.

6   Test your new code.

1.   View *Primes.aspx* in your web browser.

2.   Click *Calculate Primes*.

This time the calculation runs without any problems. Your code correctly waits for both threads to finish before binding the numbers to the *ListBox* control.

The calculation also finished in just *17* seconds this time. It took *23* seconds when working with a single thread in: *Lesson 3-4: Implement multi-threading using the Action and Task classes.*

This may not seem like a huge performance increase, but the difference would be a lot larger if you were to calculate prime numbers up to 1,000,000, for example.

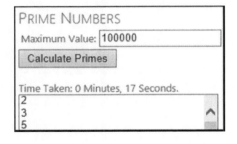

The calculations finished faster because they were shared between the processors on my computer. If your computer only contains a single processor you might not see any performance increase, as your computer has to handle both tasks on the same processor.

The *Task* class is the newest and best way to implement multi-threading in ASP.NET 4.5, but you'll cover the older *Thread* and *ThreadPool* classes in the next few lessons as you will probably encounter them in older projects.

You'll also take a closer look at the *Action* class and its partner the *Func* class in: *Lesson 4-11: Use the Func class to create delegates.*

Lesson 3-6: Implement multi-threading using the Thread class

Before the *Task* class was introduced, the *Thread* class was the easiest way to add threading to C# code. While the *Thread* class has been superseded by the *Task* class, you're still likely to see it being used in older projects.

1   Open *MathLand* from your sample files folder.

2   Open the code-behind file of *Primes.aspx*.

3   Remove the existing threading code.

Remove the following code:

Action<object> CalculatePrimesAction = new Action<object>(CalculatePrimes);
Task Thread1 = Task.Factory.StartNew (CalculatePrimesAction, new int[] { 2, MaximumValue / 2 });
Task Thread2 = Task.Factory.StartNew (CalculatePrimesAction, new int[] { (MaximumValue / 2) + 1, MaximumValue });
Thread1.Wait();
Thread2.Wait();

4   Add code to create a new thread using the *Thread* class.

1.   Add the following *using* line at the top of the code:

using System.Threading;

```
using System.Threading.Tasks;
using System.Threading;
```

The *Thread* class is in the *System.Threading* namespace, so this line will make it easier to access.

2.   In the *ButtonCalculatePrimes_Click* event handler, add the following code after the line that begins *int MaximumValue*:

Thread Thread1 = new Thread (new ParameterizedThreadStart(CalculatePrimes));

This code creates a new *Thread* object that will run the *CalculatePrimes* method.

You need to use the *ParameterizedThreadStart* object in order for the *Thread* class to run a method that has arguments. If the *CalculatePrimes* method had no arguments, you could simply use the code:

Thread Thread1 = new Thread(CalculatePrimes);

3.   Add the following code on the next line:

Thread1.Start(new int[] { 2, MaximumValue / 2 });

```
Thread Thread1 = new
    Thread(new ParameterizedThreadStart(CalculatePrimes));
Thread1.Start(new int[] { 2, MaximumValue / 2 });
```

This code tells the new thread to start running. Because you only want *Thread1* to do half of the work you are telling it to calculate prime numbers from 2 to half of the maximum value.

5 Add code to create a second thread.

Add the following code on the next line:

Thread Thread2 = new Thread
(new ParameterizedThreadStart(CalculatePrimes));
Thread2.Start
(new int[] { (MaximumValue / 2) + 1, MaximumValue });

```
Thread Thread1 = new Thread(new ParameterizedThreadStart(CalculatePrimes));
Thread1.Start(new int[] { 2, MaximumValue / 2 });
Thread Thread2 = new Thread(new ParameterizedThreadStart(CalculatePrimes));
Thread2.Start(new int[] { (MaximumValue / 2) + 1, MaximumValue });
```

This code creates and starts a second thread, which will calculate the other half of the prime numbers.

6 Add code to prevent race conditions.

This code is vulnerable to race conditions in the same way as you saw in: *Lesson 3-5: Prevent race conditions when working with the Task class.* Unfortunately, the *Thread* class doesn't offer a convenient *Wait* method, so the code to prevent a race condition is a little more complicated.

Add the following code on the next line:

while (Thread1.IsAlive || Thread2.IsAlive)
{
    Thread.Sleep(1000);
}

```
Thread2.Start(new int[] { (MaximumValue / 2) + 1, MaximumValue });

while (Thread1.IsAlive || Thread2.IsAlive)
{
    Thread.Sleep(1000);
}
```

This *while* loop will cycle as long as the *Thread1* and *Thread2* objects are both 'alive'. That is, as long as they are both still running their calculations.

Thread.Sleep tells your application's main thread to wait for a number of milliseconds before continuing. Without the *Thread.Sleep* line this *while* loop would cycle as fast as your computer could manage, which would be a waste of your computer's processing capacity.

Because of this line of code, the *while* loop will check whether the threads have finished once every second.

7 Test your new code.

1. View *Primes.aspx* in your web browser.

2. Click *Calculate Primes*.

    The calculation finished in 18 seconds. This is not quite as fast as the *Task* class, which managed to finish the calculations in 17 seconds.

    While the speed difference isn't very large, this illustrates the performance improvements that are offered by the *Task* class.

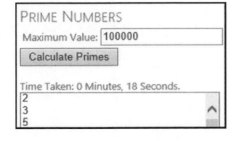

Lesson 3-7: Implement multi-threading using the ThreadPool class

Before the introduction of the *Task* class, the *ThreadPool* class offered the best way to work with large numbers of threads.

The great disadvantage of the *ThreadPool* class is that it's very difficult to tell when the threads have finished.

The *Task* class improves on the *ThreadPool* class, but you may still see *ThreadPool* being used in older projects.

1   Open *MathLand* from your sample files folder.

2   Open the code-behind file of *Primes.aspx*.

3   Remove the existing threading code.

Remove the following lines of code:

Thread Thread1 = new Thread(new ParameterizedThreadStart(CalculatePrimes));
Thread1.Start(new int[] { 2, MaximumValue / 2 });
Thread Thread2 = new Thread(new ParameterizedThreadStart(CalculatePrimes));
Thread2.Start(new int[] { (MaximumValue / 2) + 1, MaximumValue });

while (Thread1.IsAlive || Thread2.IsAlive)
{
*   Thread.Sleep(1000);*
}

4   Add code to create four threads using the *ThreadPool* class.

1. Add the following code in the space that the code you removed previously occupied:

    ThreadPool.QueueUserWorkItem(
    new WaitCallback(CalculatePrimes),
    new int[] { 2, (MaximumValue / 4) });

    ```
    int MaximumValue = Convert.ToInt32(TextBoxMaximumValue.Text); //Maximum prime number value

    ThreadPool.QueueUserWorkItem(new WaitCallback(CalculatePrimes), new int[] { 2, (MaximumValue / 4) });
    ```

    This code queues up a task using the *ThreadPool* class. The *ThreadPool* class will automatically allocate this task to a thread and execute it.

    Otherwise this code is very similar to the code that you used for the *Thread* class. This time you're dividing *MaximumValue* by 4 because you're going to use 4 threads, each one doing a quarter of the work.

2. Add the following code to allocate the other 3 tasks using the *ThreadPool* class:

    ThreadPool.QueueUserWorkItem(
    new WaitCallback(CalculatePrimes), new int[]
    { (MaximumValue / 4) + 1, (MaximumValue / 4) * 2 });

ThreadPool.QueueUserWorkItem(
new WaitCallback(CalculatePrimes), new int[]
{ ((MaximumValue / 4) * 2) + 1, (MaximumValue / 4) * 3 });
ThreadPool.QueueUserWorkItem(
new WaitCallback(CalculatePrimes), new int[]
{ ((MaximumValue / 4) * 3) + 1, MaximumValue });

```
ThreadPool.QueueUserWorkItem(new WaitCallback(CalculatePrimes), new int[] { 2, (MaximumValue / 4) });
ThreadPool.QueueUserWorkItem(new WaitCallback(CalculatePrimes), new int[] { (MaximumValue / 4) + 1, (MaximumValue / 4) * 2 });
ThreadPool.QueueUserWorkItem(new WaitCallback(CalculatePrimes), new int[] { ((MaximumValue / 4) * 2) + 1, (MaximumValue / 4) * 3 });
ThreadPool.QueueUserWorkItem(new WaitCallback(CalculatePrimes), new int[] { ((MaximumValue / 4) * 3) + 1, MaximumValue });
```

All four threads are now allocated. The only problem is that this code introduces a race condition and you don't have any way of knowing when the tasks are complete.

5   Add code to wait until all threads have finished.

The *ThreadPool* class doesn't provide any information on the status of your threads, so you will need to be a little more creative.

1.   Add a public property with the code:

public int ThreadsCompleted = 0;

Place this code outside any event handlers.

```
private List<int> PrimeNumbers = new List<int>();
public int ThreadsCompleted = 0;
```

2.   Add the following code to the end of the *CalculatePrimes* method:

ThreadsCompleted++;

```
    if (IsPrime) PrimeNumbers.Add(CurrentValue);
    CurrentValue++;
}
ThreadsCompleted++;
```

This means that the *ThreadsCompleted* property will increase by 1 each time the *CalculatePrimes* method is completed. When *ThreadsCompleted* reaches a value of 4 you will know that all 4 threads have finished.

3.   Add the following code to the *ButtonCalculatePrimes_Click* event handler, just after your *ThreadPool* code:

while (ThreadsCompleted < 4)
{
**   Thread.Sleep(1000);**
}

```
ThreadPool.QueueUserWorkItem(new WaitCallback(CalculatePrimes)

while (ThreadsCompleted < 4)
{
    Thread.Sleep(1000);
}
```

This code will wait until *ThreadsCompleted* reaches 4, waiting 1 second between checks. This will prevent a race condition.

6   Test your code.

This time you're using 4 threads to calculate the prime numbers. My computer has 4 processor cores, so this is even faster for me, but it may not be any faster if you have only 1 or 2 cores.

```
Time Taken: 0 Minutes, 11 Seconds.
2
3
5
```

Lesson 3-8: Use the lock statement to prevent threads from conflicting

Besides race conditions, other problems can occur when several threads are trying to access the same resources, especially when working with databases.

In this lesson you'll see the problem that multiple threads can cause and solve it using the *lock* statement.

1 Open *MathLand* from your sample files folder.

2 Open the code-behind file of *Primes.aspx*.

3 Add code to log the number of prime numbers that the system has calculated to the database.

Add the following code to the end of the *CalculatePrimes* method:

using (MathLandDataContext Data = new MathLandDataContext())
{
 int TotalTested = ValueFromAndToArray[1] -
 ValueFromAndToArray[0];
 var Log = Data.PrimesLogs.First();
 Log.PrimesLogTotalTests += TotalTested;
 Data.SubmitChanges();
}

```
using (MathLandDataContext Data = new MathLandDataContext())
{
    int TotalTested = ValueFromAndToArray[1] -
    ValueFromAndToArray[0];
    var Log = Data.PrimesLogs.First();
    Log.PrimesLogTotalTests += TotalTested;
    Data.SubmitChanges();
}
ThreadsCompleted++;
```

This code takes the total number of tests that the *CalculatePrimes* method made while it was running and saves it into the first record in the *PrimesLog* database table.

4 See the problem that is caused by multiple threads.

1. Click Debug→Start Debugging.

2. Enter **100** into the *Maximum Value* box.

PRIME NUMBERS
Maximum Value: 100
Calculate Primes

3. Click *Calculate Primes* several times until an error occurs.

This kind of error won't happen consistently so you may need to click 3 or 4 times before the error occurs.

```
Data.SubmitChanges();    ⚠ ChangeConflictException was unhandled
adsCompleted++;          Row not found or changed.
```

The error occurred because two threads attempted to update the database at exactly the same time.

4. Stop debugging and return to Visual Studio.

5 **Use the *lock* statement to fix the problem.**

The *lock* statement makes any code inside it exclusive. This means that it can only be executed by one thread at a time.

1. Add a private property to the class by adding the following code outside any event handlers:

private object Locker = new object();

```
public int ThreadsCompleted = 0;
private object Locker = new object();
```

This object will be used by the *lock* statement to determine whether its code is currently in use. It's best practice that the object used for the *lock* statement is not used for anything else and to use a different object for each *lock* statement.

2. Add the following code surrounding the code in the *CalculatePrimes* method that updates the database:

lock (Locker)
{
}

```
lock (Locker)
{
    using (MathLandDataContext Data = new MathLandDataContext())
    {
        int TotalTested = ValueFromAndToArray[1] -
        ValueFromAndToArray[0];
        var Log = Data.PrimesLogs.First();
        Log.PrimesLogTotalTests += TotalTested;
        Data.SubmitChanges();
    }
}
```

This *lock* statement ensures that everything inside its curly brackets can only be executed by one thread at a time (see sidebar for a more detailed explanation of how *lock* works).

6 **Test your code again.**

1. View *Primes.aspx* in your web browser.

2. Enter **100** into the *Maximum Value* box.

3. Click *Calculate Primes* repeatedly.

> PRIME NUMBERS
> Maximum Value: `100`
> [Calculate Primes]
>
> Time Taken: 0 Minutes, 1 Seconds.
> 2
> 3
> 5

No more errors occur. Your *lock* statement has stopped the threads from trying to access the database at the same time.

note

How the lock statement works

When the code in the *lock* statement is being executed, a value is placed in the *Locker* object, indicating that it is locked (in use).

If a thread reaches the *lock* statement while *Locker* is locked, it will simply wait until it becomes unlocked.

You could duplicate this functionality using a *bool* object and the *Thread.Sleep* method, as in this example:

public bool IsLocked = false;

while (IsLocked)
{
*   Thread.Sleep(1000);*
}
IsLocked = true;
//Update Database
IsLocked = false;

The *lock* statement is primarily used when working with multiple threads to prevent conflicts like the one that you saw in this lesson.

Lesson 3-9: Display a loading indicator using JavaScript

Some ASP.NET web pages can take a long time to respond to the user's input. A good example of this is the *Primes.aspx* page that you have worked with many times in this session.

In these cases, it's good practice to display an indicator to show the user that the page is loading. This reassures the user that the application has not crashed and stops them from closing their web browser.

1 Open *MathLand* from your sample files folder.

2 Open *Primes.aspx* in Design view.

3 Add a loading indicator image to the page.

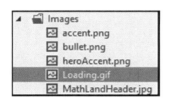

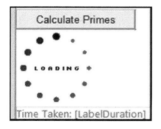

1. Expand the *Images* folder in the *Solution Explorer*.

2. Click and drag *Loading.gif* from the *Images* folder to the area beneath the *Calculate Primes* button.

   A dialog appears to allow you to provide additional information about the image.

3. Click *OK*.

   Your loading indicator has been added to the page, but you will need to add JavaScript code to display it when the user clicks the *Calculate Primes* button.

   You can't use C# code to do this because of the restrictions of ASP.NET's *Request* and *Response* system.

   When the user clicks the *Calculate Primes* button, a *Request* is sent to the web server. The web server doesn't send a *Response* back to the user until it has finished calculating all of the prime numbers, so it isn't able to display anything to the user until the calculations are already complete.

   JavaScript code runs in the user's web browser, so it can display the loading indicator to the user immediately, without needing to contact the server.

4 Hide the loading indicator and give it an *ID* of: **ImageLoading**

1. Select the loading indicator.

2. In the *Properties* window, set the *(id)* property to: **ImageLoading**

3. In the *style* property, type: **display:none**

   The loading indicator disappears. The CSS code: *display:none* hides the image from view.

5 Add JavaScript code to display the loading indicator when the *Calculate Primes* button is clicked.

note

Other web browsers can do this more easily

In this lesson you have to re-set the *Src* property of your loading image using JavaScript.

The only reason that this is necessary is because of a bug in Internet Explorer that will prevent the loading indicator from animating correctly.

In all other web browsers, you could have left the *Src* property alone and simply called the *$('#ImageLoading').show();* method to display the image.

```
function ShowLoadingIndicator() {
    $('#ImageLoading').show();
}
```

```
function ShowLoadingIndicator() {
    $('#ImageLoading').show();
    $('#ImageLoading').
        attr('src', 'Images/Loading.gif');
}
```

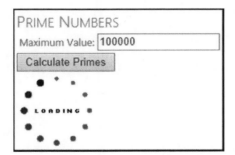

1. Select the *ButtonCalculatePrimes* control.

2. In the *Properties* window, set the *OnClientClick* property to:

   ShowLoadingIndicator();

   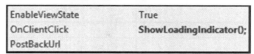

   This will call the *ShowLoadingIndicator* JavaScript function from the web page's source code whenever the button is clicked.

3. Switch to *Source* view.

   You can see that I have included a *ShowLoadingIndicator* JavaScript function near the top of the page.

   ```
   <script type="text/javascript">
       function ShowLoadingIndicator() {

       }
   </script>
   ```

4. Add the following code to the *ShowLoadingIndicator* JavaScript function:

   $('#ImageLoading').show();

   This JavaScript code calls the *show()* method of the *JQuery* JavaScript library. You'll learn more about *JQuery* in: *Lesson 9-9: Understand JQuery.*

   The *show()* method will un-hide the loading indicator image.

5. Add the following code on the next line:

   $('#ImageLoading').attr('src', 'Images/Loading.gif');

   This code uses *JQuery* to set the *src* property of the loading image so that it will display the correct image. This is necessary to work around a bug in Internet Explorer (see sidebar).

6. Test your new progress indicator.

   1. View *Primes.aspx* in your web browser.

   2. Click *Calculate Primes*.

      The loading indicator appears while the calculation is running.

      When loading is complete, the page posts back. This refreshes the page in your web browser, resetting the loading indicator so that it is hidden again.

      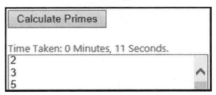

Lesson 3-10: Implement multi-threading using the Parallel class

If your multi-threading requirements are very simple, you can very easily make any *for* or *foreach* loop into a multi-threaded equivalent by using the *Parallel* class.

A 'parallel' *for* or *foreach* loop will automatically divide its iterations into separate threads.

1   Open *MathLand* from your sample files folder.

2   Open the code-behind file of *Primes.aspx*.

3   Remove the existing threading code.

Remove the following code:

ThreadPool.QueueUserWorkItem(new WaitCallback(CalculatePrimes), new int[] { 2, (MaximumValue / 4) });
*ThreadPool.QueueUserWorkItem(new WaitCallback(CalculatePrimes), new int[] { (MaximumValue / 4) + 1, (MaximumValue / 4) * 2 });*
*ThreadPool.QueueUserWorkItem(new WaitCallback(CalculatePrimes), new int[] { ((MaximumValue / 4) * 2) + 1, (MaximumValue / 4) * 3 });*
*ThreadPool.QueueUserWorkItem(new WaitCallback(CalculatePrimes), new int[] { ((MaximumValue / 4) * 3) + 1, MaximumValue });*
while (ThreadsCompleted < 4)
{
   Thread.Sleep(1000);
}

```
DateTime StartTime = DateTime.Now; //Get the time that calcul
int MaximumValue = Convert.ToInt32(TextBoxMaximumValue.Text);

ListBoxPrimes.DataSource = PrimeNumbers; //Bind the prime num
ListBoxPrimes.DataBind(); //Update the ListBox
```

4   Add code to call the *CalculatePrimes* method.

Add the following code in the space that the code you removed previously occupied:

CalculatePrimes(new int[] { 2, MaximumValue });

```
int MaximumValue = Convert.ToInt32(TextBoxMaximumValue.Text);

CalculatePrimes(new int[] { 2, MaximumValue });

ListBoxPrimes.DataSource = PrimeNumbers; //Bind the prime num
```

This code simply calls the *CalculatePrimes* method normally.

5   Add code to the *CalculatePrimes* method to implement multi-threading using the *Parallel* class.

In the *CalculatePrimes* method, replace the code:

for (int Counter = CurrentValue; Counter < IntMaxValue; Counter++)
{
   bool IsPrime = IsNumberPrime(Counter);

if (IsPrime) PrimeNumbers.Add(Counter);
}

…with:

Parallel.For(CurrentValue, IntMaxValue, Counter =>
{
   bool IsPrime = IsNumberPrime(Counter);
   if (IsPrime) PrimeNumbers.Add(Counter);
});

```
Parallel.For(CurrentValue, IntMaxValue, Counter =>
{
    bool IsPrime = IsNumberPrime(Counter);

    if (IsPrime) PrimeNumbers.Add(Counter); //If the
});
```

Notice that the code now ends with *});*.

This *Parallel.For* loop will do exactly the same thing as the *for* loop that it replaced, but it will automatically split the loops into separate threads.

As you can see, the *Parallel.For* method uses a 'lambda' expression (=>) in a very similar way to LINQ code. If you prefer, you can replace the lambda expression with an *Action* object like the one that you used in: *Lesson 3-4: Implement multi-threading using the Action and Task classes.*

You can also use the *Parallel* class to create *foreach* loops (see sidebar).

6   Test your code.

1.   View *Primes.aspx* in your web browser.

2.   Click *Calculate Primes*.

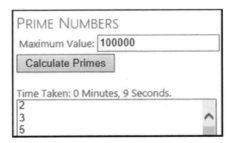

This time the calculation finishes in just 9 seconds – even faster than you saw when using 4 threads in: *Lesson 3-7: Implement multi-threading using the ThreadPool class.*

The *Parallel* class works more efficiently because it uses the same framework as the *Task* class that you worked with in: *Lesson 3-4: Implement multi-threading using the Action and Task classes.*

The best thing about the *Parallel* class is that it automatically prevents race conditions. The *Parallel.For* loop will not continue until all of the threads that it creates have finished running.

Session 3: Exercise

1   Open *Exercise3* from your sample files folder.

2   Open *SecretFiles.aspx* in Design view.

This page shows a list of files stored in the project's database and allows you to view them.

When it is finished, you will be able to encrypt and decrypt every file in the database by clicking the buttons.

3   Open the code-behind file of *SecretFiles.aspx*.

Most of the code is already in place. All that is needed is to complete the *EncryptBinary* and *DecryptBinary* methods.

4   Add *using* lines for the *System.Security.Cryptography*, *System.IO* and *System.Threading.Tasks* namespaces.

5   Add code to the *EncryptBinary* method to create a new *DES* object from the *System.Cryptography* namespace (you'll need to use the *DES.Create* method to do this). Name the object: **DESAlgorithm**

The *DES* object represents the *Data Encryption Standard*. It works identically to the *Aes* object that you used in this session.

6   Add code to set the *Key* and *IV* properties of your *DES* object to the values provided in the *EcryptionKey* and *InitializationVector* properties.

7   Add code to create a *MemoryStream* object to receive the encrypted data. Name it: **EncryptedStream**

8   Add code to create a *CryptoStream* object to encrypt the data. Remember to use the *CreateEncryptor* method of your *DES* object when supplying the arguments.

Ensure that a *using* statement is in place to automatically dispose of the *CryptoStream* object.

9   Add code to tell the *CryptoStream* object to *Write* the binary data that you want to encrypt.

10   Return the encrypted data using the *ToArray* method of the *EncryptedStream* object.

11   Copy and paste your code from the *EncryptBinary* method to the *DecryptBinary* method and modify it to decrypt the binary data that is provided to it.

12   Modify the code in the *ButtonEncryptDatabase_Click* event handler so that each call to the *EncryptSecretFile* method is handled by its own thread (change the loop into a *Parallel.ForEach* loop).

13   Add a *lock* statement to the *EncryptSecretFile* method to prevent two threads from calling *Data.SubmitChanges* at the same time.

Exercise3 - Start   Exercise3 - End

If you need help slide the page to the left ➡

Session 3: Exercise Answers

These are the three questions that students find the most difficult to answer:

Q 13	Q 12	Q 8, 9, 10

1. Add the following code outside any methods:
 	
object Locker = new object();
 	
2. In the *EncryptSecretFile* method, replace the line:
 	
Data.SubmitChanges();
 	
…with:
 	
lock (Locker)
{
   Data.SubmitChanges();
}
 	
This was covered in: *Lesson 3-8: Use the lock statement to prevent threads from conflicting.*
	Use the following code:
	
	Parallel.ForEach\<SecretFile\> (FilesToEncrypt, FileToEncrypt =>
	{
	   EncryptSecretFile (FileToEncrypt.SecretFileID);
	});
	
	This was covered in: *Lesson 3-10: Implement multi-threading using the Parallel class.*
		Use the following code:
		
		using (CryptoStream EncryptionStream = new CryptoStream (EncryptedStream, DESAlgorithm. CreateEncryptor(), CryptoStreamMode.Write))
		{
		   EncryptionStream.Write (BinaryToEncrypt, 0, BinaryToEncrypt.Length);
		}
		return EncryptedStream.ToArray();
		
		This was covered in: *Lesson 3-2: Encrypt data using the AES standard.*

If you have difficulty with the other questions, here are the lessons that cover the relevant skills:

1   **Refer to: Essential Skills Session 1.**

2   **Refer to: Essential Skills Session 1.**

3   **Refer to: Essential Skills Session 1.**

4   **Refer to: Essential Skills Session 6.**

5   **Refer to: Lesson 3-2: Encrypt data using the AES standard.**

6   **Refer to: Lesson 3-2: Encrypt data using the AES standard.**

7   **Refer to: Lesson 3-2: Encrypt data using the AES standard.**

11   **Refer to: Lesson 3-3: Decrypt data using the AES standard.**

Session Four: Advanced methods

> Success cannot come from standstill men. Methods change and men must change with them.
>
> *James Cash Penney, American businessman (1875-1971)*

You've worked with many simple methods already in this course, but C# offers a number of advanced features that enable methods to behave in more complex ways.

In this session you'll discover how to extend the functionality of your methods by adding overloads, optional arguments and output arguments. You'll also learn about the difference between sending arguments *by reference* and *by value* and how to control this behavior.

As well as extending the functionality of your methods, you'll also learn how to store references to methods in objects by using *delegates* and the *Func* class.

Session Objectives

By the end of this session you will be able to:

- Use the ref keyword
- Create a struct
- Create an enum
- Create a class library
- Add a class library to a project
- Overload a method
- Add optional arguments to a method
- Use the out keyword to get multiple values from a method
- Output multiple values from a single method
- Understand delegate methods
- Use the Func class to create delegates

note

Reference and value types

Most objects in C# are *reference types*. This means that they'll be sent by reference automatically without needing to use the *ref* keyword.

Value types are sent by value by default, but you can change this behaviour by using the *ref* keyword. Value type objects can never be *null* by default.

Here are some of the most common *value type* classes:

int
float
double
decimal
bool

structs are also sent by value by default. You'll learn about structs in the next lesson: *Lesson 4-2: Create a struct.*

While it is possible to change a value type to a reference type (as you will do in this lesson) it isn't possible to change a reference type to a value type.

trivia

The Fibonacci summation sequence

The Fibonacci sequence was first defined in *Liber Abaci* (a book written in 1202). Each subsequent number in the sequence is the sum of the previous two.

Fibonacci sequences are found everywhere in the world of nature, such as branching in trees and the arrangement of pine cones.

This has led many to regard Fibonacci sequences as having magical powers and they are widely used to predict future movements in stocks and shares (though it is not clear how successful this is)!

Lesson 4-1: Use the ref keyword

The *ref* keyword is mentioned briefly in Session 8 of the *Essential Skills* course. It's used to specifically send arguments to a method *by reference*.

When an argument is sent by *reference*, the 'actual' object is sent to the method. This means that the method is able to permanently make changes to the object.

When an argument is sent by *value*, the method only receives a copy of the object's value. Although the method will be able to make changes to the object, the object won't be modified outside the method.

Most C# objects are sent *by reference* by default. These are known as *reference types*. Objects that are sent *by value* by default are known as *value types* (see sidebar).

1   Open *MathLand* from your sample files folder.

2   View *Fibonacci.aspx* in Design view.

This page calculates numbers from the Fibonacci sequence. When it is finished, it will calculate and display as many numbers as you specify in the text box.

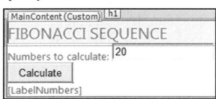

3   Open the code-behind file of *Fibonacci.aspx*.

Here you can see the method that calculates the Fibonacci numbers: *GetFibonacci*.

```
private void GetFibonacci(int Number)
{
    double Binet = (Math.Sqrt(5) + 1) / 2;
    double BinetReciprocal = Binet - 1;
    double Component1 = (Math.Pow(Binet, Number))/Math.Sqrt(5);
    double Component2 = (Math.Pow(-BinetReciprocal, Number)) / Math.Sqrt(5);
    double Fibonacci = Component1 - Component2;
    Number = (int)Math.Round(Fibonacci,0);
}
```

This method is a little unusual. Instead of returning a value with the *return* keyword, it changes the value of the *Number* argument.

The *Number* argument is an *int* variable. *int* is a *value type*, so the method will only receive a copy of the *Number* argument and any changes that are made to *Number* won't be reflected outside this method.

4   Test the page to see the problem.

1.   View *Fibonacci.aspx* in your web browser.

2.   Click *Calculate*.

Instead of returning the Fibonacci sequence, the code simply returns the numbers 1 to 20. This is because the *Number* argument was passed to the *GetFibonacci* method *by value*, so the method wasn't able to change its value outside the method.

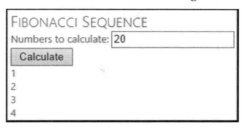

3. Close your web browser and return to Visual Studio.

5 **Change the method to receive the argument by reference.**

1. Change the code that begins the *GetFibonacci* method to the following:

*private void GetFibonacci(**ref** int Number)*

```
private void GetFibonacci(ref int Number)
{
```

All you need to do is add the keyword *ref* before *int Number*. This tells the method that the *Number* argument should be passed *by reference*.

You'll notice that an error has appeared in the *ButtonCalculate_Click* event handler where the *GetFibonacci* method is called. That's because you also need to use the *ref* keyword whenever you use an argument that is explicity sent *by reference*.

```
int Number = Counter;
GetFibonacci(Number);
LabelNumbers.Text += Number.ToString() + "<br />";
```

2. Change the line:

GetFibonacci(Number);

…to:

*GetFibonacci(**ref** Number);*

The *Number* argument will now be sent *by reference* and the *GetFibonacci* method will be able to make changes to its value that will still be visible in the *ButtonCalculate_Click* event handler.

6 **Test the page to confirm that the problem is fixed.**

1. View *Fibonacci.aspx* in your web browser.

2. Click *Calculate*.

This time the Fibonacci sequence is calculated correctly.

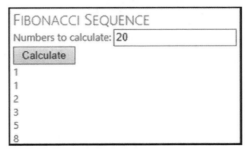

note

Memory allocation

Besides the way that reference and value types behave in methods, there's another important difference between the two.

When a reference type object is created, it's assigned to the *heap*, whereas value types are assigned to the *stack*.

The *stack* and *heap* are two different areas of memory that are used by your application.

The *stack* is smaller, but faster than the *heap*. It's for this reason that value type objects are stored in the *stack*: they're expected to need faster access and to use less space.

The *heap* can grow to any size that is required, but it's slower than the *stack*. For this reason, the larger *reference* type objects are stored in the *heap*.

```
int Number = Counter;
GetFibonacci(ref Number);
LabelNumbers.Text += Number.
```

important

Avoid using the ref keyword if possible

Although using the *ref* keyword fixed the problem in this lesson, it would still have been better programming practice to simply return a value from the *GetFibonacci* method by using the *return* keyword.

It is almost always better and more efficient to avoid using the *ref* keyword, so I'd recommend avoiding it unless you have a good reason to use it.

Lesson 4-2: Create a struct

A *struct* is a construct that is almost identical to a *class*. The major difference is that structs are *value type* objects and classes are *reference type* objects. This means that when you pass a *struct* object to a method, the method will receive a copy of the object and won't be able to make changes to it outside the method.

It's usually best to use classes instead of structs, as there are many features of classes that aren't supported by *struct* objects. However, it isn't possible to pass a *class* object by value so you may find a *struct* more appropriate if there's a special need to do this.

1 Open *MathLand* from your sample files folder.

2 View *Sequences.aspx* in Design view.

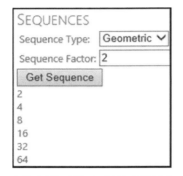

When this page is finished, it will display various mathematical sequences when the button is clicked.

3 Open *Sequences.cs*.

Note that this isn't the code-behind file for *Sequences.aspx,* but is a separate class file.

This class calculates the mathematical sequences for *Sequences.aspx*. It isn't the most efficient code, but it's a good example to demonstrate the difference between *structs* and *classes*.

4 Examine the existing code.

The *MathematicalSequences* class is the most important part of this code. In a moment you're going to change it into a *struct*.

```
private class MathematicalSequences
{
    public int Factor;
    public List<int> ArithmeticSequence;
    public List<int> GeometricSequence;
    public List<int> TriangularSequence;
    public List<int> SquareSequence;
}
```

The *PopulateSequences* method accepts a *MathematicalSequences* object as an argument and populates its properties appropriately.

```
private void PopulateSequences(MathematicalSequences ObjectToPopulate,
                              int Factor)
```

5 Change the *MathematicalSequences* class into a *struct*.

Simply replace:

private class MathematicalSequences

…with:

*private **struct** MathematicalSequences*

structs are defined in exactly the same way as classes, but using the *struct* keyword instead of *class*.

6 Test the page.

1. Open *Sequences.aspx*.

2. Click Debug→Start Debugging.

note

The use of structs is nearly always a bad idea

You may wonder why I am teaching you about structs when I don't advocate that they should ever be used.

The reason is that you may need to maintain another programmer's code which uses structs.

In my entire professional career I've never used a struct in my own real-world code because classes provide a much better solution.

```
private struct MathematicalSequences
{
    public int Factor;
    public List<int> ArithmeticSequence;
    public List<int> GeometricSequence;
    public List<int> TriangularSequence;
    public List<int> SquareSequence;
}
```

note

Limitations of structs

Structs have some limitations compared to classes:

A *struct* cannot have a constructor method without any arguments.

A *struct* cannot extend another class, nor can a class extend a struct.

You'll learn about extending classes in: *Lesson 5-1: Extend a class*.

note

Structs and memory allocation

Besides the limitations of *struct* as opposed to *class*, the only difference between the two is that structs are *value type* objects, while classes are *reference type* objects.

This means that *struct* objects are stored in the *stack*, whereas *class* objects are stored in the *heap* (see: *Lesson 4-1: Use the ref keyword (sidebar)*).

Because *struct* objects are stored in the *stack*, they will generally be processed slightly faster than *class* objects.

It's best to avoid using large structs, as there is a limited amount of space in the stack. You should only use structs for small constructs that need to be accessed quickly.

3. Click *Get Sequence*.

An error occurs.

```
Sequences.ArithmeticSequence)
⚠ NullReferenceException was unhandled by user code
```

This error indicates that the *Sequences.ArithmeticSequence* property is null. This happened because the *PopulateSequences* method failed to add the mathematical sequences to the object.

This is because structs are *value type* objects (see: *Lesson 4-1: Use the ref keyword*). The *PopulateSequences* method only received a copy of the *Sequences* object, so it was unable to place any persistent values into its properties.

4. Stop debugging and return to Visual Studio.

7 Fix the error using the *ref* keyword.

1. Return to *Sequences.cs*.

2. Change the line that begins the *PopulateSequences* method to:

private void PopulateSequences
*(**ref** MathematicalSequences ObjectToPopulate, int Factor)*

```
private void PopulateSequences
    (ref MathematicalSequences ObjectToPopulate, int Factor)
```

By adding the *ref* keyword, you're explicitly telling the method that the *ObjectToPopulate* argument will be sent *by reference*.

3. Open the code-behind file of *Sequences.aspx*.

```
MathematicalSequences Sequences = new MathematicalSequences();
PopulateSequences
    (Sequences, Convert.ToInt32(TextBoxSequenceFactor.Text));
LabelSequence.Text = "";
```

The code that calls the *PopulateSequences* method is marked with an error. That's because you also need to use the *ref* keyword when you call the method.

4. Change the line that's marked as an error to:

PopulateSequences
*(**ref** Sequences, Convert.ToInt32(TextBoxSequenceFactor.Text));*

```
PopulateSequences
    (ref Sequences, Convert.ToInt32(TextBoxSequenceFactor.Text));
```

You learned about the *ref* keyword in: *Lesson 4-1: Use the ref keyword*.

8 Test the page.

1. View *Sequences.aspx* in your web browser.

2. Click *Get Sequence*.

This time the sequence is returned without any problems. You've successfully modified the code to use a *struct* instead of a *class*.

Lesson 4-3: Create an enum

trivia

What is enum short for?

Enum is short for *enumerator*. 'Enumerating' something literally means assigning numbers to it.

An *enum* takes meaningful names and assigns numbers to them.

An *enum* is a kind of construct that you can use to make your code easier to work with.

The *enum* construct is useful when you want to create a method that has multiple 'modes'. A good example is the constructor for the *CryptoStream* class that you used in: *Lesson 3-2: Encrypt data using the AES standard*.

The *CryptoStream* constructor accepts *CryptoStreamMode.Read* or *CryptoStreamMode.Write* as one of its arguments. This is a simple *enum*.

1   Open *MathLand* from your sample files folder.

2   Open *Sequences.cs*.

3   Examine the *GetSequence* method.

This method uses an *int* argument named *SequenceType* to determine the type of sequence that it will generate.

```
if (SequenceType == 0) //Arithmetic
{
    SequenceNumber += SequenceFactor;
}
else if (SequenceType == 1) //Geometric
{
```

The code contains comments explaining the meaning of each possible *SequenceType*, but it would be very difficult to understand what is going on without these.

You can clarify the code without needing comments by using an *enum*.

4   Create a new *enum* for sequence types.

Add the following code outside any methods:

```
private enum MathSequenceType
{
    Arithmetic,
    Geometric,
    Triangular,
    Square
}
```

```
private enum MathSequenceType
{
    Arithmetic,
    Geometric,
    Triangular,
    Square
}
```

5   Use your new *enum* in the *GetSequence* method.

1.   Change the line that begins the *GetSequence* method to:

private List<int> GetSequence(
MathSequenceType *SequenceType, int SequenceFactor)*

```
private List<int> GetSequence
    (MathSequenceType SequenceType, int SequenceFactor)
```

Several errors appear, but you'll fix them shortly.

2.   Change the line:

if (SequenceType == 0) //Arithmetic

...to:

if (SequenceType == **MathSequenceType.Arithmetic***)*

If you are not completing the course incrementally use the sample file: **Lesson 4-3** to begin this lesson.

Sample files with the starting point for each lesson are also provided for all of the other lessons in this session.

tip

An enum can be converted to an int using cast

An *enum* is really just an *int* variable with meaningful names assigned to its numbers. This means that you can use the *cast* conversion method to convert an *enum* into an *int* and back again.

For example, you could convert the number 1 into a *MathSequenceType* object by using the following code:

MathSequenceType MyType = (MathSequenceType)1;

In the same way you could convert a *MathSequenceType* object back into an *int* by using the code:

int MyInt = (int)MathSequenceType .Geometric;

The *cast* conversion method is covered in Session 5 of the *Essential Skills* course in this series.

```
if (SequenceType == MathSequenceType.Arithmetic)
{
    SequenceNumber += SequenceFactor;
}
```

3. In the same way, change the *if* statements for the *Geometric, Triangular* and *Square* sequences to use the new *MathSequenceType* enum.

```
else if (SequenceType == MathSequenceType.Geometric)
{
    if (SequenceNumber == 0) SequenceNumber++;
    SequenceNumber *= SequenceFactor;
}
else if (SequenceType == MathSequenceType.Triangular)
{
    SequenceNumber = (Counter * (Counter + 1)) / 2;
}
else if (SequenceType == MathSequenceType.Square)
```

This code is now much easier to understand and doesn't need any comments to explain it.

6 Fix the problems in the *PopulateSequences* method.

Because the *GetSequence* method has changed, you'll need to change the lines that call it.

1. Change the line:

ObjectToPopulate.ArithmeticSequence = GetSequence(0, Factor);

…to:

*ObjectToPopulate.ArithmeticSequence = GetSequence(**MathSequenceType.Arithmetic**, Factor);*

```
ObjectToPopulate.ArithmeticSequence =
    GetSequence(MathSequenceType.Arithmetic, Factor);
```

2. In the same way, change the other calls to *GetSequence* to use the new *MathSequenceType* enum.

```
ObjectToPopulate.Factor = Factor;
ObjectToPopulate.ArithmeticSequence = GetSequence(MathSequenceType.Arithmetic, Factor);
ObjectToPopulate.GeometricSequence = GetSequence(MathSequenceType.Geometric, Factor);
ObjectToPopulate.TriangularSequence = GetSequence(MathSequenceType.Triangular, Factor);
ObjectToPopulate.SquareSequence = GetSequence(MathSequenceType.Square, Factor);
```

Again, this code is much easier to understand. It also reduces the chance of making a programming error.

7 Test the page.

1. View *Sequences.aspx* in your web browser.

2. Choose a sequence type and click *Get Sequence*.

   The sequence is displayed, proving that your code is working correctly.

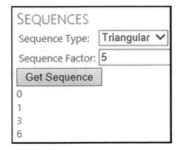

An *enum* object doesn't take up any more memory than a standard *int* variable, so there's no good reason not to use them to make your code clearer and easier to understand.

As well as making your code more readable, *enums* also make methods easier to use. This makes them particularly useful in class libraries. You'll learn more about class libraries in: *Lesson 4-4: Create a class library.*

Lesson 4-4: Create a class library

You added a reference to a class library in: *Lesson 1-2: Add references to a project*. In this lesson you'll create a brand new class library of your own.

1   Open Visual Studio.

2   Create a new class library project.

   1.   Click File→New Project.

   2.   Click *Visual C#* in the left-hand pane.

   3.   Click *Class Library* in the central pane.

   4.   In the *Name* box, enter: **EncryptionLibrary**

   5.   Click *Browse* and navigate to your sample files folder, then click *Select Folder*.

   6.   Make sure that *Create directory for solution* is ticked.

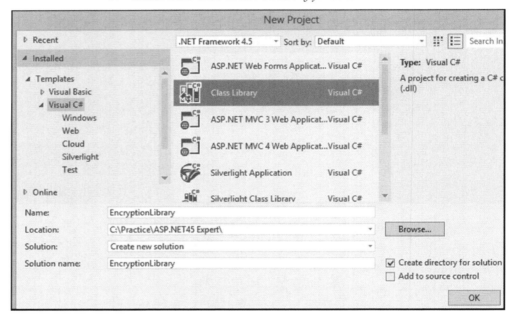

   7.   Click *OK*.

      Your class library project is created and automatically opened.

      You're going to use this class library to encapsulate the encryption code that you wrote in: *Lesson 3-2: Encrypt data using the AES standard*.

3   Make the class static and name it: **EncryptionFunctions**

   1.   Change the line:

      public class Class1

      …to:

      public static class EncryptionFunctions

```
public class EncryptionFunctions
{
    private static string EncryptString
```

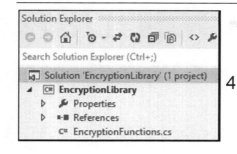

2. Right-click on *Class1* in the *Solution Explorer* and click *Rename* from the shortcut menu.

3. Type: **EncryptionFunctions.cs** and press **<Enter>**.

4 Create a new method to encrypt strings.

Add the following method to the *EncryptionFunctions* class:

public static string EncryptString(string StringToEncrypt, byte[] EncryptionKey, byte[] InitializationVector) { }

```
public static string EncryptString(string StringToEncrypt,
                                   byte[] EncryptionKey,
                                   byte[] InitializationVector)
```

5 Open the *TextLand* project from your sample files folder.

Click *Yes* if prompted to save your changes.

6 Open the code-behind file of *Encryption.aspx*.

7 Copy all code from the *ButtonEncrypt_Click* event handler.

8 Return to the *EncryptionLibrary* project.

9 Paste the copied code into the *EncryptString* method.

10 Add the required *using* lines to the top of the page.

This code requires the following *using* lines:

using System.Security.Cryptography;
using System.IO;

```
using System.Threading.Tasks;
using System.Security.Cryptography;
using System.IO;
```

11 Remove obsolete code.

Remove the lines:

string StringEncryptionKey = TextBoxEncryptionKey
.Text.PadRight(32);
byte[] EncryptionKey = Encoding.UTF8.GetBytes
(StringEncryptionKey);

These values will be provided by the method's arguments, so this code is no longer needed.

12 Fix the input value.

Replace the first instance of *TextBoxEncryption.Text* with **StringToEncrypt**

```
byte[] BytesToEncrypt = Encoding.UTF8.GetBytes(StringToEncrypt);
```

13 Fix the output value.

Replace the line:

TextBoxEncryption.Text = EncryptedString;

…with:

return EncryptedString;

```
string EncryptedString = Convert.ToBase64String(EncryptedBytes);
return EncryptedString;
```

Your class library now contains a method that is able to encrypt a string. You'll make use of this class library in the next lesson.

note

Why create class libraries?

A class library is only really useful when you want to share code across multiple projects.

Class libraries are often used to store useful functions so that every member of a development team can use them.

Lesson 4-5: Add a class library to a project

Although you can add a reference to a class library using a *dll* file, as you did in: *Lesson 1-2: Add references to a project*, you would have to rebuild the class library and replace the *dll* file every time you made changes to it.

If you add a class library project to the same solution as your target project, you can make changes to the class library much more easily.

1 Close any Visual Studio windows that are currently open.

2 Open *TextLand* from your sample files folder.

3 Add the *EncryptionLibrary* project to the solution.

1. Click File→Add→Existing Project…

2. Navigate to your sample files folder and open the *EncryptionLibrary* folder.

3. Open the *EncryptionLibrary* subfolder.

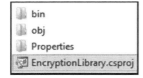

4. Click the *EncryptionLibrary.csproj* project file.

5. Click *Open*.

The *EncryptionLibrary* project is added to this *Solution*. You can now easily edit both projects at the same time.

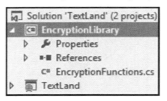

As mentioned in Session 1 of the *Essential Skills* course, a solution (*.sln*) file can link to multiple project (*.csproj*) files.

4 Build the *EncryptionLibrary* project.

Right-click *EncryptionLibrary* in the *Solution Explorer* and click *Build* from the shortcut menu.

You need to build the project before you can add a reference to it.

5 Add a reference to the *EncryptionLibrary* project in the *TextLand* project.

1. Right-click *TextLand* in the *Solution Explorer* and click *Add Reference* from the shortcut menu.

2. Click the *Solution* category if it isn't selected already.

The *EncryptionLibrary* project is listed in the central pane.

3. Tick the box next to *EncryptionLibrary* and click *OK*.

The classes from the *EncryptionLibrary* project will now be available in the *TextLand* project.

Because you referenced the project directly instead of using a *dll* file, you can be confident that the *TextLand* project will always use the latest code from the *EncryptionLibrary* project.

6   Use the *EncryptionLibrary* project's methods in the *TextLand* project.

1. Open the code-behind file of *Encryption.aspx* (from the *TextLand* project).

2. Remove all code from the *ButtonEncrypt_Click* event handler.

3. Add the following code to the *ButtonEncrypt_Click* event handler:

   string StringEncryptionKey = TextBoxEncryptionKey.Text.PadRight(32); byte[] EncryptionKey = Encoding.UTF8.GetBytes(StringEncryptionKey);

   This code retrieves the encryption key from the page.

4. Add the following code on the next line:

   string EncryptedString = EncryptionLibrary.EncryptionFunctions.EncryptString (TextBoxEncryption.Text, EncryptionKey, InitializationVector);

   This code calls the *EncryptString* method from the class library.

   You can access any of the class library's functions within the *TextLand* project as though it were part of the same project.

5. Add the following code on the next line:

   TextBoxEncryption.Text = EncryptedString;

```
protected void ButtonEncrypt_Click(object sender, EventArgs e)
{
    string StringEncryptionKey =
        TextBoxEncryptionKey.Text.PadRight(32);
    byte[] EncryptionKey =
        Encoding.UTF8.GetBytes(StringEncryptionKey);
    string EncryptedString =
        EncryptionLibrary.EncryptionFunctions.EncryptString
    (TextBoxEncryption.Text, EncryptionKey, InitializationVector);
    TextBoxEncryption.Text = EncryptedString;
}
```

The text in the *TextBoxEncryption* control can now be encrypted with much less code than was needed previously.

7   Test the project.

1. View *Encryption.aspx* in your web browser.

2. Click *Encrypt*.

ENCRYPTION

DrGqS6E2WkuQ4gIIJJR6lxaUna5m3k0/7a3qR+RKoZpTukYGCm
PeSnOUCNVtEMsxzhb/EhQJ6ZSeYO10rqpG3Vw2DnFKCPVFnAuT
c88AtHRg5i204xQQ2CNLgG851dWm8Hz3EXopNATDjQQVknoWul
NA/U7G871NIAP/MEQInjCbhOVziDg+0JJjWlwnFzYRXhi21LKi
YdMsu1QywTveCbquOKhiitQQNvNuFU3lqkTuNqGXHfbUHd1OYL
rvb1ouTXLpkwv3Lk204XXTsMPrKkIvt/Puz2ZdCz6T+ugeRDXp
WFb/uNfpAtK/gwaUjncHsQvN7sOmfYdIOT0KmVZx5CEYLKq/+I
9VV+RH279rgYGzVLuQLDX5LncpEynSletSf+1kf9f2VKYnP8Fu
4CKsp02uK8nGrsH1SjrO72EjbOiPaC1G+OakAcbwrgcDHdOuah
aywd7CP7z5tnVVL4h0Tg==

The text is encrypted without any problems.

Lesson 4-6: Overload a method

When working with the classes in the .NET framework you will have noticed that some methods are able to accept more than one set of arguments. These are known as *overloads*.

In this lesson you'll create your own overloaded method that is capable of accepting different sets of arguments and running different code.

1   Open the *TextLand* solution from your sample files folder.

Open it using the *TextLand.sln* file and not the *TextLand.csproj* file, as you will need the entire Solution for this lesson.

2   Open *EncryptionFunctions.cs* from the *EncryptionLibrary* project.

3   Add an overload for the *EncryptString* method.

At the moment the *EncryptString* method requires three arguments: a string to encrypt, an encryption key and an initialization vector.

You're going to add an *overload* to enable the *EncryptString* method to work without an encryption key or initialization vector.

1.   Copy the entire *EncryptString* method.

2.   Paste a copy of the *EncryptString* method just below the existing *EncryptString* method.

3.   Remove the *EncryptionKey* and *InitializationVector* arguments from the copy of the *EncryptString* method.

```
}
public static string EncryptString(string StringToEncrypt)
{
```

You've just created an overload for the *EncryptString* method. You did this by simply creating another method with the same name but only one argument.

4   Fix the errors in the new overload.

Replace the lines:

AESAlgorithm.Key = EncryptionKey;
AESAlgorithm.IV = InitializationVector;

…with:

AESAlgorithm.Key = Encoding.UTF8.GetBytes ("LearnASP.NETC#andVisual Studio!!");
AESAlgorithm.IV = new byte[]
{ 1, 2, 3, 4, 5, 6, 7, 8, 9, 10, 11, 12, 13, 14, 15, 16 };

```
Aes AESAlgorithm = Aes.Create();
AESAlgorithm.Key = Encoding.UTF8.GetBytes
    ("LearnASP.NETC#andVisual Studio!!");
AESAlgorithm.IV = new byte[]
{ 1, 2, 3, 4, 5, 6, 7, 8, 9, 10, 11, 12, 13, 14, 15, 16 };
```

This code is needed to tell the *AESAlgorithm* object which encryption key and initialization vector to use.

note

Limitations of overloads

You cannot create an overload that has exactly the same arguments as the method you're overloading, as there would be no way for C# to tell which overload the programmer is trying to call.

If you encounter this problem, simply create an entirely new method rather than overloading an existing one.

5 Use your new overloaded method.

1. Open the code-behind file of *Encryption.aspx*.

2. Remove the line that begins:

   string EncryptedString = EncryptionLibrary.EncryptionFunctions...

3. Type the following:

   **string EncryptedString =
   EncryptionLibrary.EncryptionFunctions.EncryptString(**

   The IntelliSense menu appears, showing the details of the *EncryptString* method.

   ```
   EncryptionLibrary.EncryptionFunctions.EncryptString(
   ▲ 1 of 2 ▼  string EncryptionFunctions.EncryptString(string StringToEncrypt)
   ```

   Notice the black arrows on the left of the *IntelliSense* menu. This indicates the presence of overloads.

4. Click the up or down arrows to cycle through your overloads.

   ```
   EncryptionLibrary.EncryptionFunctions.EncryptString(
   ▲ 1 of 2 ▼  string EncryptionFunctions.EncryptString(string StringToEncrypt)
   ```

   ```
   EncryptionLibrary.EncryptionFunctions.EncryptString(
   ▲ 2 of 2 ▼  string EncryptionFunctions.EncryptString(string StringToEncrypt, byte[] EncryptionKey, byte[] InitializationVector)
   ```

   As you can see, the *EncryptString* method is now capable of working with either a single string or with a string, encryption key and initialization vector.

5. Finish the line of code so that it reads:

   *string EncryptedString =
   EncryptionLibrary.EncryptionFunctions.EncryptString(*
   TextBoxEncryption.Text);

   ```
   string StringEncryptionKey = TextBoxEncryptionKey.Text.PadRight(32);
   byte[] EncryptionKey = Encoding.UTF8.GetBytes(StringEncryptionKey);
   string EncryptedString = EncryptionLibrary.EncryptionFunctions.
                            EncryptString(TextBoxEncryption.Text);
   TextBoxEncryption.Text = EncryptedString;
   ```

6 Test your code.

1. View *Encryption.aspx* in your web browser.

2. Click *Encrypt*.

   The text is encrypted using your method's new overload.

> **note**
>
> **Why use overloads?**
>
> You could have accomplished the same thing as you did in this lesson by simply creating a brand new method.
>
> It's down to your own judgement whether you prefer to use overloads or new methods. A good rule of thumb is to choose whichever approach will require less code.

Lesson 4-7: Add optional arguments to a method

Sometimes you want a method's arguments to be optional. You could achieve this by creating overloads for every possible combination of arguments, but that's an inefficient way to deal with the problem.

You can create optional arguments by giving them a default value, which they will use automatically unless a value is provided.

1   Open *TextLand.sln* from your sample files folder.

2   Open *EncryptionFunctions.cs* from the *EncryptionLibrary* project.

3   Remove the second overload for the *EncryptString* method.

> You're going to replace this overload's functionality by making the *EncryptionKey* and *InitializationVector* arguments optional.
>
> You learned about overloads in: *Lesson 4-6: Overload a method.*

4   Make the *EncryptionKey* and *InitializationVector* arguments optional.

> Change the line that begins the *EncryptString* method from:
>
> *public static string EncryptString(string StringToEncrypt, byte[] EncryptionKey, byte[] InitializationVector)*
>
> …to:
>
> *public static string EncryptString(string StringToEncrypt, byte[] EncryptionKey = **null**, byte[] InitializationVector = **null**)*

```
public static string EncryptString(string StringToEncrypt,
                                   byte[] EncryptionKey = null,
                                   byte[] InitializationVector = null)
{
```

> The *EncryptionKey* and *InitializationVector* arguments are now optional. If you call the method without specifying an *EncryptionKey* or *InitializationVector*, these arguments will take the default values of *null*.

5   Modify the method to work with the new optional arguments.

> 1.   Change the code:
>
>   *AESAlgorithm.Key = EncryptionKey;*
>
>   …to:
>
>   **if (EncryptionKey == null)**
>   **{**
>   **AESAlgorithm.Key = Encoding.UTF8.GetBytes**
>   **("LearnASP.NETC#andVisual Studio!!");**
>   **}**
>   **else**
>   **{**   *AESAlgorithm.Key = EncryptionKey;*   **}**

What if I wanted to specify an Initialization Vector but not an Encryption Key?

When calling a method with multiple optional arguments, you'll sometimes want to specify only one of them.

You can do this by specifying the argument by name. This is called a *Named Argument*.

Here's an example of how you'd call the *EncryptString* method with just the *StringToEncrypt* and *InitializationVector* arguments:

EncryptString(MyText, InitializationVector: MyInitializationVector);

You could even call both arguments by name for completeness, as in this example:

EncryptString(StringToEncrypt: MyText, InitializationVector: MyInitializationVector);

You can use this technique with any method. This is sometimes useful to clarify which argument is which.

```
if (EncryptionKey == null)
{
    AESAlgorithm.Key = Encoding.UTF8.GetBytes
                        ("LearnASP.NETC#andVisual Studio!!");
}
else
{
    AESAlgorithm.Key = EncryptionKey;
}
```

2. Change the code:

AESAlgorithm.IV = InitializationVector;

…to:

if (InitializationVector == null)
{
   AESAlgorithm.IV = new byte[]
   { 1, 2, 3, 4, 5, 6, 7, 8, 9, 10, 11, 12, 13, 14, 15, 16 };
}
else
{   *AESAlgorithm.IV = InitializationVector;*   **}**

```
if (InitializationVector == null)
{
    AESAlgorithm.IV = new byte[]
    { 1, 2, 3, 4, 5, 6, 7, 8, 9, 10, 11, 12, 13, 14, 15, 16 };
}
else
{
    AESAlgorithm.IV = InitializationVector;
}
```

The method will now use your default encryption key and initialization vector if one isn't specified.

6   Open the code-behind file of *Encryption.aspx.*

Notice that no errors are flagged (by red underlines). The call to *EncryptString* still works correctly with a single argument.

7   Examine the IntelliSense information for your method.

1. Add a new line to the *ButtonEncrypt_Click* event handler.

2. Type: **EncryptionLibrary.EncryptionFunctions.EncryptString(**

The IntelliSense menu appears.

```
EncryptionLibrary.EncryptionFunctions.EncryptString(
string EncryptionFunctions.EncryptString(string StringToEncrypt, [byte[] EncryptionKey = null], [byte[] InitializationVector = null])
```

Optional arguments are shown in square brackets *[ ]*. Notice that there are no longer any overloads for your method.

3. Remove the code that you just added.

8   Test your code.

View *Encryption.aspx* in your web browser and click *Encrypt.*

The text is encrypted without any problems.

ENCRYPTION

DrGqS6E2WkuQ4gIIJJR61xaUna5m3k0/7a3qR+RKoZpTukYGCm
PeSnOUCNVtEMsxzhb/EhQJ6Z5eYO10rqpG3Vw2DnFKCPVFnAuT

Lesson 4-8: Use the out keyword to get multiple values from a method

Some methods are able to return more than just a single value. One way of achieving this is by using the *out* keyword, but there are better ways (see sidebar facing page).

In this lesson you'll use the *out* keyword to retrieve multiple values from the *TryParse* method.

1   Open *TextLand.sln* from your sample files folder.

2   View *Dates.aspx* in Design view.

You may remember this page from: *Lesson 2-5: Use the TimeSpan class*. It's used to find the difference between the two specified dates.

3   See the problem with *Dates.aspx*.

1.   View *Dates.aspx* in your web browser.

2.   Enter an invalid date into one of the text boxes.

3.   Click *Get Difference*.

An error occurs because C# was unable to convert the text into a date.

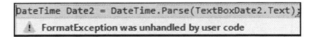

You could work around this problem by adding *try* and *catch* statements, but it's far better to eliminate any possibility of an error occurring.

You can make this code error-proof using the *TryParse* method.

4.   Stop debugging and return to Visual Studio.

4   Open the code-behind file of *Dates.aspx*.

5   Use *TryParse* to convert the dates.

1.   Remove the code:

DateTime Date1 = DateTime.Parse(TextBoxDate1.Text);

2.   Add the following code to the start of the *ButtonGetDateDifference_Click* event hander:

DateTime Date1;

This object will store the result of the *TryParse* method.

3.   Add the following code on the next line:

note

What is the difference between out and ref?

Very little. The only real difference between *out* and *ref* is that a method <u>must</u> assign values to any *out* arguments.

ref arguments can also be changed by methods, but it is not enforced by Visual Studio.

This means that using *out* instead of *ref* is slightly more resilient and less prone to error.

When you need to return multiple values from a method it is always better to return an object containing multiple properties than to use the *out* (or *ref*) keyword.

Programmers often use the *ref* (or ideally the slightly better *out*) keyword as it involves less code than creating a class to return values. In an ideal world, however, *ref* and *out* should still be avoided.

note

Other methods that use the out keyword

There are very few methods that use the *out* keyword outside of the *TryParse* methods for each data type.

Whenever an argument is used for output, it will be marked with *out* in the IntelliSense menu.

`string s, out DateTime result`

In the next lesson: *Lesson 4-9: Output multiple values from a single method,* you'll learn how to add output arguments to your own methods.

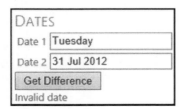

bool Date1IsValid = DateTime.TryParse(TextBoxDate1.Text, out Date1);

```
protected void ButtonGetDateDifference_Click(object sender, EventArgs e)
{
    DateTime Date1;
    bool Date1IsValid = DateTime.TryParse(TextBoxDate1.Text, out Date1);
```

Calling *DateTime.TryParse* in this way will place values in both the *Date1* and *Date1IsValid* objects.

The *out* keyword indicates that the *Date1* argument will receive a value from the method.

If the date is invalid, *Date1IsValid* will be set to *false* instead of an error occurring.

4. In the same way, replace the code:

DateTime Date2 = DateTime.Parse(TextBoxDate2.Text);

…with:

DateTime Date2;
bool Date2IsValid =
DateTime.TryParse(TextBoxDate2.Text, out Date2);

```
DateTime Date2;
bool Date2IsValid = DateTime.TryParse(TextBoxDate2.Text, out Date2);
```

This code converts the text in *TextBoxDate2* into a date.

6 Modify the method to deal with invalid dates.

1. Add the following code on the next line:

if (Date1IsValid && Date2IsValid)
{

2. Add the following code at the end of the event handler:

}
else
{
   LabelDateDifference.Text = "Invalid date";
}

```
if (Date1IsValid && Date2IsValid)
{
    TimeSpan DateDifference = Date1 - Date2;
    LabelDateDifference.Text = DateDifference.Days.ToString() + " Days";
}
else
{
    LabelDateDifference.Text = "Invalid date";
}
```

7 Test your code.

1. View *Dates.aspx* in your web browser.

2. Enter an invalid date in one of the text boxes.

3. Click *Get Difference.*

This time *Invalid Date* is displayed instead of an error occurring.

This is a better way of converting dates safely than using *try* and *catch* statements, as the code is completely error-proof.

Lesson 4-9: Output multiple values from a single method

You learned how to use the *out* keyword when calling methods in the previous lesson: *Lesson 4-8: Use the out keyword to get multiple values from a method*.

In this lesson you'll learn how to add *out* arguments to your own methods, enabling them to return more than one value.

1   Open *TextLand* from your sample files folder.

2   Open *EncryptionFunctions.cs* from the *EncryptionLibrary* project.

3   Add a new method to generate an encryption key and initialization vector.

   Add the following code outside any other methods:

   public static void GenerateKeyAndIV()
   {
      Aes AESAlgorithm = Aes.Create();
      AESAlgorithm.GenerateKey();
      AESAlgorithm.GenerateIV();
   }

```
public static void GenerateKeyAndIV()
{
    Aes AESAlgorithm = Aes.Create();
    AESAlgorithm.GenerateKey();
    AESAlgorithm.GenerateIV();
}
```

   The *GenerateKey* and *GenerateIV* methods generate a random encryption key and initialization vector.

4   Add output arguments to the method.

   In order to return two different values from this method, you'll need to use the *out* keyword.

   Add the following arguments to the *GenerateKeyAndIV* method:

   out byte[] Key, out byte[] IV

```
public static void GenerateKeyAndIV(out byte[] Key, out byte[] IV)
{
```

   An error marker appears because methods must assign values to all arguments that are marked with *out*.

5   Finish the method by setting the values of the *Key* and *IV* arguments.

   Add the following code to the end of the *GenerateKeyAndIV* method:

   Key = AESAlgorithm.Key;
   IV = AESAlgorithm.IV;

   The error marker disappears and the method is now complete.

```
public static void GenerateKeyAndIV(out byte[] Key, out byte[] IV)
{
    Aes AESAlgorithm = Aes.Create();
    AESAlgorithm.GenerateKey();
    AESAlgorithm.GenerateIV();
    Key = AESAlgorithm.Key;
    IV = AESAlgorithm.IV;
}
```

6   Use your new method.

1. Open the code-behind file of *Encryption.aspx*.

2. Add the following code to the start of the *ButtonEncrypt_Click* event handler:

    byte[] Key;
    byte[] IV;
    EncryptionLibrary.EncryptionFunctions.
    GenerateKeyAndIV(out Key, out IV);

    ```
    protected void ButtonEncrypt_Click(object sender, EventArgs e)
    {
        byte[] Key;
        byte[] IV;
        EncryptionLibrary.EncryptionFunctions.
                     GenerateKeyAndIV(out Key, out IV);
    ```

    This code calls your *GenerateKeyAndIV* method and places the returned values in the *Key* and *IV* objects.

3. Change the line:

    string EncryptedString = EncryptionLibrary.EncryptionFunctions.EncryptString(TextBoxEncryption.Text);

    …to:

    string EncryptedString = EncryptionLibrary.EncryptionFunctions.EncryptString(TextBoxEncryption.Text, **Key, IV***);*

    ```
    string EncryptedString = EncryptionLibrary.EncryptionFunctions.
        EncryptString(TextBoxEncryption.Text, Key, IV);
    TextBoxEncryption.Text = EncryptedString;
    ```

    This provides the *Key* and *IV* objects as arguments to the *EncryptString* method instead of relying on the default values.

    Your random encryption key and initialization vector won't match those used by the *ButtonDecrypt_Click* method, so the page won't be able to decrypt the text any more.

7   Test your code.

1. View *Encryption.aspx* in your web browser.

2. Click *Encrypt*.

    The text is encrypted using your new random encryption key.

3. Click *Decrypt*.

    ⚠ **CryptographicException was unhandled by user code**   ✕

    An error occurs because the *Decrypt* method is expecting a different encryption key and initialization vector.

    To fix this you would need to store the randomized encryption key and initialization vector and use them for decryption.

ENCRYPTION
zkoAClQLZMGfEA2QT2GCCqBUKZgDbAs24m1pGSv2087EK6W7uL
9Xri06EdavynKWgV+i7KKhT4oWtsDBjLiZDSswiouzuCHGuL/L
MLTCMDfyYTt6hNl7dqubAkPHkv4fHwPpMpJJzMal9CleHShYJi
22bCPviRty7GY2z/7oaNCTL19aW4VcLe8SsRWexGWrhcSGNoj9
gz8ZTFJKhLoMXYWZRKS7un4P+Z4abhA8C7+iGfsqLhldB4BVmB
EzkWpcghl9qyouhsttFMQzCXYIKxjBROXHpGAjYdZFjei0+8Lj
WwKKMRf9fQojU9s41YEj5+LdvK/FbaWJz1gB7OqRVxFeZ4q340
E4+FwPXV1c2egSbrd3dmftXKI8gZeTntH6UrDJ3/xZ4+EvCzyp
CAKEHGp6u1SqF48OPI4v1fVMOSYdWbofCsf+mF+hCFOVO48k+U
SUFMN8Upn28ZjR1mWP0Q==

Lesson 4-10: Understand delegate methods

You assigned methods to *Thread* objects in: *Lesson 3-6: Implement multi-threading using the Thread class*. To achieve this, the *Thread* class uses *delegate methods*. Delegate methods enable methods to be treated as objects.

Using delegate methods can make your code very confusing, so they're best avoided unless absolutely necessary.

In this lesson you'll create a delegate method using the *delegate* keyword.

1   Open *MathLand* from your sample files folder.

2   View *MultiCalc.aspx* in your web browser.

You may need to switch back to the *Solution Explorer* window to access the page.

This page enables you to create a batch of pending calculations by adding them to a list.

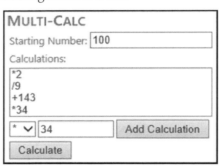

Add some calculations to the list by clicking the *Add Calculation* button. When this page is finished, you'll be able to carry out all of the calculations by clicking the *Calculate* button.

3   Close your web browser and return to Visual Studio.

4   Open *MultiCalculator.cs.*

When the *Calculate* button is clicked, the *Calculate* method runs each calculation. It does this by using a *List* collection of *Calculation* objects, each of which has a *Symbol* and a *Value* property.

This code contains *Add, Subtract, Multiply* and *Divide* methods.

You can see the spaces where the methods should be called. But instead of using ordinary method calls here, you're going to use a delegate.

```
if (Calculation.Symbol == "+")
{

}
else if (Calculation.Symbol == "-")
{

}
else if (Calculation.Symbol == "*")
{

}
else if (Calculation.Symbol == "/")
{

}
```

5   Create a delegate named: **CalculationDelegate**

Add the following code outside any event handlers:

**public delegate double CalculationDelegate(
double FirstNumber, double SecondNumber);**

```
public class MultiCalculator
{
    public delegate double CalculationDelegate
    (double FirstNumber, double SecondNumber);
```

```
foreach (Calculation Calculation in Calcula
{
    CalculationDelegate CalculatorDelegate;
    if (Calculation.Symbol == "+")
    {
        CalculatorDelegate = Add;
    }
    else if (Calculation.Symbol == "-")
    {
        CalculatorDelegate = Subtract;
    }
    else if (Calculation.Symbol == "*")
    {
        CalculatorDelegate = Multiply;
    }
    else
    {
        CalculatorDelegate = Divide;
    }
    Result = CalculatorDelegate
        (Result, Calculation.Value);
}
```

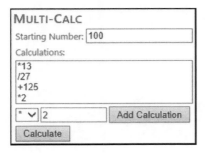

This defines a new delegate called *CalculationDelegate*.

Note that the delegate itself doesn't have any code. Delegates simply define a template rather than contain any logic themselves.

Because this delegate has exactly the same arguments and return value as the *Add, Subtract, Multiply* and *Divide* methods, it will be able to act as a 'delegate' for any of those methods.

Delegates must always have the same arguments and return value as the method they substitute for.

6   Create and use an instance of your new delegate.

1.   Add the following code on the first line of the *foreach* loop in the *Calculate* method:

CalculationDelegate CalculatorDelegate;

```
foreach (Calculation Calculation in Calculations)
{
    CalculationDelegate CalculatorDelegate;
    if (Calculation.Symbol == "+")
```

A delegate object is created just like any other C# object.

2.   Add the following code inside the first *if* statement:

CalculatorDelegate = Add;

This assigns the *Add* method to the *CalculatorDelegate* object. The *CalculatorDelegate* object now 'contains' the *Add* method and can call it on demand.

3.   Add the following code to the next *if* statement:

CalculatorDelegate = Subtract;

4.   Add the following code to the next *if* statement:

CalculatorDelegate = Multiply;

5.   Add the following code to final *if* statement:

CalculatorDelegate = Divide;

Your *CalculationDelegate* object has now been assigned the correct method depending on the kind of calculation that it needs to run. All that remains is to call the method.

6.   Add the following line of code at the end of the *foreach* loop:

Result = CalculatorDelegate(Result, Calculation.Value);

This code calls your delegate method. This will work regardless of which method the *CalculatorDelegate* object is actually calling.

7   Test your code.

1.   View *MultiCalc.aspx* in your web browser.

2.   Add some calculations to the list.

3.   Click *Calculate*.

The calculations are carried out successfully through your delegate method.

Lesson 4-11: Use the Func class to create delegates

You created an 'ordinary' delegate in the previous lesson: *Lesson 4-11: Use the Func class to create delegates*. Delegates are useful, but the code that is used to create them can be very difficult to understand.

ASP.NET 4.5 introduces the new *Action* and *Func* classes, which allow delegates to be created 'on the fly' without needing to be defined separately.

The *Action* class is used to create delegates for methods that do not return a value, while the *Func* class works with methods that do return a value.

You've already used the *Action* class in conjunction with the *Task* class in: *Lesson 3-4: Implement multi-threading using the Action and Task classes*. The *Action* class doesn't have to be used in conjunction with the *Task* class: it can also be used to create delegates for any purpose.

1 Open *MathLand* from your sample files folder.

2 Open *MultiCalculator.cs*.

This class currently uses the *CalculationDelegate* delegate to allow each of its calculation methods to be stored as objects.

```
public class MultiCalculator
{
    public delegate double CalculationDelegate
    (double FirstNumber, double SecondNumber);
```

It's a little confusing that the *CalculationDelegate* type is defined separately. The code would be easier to understand if it was all contained within the *Calculate* method.

You can do this by using the *Func* class.

3 Remove the *CalculationDelegate* code.

Remove the following code:

public delegate double CalculationDelegate(double FirstNumber, double SecondNumber);

Some errors appear, but you will fix these by using the *Func* class.

4 Modify the *Calculate* method to use the *Func* class.

Replace the code:

CalculationDelegate CalculatorDelegate;

…with:

Func<double, double, double> CalculatorDelegate;

```
foreach (Calculation Calculation in Calculations)
{
    Func<double, double, double> CalculatorFunc;
    if (Calculation.Symbol == "+")
```

Func<double, double, double> represents a method that has two *double* arguments and returns a *double* value.

This pattern matches the *Add, Subtract, Multiply* and *Divide* methods, so the new *Func* object will be able to store any of these methods.

You'll notice that there are no longer any errors. The *Func* class completely replicates the functionality of the *delegate* that was being used previously.

Note that there are some limitations to the *Func* class (see sidebar).

5   Test your code.

1.   View *MultiCalc.aspx* in your web browser.

2.   Add some calculations to the list.

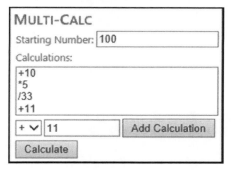

3.   Click *Calculate*.

The calculations are carried out successfully through the use of the *Func* class.

I recommend using the *Func* and *Action* classes instead of the *delegate* keyword wherever possible.

Session 4: Exercise

1   Open *Exercise4* from your sample files folder.

2   Open *MailSender.cs*.

      This is a simple class that sends e-mail messages.

3   Add an overload to the *SendEmail* method which makes the *BodyText* value into an argument.

4   Make the *ToAddress* argument of the first overload optional by giving it a default value of: **info@aspnetcentral.com**

5   Create a new class library project named: **Exercise4ClassLibrary**

6   Re-open the *Exercise4* project and add the *Exercise4ClassLibrary* project to the same solution.

7   Within the *Exercise4* project, add a reference to the *Exercise4Classlibrary* project.

8   Add a new *enum* to *Class1.cs* within the *Exercise4ClassLibrary* project. Name the enum **ColorMode** and give it the options: **Color** and **Monochrome** (add this outside the definition of *Class1*).

9   Open the code-behind file of *Grid.aspx*.

10   Add a *using* line for the *Exercise4ClassLibrary* namespace.

11   Modify the *GetRandomColor* method to use your new *ColorMode* enum instead of an *int* value.

      Some errors will appear, but you will fix them in the next step.

12   Modify the *ButtonGetColors_Click* event handler to use the *ColorMode* enum so that there are no more errors.

13   Open the code-behind file of *DateValidator.aspx* and add code to check whether the *DateEntered string* variable contains a valid date using the *DateTime.TryParse* method.

Exercise4 - Start   Exercise4 - End

If you need help slide the page to the left

Session 4: Exercise Answers

These are the four questions that students find the most difficult to answer:

Q 11	Q 8	Q 4	Q 3

1. Change the code:
 	
private Color GetRandomColor (int Mode)
 	
…to:
 	
private Color GetRandomColor (**ColorMode** *Mode)*
 	
2. Change the code:
 	
if (Mode == 0)
 	
to:
 	
if (Mode == **ColorMode.Color***)*
 	
3. Change the code:
 	
else if (Mode == 1)
 	
…to:
 	
else if (Mode == **ColorMode.Monochrome***)*
 	
This was covered in: ***Lesson 4-3: Create an enum.***
	Use the following code:
	
	public enum ColorMode
	{
	    Color,
	    Monochrome
	}
	
	Make sure to add this outside the curly brackets that define *Class1*.
	
	This was covered in: *Lesson 4-3: Create an enum.*
		Change the line:
		
		public void SendEmail(string ToAddress)
		
		…to:
		
		public void SendEmail(string ToAddress = **"info@aspnet central.com"***)*
		
		This was covered in: ***Lesson 4-7: Add optional arguments to a method.***
			Add the following code below the original *SendEmail* method (copying and pasting will speed this up):
			
			public void SendEmail(string ToAddress, string BodyText)
			{
			    using (System.Net.Mail. SmtpClient Client = new System.Net.Mail. SmtpClient())
			    {
			        string Subject = "Exercise 4";
			        Client.Send("info@ ASPNETCentral.com", ToAddress, Subject, BodyText);
			    }
			}
			
			This was covered in: *Lesson 4-6: Overload a method.*

If you have difficulty with the other questions, here are the lessons that cover the relevant skills:

1, 2   **Refer to: Essential Skills Session 1.**

5   **Refer to: Lesson 4-4: Create a class library.**

6   **Refer to: Lesson 4-5: Add a class library to a project.**

7   **Refer to: Lesson 4-5: Add a class library to a project.**

9   **Refer to: Essential Skills Session 1.**

10   **Refer to: Essential Skills Session 6.**

12   **Refer to: Lesson 4-3: Create an enum.**

13   **Refer to: Lesson 4-8: Use the out keyword to get multiple values from a method.**

Session Five: Advanced class structures

Just because you can doesn't mean you should.

Unknown Author

Classes allow you to implement your own custom objects with their own properties and methods. Basic classes are covered in the *Essential Skills* course. For most purposes, these skills are all that you will need.

The advanced class structuring skills that you'll learn in this session will rarely be needed outside of very large and complex projects. Using the techniques covered in this session can make your code much harder to work with if you use them improperly. Your goal should always be to create code that is both efficient and easy to work with. Just because you can use very complex class structures doesn't mean you should!

By the end of this session, you'll be able to confidently create and work with complex class structures, something that only a few expert programmers are able to do.

Session Objectives

By the end of this session you will be able to:

- Extend a class
- Add an extended control to a page
- Understand polymorphism
- Understand the virtual and override keywords
- Understand the abstract keyword
- Implement an interface
- Create an interface
- Use the Class View window
- Use the Object Browser window

Lesson 5-1: Extend a class

You may have noticed that some classes have different 'variants'. A good example of this is the *Stream* class. Along with *Stream* you'll find *FileStream, MemoryStream, CryptoStream* and others. These classes are all extensions of the basic *Stream* class.

In this lesson you'll learn how to extend classes and even extend classes from the .NET framework to make your own extended versions.

1   Open *StableBase* from your sample files folder.

2   View *Horses.aspx* in your web browser.

This is the main page for viewing information about horses. It uses a *GridView* control with *ButtonField*s. These are covered in Session 12 of the *Essential Skills* course in this series.

note

The partial keyword

You'll see the *partial* keyword in the code-behind file of every *aspx* page.

The *partial* keyword indicates that the class has additional code in another file. You see this in code-behind files because they also include code that is defined in the linked *aspx* page. For example, any controls on the page are considered to be part of the same class.

You can also use the *partial* keyword to spread your own classes across multiple files. This isn't usually a good idea, as it makes it harder to keep track of where the code is stored.

While I've only rarely done this in my real-world projects, I once had to create a class containing an enormous amount of code. I used the partial keyword to split the class into several files to make the code easier to work with. If you ever do this yourself, I'd recommend that you place all of the files in a single folder.

3   Close your web browser and return to Visual Studio.

4   Open the code-behind file of *Horses.aspx*.

5   See how classes are extended.

Examine the line (near the top of the page):

public partial class Horses : System.Web.UI.Page

This code tells C# that the *Horses* class *extends* the *System.Web.UI.Page* class. All ASP.NET code-behind files extend the *System.Web.UI.Page* class in this way. This code is automatically included in all code-behind files.

When one class extends another, it acquires all of the methods and properties of the class that it extends. This is also known as *inheriting from* a class. Creating a class that extends more than one other class is sometimes known as *multiple inheritance*.

See sidebar for an explanation of the *partial* keyword.

6   Examine some inconvenient code.

Look in the *GridViewHorse_RowCommand* method and notice the following code (near the top of the method):

int RowClicked = Convert.ToInt32(e.CommandArgument);
int HorseID =
Convert.ToInt32(GridViewHorse.DataKeys[RowClicked].Value);

```
PanelHorseDetails.Visible = true;
int RowClicked = Convert.ToInt32(e.CommandArgument);
int HorseID = Convert.ToInt32(GridViewHorse.DataKeys[RowClicked].Value);
```

This code is needed to retrieve the *HorseID* value from the row clicked by the user. It's rather complex and inconvenient, and it would be nicer if this code was built into the *GridView* control.

7 Create an extended *GridView* control.

1. Add a new class to the project, named: **ExtendedGridView.cs**

2. Add the following *using* line to the top of the new class:

   using System.Web.UI.WebControls;

```
using System.Web;
using System.Web.UI.WebControls;
```

3. Change the line that begins the class from:

   public class ExtendedGridView

   …to:

   public class ExtendedGridView : **GridView**

   This code tells C# that your new class will extend the *GridView* class. If you did nothing else to this class it would be identical to the *GridView* class.

8 Add a method to the *ExtendedGridView* class.

Add the following method to the class:

public int GetIDFromRow(object CommandArgument)
{
  try
  {
    int RowIndex = Convert.ToInt32(CommandArgument);
    object RowDataKey = base.DataKeys[RowIndex].Value;
    return Convert.ToInt32(RowDataKey);
  }
  catch
  {
    return 0;
  }
}

```
public class ExtendedGridView : GridView
{
    public int GetIDFromRow(object CommandArgument)
    {
        try
        {
            int RowIndex = Convert.ToInt32(CommandArgument);
            object RowDataKey = base.DataKeys[RowIndex].Value;
            return Convert.ToInt32(RowDataKey);
        }
        catch
        {
            return 0;
        }
    }
}
```

The *base* keyword allows you to access all of the methods and properties of the class that this class extends. This code uses it to access the *DataKeys* property of the base class (*GridView*).

This method will make it much easier to retrieve the ID from the *GridView* control. You'll see how to add your *ExtendedGridView* control to a page and use its new functionality in the next lesson: *Lesson 5-2: Add an extended control to a page.*

---

note

Polymorphism

Extended classes can be converted so that they impersonate the type of object they extend by using the *cast* conversion method.

For example, you could convert an *ExtendedGridView* object into a normal *GridView* object using this code:

GridView MyGridView = (GridView)MyExtendedGridView;

Allowing objects to impersonate other types is known as *polymorphism*.

You'll learn more about polymorphism in: *Lesson 5-3: Understand polymorphism.*

Lesson 5-2: Add an extended control to a page

You extended the *GridView* class from the .NET framework and added new functionality to it in the previous lesson: *Lesson 5-1: Extend a class.*

In this lesson you'll add your new *ExtendedGridView* control to a page and use its new functionality.

1   Open *StableBase* from your sample files folder.

2   Open the *Horses.aspx* page in *Source* view.

3   Examine and understand tag prefixes.

Before you can use your own classes as controls, you'll need to add a *tag prefix* to the page.

The default tag prefix is *asp*. It's currently being used by every control on this page, for example: *<asp:LinqDataSource*

```
<asp:LinqDataSource ID="LinqDataSourceHorse"
</asp:LinqDataSource>
```

The *asp* tag prefix tells ASP.NET to look in the *System.Web.UI.WebControls* namespace for the control.

4   Add a new tag prefix for your own controls.

1.   Scroll to the very top of the page.

2.   Add a new line just after the *<%@ Page* tag.

3.   Add the following code on the new line:

<%@ Register TagPrefix="tsm" Namespace="StableBase" Assembly="StableBase" %>

```
<%@ Page Title="" Language="C#" MasterPageFile="~/Site.Master" AutoEventWireup=
<%@ Register TagPrefix="tsm" Namespace="StableBase" Assembly="StableBase" %>
```

This code creates a new tag prefix named *tsm*. The *tsm* tag prefix will look in the *StableBase* namespace for its controls (this project's default namespace).

The *ExtendedGridView* class is in the *StableBase* namespace. You created the *ExtendedGridView* class in: *Lesson 5-1: Extend a class.*

5   Change the *asp:GridView* control into a *tsm:ExtendedGridView* control.

1.   Scroll down until you see the code for the *GridViewHorse* control.

```
<asp:GridView ID="GridViewHorse" runat="server" Auto
    <Columns>
        <asp:BoundField DataField="HorseName" Header
        <asp:ButtonField CommandName="ViewDetails" T
        <asp:ButtonField CommandName="ViewChecklist"
    </Columns>
</asp:GridView>
```

As you can see, this code uses the *asp:GridView* class.

2.   Change:

asp:GridView

...to:

tsm:ExtendedGridView

```
<tsm:ExtendedGridView ID="GridViewHorse" runat="serv
    <Columns>
        <asp:BoundField DataField="HorseName" Header
        <asp:ButtonField CommandName="ViewDetails" T
        <asp:ButtonField CommandName="ViewChecklist"
    </Columns>
</tsm:ExtendedGridView>
```

When you change the starting tag, Visual Studio will automatically apply your changes to the ending tag.

You have now replaced the standard *GridView* control on this page with your custom *ExtendedGridView* control.

6 Use the functionality of your new *ExtendedGridView* control.

1. Open the code-behind file of *Horses.aspx*.

2. In the *GridViewHorse_RowCommand* event handler, replace the lines:

   int RowClicked = Convert.ToInt32(e.CommandArgument);
   int HorseID =
   Convert.ToInt32(GridViewHorse.DataKeys[RowClicked].Value);

   ...with:

   int HorseID =
   GridViewHorse.GetIDFromRow(e.CommandArgument);

```
PanelHorseDetails.Visible = true;
int HorseID = GridViewHorse.GetIDFromRow(e.CommandArgument);
using (StableBaseDataContext Data = new StableBaseDataContext())
```

You created the *GetIDFromRow* method in: *Lesson 5-1: Extend a class*.

It's now much easier to retrieve the *HorseID* value and requires less code.

7 Test your code.

1. View *Horses.aspx* in your web browser.

2. Click one of the *View Details* links.

   Your *ExtendedGridView* control works perfectly and the correct horse's details are displayed.

You don't have to limit yourself to extending controls. It's possible to extend any class, including classes you've created yourself.

Extending classes can be very useful, as you've seen in this example, but it's important to be careful when extending classes. A large structure of classes extending one another can become very hard to manage.

I recommend that you only extend classes when it makes your code simpler. If extending a class makes things more complicated it is probably a step backwards.

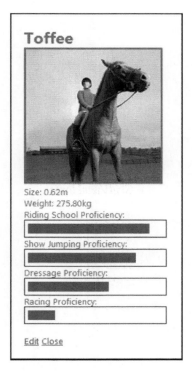

Toffee

Size: 0.62m
Weight: 275.80kg
Riding School Proficiency:

Show Jumping Proficiency:

Dressage Proficiency:

Racing Proficiency:

Edit Close

Lesson 5-3: Understand polymorphism

note

All C# objects are polymorphic

Every object in C# extends the *Object* class, so any object can be converted into the *object* type.

Because every object can impersonate a different type, it can be said that every C# object is polymorphic.

note

FindControl and MainContent

The *FindControl* method allows you to easily extract controls from a page. Because this page uses a master page, all of its controls are stored in the *MainContent* placeholder.

The *MainContent* placeholder is held in the *Page.Master.Controls* collection, but you can use the *Page.Master.FindControl* method to extract it easily.

Master pages are covered in Session 12 of the *Essential Skills* course.

Extended classes can impersonate the type of object that they extend by using the *cast* conversion method. The converted object won't have any of the additional functionality of the extended object, but if it is later converted back into its true type its methods will be available and the values of its properties will be maintained. The ability of objects to impersonate different types is known as *polymorphism*. You'll see how it works, and why it can be useful, in this lesson.

1   Open *StableBase* from your sample files folder and open the code-behind file of *HorseAdmin.aspx*.

2   Add code to the *Page_Load* event handler to extract the *ButtonAddNewHorse* control from the page.

Add the following code to the *Page_Load* event handler:

Control AddNew = Page.Master.FindControl("MainContent").FindControl("ButtonAddNewHorse");

```
protected void Page_Load(object sender, EventArgs e)
{
    Control AddNew = Page.Master.FindControl("MainContent")
                            .FindControl("ButtonAddNewHorse");
}
```

See sidebar for information on *FindControl* and *MainContent*.

Although you are treating the *AddNew* object as a *Control* object, this isn't its 'real' type. It is only impersonating a *Control* object.

3   Add code to extract and display the 'real' type of the *AddNew* object.

Add the following code to the *Page_Load* event handler:

Response.Write(AddNew.GetType().ToString());

```
Control AddNew = Page.Master.FindControl("MainContent")
Response.Write(AddNew.GetType().ToString());
```

4   Test your code.

1.   View *HorseAdmin.aspx* in your web browser.

The actual type of the *AddNew* object is displayed at the top of the page. It is in fact a *System.Web.UI.WebControls.Button* object.

All controls in ASP.NET extend the *Control* class. Because the *Button* class extends the *Control* class, any *Button* object can impersonate a *Control* object.

2.   Close your web browser and return to Visual Studio.

5   Examine the properties of the *AddNew* object.

1.   On the next line of *Page_Load*, type: **AddNew.**

The IntelliSense menu for the *AddNew* object appears.

Search for the *Text* property in the *IntelliSense* menu. You'll find that the *Text* property isn't available.

The *Control* class doesn't have a *Text* property, so you're unable to access it. To access the *Text* property of the control, you will need to convert the object back into a *Button* object.

2. Remove the *AddNew.* code that you just added.

6 Add code to convert the *AddNew* object into a *Button* object and change its *Text* property.

1. Add the following code to the *Page_Load* event handler:

Button AddNewButton = (Button)AddNew;

```
Control AddNew = MainContentHolder.FindControl("ButtonAddNewHorse");
Button AddNewButton = (Button)AddNew;
```

This code uses the *cast* conversion method to convert the *Control* object into a *Button* object (its true type).

2. Add the following code on the next line:

AddNewButton.Text = "New Record";

```
Button AddNewButton = (Button)AddNew;
AddNewButton.Text = "New Record";
```

You're now able to access the *Text* property and change its value.

7 Add code to create a new *TextBox* control.

Add the following code on the next line:

TextBox NewTextBox = new TextBox();
NewTextBox.Text = "New record name";

```
AddNewButton.Text = "New Record";
TextBox NewTextBox = new TextBox();
NewTextBox.Text = "New record name";
```

8 Add code to place the new control on the page.

Type the following code on the next line:

Page.Master.FindControl("MainContent").Controls.Add(

```
void ControlCollection.Add(Control child)
Adds the specified System.Web.UI.Control object to the collection.
child: The System.Web.UI.Control to add to the collection.
```

The *IntelliSense* menu appears, showing that only *Control* objects can be added to the *Controls* collection.

C# will automatically convert compatible objects to the type of the collection (in this case we have a collection of *Control* objects) but, as you saw earlier, you need to manually convert objects into their extended types after you remove them from a collection of polymorphic objects.

Finish the line of code so that it reads:

Page.Master.FindControl("MainContent").Controls. *Add(***NewTextBox);**

```
NewTextBox.Text = "New record name";
Page.Master.FindControl("MainContent").Controls.Add(NewTextBox);
```

9 View *HorseAdmin.aspx* in your web browser.

The *Text* property of the *ButtonAddNewHorse* control is changed and your new *TextBox* control appears on the page. To display the *TextBox* control on the page, ASP.NET automatically extracted its *Control* object from the *Controls* collection, checked its type, and then converted the object back into its extended *TextBox* type.

---

note

A better way to add controls to a page

The best way to add controls to a page using C# code is to use a *PlaceHolder* control.

You'll do this in: *Lesson 7-1: Use the Panel and PlaceHolder controls.*

| New Record | New record name |

145

Lesson 5-4: Understand the virtual and override keywords

You already know that an extended class takes on all of the functionality of the class it extends, but there may be times when the extended class needs to completely replace one or more of the base class's properties or methods.

You can do this by using the *virtual* keyword in the base class and the *override* keyword in the extended class. You'll see this in action in this lesson.

1 Open *StableBase* from your sample files folder.

2 Open *ExtendedGridView.cs*.

3 Add a *virtual* method to the *ExtendedGridView* class.

Add the following code outside any methods:

public virtual void ApplyFormatting() { }

```
public virtual void ApplyFormatting()
{
}
```

A *virtual* method is a method that can be *overridden* in any class that extends it.

Overriding a method completely replaces its functionality.

4 Create a new class named: **RedGridView**

5 Make the *RedGridView* class extend the *ExtendedGridView* class.

The line that begins the class should read:

public class RedGridView : **ExtendedGridView**

```
public class RedGridView : ExtendedGridView
```

```
using System.Web;
using System.Web.UI.WebControls;
```

6 Add a *using* line for: **System.Web.UI.WebControls**

This will save typing when accessing the *GridViewRow* class.

7 Override the *ApplyFormatting* method in the *RedGridView* class.

Add the following code to override the *ApplyFormatting* method:

public override void ApplyFormatting()
{
    foreach (GridViewRow Row in base.Rows)
    {
        Row.BackColor = System.Drawing.Color.Red;
    }
}

```
public class RedGridView : ExtendedGridView
{
    public override void ApplyFormatting()
    {
        foreach (GridViewRow Row in base.Rows)
        {
            Row.BackColor = System.Drawing.Color.Red;
        }
    }
}
```

This code overrides the *ApplyFormatting* method from the *ExtendedGridView* class and replaces it with code that makes every row red.

8 Test your new functionality.

note

Overriding without using the override keyword

If you had left out the *override* or *virtual* keywords the code would still have worked, but the code would have been marked with warnings to indicate bad coding practice.

When you replace a base class's methods without specifically overriding them, C# will complain that your new method 'hides' the old one.

It's bad practice to override methods that are not marked as virtual in the base class for two reasons:

1. It makes it difficult to understand where the method's code originates.

2. You must assume that the original programmer of the base class has judged that overriding the method could prevent the class from working properly.

note

Why use virtual?

Virtual methods and properties are particularly useful in class libraries, or any code that will be used by other programmers.

By allowing methods and properties to be overridden, you allow anyone using your code to create their own extended version and make their own changes.

For methods and properties that have no logic and are only intended to be overridden, you would usually use the *abstract* keyword instead.

You'll learn about the *abstract* keyword in the next lesson: *Lesson 5-5: Understand the abstract keyword.*

1. Open the code-behind file of *Horses.aspx*.

2. Add the following code to the *Page_Load* event handler:

   GridViewHorse.ApplyFormatting();

   ```
   protected void Page_Load(object sender, EventArgs e)
   {
       GridViewHorse.ApplyFormatting();
   }
   ```

3. View *Horses.aspx* in your web browser.

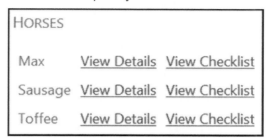

Nothing has changed as the *ExtendedGridView* control's *ApplyFormatting* method doesn't do anything.

4. Close your web browser and return to Visual Studio.

5. Open *Horses.aspx* in Source view.

6. Find the code for the *GridViewHorse* control.

7. Replace:

   tsm:ExtendedGridView

   …with:

   tsm:RedGridView

   ```
   <tsm:RedGridView ID="GridViewHorse" runat="server" A
       <Columns>
           <asp:BoundField DataField="HorseName" Header
           <asp:ButtonField CommandName="ViewDetails" T
           <asp:ButtonField CommandName="ViewChecklist"
       </Columns>
   </tsm:RedGridView>
   ```

8. View *Horses.aspx* in your web browser.

   This time the *GridView*'s rows are all shown in red. The overridden *ApplyFormatting* method has replaced the one from *ExtendedGridView*.

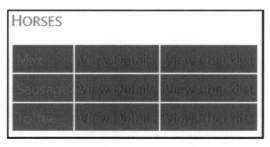

Note that the *RedGridView* class will still contain the *GetIDFromRow* method from the *ExtendedGridView* class because it extends the *ExtendedGridView* class.

Lesson 5-5: Understand the abstract keyword

The *abstract* keyword allows you to create methods that do not have any code. *abstract* methods are placeholders that are given code when the class that contains them is extended.

abstract methods must be contained in *abstract* classes, which can also contain methods and properties that are not abstract.

1   Open *StableBase* from your sample files folder.

2   Open *ExtendedGridView.cs*.

3   Make the *ApplyFormatting* method *abstract*.

Replace the code for the *ApplyFormatting* method with:

public abstract void ApplyFormatting();

```
        public abstract void ApplyFormatting();
}
```

Notice that the method no longer has any curly brackets { }.

Because an *abstract* method is designed to be overridden, it doesn't need any code.

4   Attempt to build the project.

An error is shown in the *Error List* window:

'StableBase.ExtendedGridView.ApplyFormatting()' is abstract but it is contained in non-abstract class 'StableBase.ExtendedGridView'

```
❌ 13  'StableBase.ExtendedGridView.ApplyFormatting()' is abstract but it
       is contained in non-abstract class 'StableBase.ExtendedGridView'
```

You are not allowed to create an *abstract* method or property unless the class is also *abstract*.

5   Make the *ExtendedGridView* class abstract.

Change the line that defines the class so it reads:

*public **abstract** class ExtendedGridView : GridView*

```
public abstract class ExtendedGridView : GridView
{
```

Now the *ExtendedGridView* class is defined as *abstract*.

The only purpose of *abstract* classes is to be extended. An abstract class cannot be used unless it is extended and all of its *abstract* methods and properties are overridden.

6   Open *RedGridView.cs*.

The *RedGridView* class already extends the *ExtendedGridView* class and overrides the *ApplyFormatting* method correctly.

```
public class RedGridView : ExtendedGridView
{
    public override void ApplyFormatting()
    {
        foreach (GridViewRow Row in base.Rows)
        {
            Row.BackColor = System.Drawing.Color.Red;
        }
    }
}
```

7 Comment out the *ApplyFormatting* method.

To do this easily, simply select all of the code for the *ApplyFormatting* method and click the *Comment* button on the top toolbar:

```
public class RedGridView : ExtendedGridView
{
    //public override void ApplyFormatting()
    //{
    //    foreach (GridViewRow Row in base.Rows)
    //    {
    //        Row.BackColor = System.Drawing.Color.Red;
    //    }
    //}
}
```

8 Attempt to build the project.

Another error is shown in the *Error List* window:

'StableBase.RedGridView' does not implement inherited abstract member 'StableBase.ExtendedGridView.ApplyFormatting()'

> ⊗ 13 'StableBase.RedGridView' does not implement inherited abstract member 'StableBase.ExtendedGridView.ApplyFormatting()'

When you extend an *abstract* class, you <u>must</u> override all of its *abstract* properties and methods. Failing to do so will result in this error and your project will not be able to build.

9 Uncomment the *ApplyFormatting* method.

As before, select all of the commented code and click the *Uncomment* button on the top toolbar:

```
public class RedGridView : ExtendedGridView
{
    public override void ApplyFormatting()
    {
        foreach (GridViewRow Row in base.Rows)
        {
            Row.BackColor = System.Drawing.Color.Red;
        }
    }
}
```

10 Test your code.

View *Horses.aspx* in your web browser.

The *RedGridView* class works perfectly, combining the *GetIDFromRow* functionality of *ExtendedGridView* with the *ApplyFormatting* functionality of *RedGridView*.

note

Using polymorphism and abstract to solve real-world problems

Imagine that you have an *Invoice* base class that is extended into *SalesInvoice* and *CreditNote* classes.

The base class has an abstract *Save* method which is implemented in different ways in each extended type.

If all invoices and credit notes are converted to the *Invoice* base type and placed in an *Invoices* collection, it is possible to iterate through the collection and call each object's *Save* method even though the method will work in a different way depending upon whether the extended object was originally an *Invoice* or *CreditNote* object.

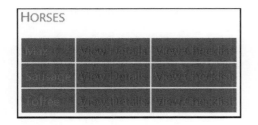

Lesson 5-6: Implement an interface

Interfaces do not contain any programming logic, but simply define a minimum set of properties and methods that a class must contain. In addition, classes may also contain properties and methods that are not specified in the interface. In this lesson you'll implement the *IDisposable* interface in one of your own classes. The *IDisposable* interface is part of the .NET framework.

1   Open *MarketTrader* from your sample files folder.

This is a relatively simple web application that is used to display stock market data.

2   Open *DataAccess.cs*.

This class is used for all database queries in the project.

Notice that this class contains an instance of the *MarketTraderDataContext* class, which is a LINQ data context.

```
public class DataAccess
{
    MarketTraderDataContext Data = new MarketTraderDataContext();
```

This object could use a lot of memory, so you should dispose of any instances of this class when they are no longer needed.

3   Open the code-behind file of *MarketData.aspx*.

The *ButtonGetData_Click* event handler uses an instance of the *DataAccess* class, but doesn't dispose of it properly.

```
protected void ButtonGetData_Click(object sender, EventArgs e)
{
    DataAccess DataClass = new DataAccess();
    int MarketID = Convert.ToInt32(DropDownListMarket.SelectedValue);
    GridViewData.DataSource = DataClass.GetMarketQuotes(MarketID);
    GridViewData.DataBind();
}
```

In *Essential Skills* Session 6 you learned that the best-practice to ensure that objects are quickly disposed of is to wrap the code in a *using* statement. The *using* statement works by calling the object's *Dispose* method.

4   Add a *using* statement to automatically dispose of the *DataClass* object.

1. Make the first line of code into a *using* statement as follows:

    using (*DataAccess DataClass = new DataAccess()***)**

2. Add curly brackets so that the rest of the event handler's code is contained in the *using* statement.

```
using (DataAccess DataClass = new DataAccess())
{
    int MarketID = Convert.ToInt32(DropDownListMarket.SelectedValue);
    GridViewData.DataSource = DataClass.GetMarketQuotes(MarketID);
    GridViewData.DataBind();
}
```

5   Attempt to build the project.

note

Interfaces and polymorphism

In *Lesson 5-3: Understand polymorphism,* you learned how objects that extend classes can impersonate (be converted into) the base types that they extend.

In a similar way, an interface can be regarded as the base class of any class that implements it.

This may sound a little confusing at first because you may be thinking that an interface is an entirely different construct to a class. In reality an interface can be thought of as a class that only contains abstract methods and properties.

Because a class that implements an interface extends the interface's base class it should be clear that you can convert an object to the same type as any interface it implements.

For example, any class that implements the *IDisposable* interface can be converted into an *IDisposable* object, as in the following code:

IDisposable MyDisposableObject = (IDisposable)DataClass;

This technique is extremely useful when you need to create a collection containing different objects that all implement the same interface.

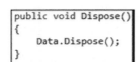

An error appears in the *Error List* window:

'MarketTrader.DataAccess': type used in a using statement must be implicitly convertible to 'System.IDisposable'

> ⊗ 1 'MarketTrader.DataAccess': type used in a using statement must be implicitly convertible to 'System.IDisposable'

The *IDisposable* interface defines a single method called *Dispose.* The error message is thus a roundabout way of saying "the *DataAccess* class does not contain a *Dispose* method".

6   Open *DataAccess.cs.*

7   Make the class implement the *IDisposable* interface.

You could simply include a *Dispose* method and the code would compile without errors, but it is best practice to explicitly implement the *IDisposable* interface. Implementing interfaces is done in exactly the same way as extending classes.

Change the code that starts the class to:

public class DataAccess : **IDisposable**

```
public class DataAccess : IDisposable
{
```

The *DataAccess* class now *implements* the *IDisposable* interface and could be grouped with any other classes that implement the same interface (see sidebar).

8   Attempt to build the project.

Another error appears in the *Error List* window:

'MarketTrader.DataAccess' does not implement interface member 'System.IDisposable.Dispose()'

> ⊗ 1 'MarketTrader.DataAccess' does not implement interface member 'System.IDisposable.Dispose()'

To implement the interface, the class must contain any methods and properties that are defined by the interface (in this case the class must have a *Dispose* method).

9   Add a *Dispose* method to the class.

Add the following method to the class:

```
public void Dispose()
{
    Data.Dispose();
}
```

10   Attempt to build the project.

This time the project builds without any problems.

11   Test your code.

1.   View *MarketData.aspx* in your web browser.

2.   Click *Get Data.*

The data is successfully returned from the database. The code is now more memory-efficient as it will dispose of the *DataAccess* object after retrieving the data.

Lesson 5-7: Create an interface

In this lesson you'll create your own custom interface and use it to group similar classes together.

1 Open *StableBase* from your sample files folder.

2 Create a new interface named: **IColoredGridView**

1. Right-click *StableBase* in the *Solution Explorer* and click Add→New Item… from the shortcut menu.

   The *Add New Item* dialog appears.

2. Click *Code* in the left-hand pane.

3. Click *Interface* in the central pane.

4. Type: **IColoredGridView.cs** into the *Name* box.

   The ASP.NET naming convention always precedes an interface's name with a capital *I*.

5. Click *Add*.

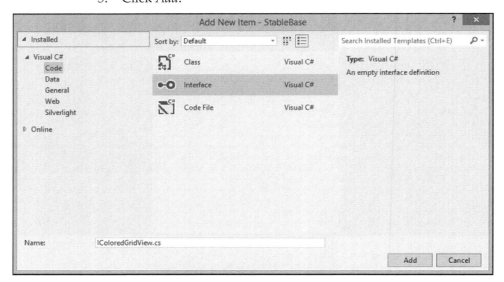

Your new interface is created and opened.

3 Add an *ApplyFormatting* method to the interface.

Add the following code to your new interface (between the curly brackets {}):

void ApplyFormatting();

This interface now requires a method named *ApplyFormatting* that does not return a value. Any class that implements the *IColoredGridView* interface must have an *ApplyFormatting* method that matches this template.

```
interface IColoredGridView
{
    void ApplyFormatting();
}
```

4 Implement the interface in the *RedGridView* class.

1. Open *RedGridView.cs*.

2. Change the code that defines the class to:

public class RedGridView : ExtendedGridView,
IColoredGridView

```
public class RedGridView : ExtendedGridView, IColoredGridView
{
```

Since the *RedGridView* class already contains an *ApplyFormatting* method, this code will compile without any errors.

5   Create a *BlueGridView* class which extends the *GridView* class and implements the *IColoredGridView* interface.

1.   Create a new class named: **BlueGridView.cs**

2.   Add a *using* line for: **System.Web.UI.WebControls**

```
using System.Web;
using System.Web.UI.WebControls;
```

3.   Add code to extend the *GridView* class and implement the *IColoredGridView* interface.

```
public class BlueGridView : GridView, IColoredGridView
{
}
```

4.   Attempt to build the project.

An error appears because the *BlueGridView* class doesn't contain the *ApplyFormatting* method that is required by the *IColoredGridView* interface.

```
⊗ 2  'StableBase.BlueGridView' does not implement interface member
      'StableBase.IColoredGridView.ApplyFormatting()'
```

5.   Add an *ApplyFormatting* method to the class using the following code:

public void ApplyFormatting()
{
    foreach (GridViewRow Row in base.Rows)
    {
       Row.BackColor = System.Drawing.Color.Blue;
    }
}

```
public void ApplyFormatting()
{
    foreach (GridViewRow Row in base.Rows)
    {
        Row.BackColor = System.Drawing.Color.Blue;
    }
}
```

6.   Attempt to build the project.

This time the project compiles without errors.

Your *RedGridView* and *BlueGridView* classes both implement the *IColoredGridView* interface.

Because both classes implement the *IColoredGridView* interface, both *RedGridView* and *BlueGridView* objects could be converted into *IColoredGridView* objects using the techniques that you learned in: *Lesson 5-3: Understand polymorphism.*

Lesson 5-8: Use the Class View window

Because extended class structures can get confusing, Visual Studio offers the *Class View* and *Object Browser* windows. These windows allow you to see a visualization of class structures.

1 Open *StableBase* from your sample files folder.

2 Display the *Class View* window.

Click View→Class View (see sidebar if this option isn't available).

The *Class View* window appears in the same area as the *Solution Explorer*.

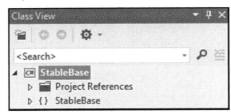

3 Examine the *RedGridView* class in the *Class View* window.

1. Expand *StableBase* in the *Class View* window.

2. Click *RedGridView* in the expanded list.

In the bottom half of the *Class View* window, you can see the *ApplyFormatting* method of this class.

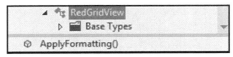

This area shows all methods and properties of the class that you have selected.

3. Expand *RedGridView*.

4. Expand *Base Types*.

The *Base Types* list shows you that the *RedGridView* class extends the *ExtendedGridView* class and implements the *IColoredGridView* interface.

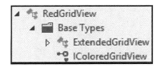

5. Expand *ExtendedGridView*.

You can now see that the *ExtendedGridView* class extends the *GridView* class.

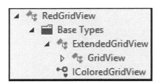

4 Quickly view the code of the *ExtendedGridView* class.

You can use the *Class View* window to quickly jump to the relevant code of each class.

Right-click *ExtendedGridView* in the *Class View* window and click *Go To Definition* from the shortcut menu.

The *ExtendedGridView* class is shown in the main Visual Studio window.

```
namespace StableBase
{
    public abstract class ExtendedGridView : GridView
    {
        public int GetIDFromRow(object CommandArgument)
        {
```

5 Create a custom folder in the *Class View* window.

The *Class View* window can be cumbersome to work with, since it will always list every class in the project.

For ease of use, you can create a custom folder that contains only the classes that you are most interested in.

1. Click the *New Folder* button at the top of the *Class View* window:

   A new folder appears, ready for you to name it.

2. Type **ColoredGridViews** and press **<Enter>**.

   Your new folder is now ready to use.

3. Click and drag the *RedGridView* class into the *ColoredGridViews* folder.

   A reference to the *StableBase.RedGridView* class is added to the folder.

   Note that the class hasn't actually been moved or changed in any way. *Class View* folders are only shortcuts for your convenience.

4. Click and drag the *BlueGridView* class into the *ColoredGridViews* folder.

   The folder now enables easy access to your two custom *GridView* classes.

6 Return to the *Solution Explorer* window.

Click the *Solution Explorer* tab beneath the *Class View* window.

Lesson 5-9: Use the Object Browser window

You've learned how to extend classes and implement interfaces, but you might still be puzzled as to how these techniques are used in practical terms.

The .NET framework makes extensive use of interfaces and extended classes. In this lesson you'll use the *Object Browser* window to see how it all fits together.

note

If the Object Browser option isn't visible

Just like *Class View*, Visual Studio must be in Expert Settings mode for you to use the *Object Browser*.

To switch to Expert Settings, click Tools→Settings→ Expert Settings.

The *Object Browser* option will now be available under the *View* menu.

1   Open *StableBase* from your sample files folder.

2   Open the *Object Browser* window.

Click View→Object Browser (see sidebar if this isn't available).

After a short delay, the *Object Browser* window appears in the central pane.

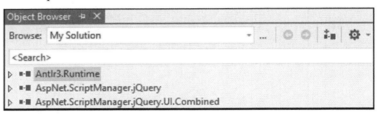

The *Object Browser* window is almost identical to the *Class View* window, but it allows you to explore the classes of the .NET framework as well as the classes in your project.

3   Examine the *TextBox* class from the .NET framework.

1.   Type: **TextBox** into the *Search* box and press **<Enter>**.

All of the objects that match the search term appear.

2.   Expand *System.Web.UI.WebControls.TextBox*.

This is the class that the *TextBox* control is based on. You've used the *TextBox* control many times in previous lessons.

3.   Expand the *Base Types* folder.

Here you can see that the *TextBox* control implements the *IEditableTextControl, IPostBackDataHandler* and *ITextControl* interfaces and extends the *WebControl* class.

4.   Expand the *WebControl* class.

note

If you still don't see the use of extending classes and implementing interfaces

Complex class and interface structures aren't often needed in ASP.NET projects, because most of the structure is already provided for you.

For example, when you create an ASP.NET page it automatically inherits a huge amount of functionality from the *System.Web.UI.Page* class.

Extending classes and implementing interfaces is far more useful when working with normal Windows desktop applications, as less functionality is provided automatically.

If you ever turn your skills to Windows desktop applications, you'll start to see the true value of the skills that you're learning in this session.

All ASP.NET controls extend the *WebControl* class.

You can see that the *WebControl* class extends the *Control* class and implements the *IAttributeAccessor* interface.

5. Expand the *Control* class.

    Here you can see that the *Control* class extends the *Object* class, as well as implementing several other interfaces.

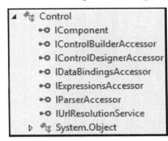

All of the classes in the .NET framework can be traced back to the *Object* class. It's for this reason that you're able to cast any object to the *object* type.

Casting to the *object* type is covered in Session 5 of the *Essential Skills* course in this series.

4   Examine the properties of the *Page* class.

1. Type **System.Web.UI.Page** into the search box and press **<Enter>**.

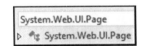

    The *System.Web.UI.Page* class appears in the *Object Browser*.

2. In the top-right pane of the *Object Browser*, scroll down and Click the *Response* property.

    Information about the property appears in the bottom-right pane.

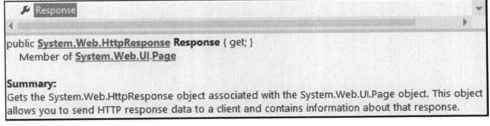

    You can see here that the *Response* property is a *System.Web.HttpResponse* object.

3. Click *System.Web.HttpResponse* in the bottom-right pane.

    You're automatically taken to the *HttpResponse* class and can now examine its properties and base types.

    The *Object Browser* can be extremely helpful when navigating the .NET framework.

Session 5: Exercise

1   Open *Exercise5* from your sample files folder.

2   Open *MailSender.cs*.

       This is a simple class that sends e-mail messages.

3   Make the *SendEmail* method *virtual*.

4   Create a new class called: **SalesMailSender.cs**

5   Make the new *SalesMailSender* class *extend* the *MailSender* class.

6   Override the *SendEmail* method in the *SalesMailSender* class and make the new method use the body text: **Thank you for your purchase.**

7   Create another new class called: **MarketingMailSender.cs**

8   Make the new *MarketingMailSender* class *extend* the *MailSender* class.

9   Add a new method to the *MarketingMailSender* class named: **SendPromotionalEmail**

10   Add code to the *SendPromotionalEmail* method that will send an e-mail message with the body text: **Here are some products that may interest you.**

       You can do this by copying and pasting the code from one of the other classes.

11   Create a new *interface* named: **IMailSender.cs**

12   Add a method to your new *interface* named: **SendEmail**

13   Ensure that the *SendEmail* method in the *IMailSender* interface returns *void* and requires a single *string* argument.

14   Make the *MailSender* class implement the *IMailSender* interface.

If you need help slide the page to the left

Exercise5 - Start   Exercise5 - End

Session 5: Exercise Answers

These are the four questions that students find the most difficult to answer:

Q 12 & 13	Q 6	Q 5	Q 3

Use the following code:
 	
void SendEmail(string FromAddress);
 	
This was covered in: *Lesson 5-7: Create an interface.*
	Use the following code:
	
	public override void SendEmail(string ToAddress = "info@ASPNETCentral.com")
	{
	    using (System.Net.Mail. SmtpClient Client = new System.Net.Mail. SmtpClient())
	    {
	        string Subject = "Exercise 5";
	        string BodyText = "Thank you for your purchase.";
	        Client.Send("info@ASPNETCentral.com", ToAddress, Subject, BodyText);
	    }
	}
	
	This was covered in: *Lesson 5-4: Understand the virtual and override keywords.*
		Change:
		
		public class SalesMailSender
		
		…to:
		
		public class SalesMailSender **: MailSender**
		
		This was covered in: *Lesson 5-1: Extend a class.*
			Change:
			
			public void SendEmail (string ToAddress)
			
			…to:
			
			public **virtual** *void SendEmail (string ToAddress)*
			
			This was covered in: *Lesson 5-4: Understand the virtual and override keywords.*

If you have difficulty with the other questions, here are the lessons that cover the relevant skills:

1, 2   **Refer to: Essential Skills Session 1.**

4   **Refer to: Essential Skills Session 6.**

7   **Refer to: Essential Skills Session 6.**

8   **Refer to: Lesson 5-1: Extend a class.**

9   **Refer to: Essential Skills Session 6.**

10   **Refer to: Lesson 2-9: Send e-mail messages using the SmtpClient class.**

11   **Refer to: Lesson 5-7: Create an interface.**

14   **Refer to: Lesson 5-6: Implement an interface.**

Session Six: Compiler directives and advanced debugging

> The Prime Directive is not just a set of rules. It is a philosophy, and a very correct one. History has proven again and again that whenever mankind interferes with a less developed civilization, no matter how well intentioned that interference may be, the results are invariably disastrous.
>
> *Jean-Luc Picard (fictional Star Trek character)*
> *Captain of the USS Enterprise (born 2305)*

When you build your project, all of its C# code is turned into a binary *dll* file. The program that does this is called the *compiler*. By using *compiler directives*, you can send instructions to the compiler when it builds your code.

Unlike Star Trek's Prime Directive, interfering with the normal operation of the compiler can be very beneficial to programming productivity!

The only compiler directive that you're likely to have seen before is the *#region* directive, as it's often used to help organize code. Many developers use the *#region* directive without even realizing that it's a compiler directive.

In this session you'll explore compiler directives and their uses, as well as some advanced debugging techniques.

Session Objectives

By the end of this session you will be able to:

- Create code regions with the #region directive
- Use the #if directive to selectively compile code
- Use the #if directive with the TRACE constant
- Use the #define directive to create a new constant
- Use the #else and #elif directives
- Use the #warning directive to show warnings when compiling
- Use the #error directive to cause a compile error
- Use System.Diagnostics to write Debug messages
- Use a listener to save diagnostic information to a file
- Enable tracing

Lesson 6-1: Create code regions with the #region directive

The simplest compiler directive is the *#region* directive. It is the only compiler directive that doesn't actually have any effect upon the compilation process.

You could even argue that the *#region* directive isn't a true compiler directive because its only purpose is to help organize your code.

1   Open *MathLand* from your sample files folder.

2   Open the code-behind file of *Primes.aspx*.

This is the code that you used to test multi-threading in: *Lesson 3-10: Implement multi-threading using the Parallel class*. There's a lot of code here doing a lot of different things. It could make it easier to work with if you split it into regions.

3   Collapse the code to definitions.

Click Edit→Outlining→Collapse to Definitions.

The code is collapsed to the definitions of its methods and properties (see sidebar if the option is not available).

This view is easier to work with as it allows you to expand only the code you want, but by adding regions you can create your own collapsible groups.

note

If the Outlining option isn't visible

Visual Studio must be in Expert Settings mode for you to use the *Outlining* options in the *Edit* menu.

To switch to Expert Settings, click Tools→Settings→ Expert Settings.

The *Outlining* option will now be available under the *Edit* menu.

4   Add a region for the event handlers and properties.

1.   Add the following code just before the *Page_Load* event handler:

#region Event Handlers and Properties

```
#region Event Handlers and Properties
protected void Page_Load(object sender, EventArgs e)...
```

This code is used to begin a region.

2.   Add the following code after the end of the *ButtonCalculatePrimes_Click* event handler:

#endregion

```
#region Event Handlers and Properties
protected void Page_Load(object sender, EventArgs e)...

private List<int> PrimeNumbers = new List<int>(); //Colle
public int ThreadsCompleted = 0;
private object Locker = new object();

protected void ButtonCalculatePrimes_Click(object sender,
#endregion
```

If you are not completing the course incrementally use the sample file: **Lesson 6-1** to begin this lesson.

Sample files with the starting point for each lesson are also provided for all of the other lessons in this session.

5   Collapse your new region.

Click the minus sign next to the *#region* line to collapse the region (⊟).

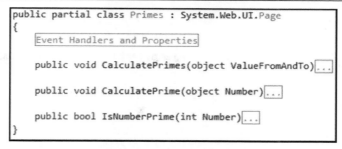

```
public partial class Primes : System.Web.UI.Page
{
    Event Handlers and Properties

    public void CalculatePrimes(object ValueFromAndTo)...

    public void CalculatePrime(object Number)...

    public bool IsNumberPrime(int Number)...
}
```

Now all of the event handlers and properties are hidden away, allowing you to concentrate on the other methods.

6   Add a region for the calculation methods.

1.   Add the following code just before the *CalculatePrimes* method:

#region Calculation methods

```
#region Calculation methods
public void CalculatePrimes(object ValueFromAndTo)...
```

2.   Add the following code after the end of the *IsNumberPrime* method:

#endregion

```
#region Calculation methods
public void CalculatePrimes(object ValueFromAndTo)...

public void CalculatePrime(object Number)...

public bool IsNumberPrime(int Number)...
#endregion
```

7   Collapse the *Calculation methods* region.

Just as you did for the *Event Handlers and Properties* region, collapse the new region by clicking the minus sign immediately before *Calculation methods*.

```
public partial class Primes : System.Web.UI.Page
{
    Event Handlers and Properties

    Calculation methods
}
```

Your code is now conveniently grouped to allow for quick access to the code that you are looking for.

Lesson 6-2: Use the #if directive to selectively compile code

note

The DEBUG constant and the System.Diagnostics namespace

As well as being useful for selectively compiling code using the *#if* directive, the DEBUG constant is also relevant to the *System.Diagnostics* namespace.

Some of the methods in the *System.Diagnostics* namespace are able to detect the DEBUG constant and react accordingly.

You'll see how this works in: *Lesson 6-8: Use System.Diagnostics to write Debug messages.*

Compiler directives are often used to make an application work differently depending on the build profile.

You learned about build profiles in: *Lesson 1-3: Use the Debug and Release profiles.*

In this lesson you'll use the *#if* directive to compile certain code only if the project is compiled using a build profile that defines the DEBUG constant.

By default the *Debug* profile defines the DEBUG constant. You'll learn more about constants later in: *Lesson 6-4: Use the #define directive to create a new constant.*

1   Open *MarketTrader* from your sample files folder.

2   Open *Site.Master* in Design view.

This is a master page. Master pages are covered in Session 12 of the *Essential Skills* course in this series.

Every page that is associated with a master page inherits both the layout and any C# code that is included in the master page. Every page in this project is associated with this master page.

Notice that there is a *Label* control in the top-right corner named: *LabelDebug*

You're going to add a compiler directive that will show a message in this Label only if the project is built using the *Debug* profile.

3   Open the code-behind file of *Site.Master*.

4   Add code to display a message in the *LabelDebug* control.

Scroll down and add the following code to the *Page_Load* event handler:

LabelDebug.Text = "DEBUG MODE - NOT FOR RELEASE";

```
protected void Page_Load(object sender, EventArgs e)
{
    LabelDebug.Text = "DEBUG MODE - NOT FOR RELEASE";
}
```

This code will run regardless of which profile is used to build the project. You'll need to add a compiler directive in order to change this.

5   Add a compiler directive to compile the code only if the *DEBUG* constant is present.

1.   Add a new line to the start of the *Page_Load* event handler with the following code:

#if DEBUG

2. Add a new line to the end of the *Page_Load* event handler with the following code:

#endif

```
            protected void Page_Load(object sender, EventArgs e)
            {
#if DEBUG
            LabelDebug.Text = "DEBUG MODE - NOT FOR RELEASE";
#endif
            }
```

The compiler directives appear to the far left of the rest of the code. This is to indicate that they will only affect the compiler and aren't part of the programming logic itself.

When the compiler runs, it will see the *#if* directive and will compile the *LabelDebug.Text…* line of code only if the DEBUG constant is present.

This means that the code will be entirely omitted from the built version of the site if the DEBUG constant is not enabled.

You may remember seeing the option for the DEBUG constant in: *Lesson 1-5: Change Build options.*

6 View the project using the *Debug* profile.

1. Make sure that *Debug* is selected from the drop-down menu on the top toolbar.

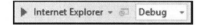

2. Click Debug→Start Debugging.

Your message appears in the top-right corner, as expected.

When you run the project in Debug mode, it is automatically built using your selected build profile.

Because the *Debug* profile has the DEBUG constant enabled, your compiler directive allowed the code to be compiled.

3. Close your web browser and return to Visual Studio.

7 Compile and run the project using the *Release* profile.

1. Select *Release* from the drop-down menu on the top toolbar.

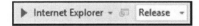

2. Click Debug→Start Debugging.

This time there is no message in the top-right corner.

Your compiler directive did not find the DEBUG constant, because it isn't enabled in the *Release* profile.

This is a good way to ensure that you don't accidentally release an unoptimized Debug version of your code.

Lesson 6-3: Use the #if directive with the TRACE constant

The TRACE constant is very similar to the DEBUG constant. You saw it when you examined the different Build options in: *Lesson 1-5: Change Build options*.

The TRACE constant is enabled on both the *Debug* and *Release* profiles by default.

1   Open *MarketTrader* from your sample files folder.

2   Open the code-behind file of *Site.Master*.

3   Add code to display a message if the TRACE constant is present.

Add the following code to the bottom of the *Page_Load* event handler (outside the existing *#if* directive):

**LabelDebug.Text += "
TRACE MODE ENABLED";**

```
#if DEBUG
            LabelDebug.Text = "DEBUG MODE - NOT FOR RELEASE";
#endif
            LabelDebug.Text += "<br />TRACE MODE ENABLED";
```

4   Add an *#if* directive to compile the code only if the TRACE constant is present.

1.   Add the following code on a new line after the *#endif* directive:

#if TRACE

2.   Add the following code on a new line at the end of the *Page_Load* event handler:

#endif

```
#if TRACE
            LabelDebug.Text += "<br />TRACE MODE ENABLED";
#endif
```

5   Disable the TRACE constant on the *Release* profile.

1.   Make sure that *Release* is selected from the drop-down menu on the top toolbar.

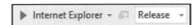

2.   Right-click *MarketTrader* in the *Solution Explorer* and click *Properties* in the shortcut menu.

The project's properties appear in the main panel.

3.   Click the *Build* tab in the project properties window (if it isn't selected already).

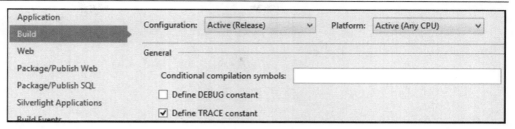

Here you can see the checkboxes that enable and disable the DEBUG and TRACE constants.

You can also see the *Conditional compilation symbols* box, which allows you define custom constants. You'll learn more about creating custom constants in: *Lesson 6-4: Use the #define directive to create a new constant.*

4. Un-tick the *Define TRACE constant* checkbox.

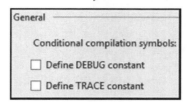

The DEBUG and TRACE constants are both now disabled in the *Release* profile, but both remain enabled in the *Debug* profile.

6   Test your code.

1. Make sure that *Debug* is selected from the drop-down menu on the top toolbar.

2. Click Debug→Start Debugging.

   Both messages appear in the top-right corner, as expected.

3. Close your web browser and return to Visual Studio.

4. Select *Release* from the drop-down menu on the top toolbar.

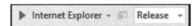

5. Click Build→Rebuild Solution.

   You learned about rebuilding in: *Lesson 1-4: Build, Rebuild and Clean a project.*

6. Click Debug→Start Debugging.

   This time neither message appears in the top-right corner. Your *#if* directives did not find either the TRACE or DEBUG constants, so the code within them was not compiled when the project was rebuilt.

note

What's the difference between TRACE and DEBUG?

The TRACE and DEBUG constants are simply values that are either present or not present.

They become important when working with the *System.Diagnostics* namespace.

The *System.Diagnostics* namespace behaves differently depending upon whether the TRACE and DEBUG constants are present.

You'll work with the *System.Diagnostics* namespace in: *Lesson 6-8: Use System.Diagnostics to write Debug messages.*

Lesson 6-4: Use the #define directive to create a new constant

As well as using the DEBUG and TRACE constants, you can create new constants of your own by using the *#define* compiler directive.

The DEBUG and TRACE constants are usually sufficient for most projects so it's rare to see this done, but it's included in this lesson for completeness.

Constants can also be defined for the entire project by using the *Conditional compilation symbols* setting in the project's properties (see sidebar).

1   Open *MarketTrader* from your sample files folder.

2   Open the code-behind file of *Site.Master*.

3   Add code to define a new constant named: **TRIALVERSION**

Add the following code to the very top of the page, before the *using* lines:

#define TRIALVERSION

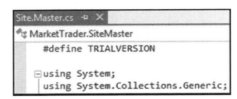

This code creates a new constant named *TRIALVERSION*.

You can use your new constant in exactly the same way as you used the DEBUG and TRACE constants in earlier lessons.

4   Add code to display a message indicating whether this is a trial version.

Add the following code to the end of the *Page_Load* event handler:

LabelDebug.Text = "TRIAL VERSION";

```
        protected void Page_Load(object sender, EventArgs e)
        {
#if DEBUG
            LabelDebug.Text = "DEBUG MODE - NOT FOR RELEASE";

#endif
#if TRACE
            LabelDebug.Text += "<br />TRACE MODE ENABLED";

#endif
            LabelDebug.Text = "TRIAL VERSION";

        }
```

5   Add a compiler directive to check for the TRIALVERSION constant.

1. Add a new line before *LabelDebug.Text = "TRIAL VERSION";* with the following code:

    #if TRIALVERSION

note

Defining a custom constant for your entire project

You may have noticed the *Conditional compilation symbols* box when viewing the *Build* properties of your project.

You can use this box to define custom constants for your entire project.

General
Conditional compilation symbols:

If you were to enter *TRIALVERSION* in this box, a *TRIALVERSION* constant would be automatically defined on every page of your project.

This is the equivalent of adding *#define TRIALVERSION* to every class.

2. Add a new line to the end of the *Page_Load* event handler with the following code:

#endif

```
#if TRACE
            LabelDebug.Text += "<br />TRACE MODE ENABLED";
#endif
#if TRIALVERSION
            LabelDebug.Text = "TRIAL VERSION";
#endif
```

Now this code will only be compiled if the TRIALVERSION constant is present.

6 Test your code.

1. Click Debug→Start Debugging.

The *TRIAL VERSION* indicator is displayed in the top-right corner.

2. Close your web browser and return to Visual Studio.

7 Use the #undef directive to undefine a constant.

Add the following code at the top of the page, just after the *#define* line:

#undef TRIALVERSION

This code removes the TRIALVERSION constant, so it will no longer be detected.

You could, of course, have simply removed the *#define* directive but this example illustrates the use of the *#undef* directive.

As well as your own constants, you could also use the *#undef* directive to undefine the DEBUG or TRACE constants.

8 Test your code again.

Run the project in Debug mode once more.

This time the *TRIAL VERSION* text isn't displayed because you have undefined the *TRIALVERSION* constant.

Custom compilation symbols are useful when you have a project that you want to compile in different ways. A common example of this would be a project that needs to be compiled into both a restricted trial version and a full unrestricted version.

By using custom compilation constants, you could build different versions of your application for trial and commercial purposes.

Lesson 6-5: Use the #else and #elif directives

The *#else* and *#elif* compilation directives are the compiler directive equivalents of the *else* and *else if* statements.

By using *#else* and *#elif*, you can expand the logic of your compiler directives.

1 Open *MarketTrader* from your sample files folder.

2 Open the code-behind file of *Site.Master* and scroll down to the *Page_Load* event handler.

At the moment there are three *#if* directives in the *Page_Load* event handler.

```
#if DEBUG
            LabelDebug.Text = "DEBUG MODE - NOT FOR RELEASE";
#endif
#if TRACE
            LabelDebug.Text += "<br />TRACE MODE ENABLED";
#endif
#if TRIALVERSION
            LabelDebug.Text = "TRIAL VERSION";
#endif
```

3 Add an *#elif* directive to check for the *PROVERSION* constant.

1. Remove the last *#endif* directive.

```
#if TRIALVERSION
            LabelDebug.Text = "TRIAL VERSION";

        }
```

2. Add the following code:

#elif PROVERSION
     LabelDebug.Text = "PRO VERSION";
#endif

```
#if TRIALVERSION
            LabelDebug.Text = "TRIAL VERSION";
#elif PROVERSION
            LabelDebug.Text = "PRO VERSION";
#endif
```

The compiler will now check for the *PROVERSION* constant, but only if it isn't able to find the *TRIALVERSION* constant.

The *#elif* directive is very similar to the *else if* statement.

if and *else if* statements are covered in Session 7 of the *Essential Skills* course in this series.

4 Define the *PROVERSION* constant.

1. Remove the following code from the top of the page:

#define TRIALVERSION
#undef TRIALVERSION

2. Add the following code in its place:

#define PROVERSION

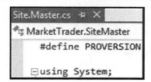

5   Test your code.

1.   Run the project in Debug mode.

The *PRO VERSION* message is shown in the top-right corner, as expected.

2.   Close your web browser and return to Visual Studio.

6   Add an *#else* directive for the standard version.

Remove the last *#endif* directive from the *Page_Load* event handler and add the following code in its place:

#else
        LabelDebug.Text = "STANDARD VERSION";
#endif

```
#if TRIALVERSION
        LabelDebug.Text = "TRIAL VERSION";
#elif PROVERSION
        LabelDebug.Text = "PRO VERSION";
#else
        LabelDebug.Text = "STANDARD VERSION";
#endif
```

This completes your logical chain. If neither the *TRIALVERSION* nor *PROVERSION* constants are found, *STANDARD VERSION* will be displayed.

7   Remove the *PROVERSION* constant.

Remove the following code from the top of the page:

#define PROVERSION

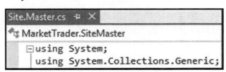

8   Test your code.

1.   Run the project in Debug mode.

This time neither the *TRIALVERSION* nor *PROVERSION* constants were found, so *STANDARD VERSION* is displayed as expected.

2.   Close your web browser.

Lesson 6-6: Use the #warning directive to show warnings when compiling

You used the *Output* window to view the messages that were generated by the compiler and debugger in: *Lesson 1-10: Understand the Output window.*

By using the *#warning* compiler directive, you can add your own warning messages that will appear in the *Output* window. This is of limited utility as most developers pay little attention to the *Output* window, but it could be useful if used in a very tightly controlled development environment.

1 Open *MarketTrader* from your sample files folder.

2 Open the code-behind file of *Site.Master*.

3 Add a *#warning* directive to display a warning if building in *Debug* mode.

    1. Remove the following code:

      LabelDebug.Text = "DEBUG MODE - NOT FOR RELEASE";

    2. Add the following code in its place:

      #warning COMPILING IN DEBUG MODE!

```
#if DEBUG
#warning COMPILING IN DEBUG MODE!
#endif
```

4 Test your new warning.

    1. Ensure that the *Debug* build profile is selected in the drop-down menu on the top toolbar.

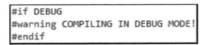

    2. Build your project.

      To do this, right-click *MarketTrader* in the *Solution Explorer* and click *Build* from the shortcut menu or click Build→ Build MarketTrader.

      The *Output* window appears, displaying the messages that were generated by the compiler.

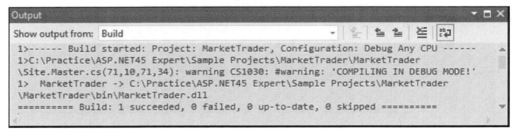

Notice that your warning is displayed in the *Output* window, indicating that you are building the project using the *Debug* profile.

Of course, this is only useful if the developer is paying close attention to the *Output* window.

5 Examine your warning in the *Error List* window.

Warnings also appear in the *Error List* window.

If the *Error List* window isn't available on your screen, you may need to click View→Error List to display it.

Warnings do not prevent your project from compiling. Their only purpose is to provide information.

6 Build the project using the *Release* profile.

1. Switch to the *Release* profile in the build profiles drop-down menu.

2. Build the project.

This time no warnings are displayed in the *Output* window.

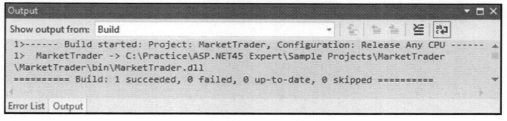

7 Examine the *Error List* window.

The warning has also disappeared from the *Error List* window, as your *#warning* directive will no longer be reached by the compiler.

Lesson 6-7: Use the #error directive to cause a compile error

The *#error* directive is similar to the *#warning* directive, but it will prevent the project from compiling rather than simply showing a warning message.

#error directives should be used to prevent a project from being compiled incorrectly.

1   Open *MarketTrader* from your sample files folder.

2   Open the code-behind file of *Site.Master*.

At the moment this code will display a warning message if it is compiled using the *Debug* profile, but it will not prevent the project from being built.

```
#if DEBUG
#warning COMPILING IN DEBUG MODE!
#endif
```

If this were the absolute final version of this application, you might want to prevent it from ever being built with the *Debug* profile. You can do this with the *#error* directive.

3   Replace the *#warning* directive with an *#error* directive.

Replace:

#warning COMPILING IN DEBUG MODE!

…with:

#error CANNOT COMPILE IN DEBUG MODE!

```
#if DEBUG
#error CANNOT COMPILE IN DEBUG MODE!
#endif
```

4   Test your new *#error* directive.

1.   Select the *Debug* profile from the build profiles drop-down menu on the top toolbar.

2.   Attempt to build your project.

The *Error List* window appears (if it wasn't visible already), showing your error message.

As long as your *#error* directive is present, the project will never allow you to build it with a profile that has the DEBUG constant.

5 Examine the code in the *Site.Master.cs* file.

You'll notice that your *#error* directive line is underlined in red, indicating an error.

```
#if DEBUG
#error CANNOT COMPILE IN DEBUG MODE!
#endif
```

This doesn't mean that you've made a mistake in the directive. The *#error* directive is supposed to cause an error.

6 Switch to the *Release* profile and test your code.

1. Select the *Release* build profile from the build profiles drop-down menu on the top toolbar.

2. Examine the code in *Site.Master.cs*.

The red underline has disappeared. The DEBUG constant is no longer enabled, so the *#error* directive does not cause an error.

```
#if DEBUG
#error CANNOT COMPILE IN DEBUG MODE!
#endif
```

3. Build your project.

The *#error* directive isn't reached by the compiler, so this time the project builds without any problems.

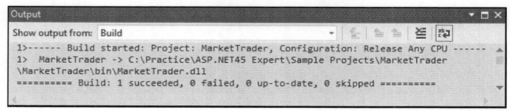

Lesson 6-8: Use System.Diagnostics to write Debug messages

The DEBUG and TRACE constants have another use besides conditionally compiling code. The *System.Diagnostics.Debug* and *System.Diagnostics.Trace* classes are enabled and disabled by the DEBUG and TRACE constants.

In this lesson, you'll use the *System.Diagnostics.Debug* class to display useful information to the developer. See sidebar for more on the *System.Diagnostics.Trace* class.

note

System.Diagnostics. Trace

The *Trace* class is identical to the *Debug* class, but it looks for the TRACE constant instead of the DEBUG constant.

The two classes exist because the DEBUG constant is only expected to be present when the project is built using the *Debug* build profile (see: *Lesson 1-3: Use the Debug and Release profiles*).

The *Debug* class should be used for debugging while the site is in development, and the *Trace* class should be used for logging diagnostic information once the site is live.

note

Storing diagnostic messages in a log file

By adding a *listener*, you can save your *Debug* and *Trace* messages to a file on the web server.

You'll learn how to do this in: *Lesson 6-9: Use a listener to save diagnostic information to a file.*

1 Open *MarketTrader* from your sample files folder.

2 Open the code-behind file of *Site.Master*.

3 Add a *using* line for the *System.Diagnostics* namespace.

Add the following code to the *using* lines at the top of the page:

using System.Diagnostics;

```
using System.Web.UI.WebControls;
using System.Diagnostics;
```

This will make it easier to access the *System.Diagnostics.Debug* class.

4 Remove all code from the *Page_Load* event handler.

5 Add code to inform the developer when a page is loaded.

Add the following code to the *Page_Load* event handler:

Debug.WriteLine("Loaded page: " + Request.Url);

```
protected void Page_Load(object sender, EventArgs e)
{
    Debug.WriteLine("Loaded page: " + Request.Url);
}
```

Because this code is in the master page, it will run whenever any page is loaded.

When this code runs, it will display the URL that was requested by the user in the *Output* window.

Because you are using the *Debug* class, this will only happen if the DEBUG constant is enabled.

6 Test your new code.

1. Ensure that the *Debug* build profile is selected from the build profiles drop-down menu on the top toolbar.

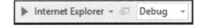

2. Click Debug→Start Debugging.

3. Return to Visual Studio without closing your web browser.

4. Examine the *Output* window.

Near the bottom of the *Output* window, you can see your debug message (you may need to use the *Output* window's scrollbar to see the message).

5. Return to your web browser without stopping debugging.

6. Click the *Data* button on the page's navigation bar.

7. Return to Visual Studio without closing your web browser and examine the *Output* window again.

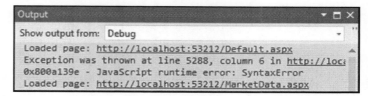

As expected, another line has appeared, showing that *MarketData.aspx* was loaded.

Again, you may need to scroll through the messages in the *Output* window in order to find this message.

8. Close your web browser and return to Visual Studio.

7   Test your code in the Release profile.

1. Select the *Release* build profile from the build profiles drop-down menu on the top toolbar.

2. Click Debug→Start Debugging.

3. Return to Visual Studio without closing your web browser and examine the *Output* window.

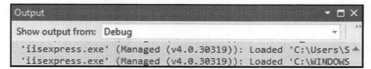

This time there are no custom messages. The *Debug* class only works if the DEBUG constant is present.

Debug messages can be very useful when you want to monitor the status of your application without using breakpoints and watches.

Lesson 6-9: Use a listener to save diagnostic information to a file

It's sometimes useful to be able to save diagnostic information to a file. You can do this using a *listener*.

1 Open *MarketTrader* from your sample files folder.

2 Open *Web.config*.

3 Add a <system.diagnostics> tag.

Add the following tag inside the *<configuration>* tag, just after the *</configSections>* tag:

<system.diagnostics>
</system.diagnostics>

```
</configSections>
<system.diagnostics>

</system.diagnostics>
```

4 Add a <trace> tag inside the <system.diagnostics> tag.

Add the following tag inside the *<system.diagnostics>* tag:

<trace autoflush="true">
</trace>

```
<system.diagnostics>
  <trace autoflush="true">

  </trace>
</system.diagnostics>
```

The *autoflush* property must be set to *true* in order for diagnostic messages to be automatically written to the log file.

5 Add a <listeners> tag inside the <trace> tag.

Add the following tag inside the *<trace>* tag:

<listeners>
</listeners>

```
<system.diagnostics>
  <trace autoflush="true">
    <listeners>

    </listeners>
  </trace>
</system.diagnostics>
```

6 Add a *TextWriterTraceListener* inside the <listeners> tag.

Add the following tag inside the *<listeners>* tag:

<add name="MarketTraderLog"
type="System.Diagnostics.TextWriterTraceListener, System,
Version=2.0.3600.0, Culture=neutral,
PublicKeyToken=b77a5c561934e089" initializeData=
"C:\Practice\ASP.NET45 Expert\MarketTrader.log" />

```
<listeners>
 <add name="MarketTraderLog"
      type="System.Diagnostics.TextWriterTraceListener,
      System, Version=2.0.3600.0, Culture=neutral,
      PublicKeyToken=b77a5c561934e089"
      initializeData="C:\Practice\ASP.NET45 Expert\MarketTrader.log" />
</listeners>
```

This (incredibly long-winded) tag adds a listener that will save any information that is written using the *System.Diagnostics.Debug* or *System.Diagnostics.Trace* classes into a log file in your sample files folder.

You learned about the *Debug* and *Trace* classes in: *Lesson 6-8: Use System.Diagnostics to write Debug messages.*

7 Test the diagnostic logging.

1. Ensure that the *Debug* build profile is selected from the build profiles drop-down menu on the top toolbar.

The *System.Diagnostics.Debug* class only works when the DEBUG constant is present, so you will need to use the *Debug* profile for any messages to be generated.

2. Run the project in Debug mode.

3. Click the *Charts* button on the navigation bar.

4. Close your web browser.

5. Using Windows Explorer, navigate to:
C:\Practice\ASP.NET45 Expert

A new file named *MarketTrader.log* has appeared.

This file contains the messages that were logged by your *TextWriterTraceListener*.

6. Open *MarketTrader.log*.

The file contains messages indicating that the *default.aspx* and *MarketCharts.aspx* pages were loaded.

You added the code that created these messages in: *Lesson 6-8: Use System.Diagnostics to write Debug messages.*

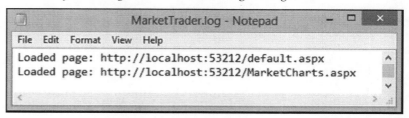

Lesson 6-10: Enable tracing

When *tracing* is enabled, your application will automatically gather information about every request that it receives.

This information can be extremely useful when analyzing your application's performance or trying to determine the source of an error.

1   Open *MathLand* from your sample files folder.

2   Enable tracing on the *Primes.aspx* page.

1.   Open *Primes.aspx* in Design view.

2.   Click the drop-down menu in the *Properties* window and select *Document*.

3.   Set the *Trace* property to: **true**

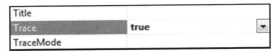

Tracing is now enabled on this page.

You'll also notice the *TraceMode* property. See sidebar for more on this.

3   View the new tracing information.

1.   View *Primes.aspx* in your web browser.

A huge amount of information is displayed at the bottom of the page.

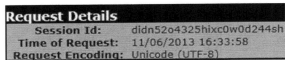

This information includes everything from the information that the user sent to the server to the amount of time it took for each method to execute.

2.   Close your web browser and return to Visual Studio.

4   Enable tracing for the entire application.

1.   Open *Web.config*.

2.   Add the following code inside the *<system.web>* tag:

<trace enabled="true" pageOutput="true" localOnly="true" requestLimit="10" />

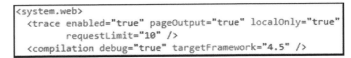

```
<system.web>
  <trace enabled="true" pageOutput="true" localOnly="true"
      requestLimit="10" />
  <compilation debug="true" targetFramework="4.5" />
```

This tag enables tracing for your entire application.

The *pageOutput* property allows the tracing information to appear on the pages, as you saw in the previous step.

note

The TRACE constant

You learned about the TRACE constant in: *Lesson 6-3: Use the #if directive with the TRACE constant.*

The TRACE constant is completely unrelated to the tracing features that you use in this lesson.

The tracing features will work regardless of whether the TRACE constant is present or not.

note

Saving tracing information to a file

If you set the *writeToDiagnosticsTrace* property to *true* when adding the *trace* tag to your *Web.config* file, all tracing information will be automatically sent to the *System.Diagnostics.Trace* class.

You learned about the *Trace* class in: *Lesson 6-8: Use System.Diagnostics to write Debug messages.*

You can then add a *listener* to save the information to a file.

You learned about listeners in: *Lesson 6-9: Use a listener to save diagnostic information to a file.*

Setting *localOnly* to *true* means that tracing will only be visible to users who are using the application from the web server itself. It won't be visible to users on the internet.

Finally, the *requestLimit* property limits the number of requests that are stored in the trace log. In this case, only the last 10 requests will be logged.

5 View tracing information using the Trace Viewer.

1. View *Default.aspx* in your web browser.

   Tracing information appears at the bottom of the screen and will now appear on every page in the application.

   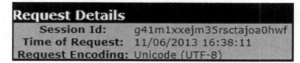

   While this is useful, it only displays information about your own requests, and only the request you made for this page.

   It would be more useful if you could see every request that has been logged. You can do this with the *Trace Viewer*.

2. Using your web browser's address bar, navigate to *Trace.axd* in the root of your application.

   The Trace Viewer tool appears. *Trace.axd* is only available if tracing is enabled.

   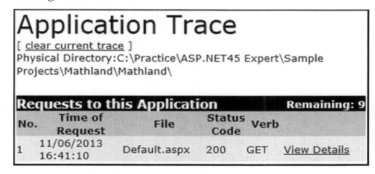

   The Trace Viewer shows you the request that your web browser sent for the *Default.aspx* page.

   You might expect that the browser would send more requests in order to retrieve CSS and JavaScript files, but Internet Explorer keeps a "cached" copy of these files after receiving them for the first time, meaning that they do not need to be requested again. It's possible that you will see requests for these files if you are not working through this course sequentially.

   You can view the full details of each request in the Trace Viewer by clicking the *View Details* links.

Session 6: Exercise

1   Open *Exercise6* from your sample files folder.

2   Open the code-behind file of *Site.Master*.

3   Add an *#if* directive to the *Page_Load* event handler to display *DEBUG* in the *LabelCompileType* control if the DEBUG constant is found.

4   Add an *#elif* directive to display *FINAL VERSION* in the *LabelCompileType* control if a constant named FINALVERSION is found.

5   Add an *#else* directive to display *STANDARD* in the *LabelCompileType* control if neither DEBUG nor FINALVERSION constants are found.

6   Use the *#define* directive to define the *FINALVERSION* constant on this page.

7   Open the code-behind file of *RandomColors.aspx*.

8   Use the *#region* directive to enclose the *Page_Load* method in a region named: **Event Handlers**

9   Use the *#region* directive to enclose the *ColorTable* and *GetRandomColor* methods in a region named: **Random Color Generator**

10   Add a *using* line for: **System.Diagnostics**

11   Add code to the end of the *GetRandomColor* method to output the *ColorCode* variable using the *Debug.WriteLine* method.

12   Open *RandomColors.aspx* in Design view and enable tracing.

13   Open *Web.config* and add a *TextWriterTraceListener* to log debug information to: **C:\Practice\ASP.NET45 Expert\Exercise6.log**

If you need help slide the page to the left

Session 6: Exercise Answers

These are the four questions that students find the most difficult to answer:

Q 11	Q 8	Q 6	Q 3

Add the following line of code on the line after *string ColorCode...*: **Debug.WriteLine(ColorCode);** This was covered in: *Lesson 6-8: Use System.Diagnostics to write Debug messages.*	Enclose the *Page_Load* event handler in the tags: **#region Event Handlers** ...and: **#endregion**
	 ```#region Event Handlers```
	```protected void Page_Load(object```
	```{```
	```}```
	```#endregion```
	 This was covered in: *Lesson 6-1: Create code regions with the #region directive.*
		Add the following code to the very top of the page, before the *using* lines: **#define FINALVERSION** This was covered in: *Lesson 6-4: Use the #define directive to create a new constant.*	Use the following code: **#if DEBUG** **LabelCompileType .Text = "DEBUG";** **#endif** This was covered in: *Lesson 6-2: Use the #if directive to selectively compile code.*

If you have difficulty with the other questions, here are the lessons that cover the relevant skills:

1   Refer to: Essential Skills Session 1.

2   Refer to: Essential Skills Session 1.

4   Refer to: Lesson 6-5: Use the #else and #elif directives.

5   Refer to: Lesson 6-5: Use the #else and #elif directives.

7   Refer to: Essential Skills Session 1.

9   Refer to: Lesson 6-1: Create code regions with the #region directive.

10   Refer to: Lesson 6-8: Use System.Diagnostics to write Debug messages.

12   Refer to: Lesson 6-10: Enable tracing.

13   Refer to: Lesson 6-9: Use a listener to save diagnostic information to a file.

Session Seven: Advanced ASP.NET controls

Inside every well-written large program is a well-written small program.

Charles Antony Richard Hoare, British computer scientist (born 1934)

The most basic ASP.NET controls were covered in the *Essential Skills* course, but ASP.NET also contains some more complex controls with advanced features.

Using appropriate controls can give your users a rich, intuitive and productive user interface to get the very most out of your applications. Charles Antony Richard Hoare would greatly approve of controls, as they are well-written pieces of code that can be used within larger projects.

In this session you'll learn how to use the more advanced ASP.NET controls, including the *Calendar*, *Chart* and *ListView* controls.

Session Objectives

By the end of this session you will be able to:

- Use the Panel and PlaceHolder controls
- Use the Calendar control
- Use the FileUpload control
- Create a Chart control
- Customize the Chart control
- Use the View and MultiView controls
- Understand primary and foreign keys
- Use the GridView TemplateField
- Use the GridView EditItemTemplate
- Create a ListView control
- Add editing features to a ListView control
- Add resources files to a project
- Use the Localize control
- Add a sitemap file to a project
- Use the SiteMapPath control
- Use the TreeView and SiteMapDataSource controls
- Use the Menu control

Lesson 7-1: Use the Panel and PlaceHolder controls

You've seen the *Panel* control before, although there hasn't been a lesson dedicated to it. *Panel* controls are perfect for splitting your page into areas that can be selectively shown and hidden using the *Visible* property.

The *PlaceHolder* control is much lesser-known, but very similar to the *Panel* control. *PlaceHolder* controls are used to reserve a space on the page where controls will be added using C# code.

In this lesson you'll use the *Panel* and *PlaceHolder* controls and see the difference between them.

1   Open *ForestWalks* from your sample files folder.

This is a relatively simple site that displays information and pictures about forest walks.

2   Open *DreamFalls.aspx* in Design view.

3   Add a *Panel* control to the page.

You'll find the *Panel* control in the *Standard* category of the *Toolbox*.

4   Set the *ID* property of the new control to: **PanelFirstImage**

5   Add a *PlaceHolder* control to the page.

You'll also find the *PlaceHolder* control in the *Standard* category.

6   Switch to *Source* view and ensure that the *PlaceHolder* control is not nested inside the *Panel* control.

The code should appear as below.

```
<asp:Content ID="Content2" ContentPlaceHolderID="MainContent" runat="server">
    <asp:Panel ID="PanelFirstImage" runat="server"></asp:Panel>
    <asp:PlaceHolder ID="PlaceHolder1" runat="server"></asp:PlaceHolder>
</asp:Content>
```

7   Switch back to *Design* view.

8   Set the *ID* property of the new *PlaceHolder* control to: **PlaceHolderSecondImage**

9   Open the code-behind file of *DreamFalls.aspx*.

10 Add code to the *Page_Load* event handler to create a new *Image* control.

Use the following code:

Image FirstImage = new Image();
FirstImage.ImageUrl = "~/Images/dreamfalls.jpg";

```
protected void Page_Load(object sender, EventArgs e)
{
    Image FirstImage = new Image();
    FirstImage.ImageUrl = "~/Images/dreamfalls.jpg";
}
```

Note that the *Image* class is the same as the *Image* control that is available from the *Toolbox*.

11 Add code to create a second new *Image* control.

> If you are not completing the course incrementally use the sample file: **Lesson 7-1** to begin this lesson.
>
> Sample files with the starting point for each lesson are also provided for all of the other lessons in this session.

Use the following code:

Image SecondImage = new Image();
SecondImage.ImageUrl = "~/Images/dreamfalls2.jpg";

```
Image FirstImage = new Image();
FirstImage.ImageUrl = "~/Images/dreamfalls.jpg";
Image SecondImage = new Image();
SecondImage.ImageUrl = "~/Images/dreamfalls2.jpg";
```

12 Add code to place the *FirstImage* control inside the *PanelFirstImage* control.

Use the following code:

PanelFirstImage.Controls.Add(FirstImage);

```
Image SecondImage = new Image();
SecondImage.ImageUrl = "~/Images/dreamfalls2.jpg";
PanelFirstImage.Controls.Add(FirstImage);
```

The *Controls* property allows you to easily add controls to a *Panel* control. You can also use the *Page.Controls* property to add controls directly to a page. (You did this in: *Lesson 5-3: Understand polymorphism*).

13 Add code to place the *SecondImage* control inside the *PlaceHolderSecondImage* control.

Use the following code:

PlaceHolderSecondImage.Controls.Add(SecondImage);

```
PanelFirstImage.Controls.Add(FirstImage);
PlaceHolderSecondImage.Controls.Add(SecondImage);
```

14 Test your code and see the difference between the *Panel* and *PlaceHolder* controls.

1. View *DreamFalls.aspx* in your web browser.

   The images appear on the page as expected.

2. View the page's HTML code.

   To do this in Internet Explorer, right-click the page and click *View Source* from the shortcut menu.

```
    <div id="MainContent_PanelFirstImage">
        <img src="Images/dreamfalls.jpg" />
</div>
    <img src="Images/dreamfalls2.jpg" />
```

As you can see, the only difference between the *Panel* and *PlaceHolder* controls is that the *Panel* control places its contents inside an HTML *<div>* tag.

Because the *Panel* control creates a *<div>* tag, it can offer many formatting options that are not available to the *PlaceHolder* control. The *PlaceHolder* control never adds any additional code to its contents.

Although the two controls are almost functionally identical, the *Panel* control is easier to work with in Design view so it's a better choice to separate your pages into sections (see sidebar).

The *PlaceHolder* control is a better choice when adding controls to the page using C# code, as you did in this lesson.

Lesson 7-2: Use the Calendar control

The *Calendar* control was covered briefly in Session 1 of the *Essential Skills* course, but the *Calendar* control has some more advanced features that you'll use in this lesson.

1   Open *MarketTrader* from your sample files folder.

2   Open *MarketDataByDate.aspx* in Design view.

This page will be used to display market quotes between two dates.

3   Add a *Calendar* control to the table cell beneath *Start Date*.

4   Set the *ID* property of the new *Calendar* control to: **CalendarStartDate**

5   Add another *Calendar* control in the table cell beneath *Finish Date*.

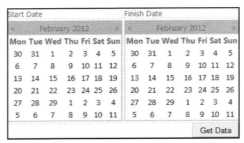

6   Set the *ID* property of the new *Calendar* control to: **CalendarFinishDate**

7   Open the code-behind file of *MarketDataByDate.aspx*.

8   Add code to the *ButtonGetData_Click* event handler to retrieve the data for the page.

Use the following code (see sidebar if an error occurs):

```
using (DataAccess Data = new DataAccess())
{
    GridViewData.DataSource = Data.GetMarketQuotesByDate(
    CalendarStartDate.SelectedDate,
    CalendarFinishDate.SelectedDate);
    GridViewData.DataBind();
}
```

```
protected void ButtonGetData_Click(object sender, EventArgs e)
{
    using (DataAccess Data = new DataAccess())
    {
        GridViewData.DataSource = Data.GetMarketQuotesByDate(
            CalendarStartDate.SelectedDate,
            CalendarFinishDate.SelectedDate);
        GridViewData.DataBind();
    }
}
```

The *SelectedDate* property contains the *Calendar* control's currently selected date.

note

Other useful properties of the Calendar control

The *SelectionMode* property of the *Calendar* control allows you to change the way that dates are selected.

In *Day* mode, the user can only select a single date, but *DayWeekMonth* mode makes selectors appear for weeks and months.

The *FirstDayOfWeek* property allows you to change which day the *Calendar* control uses as the first day of the week.

9 Add code to the *Page_Load* event handler to set the default dates of the *Calendar* controls.

Use the following code:

if (!Page.IsPostBack)
{
  CalendarStartDate.SelectedDate = new DateTime(2011, 12, 1);
  CalendarFinishDate.SelectedDate = new DateTime(2011, 12, 31);
}

```
protected void Page_Load(object sender, EventArgs e)
{
    if (!Page.IsPostBack)
    {
        CalendarStartDate.SelectedDate = new DateTime(2011, 12, 1);
        CalendarFinishDate.SelectedDate = new DateTime(2011, 12, 31);
    }
}
```

This code sets the *SelectedDate* properties of the *CalendarStartDate* and *CalendarFinishDate* controls to *01-Dec-2011* and *31-Dec-2011*.

Note that the *Page.IsPostBack* property is used to ensure that this code only runs once and does not overwrite any values selected by the user. This is needed because the *Calendar* control causes a post back whenever the user changes the date. (*PostBack* was covered in Session 3 of the *Essential Skills* course in this series).

10 Test your code.

1. View *MarketDataByDate.aspx* in your web browser.

2. Examine the *Calendar* controls.

    Although the *Page_Load* event handler set their *SelectedDate* properties to December 2011, the *Calendar* controls are still showing the current month.

    This is because you also need to set their *VisibleDate* properties.

3. Close your web browser and return to Visual Studio.

11 Add code to the *Page_Load* event handler to set the *VisibleDate* properties of the *Calendar* controls.

Add the following code inside the *if* statement:

CalendarStartDate.VisibleDate =
CalendarStartDate.SelectedDate;
CalendarFinishDate.VisibleDate =
CalendarFinishDate.SelectedDate;

```
if (!Page.IsPostBack)
{
    CalendarStartDate.SelectedDate = new DateTime(2011, 12, 1);
    CalendarFinishDate.SelectedDate = new DateTime(2011, 12, 31);
    CalendarStartDate.VisibleDate = CalendarStartDate.SelectedDate;
    CalendarFinishDate.VisibleDate = CalendarFinishDate.SelectedDate;
}
```

12 Test your code again.

This time the selected dates are displayed correctly.

Lesson 7-3: Use the FileUpload control

The *FileUpload* control is the only way for a user to transfer a file to a web application using an un-modified web browser. You've encountered the *FileUpload* control a few times previously, but you'll take a closer look at it in this lesson.

1 Open *TextLand* from your sample files folder.

2 Open *XML.aspx* in Design view.

In this lesson you'll add a *FileUpload* control to this page to enable the user to upload a file.

You'll use this page to read data from XML files in: *Lesson 10-10: Read data from an XML file.* This is the only reason that XML is mentioned in this lesson.

3 Add a *FileUpload* control to the page.

You'll find the *FileUpload* control in the *Standard* category of the *Toolbox*.

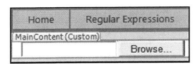

4 Set the *ID* property of the *FileUpload* control to: **FileUploadXML**

5 Add a *Button* control to the page, just after the *FileUpload* control.

While the *FileUpload* control allows the user to select a file to upload, it doesn't offer a way to send the file to the web server. You will need a *Button* control to submit the file.

When the *Button* control is clicked, the file that the user has selected will be sent to the web server as part of the user's *Request*.

6 Set the *ID* property of the *Button* control to: **ButtonUploadXML**

7 Set the *Text* property of the *Button* control to: **Upload XML**

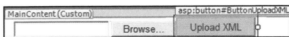

8 Add a *Click* event handler to the *ButtonUploadXML* control.

You can do this quickly by simply double-clicking the *Upload XML* button in Design view.

9 Add code to the *ButtonUploadXML_Click* event handler to check whether a file has been selected for upload.

1. Add the following code to the *ButtonUploadXML_Click* event handler:

```
if (FileUploadXML.HasFile)
{   }
```

```
protected void ButtonUploadXML_Click(object
{
    if (FileUploadXML.HasFile)
    {
    }
}
```

The *HasFile* property of the *FileUpload* control will be *true* if the user has selected a file to upload.

10   Add code to retrieve the uploaded file's binary data.

Add the following code inside the *if* statement:

byte[] FileBytes = FileUploadXML.FileBytes;

```
if (FileUploadXML.HasFile)
{
    byte[] FileBytes = FileUploadXML.FileBytes;
}
```

11   Add code to save the file onto the web server.

Add the following code on the next line:

string FileName = FileUploadXML.FileName;
string SavePath = Server.MapPath("~") + FileName;
System.IO.File.WriteAllBytes(SavePath, FileBytes);

```
if (FileUploadXML.HasFile)
{
    byte[] FileBytes = FileUploadXML.FileBytes;
    string FileName = FileUploadXML.FileName;
    string SavePath = Server.MapPath("~") + FileName;
    System.IO.File.WriteAllBytes(SavePath, FileBytes);
}
```

The *FileName* property of the *FileUpload* control contains the name of the uploaded file.

The *Server.MapPath* method converts a 'relative' path into a 'physical' path.

The tilde ~ indicates the root folder of your web application. The *Server.MapPath* method converts this to something like:
C:\Practice\ASP.NET45 Expert\Sample Projects\TextLand

12   Test your code.

1.   View *XML.aspx* in your web browser.

2.   Click *Browse* and navigate to your sample files folder.

3.   Select *MailModule.xml* and click *Open*.

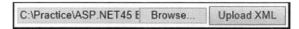

4.   Click *Upload XML*.

Nothing appears to happen, but the file was successfully uploaded and written to the *TextLand* folder.

5.   Close your web browser and, using Windows Explorer, navigate to the *TextLand* folder in your sample files folder.

6.   Open the *TextLand* subfolder.

MailModule.xml appears in this folder. Your code saved the file successfully.

Lesson 7-4: Create a Chart control

The *Chart* control was introduced in ASP.NET 4.0.

Before the *Chart* control, developers had to either pay for expensive third-party charting products or try to create their own charts using the classes in the *System.Drawing* namespace.

The *Chart* control makes it really easy to add charts to your pages.

1 Open *MarketTrader* from your sample files folder.

2 Open *MarketCharts.aspx* in Design view.

At the moment this page contains only a *SqlDataSource* control. See sidebar for an explanation of where the data comes from.

This control will provide the data for your *Chart* control.

3 Add a *Chart* control to the page.

You'll find this in the *Data* category of the *Toolbox*.

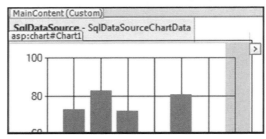

4 Set the *ID* property of your new chart to: **ChartQuotes**

5 Set the data source of the *ChartQuotes* control.

1. Select the control and open the *QuickTasks* menu for the control by clicking the arrow in the top-right corner.

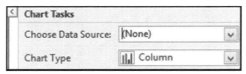

2. Select *SqlDataSourceChartData* from the *Choose Data Source* drop-down menu.

The *QuickTasks* menu changes, allowing you to select which data will be displayed on the chart.

3. Choose *QuoteDate* from the *X Value Member* drop-down menu.

If there are no entries in the menu, click *Refresh Schema* and the items will appear.

4. Choose *DowJonesValue* from the *Y Value Member* drop-down.

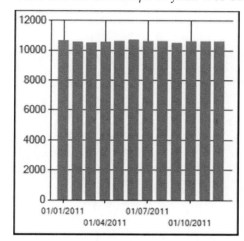

6   Test your new chart.

1.   View *MarketCharts.aspx* in your web browser.

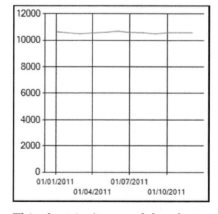

Your chart works, returning the Dow Jones figures from the database. You'll improve this chart in the coming lessons.

2.   Close your web browser and return to Visual Studio.

7   Change the chart type to *Line*.

This chart would look nicer as a line chart. It's very easy to change the chart type.

1.   Open the *QuickTasks* menu of the *Chart* control.

2.   Select *Line* from the *Chart Type* drop-down menu.

8   Test your chart again.

Once again, view *MarketCharts.aspx* in your web browser.

You now have a line chart.

This chart isn't as useful and attractive as it could be. In the next lesson you'll improve this chart by adjusting the scale and adding more data.

Lesson 7-5: Customize the Chart control

You created a *Chart* control and worked with its basic settings in the previous lesson: *Lesson 7-4: Create a Chart control*.

In this lesson you'll use some of the more advanced features of the *Chart* control to make your chart more useful and attractive.

1   Open *MarketTrader* from your sample files folder.

2   Open *MarketCharts.aspx* in Design view.

3   Fix the scale of the *ChartQuotes* control.

One of the major problems with the chart is that its Y axis starts at zero, making the differences in value hard to see.

1. Select the *Chart* control.

2. Find the *ChartAreas* property in the *Properties* window and click its browse icon.

The *ChartArea Collection Editor* dialog appears.

3. Find the *Axes* property in the right-hand pane of the dialog and click its browse icon.

The *Axis Collection Editor* dialog appears. This dialog contains the properties that control the formatting of your chart's axes.

4. Select *Y (Value) axis* in the left-hand pane.

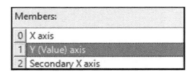

5. Find the *Scale* group in the right-hand pane of the dialog.

6. Set the *IsStartedFromZero* property to: **False**

7. Set the *Minimum* property to: **10400**

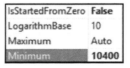

Your chart's Y axis will now start at 10,400 instead of starting at zero. This will make the chart much more readable.

8. Click *OK* twice to close both dialogs.

4 Test the page.

1. View the page in your web browser.

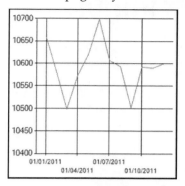

The chart is now much more informative.

2. Close your web browser and return to Visual Studio.

5 Add a second series to the chart to show the *NASDAQValue*.

1. Select the *Chart* control.

2. Find the *Series* property in the *Properties* window and click its browse button.

The *Series Collection Editor* dialog appears. This dialog allows you to customize the data series that are used by your chart.

3. Click the *Add* button to add a new series.

4. Set the *ChartType* property of the new series to: **Line**

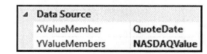

5. Find the *Data Source* category in the right-hand pane.

6. Set the *XValueMember* property to: **QuoteDate**

7. Set the *YValueMembers* property to: **NASDAQValue**

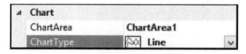

8. Click *OK*.

6 Test your chart.

View *MarketCharts.aspx* in your web browser.

Your chart now shows a comparison between the Dow Jones and NASDAQ, on a scale that is easier to read.

The *Chart* control has many more properties, allowing you to create almost any chart you can imagine. With the skills you've learned in this lesson you will be able to further explore the enormous number of features available in the *Chart* control.

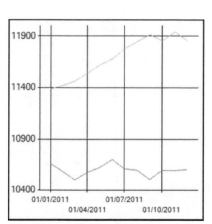

Lesson 7-6: Use the View and MultiView controls

The *View* and *MultiView* controls are always used together: they can't be used individually.

In this lesson you'll use the *View* and *MultiView* controls to display a series of images.

1   Open *ForestWalks* from your sample files folder.

2   Open *SunbeamHill.aspx* in *Design* view.

3   Add a *MultiView* control to the page just above the *LabelWalkInfo* control.

You'll find it in the *Standard* category of the *Toolbox*.

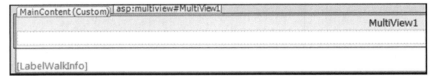

4   Set the *ID* property of your new *MultiView* control to: **MultiViewImages**

5   Add four *View* controls inside your *MultiView* control.

Click and drag four *View* controls into your *MultiView* control.

This can be difficult to do, as the *View* controls must not be placed inside one another. It is possible to place the controls correctly by dragging them to the far right side of the *MultiView*.

If you find it too difficult to drag and drop the controls, switch to Source view and add the controls there.

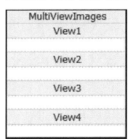

6   Add images to each of your *View* controls.

1.   Expand the *Images* folder in the *Solution Explorer*.

2.   Click and drag *sunbeamhill.jpg* from the *Images* folder into the box below the first *View* control.

A dialog appears, allowing you to provide additional image information.

3.   Click *OK*.

Your first *View* control is now ready. When it is active, it will display the *sunbeamhill.jpg* image.

4. In the same way, drag the *sunbeamhill2.jpg* image into the *View2* control.

5. Drag the *sunbeamhill3.jpg* image into the *View3* control.

6. Drag the *sunbeamhill4.jpg* image into the *View4* control.

Each of your *View* controls now contains a different image.

7   Set the *MultiView* control's default view.

Set the *ActiveViewIndex* property of the *MultiView* control to: **0**

An index number is assigned to each *View* control inside the *MultiView* control. The first view is *0*, the second *1*, the third *2* and so on.

Setting the *ActiveViewIndex* property to *0* displays the first *View* control inside the *MultiView* control.

8   Add a *LinkButton* control to move between images.

1. Add a *LinkButton* control to the page, just before the *LabelWalkInfo* Label control.

2. Set the *ID* property of the new control to: **LinkButtonNextImage**

3. Set the *Text* property of the new control to: **Next Image**

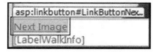

9   Add code to the new control to move between images.

1. Add a *Click* event handler to the *LinkButtonNextImage* control.

2. Add the following code to the new event handler:

if (MultiViewImages.ActiveViewIndex < 3)
MultiViewImages.ActiveViewIndex++;
else MultiViewImages.ActiveViewIndex = 0;

```
protected void LinkButtonNextImage_Click(object sender,
{
    if (MultiViewImages.ActiveViewIndex < 3)
        MultiViewImages.ActiveViewIndex++;
    else MultiViewImages.ActiveViewIndex = 0;
}
```

This code increases the *ActiveViewIndex* property when the user clicks the *LinkButton* control.

Changing the *ActiveViewIndex* property changes which *View* control is visible. When the *ActiveViewIndex* reaches 4 it is reset back to zero, allowing the images to rotate.

10   Test your code.

1. View *Sunbeamhill.aspx* in your web browser.

2. Click the *Next Image* button repeatedly.

Clicking the button allows you to cycle through the images.

---

note

MultiView and Panel

You could have done everything that you did in this lesson by using several *Panel* controls instead of the *MultiView* and *View* controls.

The advantage of the *MultiView* control is that its views are organized through the *ActiveViewIndex* property, making it easier to switch between them.

If you prefer to work with the *Panel* control you can completely ignore the *MultiView* control.

It's down to your own judgement to choose the best control for the situation.

Lesson 7-7: Understand primary and foreign keys

Up to now in the course you've used LINQ to access single tables in a database. In later lessons you'll work with data that is contained in more than one database table (relational data).

This book is not intended to teach the reader database design skills, but you'll need an insight into how databases work behind the scenes in order to understand the coming lessons. Specifically, you will need to understand how tables are related using *primary* and *foreign* key fields. By the end of this lesson you'll completely understand the concept of *primary* and *foreign* keys.

1   Open *MarketTrader* from your sample files folder.

2   Examine a primary key.

1.   Expand the *App_Data* folder in the *Solution Explorer*.

2.   Double-click *MarketTrader.mdf*.

After a short delay, the *MarketTrader* database is displayed in the *Database Explorer* window.

3.   Expand *Tables* in the *Database Explorer* window.

4.   Right-click the *Market* table and click *Show Table Data* from the shortcut menu.

The *Market* table's contents are displayed in the main Visual Studio pane.

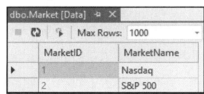

The *MarketID* field is this table's *primary key*. The primary key is used to uniquely identify each record.

Without this unique identifier it would be very hard to find a record again if its values changed. Primary keys never change, ensuring that the same record is always retrieved for each key.

The primary keys are sequential numbers in this example, but this isn't always the case as records may be deleted and re-sorted during the table's life. Primary keys also don't have to be numbers. You'll often see them as long strings of text known as GUIDs (globally unique identifiers).

The most important thing to remember about primary keys is that they are always unique for each record in a database table.

3   Examine a foreign key.

In this database, every *Market* can have many *Quotes*. For example, the *Nasdaq* market has many *Quote* records showing the value of the *Nasdaq* market on different dates.

To link the records in the *Market* table to the records in the *Quote* table, a *foreign key* is used.

1. Right-click the *Quote* table in the *Database Explorer* and click *Show Table Data* from the shortcut menu.

   The *Quote* table's contents are displayed in the main Visual Studio pane.

	QuoteID	MarketID	QuoteDate	QuoteValue
	1	1	01/01/2011 00:0...	11389.3700
	2	1	01/02/2011 00:0...	11423.4800

   Here you can see that the *Quote* table also has a primary key. The primary key of the *Quote* table is *QuoteID*.

   You can also see a *MarketID* field in the *Quote* table. This is the foreign key that links each record in the *Quote* table with a record in the *Market* table. It is called a foreign key because the key really belongs to a different table (in this case the *Market* table).

   The first record in the *Quote* table has a *MarketID* of *1*.

2. Return to the *Market* database table.

	MarketID	MarketName
▶	1	Nasdaq
	2	S&P 500

   Here you can see that *MarketID 1* corresponds with the *Nasdaq* market. This means that the first record in the *Quote* table belongs to the *Nasdaq* market.

4 **Examine a relationship.**

1. Return to the *Solution Explorer* window.

2. Open *MarketTrader.dbml*.

   This is a LINQ data class. Creating LINQ data classes is covered in Session 10 of the *Essential Skills* course in this series.

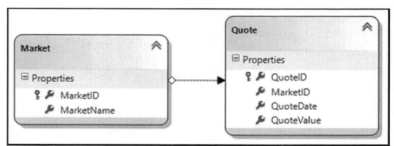

You can see an arrow between the *Market* and *Quote* tables. This indicates the presence of a *relationship*.

The relationship tells LINQ that the two tables are linked by the *MarketID* primary and foreign keys. This relationship allows LINQ to extract the *Market* record for every *Quote* and to extract all *Quote* records for every *Market*.

You'll see this behaviour in action in the coming lessons.

important

Limitations of the GridView control's editing features

GridView controls can automatically provide editing features when you provide them with data.

In this example, the *GridView* control is receiving records from a *LinqDataSource* control linked to the *Quote* database table. The *Quote* table contains details of quotes, but it doesn't contain details of markets. Market data is held in the *Market* table.

You could solve this by creating a stored procedure that returned data from both the *Quote* and *Market* database tables, but the *GridView* control would not be able to apply automatic editing features. The *GridView* control can only automatically edit data that originates from a single table.

The technique used in this lesson enables you to extract data from the *Quote* table and related data from the *Market* table without interfering with the *GridView* control's automatic editing features.

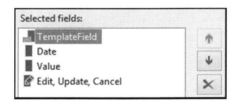

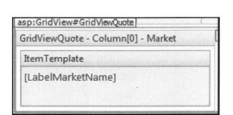

Lesson 7-8: Use the GridView TemplateField

The basics of the *GridView* control are covered in Session 11 of the *Essential Skills* course, but the basic features of the *GridView* control can be rather limiting. In this lesson you'll use *templates* to fully customize a *GridView* control.

1 Open *MarketTrader* from your sample files folder.

2 See the limitations of basic *GridView* controls.

1. View *QuoteAdmin.aspx* in your web browser.

    This is a simple admin page for the *Quote* database table.

    Notice that the *GridView* control displays the *MarketID* foreign key. It would be better if you could see the *MarketName* here.

    You could use a stored procedure to extract the *MarketName* field, but this would interfere with the *GridView* control's automatic features (see sidebar).

2. Close your web browser and return to Visual Studio.

3 Open *QuoteAdmin.aspx* in Design view.

4 Replace the *MarketID* field with a *TemplateField* called *Market*.

1. Open the *QuickTasks* menu of the *GridViewQuote* control and click *Edit Columns*.

2. Remove the *MarketID* field from the *Selected fields* list.

3. Add a new *TemplateField* from the *Available fields* list.

4. Use the arrow buttons to move the new *TemplateField* to the top of the list.

5. Set the *HeaderText* property of the *TemplateField* to: **Market**

6. Click *OK*.

    If you're having trouble with any of these steps, refer to Session 11 of the *Essential Skills* course.

5 Customize your new *TemplateField*.

1. Open the *QuickTasks* menu of the *GridViewQuote* control and click *Edit Templates*.

    The *GridView* control switches to template editing mode.

2. Add a *Label* control to the *ItemTemplate* by dragging and dropping it into the *ItemTemplate* box.

3. Set the *ID* property of the new *Label* control to: **LabelMarketName**

4. Open the *QuickTasks* menu for the new *Label* control and click *Edit DataBindings…*

A dialog appears, allowing you to select a data field to display in the control. You're going to use a *custom binding* to find the related record in the *Market* table and return its *MarketName* field.

5. Click the *Custom binding* radio button.

6. Type the following code into the *Code expression* box:

    Eval("Market.MarketName")

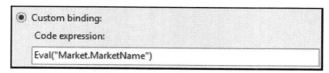

This code works because LINQ is aware of the relationship between the *Quote* table and the *Market* table. You can retrieve fields from any related database table in this way.

7. Click *OK*.

8. Switch to *Source* view and examine the code that has been generated.

    Notice the following code:

    Text='<%# Eval("Market.MarketName") %>'

    ```
    <asp:TemplateField HeaderText="Market">
        <ItemTemplate>
            <asp:Label ID="LabelMarket" runat="server"
            Text='<%# Eval("Market.MarketName") %>'>
            </asp:Label>
    ```

    % tags are used to insert C# code directly into the page's HTML code.

    The *Eval* method runs during the *RowDataBound* event of the *GridView* control. It is used to display values from the *GridView* control's data source.

    You could achieve the same result by adding C# code to the *RowDataBound* event handler of the *GridView* control, but the technique that you've used requires less code.

6   Test the page.

1. View *QuoteAdmin.aspx* in your web browser.

    The *MarketName* field is displayed as expected.

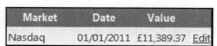

2. Click one of the *Edit* buttons next to a record.

Market	Date	Value
Nasdaq	01/01/2011 00:00:00	11389.3700

    The *Date* and *Value* fields are automatically made editable.

    The *Market* field is not editable as you have only added a control to the *ItemTemplate* of the *TemplateField*.

    To enable the user to edit the record you would need to add an editable control to the *EditItemTemplate* of the *TemplateField*. You'll do this in the next lesson: *Lesson 7-9: Use the GridView EditItemTemplate*.

Lesson 7-9: Use the GridView EditItemTemplate

note

GridView TemplateField templates

TemplateFields provide several different templates:

ItemTemplate
The standard template used for each row in the *GridView* control. If another template is missing, this one will be used instead.

AlternatingItemTemplate
A template to be used for every other row. This is often used to create a 'striped' effect by using a different background color.

EditItemTemplate
The template to be used when the row is being edited. This will typically contain editable controls such as the *TextBox* and *DropDownList* controls.

HeaderTemplate
The template for the heading of the column in the *GridView* control. If you leave this template blank, the *HeaderText* property will be used instead.

FooterTemplate
The template for the footer of the column in the *GridView* control.

Other GridView templates

As well as the *TemplateField* templates, you'll notice the *EmptyDataTemplate* and *PagerTemplate* options. These templates are always available, even without any *TemplateField* columns.

The *EmptyDataTemplate* is displayed if the *GridView* control has no data to display.

The *PagerTemplate* is used to switch between pages of data. You would use this if you wanted to implement your own custom paging system.

1   Open *MarketTrader* from your sample files folder.

2   Open *QuoteAdmin.aspx* in Design view.

3   Edit the *EditItemTemplate* for the *Market* field.

   1.   Open the *QuickTasks* menu for the *GridView* control.

     If you've just finished the previous lesson, the *QuickTasks* menu will already be in *Template Editing Mode*.

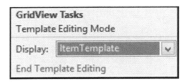

     If this isn't what you see, click *Edit Templates* from the *QuickTasks* menu that is displayed.

   2.   Click the *Display* drop-down menu.

     A list of templates is displayed.

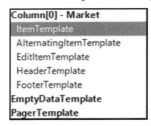

     Notice the text: *Column[0] – Market*.

     This is a reference to the *TemplateField* that you created in the previous lesson. If there was more than one *TemplateField* in this *GridView* control you would see *Column[1], Column[2],* etc.

   3.   Click the *EditItemTemplate* option.

     This template allows you to customize the editing controls that will appear when the user clicks one of the *GridView* control's *Edit* buttons.

     See sidebar for information about the other templates.

4   Add a *DropDownList* control to the *EditItemTemplate* and set its ID property to: **DropDownListMarket**

When the user clicks one of the *Edit* buttons next to a *Quote* record in the *GridView* control, this *DropDownList* control will appear in the *Market* column. You're going to configure this *DropDownList* control to allow the user to change which *Market* record is linked to each *Quote* record.

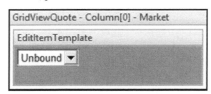

5   Add a *LinqDataSource* control to the *EditItemTemplate*.

The *DropDownList* control will use this data source to display a list of all markets from the *Market* table.

6   Set the *ID* property of the new *LinqDataSource* control to: **LinqDataSourceMarket**

7   Configure the new *LinqDataSource* control to retrieve records from the *Market* table, sorted by *MarketName*.

Configuring *LinqDataSource* controls is covered in Session 11 of the *Essential Skills* course.

8   Configure the *DropDownList* control to display the list of markets.

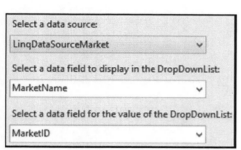

1. Click *Choose Data Source…* from the *QuickTasks* menu of the *DropDownList* control.

2. Select *LinqDataSourceMarket* from the first drop-down menu.

3. Select *MarketName* from the second drop-down menu.

4. Select *MarketID* from the third drop-down menu.

    The *MarketID* is the primary key of the *Market* table. You'll use this to connect (*bind*) the *DropDownList* control to the *Quote* record that is being edited in the *GridView* control.

5. Click *OK*.

Your *DropDownList* control is now configured to retrieve the list of markets, but in order to actually update records it will need to be connected (*bound*) to the *Quote* record that is being edited.

9   Bind the *DropDownList* control to the *MarketID* field of the *Quote* database table.

1. Click *Edit Databindings…* from the *QuickTasks* menu of the *DropDownList* control.

2. Select *MarketID* from the *Bound to* drop-down menu.

    If this option is not available, click *Refresh Schema*.

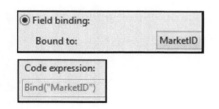

3. Examine the *Code expression* text box.

    The code in the box is very similar to the *Eval* expression that you used in: *Lesson 7-8: Use the GridView TemplateField*.

    The *Eval* expression simply extracts a value from the database, while the *Bind* expression also allows the value to be updated.

4. Click *OK*.

10   Test the page.

1. Click Debug→Start Debugging.

2. Click *Edit* next to a record.

    You can now edit the *Market* foreign key field using the *DropDownList* control. Because it was correctly *bound* to the *MarketID* field, it will display the current market of each record as well as allowing you to change it.

Lesson 7-10: Create a ListView control

The *ListView* control is very similar to the *GridView* control, but without most of the convenient automated *QuickTasks* features.

For simple tasks, the *GridView* control is easier to use as it automatically provides many of the features you need. However, the *ListView* control can be customized to a far greater extent, making it useful when user requirements demand more sophisticated customization.

<table>
<tr><td>

note

If Configure ListView isn't available

There is a bug in the *QuickTasks* menu of the *ListView* control that sometimes prevents the *Configure ListView* option from appearing.

If you experience this problem:

1. Click *Refresh Schema*.

2. Click *No* when prompted.

3. Select *(None)* from the *Choose Data Source* drop-down menu.

4. Re-select *LinqDataSourceQuote*.

The *Configure ListView* option should then appear.

If the option is still unavailable, close *QuoteAdmin.aspx* and reopen it.

</td></tr>
</table>

1   Open *MarketTrader* from your sample files folder.

2   Open *QuoteAdmin.aspx* in Design view.

You're going to try to duplicate the functionality of the *GridView* control on this page with a *ListView* control.

3   Add a *ListView* control to the page, above the existing *GridView* control.

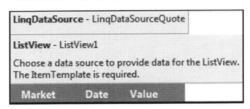

Don't delete the *GridView* control as it contains some useful code that you'll need later.

4   Configure the new *ListView* control.

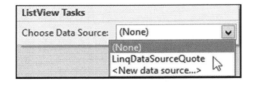

1.   Set the *ID* property of the new control to: **ListViewQuote**

2.   Open the *QuickTasks* menu of the *ListView* control and select *LinqDataSourceQuote* from the drop-down menu.

The *QuickTasks* menu changes, enabling more options.

3.   Click *Configure ListView…* (see sidebar if this isn't available)

Although the *ListView* control's layout is entirely controlled by templates, this dialog allows you to generate a basic set of templates to use as a starting point.

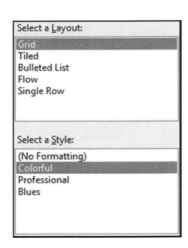

4.   Click the different options in the *Select a Layout* box to see a preview of each layout.

As you can see, the *ListView* control can provide much more flexible layouts than the *GridView* control.

5.   In the *Select a Layout* box, click: *Grid*

6.   In the *Select a Style* box, click: *Colorful*

7.   Click *OK*.

Automatically-generated templates are added to your *ListView* control. If you test this page, the records from the database will be displayed in your *ListView* control.

5   Examine the automatically-generated templates.

1. Switch to *Source* view.

   The *ListView* control has added a lot of code. Unlike the *GridView* control, the *ListView* control requires templates for everything that it will display.

2. Find the *<LayoutTemplate>* tag.

   You will find it about half-way down the page.

   The *LayoutTemplate* is the template for the *ListView* control's overall table structure. It contains the basic HTML *<table>* tag, and the headings of each column.

   The most important element here is the tag with the *ID*: *itemPlaceHolder*

   The *itemPlaceHolder* tag is automatically replaced with the contents of the *ItemTemplate, AlternatingItemTemplate, EditItemTemplate* or *InsertItemTemplate* as appropriate.

```
</ItemTemplate>
<LayoutTemplate>
    <table runat="server">
```

```
<tr runat="server" style="background-cold
    <th runat="server">
        QuoteID</th>
    <th runat="server">
        MarketID</th>
    <th runat="server">
        QuoteDate</th>
    <th runat="server">
        QuoteValue</th>
    <th runat="server">
        Market</th>
</tr>
<tr ID="itemPlaceholder" runat="server">
</tr>
```

```
</InsertItemTemplate>
<ItemTemplate>
```

3. Find the *<ItemTemplate>* tag.

   You'll find it just before the *<LayoutTemplate>* tag.

   As long as the user is not editing or inserting an item, this template will be displayed in the *itemPlaceHolder*.

   The *ItemTemplate* uses *Label* controls and the *Eval* method in the same way as you did in: *Lesson 7-8: Use the GridView TemplateField*.

6   Add code to format the *ListView* control's *QuoteDate* field.

   1. Find the *QuoteDateLabel* control within the *<ItemTemplate>* tag.

   2. Change its *Text* property to:

      <%# Eval("QuoteDate","{0:d}") %>

```
<asp:Label ID="QuoteDateLabel" runat="server"
Text='<%# Eval("QuoteDate","{0:d}") %>' />
```

   Because the *ListView* control doesn't have a convenient *Edit Fields* dialog, this is the only way to apply a format to its fields.

   Data format strings like this one are covered in Session 11 of the *Essential Skills* course in this series.

7   Test your code.

   View *QuoteAdmin.aspx* in your web browser.

QuoteID	MarketID	QuoteDate	QuoteValue	Market
1	1	01/01/2011	11389.3700	MarketTrader.Market
13	2	01/01/2011 00:00:00	11350.2700	MarketTrader.Market

Although every alternating row is now formatted correctly, the other rows aren't. This is because you didn't apply the format to the *AlternatingItemTemplate*.

You'd need to do a lot more work to make this *ListView* control look as presentable as your *GridView* control, but you'd be able to do so with the skills that you've learned in this lesson.

In the next lesson you'll add the same editing features to this *ListView* control that are available in the *GridView* control.

Lesson 7-11: Add editing features to a ListView control

Adding editing features to a *GridView* control is a simple matter of adding a field.

Adding editing features to a *ListView* control requires a lot more work, as you'll see in this lesson.

1 Open *MarketTrader* from your sample files folder.

2 Open *QuoteAdmin.aspx* in Source view.

3 Remove the *AlternatingItemTemplate* from your *ListView* control.

Delete everything from *<AlternatingItemTemplate>* to *</AlternatingItemTemplate>*, including the tags themselves.

This control doesn't need an alternating item template.

4 Add an editing button.

1. Find the *<ItemTemplate>* tag.

2. Add the following code after the last *</td>* tag inside the *<ItemTemplate>* tags:

```
<td>
   <asp:Button ID="EditButton" runat="server"
   CommandName="Edit" Text="Edit" />
</td>
```

```
            <td>
                <asp:Button ID="EditButton" runat="server"
                CommandName="Edit" Text="Edit" />
            </td>
        </tr>
</ItemTemplate>
```

This code adds a new column to the *ItemTemplate* containing a *Button* control.

Notice the *CommandName* property. You may remember using this property in the *RowCommand* event of the *GridView* control.

The *ListView* control has an *ItemCommand* event which works in the same way as the *RowCommand* event of the *GridView* control. However, the *Edit* command is a special command that will be automatically recognized without needing to add any code.

5 Test your code.

1. View *QuoteAdmin.aspx* in your web browser.

QuoteID	MarketID	QuoteDate	QuoteValue	Market	
1	1	01/01/2011	11389.3700	MarketTrader.Market	Edit

2. Click one of the *Edit* buttons.

The *ListView* control switches to edit mode and the *EditItemTemplate* is displayed.

Update	Cancel	1	1	01/01/2011 00:00:00	11389.3700

3. Close your web browser and return to Visual Studio.

6 Add a drop-down menu to the *ListView* control's *EditItemTemplate*.

In *Lesson 7-9: Use the GridView EditItemTemplate,* you added a *DropDownList* control to a *GridView* control's *EditItemTemplate*.

Your *ListView* control can do the same thing using exactly the same code.

1. Scroll down to your *GridView* control's code.

2. Copy all of the code <u>between</u> the *GridView* control's *<EditItemTemplate>* tags, <u>not</u> including the tags themselves.

```
<EditItemTemplate>
    <asp:LinqDataSource ID="LinqDataSourceMarket"
    </asp:LinqDataSource>
    <asp:DropDownList ID="DropDownListMarket" run
    </asp:DropDownList>
</EditItemTemplate>
```

3. Scroll up to the *ListView* control's *<EditItemTemplate>* tags.

4. Select the code for the *MarketTextBox* control.

```
<td>
    <asp:TextBox ID="MarketTextBox" runat="server" Text='<%# Bind("Market") %>' />
</td>
```

5. Paste the copied code so that it replaces the selected code.

```
<td>
    <asp:LinqDataSource ID="LinqDataSourceMarket" runat="server"
    </asp:LinqDataSource>
    <asp:DropDownList ID="DropDownListMarket" runat="server" Dat
    </asp:DropDownList>
</td>
```

7 Test your code.

1. View *QuoteAdmin.aspx* in your web browser.

2. Click one of the *Edit* buttons.

Your modified *EditItemTemplate* is displayed.

QuoteValue	Market	
01/01/2011 00:00:00	11389.3700	Nasdaq ⌄

The *DropDownList* control list appears on the right-hand side, allowing you to change this record's market.

This *ListView* control is still nowhere near as presentable as the *GridView* control you worked with in: *Lesson 7-9: Use the GridView EditItemTemplate.*

It would take a lot of effort to reformat this *ListView* control to look exactly the same as the *GridView* control, but it is certainly possible using the skills you've learned in the last two lessons.

Lesson 7-12: Add resources files to a project

Resources files offer a very simple way to store information without a database.

As well as general information storage, resources files can be used to automatically 'localize' a page by providing text in different languages.

In this lesson you'll create resources files to store text in English and French.

1   Open *ForestWalks* from your sample files folder.

2   Add an *App_GlobalResources* folder to the project.

Right-click *ForestWalks* in the *Solution Explorer* and click Add→Add ASP.NET Folder→App_GlobalResources from the shortcut menu.

The *App_GlobalResources* folder is a special folder that is used to store resources files.

You might also have noticed the option for *App_LocalResources*. See sidebar for more on this.

3   Add a new resources file named: **WebResources.resx**

1.   Right-click *App_GlobalResources* in the *Solution Explorer* and click Add→New Item… from the shortcut menu.

2.   Click *General* in the left-hand pane.

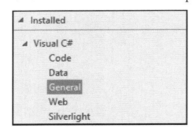

3.   Click *Resources File* in the central pane.

4.   In the *Name* box, type: **WebResources.resx**

5.   Click *Add*.

Your new resources file is created and opened, ready for you to add information to it.

WebResources.resx is automatically recognized by ASP.NET as the default resources file.

4   Set the *Name* of your first record to: **DreamFalls**

Simply enter **DreamFalls** under *Name*.

note

App_GlobalResources and App_LocalResources

Resources files stored in the *App_GlobalResources* folder are available to every page in your web application.

Resources files stored in the *App_LocalResources* folder are only available to pages that are in the same folder as the *App_LocalResources* folder. You would need to create a separate *App_LocalResources* folder for each subfolder of your web application that required resources files.

Placing resources files in these special folders allows the contents to be easily accessed.

You don't have to keep your resources files in either of these special folders, but if you don't you will have to use the *System.Resources* class to retrieve any information from them. I can't think of any real-world scenario where you'd actually want to do this.

This value works as a key that you will use to retrieve the *Value* later.

5 Set the *Value* of your first record to: **The most beautiful waterfalls**

This is the actual value of your resource. You'll use this text for the English version of *DreamFalls.aspx*.

6 Set the *Comment* of the record to: **Dream falls description**

Name	▲ Value	Comment
DreamFalls	The most beautiful waterfalls	Dream falls description

The *Comment* field is used to explain the purpose of each record in your resources file. Comments aren't required, but they can be useful if a record's purpose isn't obvious.

7 Add a resources file for the French language, named: **WebResources.fr.resx**

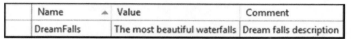

Because you added *.fr* to the name, ASP.NET will automatically use this resource file for the French language.

8 Add a record to the new file for the French language.

1. On the first line, set the *Name* field to: **DreamFalls**

2. Set the *Value* field to: **Les plus belles cascades**

3. Set the *Comment* field to: **Dream falls description**

Name	▲ Value	Comment
DreamFalls	Les plus belles cascades	Dream falls description

Using these resources files, you can automatically populate a web page with the correct language. You'll do this in the next lesson: *Lesson 7-13: Use the Localize control*.

Resources files are also useful for storing other information if your needs are very basic. However, a database is a better choice for anything but the most basic purposes.

Resources files are not the best option for storing settings for your application. You'll discover a better solution for storing settings in: *Lesson 8-1: Work with application settings*.

Lesson 7-13: Use the Localize control

The *Localize* control is only ever used to localize your pages. That is, to automatically populate them with text for different languages.

The *Localize* control is functionally identical to the *Literal* control. The only reason that a separate control exists is to emphasize that it is being used to localize the page.

1 Open *ForestWalks* from your sample files folder.

2 Open *DreamFalls.aspx* in Source view.

3 Add a *Localize* control to the page, just before the *</asp:Content>* tag.

```
<asp:PlaceHolder ID="PlaceHolderSecondImage" runat="server">
    <asp:Localize ID="Localize1" runat="server"></asp:Localize>
</asp:Content>
```

Do this by simply dragging the *Localize* control from the *Standard* category of the *Toolbox* onto the code.

4 Set the *ID* property of the new control to: **LocalizeDescription**

```
<asp:PlaceHolder ID="PlaceHolderSecondImage" runat="server">
    <asp:Localize ID="LocalizeDescription" runat="server"></asp:
</asp:Content>
```

5 Set the *Text* property of the control to retrieve the *DreamFalls* resource from the resources files.

Set the *Text* property with the following code:

Text="<%$ Resources:WebResources, DreamFalls %>"

```
<asp:Localize ID="LocalizeDescription"
Text="<%$ Resources:WebResources, DreamFalls %>"
runat="server"></asp:Localize>
```

This code tells the *Localize* control to retrieve the *DreamFalls* resource from the *WebResources* resources file.

Note that this will recognize both the *WebResources.resx* file and the *WebResources.fr.resx* file that you created in: *Lesson 7-12: Add resources files to a project*. ASP.NET will automatically select the correct file for the page's language.

6 Test your code.

View *DreamFalls.aspx* in your web browser.

The value from *WebResources.resx* is displayed, as the page is not using the French language.

The most beautiful waterfalls

Note that if your computer is set to use the French language you may see the French text immediately, as it will be your computer's default language.

Notice the flags in the top-right corner.

When they are clicked, these buttons set a value in *Session[Language]*. You'll use this value to set the language when the page loads.

7 Close your web browser and return to Visual Studio.

8 Open the code-behind file of *DreamFalls.aspx*.

9 Add code to set the language of the page.

Add the following new event handler:

protected override void InitializeCulture()
{
**   if (Session["Language"] == null) Page.UICulture = "en-US";**
**   else if (Session["Language"].ToString() == "FR")**
**   Page.UICulture = "FR-fr";**
**   else Page.UICulture = "en-US";**
**   base.InitializeCulture();**
}

```
protected override void InitializeCulture()
{
    if (Session["Language"] == null) Page.UICulture = "en-US";
    else if (Session["Language"].ToString() == "FR")
        Page.UICulture = "FR-fr";
    else Page.UICulture = "en-US";
    base.InitializeCulture();
}
```

This code uses the *override* keyword to replace the *System.Web.UI.Page* class's default *InitializeCulture* event handler with your own code. You learned about the *override* keyword in: *Lesson 5-4: Understand the virtual and override keywords*.

The *InitializeCulture* event is used to set the page's culture (language). It occurs before the *Page_Load* event, so setting the culture in the *Page_Load* event handler would be too late for it to affect the page.

For this code to work correctly, you must also call *base.InitializeCulture* to run the original *InitializeCulture* method after the *Page.UICulture* property has been set (see sidebar).

10 Test your code.

1. View *DreamFalls.aspx* in your web browser.

2. Click the French flag in the top-right corner.

    The French text is displayed on the page.

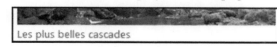

Les plus belles cascades

3. Click the American flag in the top-right corner.

    The English text is displayed again.

The most beautiful waterfalls

note

How the InitializeCulture method works

The *InitializeCulture* method reads the *Page.UICulture* property and applies the correct language to a page.

In this lesson you override the *InitializeCulture* method, replacing the original *InitializeCulture* method with a method that changes the *Page.UICulture* property.

If this was all you did, your language settings would not be applied to the page. In order to apply the correct language to the page, the original unaltered *InitializeCulture* method must run after your overridden version of the *InitializeCulture* method.

To call the original method, you call the *base.InitializeCulture()* method at the end of your overridden method. This allows both methods to run sequentially.

Lesson 7-14: Add a sitemap file to a project

note

Search engine sitemaps

Some search engines are able to read an XML file to determine a site's structure, but these XML files are not the same as the *Web.sitemap* file created in this lesson.

The *Web.sitemap* file is only used as a data source for ASP.NET's navigation controls.

If you want a search engine sitemap you will have to create separate XML files for each search engine that you need to support (the different search engines haven't yet agreed upon a universal sitemap specification).

The *sitemap* file is an XML file that ASP.NET navigation controls can use to automatically generate a navigation structure. You learned about XML files in Session 3 of the *Essential Skills* course in this series.

In this lesson you'll create a *sitemap* file for the *ForestWalks* project.

1 Open *ForestWalks* from your sample files folder.

2 Add a sitemap file to the project.

1. Right-click *ForestWalks* in the *Solution Explorer* and click Add→New Item… from the shortcut menu.

2. Click *Web* in the left-hand pane.

3. Scroll down and click *Site Map* in the central pane.

4. Click *Add*.

The new *Web.sitemap* file is created and opened.

```
Web.sitemap  ⊡ ✕
        <?xml version="1.0" encoding="utf-8" ?>
    <siteMap xmlns="http://schemas.microsoft.com/AspNet/Site
        <siteMapNode url="" title=""  description="">
            <siteMapNode url="" title=""  description="" />
            <siteMapNode url="" title=""  description="" />
        </siteMapNode>
    </siteMap>
```

A *sitemap* file consists of a series of *siteMapNode* tags that define the navigation structure of your website.

3 Remove the existing *SiteMapNode* tags.

You want to start with an empty *sitemap* file, so delete all of the *SiteMapNode* tags.

```
<?xml version="1.0" encoding="utf-8" ?>
<siteMap xmlns="http://schemas.microsoft.com/AspNet/SiteMap-File-1.0" >

</siteMap>
```

4 Add a *SiteMapNode* tag for the root of the site.

Add the following code between the *<sitemap>* and *</sitemap>* tags:

**\<siteMapNode url="~" title="Root">
\</siteMapNode>**

```
<?xml version="1.0" encoding="utf-8" ?>
<siteMap xmlns="http://schemas.microsoft.com/AspNet/SiteMap-File-1.0" >
  <siteMapNode url="~" title="Root">
  </siteMapNode>
</siteMap>
```

Every *sitemap* file must have a root tag (or 'node') that contains every other tag. The tilde (~) indicates the site's root folder.

5 Add a *SiteMapNode* tag for the site's homepage.

Add the following code between the *<siteMapNode>* and *</siteMapNode>* tags you added in the previous step.

<siteMapNode url="Default.aspx" title="Home" />

```xml
<?xml version="1.0" encoding="utf-8" ?>
<siteMap xmlns="http://schemas.microsoft.com/AspNet/SiteMap-File-1.0" >
  <siteMapNode url="~" title="Root">
    <siteMapNode url="Default.aspx" title="Home" />
  </siteMapNode>
</siteMap>
```

This is a self-closing tag, as it doesn't contain any other tags.

6   Add a *SiteMapNode* tag to act as a container for the other pages.

Add the following code on the next line:

<siteMapNode title="Walks">
</siteMapNode>

```xml
<?xml version="1.0" encoding="utf-8" ?>
<siteMap xmlns="http://schemas.microsoft.com/AspNet/SiteMap-File-1.0" >
  <siteMapNode url="~" title="Root">
    <siteMapNode url="Default.aspx" title="Home" />
    <siteMapNode title="Walks">
    </siteMapNode>
  </siteMapNode>
</siteMap>
```

This node doesn't have a *url* property as its only purpose is to act as a container.

7   Add *SiteMapNode* tags for the other pages in the site.

Add the following tags nested inside the *Walks* tag that you just added:

<siteMapNode url="DreamFalls.aspx"
title="Dream Falls" />
<siteMapNode url="SunbeamHill.aspx"
title="Sunbeam Hill" />
<siteMapNode url="WinterMountain.aspx"
title="Winter Mountain" />

```xml
<?xml version="1.0" encoding="utf-8" ?>
<siteMap xmlns="http://schemas.microsoft.com/AspNet/SiteMap-File-1.0" >
  <siteMapNode url="~" title="Root">
    <siteMapNode url="Default.aspx" title="Home" />
    <siteMapNode title="Walks">
      <siteMapNode url="DreamFalls.aspx" title="Dream Falls" />
      <siteMapNode url="SunbeamHill.aspx" title="Sunbeam Hill" />
      <siteMapNode url="WinterMountain.aspx" title="Winter Mountain" />
    </siteMapNode>
  </siteMapNode>
</siteMap>
```

These self-closing tags represent the last three pages in the project.

Your *sitemap* file is now complete and ready to be used with the *Menu, SiteMapPath* and *TreeView* controls. You'll use these in the coming lessons.

This XML file will make a lot more sense when you use it with the ASP.NET navigation controls.

Lesson 7-15: Use the SiteMapPath control

The *SiteMapPath* control allows you to automatically create a "breadcrumb trail" navigation structure based on your *sitemap* file.

You created a *sitemap* file in: *Lesson 7-14: Add a sitemap file to a project*

1   Open *ForestWalks* from your sample files folder.

2   Open *Site.Master* in Design view.

As this is the site's master page, it's the ideal location for navigation controls.

Controls that are placed on the master page will be displayed on every other page that uses the master page. Every page in this project uses the *Site.master* master page.

Master pages are covered in Session 12 of the *Essential Skills* course.

3   Add a *SiteMapPath* control to the area just below the banner.

You'll find this control in the *Navigation* category of the *Toolbox*.

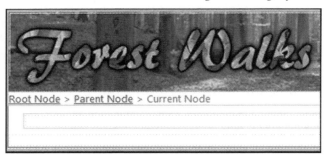

The *SiteMapPath* control automatically reads your *Web.sitemap* file to build a 'breadcrumb trail' navigation structure.

4   Test your new *SiteMapPath* control.

1.   View *DreamFalls.aspx* in your web browser.

The breadcrumb trail appears at the top of the page, indicating that you are on the *Dream Falls* page inside the *Walks* category.

The *Walks* item isn't a hyperlink because you didn't assign a *url* property to the corresponding tag in the *sitemap* file (see: *Lesson 7-14: Add a sitemap file to a project*).

2. Click the *Root* link on the breadcrumb trail.

You're returned to the homepage.

3. Close your web browser and return to Visual Studio.

5 Open *Web.sitemap*.

6 Compare the *sitemap* file with the resulting navigation structure.

This *sitemap* code:

```
<siteMapNode url="~" title="Root">
  <siteMapNode url="Default.aspx" title="Home" />
  <siteMapNode title="Walks">
    <siteMapNode url="DreamFalls.aspx" title="Dream Falls" />
    <siteMapNode url="SunbeamHill.aspx" title="Sunbeam Hill" />
    <siteMapNode url="WinterMountain.aspx" title="Winter Mountain" />
  </siteMapNode>
</siteMapNode>
```

Produces this navigation structure for the *DreamFalls.aspx* page:

You can see that the *Root* node is the 'master' node that contains all of the others and refers to the 'top level' of the site.

The *Walks* node is on the next level, but doesn't have a *url* property.

DreamFalls.aspx is on the third level, and this is accurately reflected in the *SiteMapPath* control's navigation structure.

Lesson 7-16: Use the TreeView and SiteMapDataSource controls

Like the *SiteMapPath* control, the *TreeView* control is capable of using information from your *Web.sitemap* file. Doing this requires a *SiteMapDataSource* control.

Unlike the *SiteMapPath* control, you can also choose to customize a *TreeView* control manually by using its *QuickTasks* menu.

1   Open *ForestWalks* from your sample files folder.

2   Open *Site.Master* in Design view.

3   Add a *SiteMapDataSource* control to the page, just after the *SiteMapPath* control.

You'll find it in the *Data* category of the *Toolbox*.

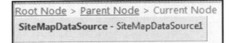

4   Set the *ID* property of the new control to: **SiteMapDataSourceForestWalks**

You don't need to change any more properties. The *SiteMapDataSource* control will automatically detect your *Web.sitemap* file.

5   Add a *TreeView* control to the page, just after the *SiteMapDataSource* control.

You'll find it in the *Navigation* category of the *Toolbox*.

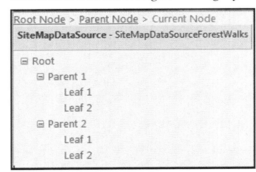

As you can see, this control will display your site's navigation structure in a 'tree' structure.

6   Set the *ID* property of your new *TreeView* control to: **TreeViewNavigation**

7   Set the data source of your new *TreeView* control.

1. Open the *QuickTasks* menu of your new *TreeView* control.

2. Choose *SiteMapDataSourceForestWalks* from the drop-down menu.

note

Custom site map providers

If you want a more complex solution than the *Web.sitemap* file, it's possible to create your own site map provider class.

To do this, you would create a class that extends the *System.Web.SiteMapProvider* class.

You learned about extending classes in: *Lesson 5-1: Extend a class*.

You can specify a custom site map provider by setting the *SiteMapProvider* property in the *SiteMapPath* and *SiteMapDataSource* controls.

8   Test the site.

1. View *Default.aspx* in your web browser.

The navigation structure from your *Web.sitemap* file is now shown in a tree structure.

This navigation structure isn't really ideal for this site. It would look better on a site with a vertical navigation bar.

2. Try expanding and collapsing the groups by clicking the + and – buttons.

3. Click *Dream Falls* from the *Walks* category.

You're taken to the correct page.

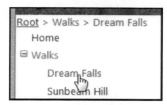

4. Close your web browser and return to Visual Studio.

9   Configure the *SiteMapDataSource* control to hide the *Root* element.

Your *Web.sitemap* file contains both *Root* and *Home* elements, which could be a little confusing for your users.

Set the *ShowStartingNode* property of your *SiteMapDataSource* control to: **False**

Your *TreeView* control now looks less confusing.

The techniques that you used in this lesson apply equally to the *Menu* control, which you'll use in the next lesson: *Lesson 7-17: Use the Menu control.*

Lesson 7-17: Use the Menu control

The *Menu* control is very similar to the *TreeView* control. The only difference is the way that it displays your navigation structure.

You can configure the *Menu* control to use information from your *Web.sitemap* file using the techniques that you learned in: *Lesson 7-16: Use the TreeView and SiteMapDataSource controls.*

In this lesson you'll learn how to customize a *Menu* control manually without using a *Web.sitemap* file.

1   Open *ForestWalks* from your sample files folder.

2   Open *Site.Master* in Design view.

3   Delete the existing *TreeView* control.

4   Add a *Menu* control to the same location.

You'll find it in the *Navigation* category of the *Toolbox*.

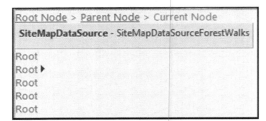

5   Set the *ID* property of the *Menu* control to: **MenuNavigation**

6   Configure the *Menu* control to display links horizontally instead of vertically.

To do this, set the *Orientation* property of your *Menu* control to: **Horizontal**

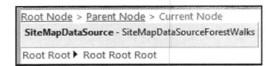

7   Manually add links to your *Menu* control.

1.   Click *Edit Menu Items...* from the *QuickTasks* menu of your *Menu* control.

The *Menu Item Editor* dialog appears.

An identical dialog is available for the *TreeView* control that you worked with in: *Lesson 7-16: Use the TreeView and SiteMapDataSource controls.*

2.   Click the *Add a root item button* in the top-left of the dialog.

A new item appears in the dialog and its properties are displayed on the right.

3. Set the *Text* property of the new item to: **Home**

4. Set the *NavigateUrl* property to: **~/Default.aspx**

   Note that this property has a browse button, allowing you to select the target page using a dialog.

   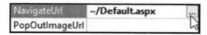

5. Click the *Add a root item* button again to add another item.

6. Set the *Text* property of the new item to: **Walks**

7. Click the *Add a child item* button to add an item 'inside' the *Walks* category.

8. Set the *Text* property of the new item to: **Dream Falls**

9. Set the *NavigateUrl* property of the new item to: **~/DreamFalls.aspx**

10. Click *OK*.

8 Apply a custom style to your *Menu* control.

1. Set the *CssClass* property of your *Menu* control to: **menu**

   This CSS class originates from the *Site.css* file in the *Styles* folder. CSS classes are covered in Session 2 of the *Essential Skills* course.

2. Set the *IncludeStyleBlock* property of your *Menu* control to: **false**

   The *IncludeStyleBlock* property controls whether the *Menu* control will add any CSS code of its own. By setting it to *false*, you ensure that only your own CSS will be applied to the control.

9 View *Default.aspx* in your web browser.

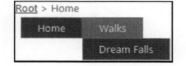

Your *Menu* control now offers an attractive and easy to use navigation menu.

Notice that the *Walks* menu automatically expands when you move your mouse cursor over it.

Session 7: Exercise

1 Open *Exercise7* from your sample files folder and open *SalesAdmin.aspx* in Design view.

2 In the *GridView* control, replace the *Product* field with a *TemplateField* called: **Product**

3 Add a *Label* control to the *ItemTemplate* of your new *TemplateField* and configure it to display the *Product.ProductName* data field using the *Eval* method.

4 In the *EditItemTemplate* of your *TemplateField*, add a *LinqDataSource* control that retrieves all records from the *Product* table. Set an appropriate ID property for the control for easy identification.

5 Add a *DropDownList* control to the *EditItemTemplate* and link it to the *LinqDataSource* control that you created in the previous step.

6 Configure your *DropDownList* control to use *ProductName* as its display field and *ProductID* as its value field.

7 Bind the *DropDownList* control to the *ProductID* data field using the *Bind* method.

8 Open *IronData.aspx* in Design view and add a *ListView* control to the page, linked to the *LinqDataSourceIronSales* data source.

9 Generate templates for your new *ListView* control using the *Configure ListView* option with the default settings.

10 Open *IronChart.aspx* in Design view and add a *Chart* control to the page, linked to the *SqlDataSourceIronSales* data source.

11 In the *QuickTasks* menu of the *Chart* control, set the *X Value Member* property to **SaleMonth** and the *Y Value Member* to **SaleValue**.

12 Open the *Web.sitemap* file and add a new pair of *siteMapNode* tags (similar to, and at the same level as, the *Iron* tag) with a *title* property of: **Admin**

13 Add a new *siteMapNode* tag inside the *Admin* tag with a *url* property of: **SalesAdmin.aspx** and a *title* property of: **Sales Admin**

14 Open *Site.Master* in Design view and add a *SiteMapDataSource* control in the blue area near the top of the page.

15 Configure the new *SiteMapDataSource* control to hide the starting node.

16 Add a *Menu* control in the same area and link it to the *SiteMapDataSource* control.

17 Set the *CssClass* property of the new *Menu* control to: **menu**

18 Configure the *Menu* control to display items horizontally instead of vertically.

19 Configure the *Menu* control not to generate any CSS code of its own.

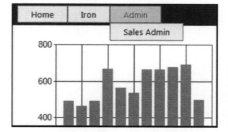

Session 7: Exercise Answers

These are the four questions that students find the most difficult to answer:

Q 12 & 13	Q 7	Q 3	Q 2

Use the following code:
 	
`<siteMapNode title="Admin">`
 `<siteMapNode url="SalesAdmin.aspx" title="Sales Admin" />`
`</siteMapNode>`
 	
This was covered in: *Lesson 7-14: Add a sitemap file to a project.*
	1. Open the *QuickTasks* menu of the *DropDownList* control and click *Edit Databindings…*
	
	2. Click the *Bound to* drop-down menu and select *ProductID.*
	
	3. Click *OK.*
	
	This was covered in: *Lesson 7-9: Use the GridView EditItemTemplate.*
		1. Open the *QuickTasks* menu of the *GridView* control and click *Edit Templates.*
		
		2. Drag a *Label* control into the *ItemTemplate* area.
		
		3. Open the *QuickTasks* menu of the *Label* control and click *Edit DataBindings…*
		
		4. Click *Custom binding.*
		
		5. In the *code expression* box, type:
		
		Eval("Product.ProductName")
		
		6. Click *OK.*
		
		This was covered in: *Lesson 7-8: Use the GridView TemplateField.*
			1. Open the *QuickTasks* menu of the *GridView* control and click *Edit Columns…*
			
			2. Click the *Product* column in the *Selected fields* pane and click the delete button.
			
			3. Click *TemplateField* in the *Available fields* pane and click *Add.*
			
			4. Set the *HeaderText* property to: **Product**
			
			5. Click *OK.*
			
			This was covered in: *Lesson 7-8: Use the GridView TemplateField.*

If you have difficulty with the other questions, here are the lessons that cover the relevant skills:

1   Refer to: **Essential Skills Session 1.**

4   Refer to: **Lesson 7-9: Use the GridView EditItemTemplate.**

5   Refer to: **Lesson 7-9: Use the GridView EditItemTemplate.**

6   Refer to: **Lesson 7-9: Use the GridView EditItemTemplate.**

8   Refer to: **Lesson 7-10: Create a ListView control.**

9   Refer to: **Lesson 7-10: Create a ListView control.**

10   Refer to: **Lesson 7-4: Create a Chart control.**

11   Refer to: **Lesson 7-4: Create a Chart control.**

14   Refer to: **Lesson 7-16: Use the TreeView and SiteMapDataSource controls.**

15   Refer to: **Lesson 7-16: Use the TreeView and SiteMapDataSource controls.**

16   Refer to: **Lesson 7-17: Use the Menu control.**

17   Refer to: **Lesson 7-17: Use the Menu control.**

18   Refer to: **Lesson 7-17: Use the Menu control.**

19   Refer to: **Lesson 7-17: Use the Menu control.**

8

Session Eight: Advanced ASP.NET techniques

The most perfect technique is that which is not noticed at all.

Pablo Casals, Spanish musician (1876-1973)

By this stage you have a good understanding of how ASP.NET works, using controls, event handlers and the .NET framework.

In this session you'll learn about some of the more advanced components and capabilities of ASP.NET, allowing you to take greater control of your web applications.

The techniques that you'll learn in this session allow you to take absolute control of ASP.NET and provide your users with advanced interfaces that aren't constrained by the limits of ASP.NET's automated features.

Your users won't notice that you're using these advanced features, but they will notice the improvements in usability that they can provide.

Session Objectives

By the end of this session you will be able to:

- Work with application settings
- Create a skin
- Work with multiple themes
- Create a Web User Control
- Create an HTTP Handler
- Apply an HTTP Handler to a folder
- Use routes to create virtual paths
- Create an HTTP Module
- Implement custom security with an HTTP Module
- Enable caching
- Use the Substitution control to enable partial caching

Lesson 8-1: Work with application settings

Sometimes you'll want to specify your own custom application settings so that you can change your application's behavior without needing to rebuild it.

You could achieve this by using a database, but ASP.NET also offers you the ability to add your own custom settings to the *Web.config* file.

1   Open *MathLand* from your sample files folder.

2   Open the ASP.NET Configuration utility.

To do this, click Project→ASP.NET Configuration.

The ASP.NET Configuration utility is covered in depth in Session 9 of the *Essential Skills* course.

3   Click the Application tab at the top of the screen.

4   Create an application setting to store the application's name.

1.   Click *Create application settings*.

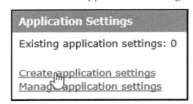

2.   In the *Name* box, enter: **ApplicationName**

3.   In the *Value* box, enter: **MathLand**

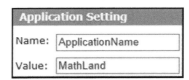

4.   Click *Save*.

Your new application setting is added and a confirmation message appears.

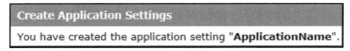

If you are not completing the course incrementally use the sample file: **Lesson 8-1** to begin this lesson.

Sample files with the starting point for each lesson are also provided for all of the other lessons in this session.

5   Close the ASP.NET Configuration utility and return to Visual Studio.

6   Open *Web.config* and examine your new setting.

When you create an application setting, it is added to your *Web.config* file within the *<appSettings>* tag.

```
</configSections>
<appSettings>
  <add key="ApplicationName" value="MathLand" />
</appSettings>
```

You don't need to use the ASP.NET Configuration utility to add application settings. If you prefer, you can simply type them into your *Web.config* file.

7 Open *Global.asax*.

I've added some code to the *Application_Error* event handler that will log any errors to a database.

```
void Application_Error(object sender, EventArgs e)
{
    // Code that runs when an unhandled error occurs
    using (MathLandDataContext Data = new MathLandDataContext())
    {
        Exception ErrorToLog = Server.GetLastError();
```

If the error logs were being saved into a central database, you would need to log the name of the application.

Without the name of the application, you wouldn't be able to tell which application each error originated from.

8 Add a *using* line for *System.Configuration*.

```
using Mathland;
using System.Configuration;
```

The classes that are needed to retrieve application settings are in the *System.Configuration* namespace, so this will make them easier to access.

9 Add code to retrieve your application setting.

Add the following code in the area that is marked with a *TODO* comment:

Log.ErrorLogAppName = ConfigurationManager.AppSettings["ApplicationName"];

```
Log.ErrorLogDate = DateTime.Now;
Log.ErrorLogAppName =
    ConfigurationManager.AppSettings["ApplicationName"];
Data.ErrorLogs.InsertOnSubmit(Log);
Data.SubmitChanges();
```

This code extracts the *ApplicationName* setting from *Web.config*.

10 Test your code.

1. Run the project in Debug mode.

2. Using your web browser's address bar, attempt to navigate to a page that does not exist (as shown below).

> http://localhost:53754/qqq.aspx
> *The resource cannot be found.*

3. Close your web browser.

4. Use the *Database Explorer* window to view the contents of the *ErrorLog* database table.

The error has been logged and the *ApplicationName* setting was retrieved correctly.

ErrorLogID	ErrorLogAppName	ErrorLogDate	ErrorLogMessage
11	MathLand	28/06/2013 15:09:38	The file '/qqq.aspx' does not exist.

---

note

Why are application settings useful?

Application settings are useful because they allow settings to be changed without needing to rebuild the project.

Even after the project is built, you can modify the *Web.config* file to change its behaviour.

If you want users to be able to change your application's settings through the application itself, it is a better choice to store your settings in a database.

Although it is possible to change the *Web.config* file using C# code, doing so can cause problems.

You would not be able to store settings for individual users in the *Web.config* file. To store settings for each user, you would need to create a database with a *UserSettings* table that contained settings for each user.

Lesson 8-2: Create a skin

When adding controls to pages, you often need to set many different properties. This can be time-consuming when you need many controls to have the same appearance.

The *CssClass* property is a partial solution to this problem, but there are many properties that you cannot set using CSS code alone.

Using skins, you can create presets for almost every property of a control.

1   Open *MarketTrader* from your sample files folder.

2   Add a skin file to the project, named: **BlueGridViews**

1. Right-click *MarketTrader* in the *Solution Explorer* and click Add→New Item… from the shortcut menu.

2. Click *Web* in the left-hand pane.

3. Scroll down and click *Skin File* in the central pane.

4. In the *Name* box, type: **BlueGridViews.skin**

5. Click *Add*.

You are prompted to place your new *skin* file inside a special *App_Themes* folder.

note

The default project does not use skins

If you look in the *Content* folder of this project, you will see that it contains a *themes* folder. The contents of this folder are unrelated to ASP.NET's themes feature.

The *Content/themes* folder contains resources that are used by the *jQuery user interface* library, which provides extended JavaScript user interface features.

You don't have to use the *jQuery user interface* library, but it is included with every new ASP.NET 4.5 Web Forms Application project.

6. Click *Yes*.

Your new skin is created and opened.

If you look in the *Solution Explorer*, you can see that two new folders have been created along with your *skin* file.

The *App_Themes* folder is one of ASP.NET's special folders. Just as the *App_Data* folder contains databases, the *App_Themes* folder is intended to contain only *skin* files and CSS stylesheets.

The *BlueGridViews* folder represents a *theme*. Because the *BlueGridViews.skin* file is in the *BlueGridViews* folder, it's treated as part of the *BlueGridViews* theme.

You'll learn more about themes later in this lesson and in: *Lesson 8-3: Work with multiple themes.*

3 Configure your new skin to format the *GridView* control.

Add the following code to the bottom of your new *skin* file:

```
<asp:GridView runat="server" SkinId="BlueGridView"
ForeColor="White" >
  <HeaderStyle BackColor="SlateBlue" />
  <RowStyle BackColor="Navy" />
  <AlternatingRowStyle BackColor="Blue" />
</asp:GridView>
```

```
<asp:Image runat="server" ImageUrl="~/images/image1.jpg" />
--%>

<asp:GridView runat="server" SkinId="BlueGridView" ForeColor="White" >
    <HeaderStyle BackColor="SlateBlue" />
    <RowStyle BackColor="Navy" />
    <AlternatingRowStyle BackColor="Blue" />
</asp:GridView>
```

Ensure that the code is outside the % tags that appear by default.

This skin will apply a blue color scheme to any *GridView* control that uses it.

4 Apply your new skin to the *GridView* control on the *MarketData.aspx* page.

1. Open *MarketData.aspx* in Design view.

2. Click the drop-down menu in the *Properties* window and select *DOCUMENT*.

3. Set the *Theme* property to: **BlueGridViews**

This applies the *BlueGridViews* theme to this page only.

Note that the *StyleSheetTheme* property can also be used to apply a theme in a slightly different way (see sidebar).

4. Set the *SkinID* property of the *GridView* control on this page to: **BlueGridView**

Note that this matches the *SkinId* property that you specified in the *skin* file.

If you had not specified a *SkinId* property in the *skin* file, you would not need to set this property. The skin would be automatically applied to all *GridView* controls on this page (and on any other pages that use the *BlueGridViews* theme).

5 Test your new theme.

1. View *MarketData.aspx* in your web browser.

2. Click *Get Data*.

The *GridView* control appears, showing the blue formatting that you specified in the *skin* file.

---

note

Limitations of skins

Skins are only able to specify values for properties that affect the appearance of a control.

Properties that only affect the behaviour of controls cannot be set using skins.

note

The StyleSheetTheme property

The *StyleSheetTheme* property is nearly identical to the *Theme* property.

The difference is that the *Theme* property will allow the theme to override any properties of the controls on the page that have been manually set, while the *StyleSheetTheme* property will leave any manually-set properties as they are.

Lesson 8-3: Work with multiple themes

1   Open *MarketTrader* from your sample files folder.

2   Add a second theme, named: **RedGridViews**

     1.   Right-click *App_Themes* in the *Solution Explorer* and click Add→Add ASP.NET Folder→Theme from the shortcut menu.

       A new theme folder appears, ready to be named.

     2.   Type: **RedGridViews** and press **<Enter>**.

       You have just added a second theme to your project.

3   Add a skin to the *RedGridViews* theme, named: **RedGridViews.skin**

     1.   Right-click the *RedGridViews* folder in the *Solution Explorer* and click Add→New Item… from the shortcut menu.

     2.   Click *Web* in the left-hand pane.

     3.   Click *Skin File* in the central pane.

     4.   In the *Name* box, type: **RedGridViews.skin**

     5.   Click *Add*.

       The new *skin* file appears in the *RedGridViews* theme folder and is automatically opened.

4   Add code to your new skin to apply a red color scheme to all *GridView* controls on pages that use the theme.

     Add the following code to your new *skin* file:

<asp:GridView runat="server" ForeColor="White" >
   <HeaderStyle BackColor="Crimson" />
   <RowStyle BackColor="Red" />
   <AlternatingRowStyle BackColor="DarkRed" />
</asp:GridView>

```
<asp:GridView runat="server" ForeColor="White" >
    <HeaderStyle BackColor="Crimson" />
    <RowStyle BackColor="Red" />
    <AlternatingRowStyle BackColor="DarkRed" />
</asp:GridView>
```

---

note

Themes and CSS files

You can add both *skin* and *css* files to a theme.

If you add a *css* file to a theme it will be automatically included in any page that uses the theme.

Using themes can be a very convenient way to manage your site's styles.

---

note

Allowing users to select a theme

You may have encountered websites on the internet that allow you to choose between a number of visual themes (sometimes simply referred to as skins).

To do this in ASP.NET, you would first need to create a database table to store each user's choice of theme.

To apply the user's chosen theme to each page, you would add some code to the *Page_Load* event handler of each page to set the *Page.Theme* property to their chosen theme.

You could do this more easily by adding code to the *Page_Load* event handler of a master page that was used by every page in the application.

---

note

Themes and the Machine.config file

Every ASP.NET (IIS) web server has a file called *Machine.config* which controls the behavior of the server.

By using the *pages* tag in the *Machine.config* file, you can apply a theme to every web site running on that server.

This code is very similar to the code that you used in: *Lesson 8-2: Create a skin.* The important difference is that you haven't specified a *SkinId* property this time. This means that this skin will be automatically applied to any *GridView* controls on pages that use the *RedGridViews* theme.

5　Set the entire project to use the *RedGridViews* theme.

You learned how to set a single page to use a theme in: *Lesson 8-2: Create a skin,* but it's also possible to apply a theme to your entire project.

1. Open *Web.config.*

   There's a lot more code here than you're used to seeing. Most of this was automatically added to support the *Chart* control that you created in: *Lesson 7-4: Create a Chart control.*

2. Find the *<pages>* tag.

   ```
   <httpRuntime targetFramework="4.5"/>
   <pages>
       <namespaces>
   ```

3. Add a *theme* property to the *<pages>* tag using the following code:

   <pages **theme="RedGridViews">**

   ```
   <httpRuntime targetFramework="4.5"/>
   <pages theme="RedGridViews">
       <namespaces>
   ```

   This applies the *RedGridViews* theme to every page in this project, unless the page has been configured to use a different theme.

6　Test the theme.

1. View *MarketDataByDate.aspx* in your web browser.

2. Click *Get Data.*

   The *GridView* control on this page now has the red formatting from your *RedGridViews* theme.

3. Click the *Data* button on the navigation bar to navigate to *MarketData.aspx.*

4. Click *Get Data.*

   The *GridView* control on this page still uses the *BlueGridViews* theme.

   This is because you specifically told this page to use the *BlueGridViews* theme in: *Lesson 8-2: Create a skin.*

Date	Value
01/12/2011	£11,858.24
01/12/2011	£11,406.50
01/12/2011	£14,489.97
01/12/2011	£12,807.02
01/12/2011	£12,894.37
01/12/2011	£11,731.74
01/12/2011	£10,599.49

Date	Value
01/01/2011	£12,880.91
01/02/2011	£12,808.21
01/03/2011	£12,769.85
01/04/2011	£12,684.88
01/05/2011	£12,778.19
01/06/2011	£12,861.72

Lesson 8-4: Create a Web User Control

In *Session Five: Advanced class structures,* you created an extended version of the *GridView* control, adding additional logic to it.

Web User Controls allow you to do the same thing a lot more easily and allow you to create even more advanced controls. *Web User Controls* are usually the best way to create custom controls.

1   Open *JoesBarWebApplication.sln* from your sample files folder.

2   Create a new *Web User Control* named: **MailControl.ascx**

1. Right-click *JoesBarWebApplication* in the *Solution Explorer* and click Add→New Item… from the shortcut menu.

2. Click *Web* in the left-hand pane.

3. Click *Web User Control* in the central pane.

4. In the *Name* box, type: **MailControl.ascx**

5. Click *Add.*

    Your new *Web User Control* is created and its code is automatically opened.

3   Switch to Design view and add controls to your Web User Control.

A *Web User Control* can be edited in exactly the same way as an *aspx* page.

1. Click the *Design* button in the bottom-left corner of the main Visual Studio pane to switch to Design view.

2. Add a *TextBox* control to the *Web User Control.*

3. Set the *ID* property of the new *TextBox* control to: **TextBoxEmailAddress**

4. Add a *Button* control to the *Web User Control,* just after the *TextBox* control.

5. Set the *ID* property of the new *Button* control to: **ButtonSignUp**

6. Set the *Text* property of the new *Button* control to: **Sign Up**

4   Add e-mail code to your Web User Control.

1. Add a *Click* event handler to the *ButtonSignUp* control.

2. Add the following code to the new event handler:

    System.Net.Mail.SmtpClient Client = new System.Net.Mail.SmtpClient();

string AddressToSignUp = TextBoxEmailAddress.Text;
Client.Send("SimonSmart@ASPNETCentral.com",
"Info@ASPNETCentral.com", "Discount Sign-Up", "Sign up "
+ AddressToSignUp);
TextBoxEmailAddress.Text = "Thanks for signing up!";
ButtonSignUp.Enabled = false;
TextBoxEmailAddress.Enabled = false;

```
protected void ButtonSignUp_Click(object sender, EventArgs e)
{
    System.Net.Mail.SmtpClient Client = new System.Net.Mail.SmtpClient();
    string AddressToSignUp = TextBoxEmailAddress.Text;
    Client.Send("SimonSmart@ASPNETCentral.com", "Info@ASPNETCentral.com",
        "Discount Sign-Up", "Sign up " + AddressToSignUp);
    TextBoxEmailAddress.Text = "Thanks for signing up!";
    ButtonSignUp.Enabled = false;
    TextBoxEmailAddress.Enabled = false;
}
```

This code sends an e-mail message when the button is clicked.

5   Add your Web User Control to a page.

1.   Open *Default.aspx* in Design view.

2.   Click and drag *MailControl.ascx* from the *Solution Explorer* onto the bottom of the page.

Your *Web User Control* is added to the page just like any other control.

6   Switch to Source view and examine the code.

Near the top of the page, notice the line:

<%@ Register src="MailControl.ascx" tagname="MailControl" tagprefix="uc1" %>

You used some very similar code when you added an extended *GridView* control to a page in: *Lesson 5-2: Add an extended control to a page*.

Dragging and dropping a *Web User Control* onto a page adds this code automatically.

7   Test your new control.

View *Default.aspx* in your web browser.

Your new control appears at the bottom of the page.

Note that the *Sign Up* button will not work unless a mail server is available. You learned about this in: *Lesson 2-9: Send e-mail messages using the SmtpClient class*.

Lesson 8-5: Create an HTTP Handler

ASP.NET web applications automatically handle requests from web users, sending the user to the appropriate page or showing an error if the page does not exist.

By using an HTTP handler, you can take control of this functionality. In this lesson you'll use an HTTP handler to redirect the user to different pages according to their request.

1   Open *ForestWalks* from your sample files folder.

2   Add a new HTTP handler, named: **WalkHandler.cs**

   1.   Right-click *ForestWalks* in the *Solution Explorer* and click Add→New Item… from the shortcut menu.

   2.   Click *Web* in the left-hand pane.

   3.   Click *ASP.NET Handler* in the central pane.

   4.   In the *Name* box, type: **WalkHandler.cs**

   5.   Click *Add*.

   Your new HTTP Handler is created and opened.

   ```
   namespace ForestWalks
   {
       public class WalkHandler : IHttpHandler
       {
           /// <summary>
   ```

   An HTTP Handler is simply a class that implements the *IHttpHandler* interface. You learned about implementing interfaces in: *Lesson 5-6: Implement an interface*.

3   Add code to your new HTTP handler.

   1.   Expand the *IHttpHandler Members* region.

   You learned about the *#region* directive in: *Lesson 6-1: Create code regions with the #region directive*.

   ```
   public bool IsReusable
   {
       // Return false in case your Managed Handler cannot
       // Usually this would be false in case you have some
       get { return true; }
   }

   public void ProcessRequest(HttpContext context)
   {
       //write your handler implementation here.
   }
   ```

   The *IsReusable* property and *ProcessRequest* methods are required by the *IHttpHandler* interface.

note

The context object

The *context* object in the *ProcessRequest* method is an *HttpContext* object.

The *context* object is the bridge connecting your HTTP Handler with the rest of your ASP.NET application.

Whenever your HTTP Handler handles a request from a web user, the details of the request will be made available in the *context.Request* object.

The *context.Response* object can then be used to control the response that is sent back to the user by the HTTP Handler.

note

The Url.Segments property

The *Url* property contains the web address that was requested by the user. For example:

www.aspnetcentral.com/ Lessons/HttpHandlers.aspx

The *Url.Segments* property allows you to access the different parts of this request.

For example, *Url.Segments[0]* would contain:

www.aspnetcentral.com

…*Url.Segments[1]* would contain:

Lessons

…and *Url.Segments[2]* would contain:

HttpHandlers.aspx

2.   Add the following code to the *ProcessRequest* method:

string RequestedPage = context.Request.Url.Segments[2].ToLower();

```
public void ProcessRequest(HttpContext context)
{
    //write your handler implementation here.
    string RequestedPage = context.Request.Url.Segments[2].ToLower();
}
```

The *context.Request* object is the same type of object as the *Page.Request* object. The *Page.Request* object is covered in Session 3 of the *Essential Skills* course. See sidebar for more on the *context* object.

The *Url.Segments[2]* property is used to retrieve the last segment of the web address that was requested by the user (see sidebar).

By using the *ToLower* method, you are converting the user's request into lower case. This will allow the HTTP handler to work regardless of whether the user uses capital letters or not.

Add the following code on the next line:

if (RequestedPage == "dreamfalls")
    context.Response.Redirect("~/DreamFalls.aspx");
else if (RequestedPage == "wintermountain")
    context.Response.Redirect("~/WinterMountain.aspx");
else if (RequestedPage == "sunbeamhill")
    context.Response.Redirect("~/SunbeamHill.aspx");
else context.Response.Redirect("~/Default.aspx");

```
if (RequestedPage == "dreamfalls")
    context.Response.Redirect("~/DreamFalls.aspx");
else if (RequestedPage == "wintermountain")
    context.Response.Redirect("~/WinterMountain.aspx");
else if (RequestedPage == "sunbeamhill")
    context.Response.Redirect("~/SunbeamHill.aspx");
else
    context.Response.Redirect("~/Default.aspx");
```

Even though there are no 'real' pages in the *Walks* folder, this code will allow users to navigate to any of the following addresses:

www.[domain name]/Walks/DreamFalls
www.[domain name]/Walks/WinterMountain
www.[domain name]/Walks/SunbeamHill

The user will be appropriately redirected based on the page that they requested. If the user does not request one of these three addresses, they will be sent to *Default.aspx*.

Before this handler will be functional you will need to configure your project to use it for any requests that are made for pages in the *Walks* folder.

You'll apply your HTTP Handler to the *Walks* folder in the next lesson: *Lesson 8-6: Apply an HTTP Handler to a folder*.

Lesson 8-6: Apply an HTTP Handler to a folder

You created a simple HTTP Handler that redirects a user's requests in the previous lesson: *Lesson 8-5: Create an HTTP Handler*.

In this lesson you'll apply your HTTP Handler to the *Walks* folder in the *ForestWalks* project.

An HTTP Handler won't do anything unless you configure a *Web.config* file to apply it to a folder.

1   Open *ForestWalks* from your sample files folder.

2   Add a new *Web.config* file to the *Walks* folder.

    1.   Right-click the *Walks* folder and click Add→New Item… from the shortcut menu.

    2.   Click *Web* in the left-hand pane.

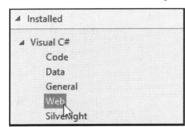

    3.   Click *Web Configuration File* in the central pane.

    4.   Click *Add*.

    A new *Web.config* file appears in the *Walks* folder.

    The new file is automatically opened.

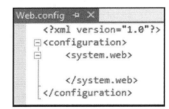

3   Add code to apply your HTTP Handler to the *Walks* folder.

Add the following code inside the *<configuration>* tag, but outside the *<system.web>* tag:

```
<system.webServer>
 <handlers>
  <add verb="*" path="*" name="WalkHandler"
  type="ForestWalks.WalkHandler" />
 </handlers>
</system.webServer>
```

```
Web.config + X
    <?xml version="1.0"?>
  <configuration>
    <system.webServer>
      <handlers>
        <add verb="*" path="*" name="WalkHandler" type="ForestWalks.WalkHandler" />
      </handlers>
    </system.webServer>
    <system.web>

    </system.web>
  </configuration>
```

note

Uses for HTTP Handlers

The system that you created in this lesson could have been created more easily by using ASP.NET 4.5's new *FriendlyUrls* feature. This is covered in Session 12 of the Essential Skills course in this series.

While *FriendlyUrls* makes simple redirection easy, HTTP Handlers have many more potential uses.

HTTP Handlers are often used to apply custom security features to sites. For example, the *aspnetcentral.com* website uses an HTTP Handler to display different content depending on whether the user is logged in.

HTTP Handlers can also be used to create 'virtual' files. By intercepting a request for a file and populating the *context.Response* object with appropriate data, you can create the illusion of a file.

This can be useful when you are storing files in a database and want to make them easily accessible.

You'll use an HTTP Handler to create a 'virtual' image in: *Lesson 12-10: Create a Captcha image system.*

These are just a few of the possibilities. By using HTTP Handlers you can take full control of the web server's response to any request.

This code configures your application to handle all web requests for the *Walks* folder with your *WalkHandler* HTTP Handler.

The *verb* property indicates the type of request. The * indicates that the handler should handle all types of request. See sidebar for other *verb* options.

The *path* property indicates the file name that the handler should handle. For example, a *path* property of **.jpg* would only handle requests for files with names ending in *.jpg*.

Note that you cannot use the *path* property to specify sub-folders, so you couldn't use a *path* property of: */walks/**. This is the reason that you can't add the handler to the project's main *Web.config* file.

The *name* property simply specifies a unique name for the handler.

Finally, the *type* property specifies which class contains the HTTP Handler. Your HTTP Handler is the *ForestWalks.WalkHandler* class.

4   Test your code.

1.   Run the project in Debug mode.

2.   Using your web browser's address bar, attempt to navigate to: **/Walks/DreamFalls**

http://localhost:63170/Walks/DreamFalls

Your HTTP Handler automatically redirects you to *DreamFalls.aspx* in your web application's root folder.

http://localhost:63170/DreamFalls.aspx

3.   Attempt to navigate to: **/Walks/SunbeamHill**

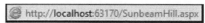
http://localhost:63170/Walks/SunbeamHill

Your HTTP Handler automatically redirects you to *SunbeamHill.aspx* in your web application's root folder.

http://localhost:63170/SunbeamHill.aspx

4.   Attempt to navigate to: **/Walks/badpage**

http://localhost:63170/Walks/badpage

The HTTP Handler redirects you back to *Default.aspx*.

http://localhost:63170/Default.aspx

Lesson 8-7: Use routes to create virtual paths

You created an HTTP Handler that redirects a user's requests earlier in this session, in: *Lesson 8-5: Create an HTTP Handler*.

HTTP Handlers allow you to take complete control of ASP.NET's Request/Response system, making them the best choice for complex systems. If you only want to redirect users, however, you can use the new *System.Web.Routing* namespace to do the same thing with less code.

1 Open *MarketTrader* from your sample files folder.

2 Open *Global.asax*.

The *Global.asax* file contains event handlers that affect your entire web application. *Global.asax* is explained in more depth in Session 12 of the Essential Skills course in this series.

You'll notice that some code has been automatically included in the *Application_Start* event handler. This code is included in all new ASP.NET 4.5 Web Forms Application projects.

```
void Application_Start(object sender, EventArgs e)
{
    // Code that runs on application startup
    BundleConfig.RegisterBundles(BundleTable.Bundles);
    AuthConfig.RegisterOpenAuth();
    RouteConfig.RegisterRoutes(RouteTable.Routes);
}
```

This code runs when your web application is started by the web server and enables some of the new features of ASP.NET 4.5. This code is also explained in Session 12 of the Essential Skills course.

The important line here is:

RouteConfig.RegisterRoutes(RouteTable.Routes);

This code refers to the *RegisterRoutes* method that can be found in *RouteConfig.cs* in the *App_Start* folder.

note

The App_Start folder is an ordinary folder

The *App_Start* folder follows the same naming convention as some of ASP.NET's 'special' folders (such as *App_Data*), so you might expect it to be special in some way.

In fact, *App_Start* is a completely ordinary folder and its contents are not treated any differently by ASP.NET.

3 Open *RouteConfig.cs* from the *App_Start* folder.

Currently, this file contains some code that simply enables the new *FriendlyUrls* feature.

```
public static void RegisterRoutes(RouteCollection routes)
{
    routes.EnableFriendlyUrls();
}
```

4 Add some code to create a new route linking */Reports/Charts* to the *MarketCharts.aspx* page.

Add the following code to the *RegisterRoutes* method:

routes.MapPageRoute
   ("Reports", "Reports/Charts", "~/MarketCharts.aspx");

```
routes.EnableFriendlyUrls();
routes.MapPageRoute
    ("Reports", "Reports/Charts", "~/MarketCharts.aspx");
```

note

Routes with parameters

You can use routing to easily create separate routes for multiple parameters.

For example, you might have a *products.aspx* page that accepts a *type* query string parameter.

This means that your *products.aspx* page could be accessed using:

products.aspx?type=dvds
products.aspx?type=books
...etc.

You could create routes for both of these values with a single line of code:

**routes.MapPageRoute
("Products", "Products/{type}",
"~/products.aspx");**

Placing *{type}* in curly brackets enables the route to accept any text for the *{type}* parameter. Your users could now access:

/Products/DVDs
/Products/Books
...etc.

To check which value was provided, you must use the *Page.RouteData.Values["type"]* property instead of *Page.QueryString*.

Creating routes like this not only makes your site's URLs friendlier to users, but can also be beneficial to search engines.

This code creates a route that will send any requests for */Reports/Charts* to the *MarketCharts.aspx* page.

The new *FriendlyUrls* feature allows you to do something very similar, but often requires additional *aspx* pages to be created. *FriendlyUrls* is covered in Session 12 of the Essential Skills course in this series.

The code that Microsoft has provided is a little hard to understand because it is passing in the *routes* object from the *Global.asax* file. Here's how the line of code looks when providing the complete namespaces:

*System.Web.Routing.RouteTable.Routes.MapPageRoute
("Reports", "Reports/Charts", "~/MarketCharts.aspx");*

5   Test your new route.

1.   Click Debug→Start Debugging.

2.   Using your web browser's address bar, navigate to:
     /Reports/Charts

    http://localhost:53212/Reports/Charts

MarketCharts.aspx is displayed using your new route.

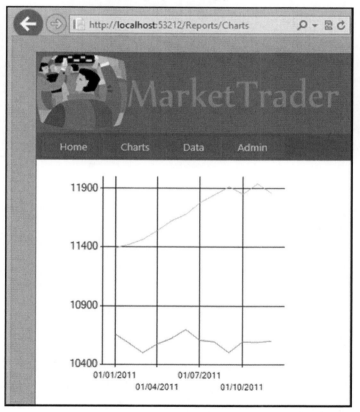

This new *routes* feature makes it very easy to create alternate routes to pages without needing to create any additional pages or HTTP Handlers.

If you only need to re-direct users, *routing* or *FriendlyUrls* are the best choice. If you need more complex functionality, it is better to use HTTP Handlers.

Lesson 8-8: Create an HTTP Module

HTTP Modules are very similar to HTTP Handlers. The main difference is that HTTP Modules cannot be configured to handle specific requests. Instead, HTTP Modules intercept every request that your application receives.

HTTP Modules also allow you to work with additional events that occur between the user's request and the web server's response.

1   Open *SecFile* from your sample files folder.

The *SecFile* project allows users to upload and retrieve files. You're going to use an HTTP Module to add custom security features to the project.

2   Add a new HTTP Module to the project, named: **SecurityModule.cs**

1. Right-click *SecFile* in the *Solution Explorer* and click Add→New Item… from the shortcut menu.

2. Click *Web* in the left-hand pane.

3. Click *ASP.NET Module* in the central pane.

4. In the *Name* box, type: **SecurityModule.cs**

5. Click *Add*.

Your new HTTP Module is created and opened.

```
namespace SecFile
{
    public class SecurityModule : IHttpModule
    {
```

An HTTP Module is simply a class that implements the *IHttpModule* interface.

3   Expand the *IHttpModule Members* region.

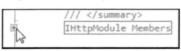

4   Remove all existing code from the *Init* method.

The code that currently exists in the *Init* method may cause errors, so remove it before continuing.

```
public void Init(HttpApplication context)
{

}
```

5   Add code to intercept the *AuthorizeRequest* event.

HTTP Modules are able to intercept any part of the process that occurs when the web server receives a request.

note

Global.asax as an alternative to HTTP Modules

The *Global.asax* file is capable of adding code to the same events as an HTTP Module.

If your requirements are simple, you can simply use *Global.asax* instead of creating an HTTP Module.

The advantage of HTTP Modules over the *Global.asax* file is the ability to attach more than one module to a project.

Global.asax is covered in depth in Session 12 of the *Essential Skills* course in this series.

The part of this lifecycle that you're interested in is the *AuthorizeRequest* event. The *AuthorizeRequest* event happens immediately after the user's credentials have been established, making it an ideal place to check their access rights.

See sidebar if you want to know which credentials can be established.

Add the following code to the *Init* method:

context.AuthorizeRequest += new EventHandler(CustomSecurity);

```
public void Init(HttpApplication context)
{
    context.AuthorizeRequest += new EventHandler(CustomSecurity);
}
```

This code tells ASP.NET to run the *CustomSecurity* method when the *AuthorizeRequest* event occurs.

The code is marked with an error because you have not yet created the *CustomSecurity* method.

EventHandler is a *delegate* type that allows event handler methods to be passed as objects. You learned about delegates in: *Lesson 4-10: Understand delegate methods.*

Methods must contain the *object sender* and *EventArgs args* arguments to be used by the *EventHandler* delegate type.

6   Create the *CustomSecurity* method.

Add the following new method to your HTTP Module:

public void CustomSecurity(object sender, EventArgs args)
{
  HttpApplication CurrentApplication =
  (HttpApplication)sender;
}

```
public void CustomSecurity(object sender, EventArgs args)
{
    HttpApplication CurrentApplication = (HttpApplication)sender;
}
```

The *HttpApplication* object contains the *Request* and *Response* objects that you're already familiar with, as well as the *User* property.

You'll finish implementing your custom security module in the next lesson: *Lesson 8-9: Implement custom security with an HTTP Module.*

note

Why implement security when ASP.NET has its own security system?

In Session 9 of the *Essential Skills* course you learned that ASP.NET has its own security system that works well and is easy to implement.

In this lesson you use an HTTP module to create your own custom security system that works entirely outside the built-in system (though it still uses ASP.NET to manage user login).

There are two reasons to implement a custom security system:

1. The built-in security system only manages security by folder. Often there is a requirement to implement security at page level (or even by specific items on pages).

2. When you need remote users to be able to manage security permissions. The built-in security uses the ASP.NET Configuration utility, meaning that you need to access the server itself to manage them.

Using a custom security module, you can create elegant admin pages that enable your remote users to manage security permissions from within your applications.

The *CheckAccess* method used in this lesson checks to see whether the logged-in user has a record in a *SecureUsers* table that I have created in the *SecFile* database. If a record exists, the user is allowed access to all pages. If the record does not exist, the user may only access the *Default.aspx* and *UserAdmin.aspx* pages.

In a real-world system the user would only be given access to the *Default.aspx* page. You're allowing access to the *UserAdmin.aspx* page only so that you are able to add yourself to the *SecureUsers* table.

Lesson 8-9: Implement custom security with an HTTP Module

1   Open *SecFile* from your sample files folder.

2   Open *SecurityModule.cs*.

In this lesson you will implement custom security to apply more sophisticated security than is available with ASP.NET's built-in security system (see sidebar).

3   Add code to retrieve information about the requested file.

Add the following code to the *CustomSecurity* method:

string FilePath = CurrentApplication.Request. AppRelativeCurrentExecutionFilePath;
string FileName = System.IO.Path.GetFileName(FilePath);
string FileExtension = System.IO.Path.GetExtension(FileName);

```
HttpApplication CurrentApplication = (HttpApplication)sender;
string FilePath = CurrentApplication.Request.
    AppRelativeCurrentExecutionFilePath;
string FileName = System.IO.Path.GetFileName(FilePath);
string FileExtension = System.IO.Path.GetExtension(FileName);
```

This code retrieves information about the file that was requested by the user (such as */Contacts/HeadOffice.aspx*).

The file name and extension will be needed to filter out file types that you don't want to be secured (see sidebar on facing page).

4   Add an *if* statement to exclude the *Default.aspx* and *UserAdmin.aspx* files from security checks, along with any files that are not *.aspx* pages.

Add the following *if* statement on the next line of the *CustomSecurity* method:

if (FileExtension == ".aspx" && FileName != "Default.aspx"
   && FileName != "UserAdmin.aspx") { }

```
string FileExtension = System.IO.Path.GetExtension(FileName);
if (FileExtension == ".aspx" && FileName != "Default.aspx"
    && FileName != "UserAdmin.aspx")
{

}
```

This *if* statement will only execute if the requested file is an *aspx* page and is not *Default.aspx* or *UserAdmin.aspx*.

5   Add code to check whether the user is authorized and redirect unauthorized users to *AccessDenied.aspx*.

Add the following code inside the *if* statement:

string UserName = CurrentApplication.User.Identity.Name;
if (!Utilities.CheckAccess(UserName))
{
   CurrentApplication.Server.Transfer("~/AccessDenied.aspx");
}

```
if (FileExtension == ".aspx" && FileName != "Default.aspx" && FileN
{
    string UserName = CurrentApplication.User.Identity.Name;
    if (!Utilities.CheckAccess(UserName))
    {
        CurrentApplication.Server.Transfer("~/AccessDenied.aspx");
    }
}
```

This code retrieves the username from the *CurrentApplication* object and checks whether the user is authorized by using the *CheckAccess* method from this project's *Utilities.cs* class.

Note that the *Utilities.cs* class is a part of this project and not part of the .NET framework. *Utilities.cs* is visible in the *Solution Explorer*.

If the *CheckAccess* method returns *false*, the user will be redirected to *AccessDenied.aspx*.

6   Apply your HTTP Module to this project's *Web.config* file.

Before an HTTP Module will do anything, you must apply it to the project by editing the *Web.config* file.

Open *Web.config* and add the following code just after the *</configsections>* tag:

<system.webServer>
 <modules>
  <add name="SecurityModule" type="SecFile.SecurityModule" />
 </modules>
</system.webServer>

```
<system.webServer>
  <modules>
    <add name="SecurityModule" type="SecFile.SecurityModule" />
```

7   Test your new security module.

1. View *Default.aspx* in your web browser.

    If you are prompted to log in, log in with your Windows username and password.

    > **WELCOME TO SECFILE**
    >
    > Only authorized users are allowed to access the files in this application.

    The page is displayed without any problems.

2. Click the *Files* button on the navigation bar.

    Notice that the text on the page has changed.

    Your username is not on the list of approved users, so the HTTP Module redirects you to *AccessDenied.aspx*. Make a note of your username as you'll now add it to the list of approved users.

3. Click the *Admin* button on the navigation bar.

4. Enter the username that you noted earlier into the textbox and click *Add User*.

5. Click *Files* on the navigation bar once again.

    You are now allowed to access the page.

> Sorry, but you do not have access to this page.
>
> **Your username is: SSmart**

> **ADD USER**
>
> SSmart   [Add User]

Lesson 8-10: Enable caching

Some ASP.NET pages can be slow to load, especially those that rely on complex database queries.

One way to mitigate this problem is to enable *caching*. When caching is enabled, ASP.NET will not recreate the page's HTML code every time it is requested. Instead it will keep a copy of the last version of the page.

Displaying the cached copy of the page is much faster than running the page's C# code and rebuilding its HTML code.

You'll apply caching to a page in this lesson.

1   Open *TextLand* from your sample files folder.

2   Examine *TimeZones.aspx* without caching.

   1.   View *TimeZones.aspx* in your web browser.

     This page displays the current time in several different time zones.

> **TIME ZONES**
> Greenwich Mean Time (GMT): 13:48:01
> Eastern Standard Time (EST): 08:48:01
> Central Standard Time (CST): 07:48:01
> Mountain Standard Time (MT): 06:48:01

   2.   After a few seconds, click your web browser's Refresh button to refresh the page.

     The page's code is executed and the times are updated.

> **TIME ZONES**
> Greenwich Mean Time (GMT): 13:48:14
> Eastern Standard Time (EST): 08:48:14
> Central Standard Time (CST): 07:48:14
> Mountain Standard Time (MT): 06:48:14

   3.   Close your web browser and return to Visual Studio.

3   Enable caching on *TimeZones.aspx*.

   1.   Open *TimeZones.aspx* in Source view.

   2.   Add the following code to the top of the page, just after the *<%@ Page>* tag:

<%@ OutputCache Duration="60" VaryByParam="None" %>

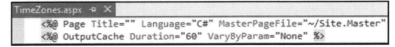

```
TimeZones.aspx
    <%@ Page Title="" Language="C#" MasterPageFile="~/Site.Master"
    <%@ OutputCache Duration="60" VaryByParam="None" %>
```

This code tells ASP.NET to keep a cached copy of this page for 60 seconds.

This means that the page's HTML code will only be regenerated if it has been at least 60 seconds since the last request for the page.

See sidebar for an explanation of *VaryByParam*.

note

Why isn't the page cached after my first request?

The *GET* verb is used when you first request an *aspx* page. If you then post-back (or refresh) the page, the *POST* verb is used.

For an explanation of verbs, see: *Lesson 8-6: Apply an HTTP Handler to a folder (sidebar)*.

ASP.NET creates a separate cached copy of the page for each verb.

When you first loaded the page, a cached copy of the page was created for the *GET* verb.

When you refreshed the page for the first time, a cached copy was created for the *POST* verb.

When you refreshed the page for the second time, ASP.NET saw that a cached copy existed for the *POST* verb and displayed it.

tip

Caching only part of a page

There are two ways to create a page that is only partially cached.

The first option is to create a *Web User Control* and add the *<%@ OutputCache>* tag to its code. If you do this, only the contents of the *Web User Control* will be cached.

You learned about Web User Controls in: *Lesson 8-4: Create a Web User Control*.

The second option is to enable caching on the page as you have in this example and then use the *Substitution* control to create areas that are exempt from caching.

You'll learn about the *Substitution* control in: *Lesson 8-11: Use the Substitution control to enable partial caching*.

4 Examine the page with caching enabled.

1. View *TimeZones.aspx* in your web browser again.

    Once again, the times are displayed.

    TIME ZONES
Greenwich Mean Time (GMT):	13:52:33
Eastern Standard Time (EST):	08:52:33
Central Standard Time (CST):	07:52:33
Mountain Standard Time (MT):	06:52:33

2. After a few seconds, press your web browser's *Refresh* button to refresh the page, then wait a few more seconds and refresh again.

    See sidebar for an explanation of why you need to refresh the page twice.

    Instead of updating the page, ASP.NET uses a cached copy. This page will not update again until 60 seconds have elapsed.

    TIME ZONES
Greenwich Mean Time (GMT):	13:52:33
Eastern Standard Time (EST):	08:52:33
Central Standard Time (CST):	07:52:33
Mountain Standard Time (MT):	06:52:33

    Because a cached version of the page is used, none of the page's C# code runs.

    If this page contained intensive C# code or slow database queries, this could significantly improve the user's experience. The cached copies would be much faster to load as they would not need to re-run any code.

    You should also consider that there may be a large number of other users accessing this page. By caching the page you will drastically speed up access for all users.

3. Close your web browser and return to Visual Studio.

    Caching is not always the best choice. In this example, the times shown on the page may be up to 60 seconds away from the actual time. Caching shouldn't be used when real-time results are important.

Lesson 8-11: Use the Substitution control to enable partial caching

The *Substitution* control is one of those mysterious controls that few developers know the purpose of.

The *Substitution* control is used on cached pages to define areas that will not be cached. This allows you to create pages that are only partially cached.

note

An alternative way to partially cache pages

Web User Controls can also be used to enable partially cached pages.

For more details, see: *Lesson 8-10: Enable caching (sidebar).*

1   Open *TextLand* from your sample files folder.

2   Open *TimeZones.aspx* in Design view.

You enabled caching on this page in: *Lesson 8-10: Enable caching.*

3   Replace the *LabelGMT* control with a *Substitution* control.

1.   Delete the *LabelGMT* control.

2.   Add a *Substition* control in its place.

```
Greenwich Mean Time (GMT):  [ Substitution "Substitution1" ]
Eastern Standard Time (EST):  [LabelEST]
Central Standard Time (CST):  [td]belCST]
Mountain Standard Time (MT): [LabelMT]
```

You'll find it in the *Standard* category of the *Toolbox.*

3.   Set the *ID* property of your new *Substitution* control to: **SubstitutionGMT**

```
Greenwich Mean Time (GMT):  [ Substitution "SubstitutionGMT" ]
Eastern Standard Time (EST):  [LabelEST]
```

4   Fix an error that has been introduced.

Because you deleted the *LabelGMT* control, the code that refers to it will cause an error.

1.   Open the code-behind file of *TimeZones.aspx.*

2.   Remove the following line of code from the *Page_Load* event handler.

LabelGMT.Text = DateTime.UtcNow.ToLongTimeString();

```
protected void Page_Load(object sender, EventArgs e)
{
    LabelEST.Text = DateTime.UtcNow.AddHours(-5).ToLongTimeString();
```

5   Create a method for your *Substitution* control.

It's necessary for a *Substitution* control to use a *delegate* method, as it is the only way it can bypass caching (its only purpose). You learned about *delegate* methods in: *Lesson 4-10: Understand delegate methods.*

Add the following code to create a method for the *Substitution* control to use:

```
public static string GetGMTTime(HttpContext context)
{
    return DateTime.UtcNow.ToLongTimeString();
}
```

```
public static string GetGMTTime(HttpContext context)
{
    return DateTime.UtcNow.ToLongTimeString();
}
```

The *HttpContext* argument is required because *Substitution* delegate methods must have the same arguments and return value as the *System.Web.HttpResponseSubstitutionCallback* method.

6   Apply your method to the *Substitution* control.

1.   Open *TimeZones.aspx* in *Design* view.

2.   Set the *MethodName* property of the *SubstitutionGMT* control to: **GetGMTTime**

EnableViewState	True
MethodName	**GetGMTTime**
ValidateRequestMode	Inherit

The *Substitution* control will now automatically call the *GetGMTTime* method each time the page is loaded and display the result on the page.

7   Test your *Substitution* control.

1.   View *TimeZones.aspx* in your web browser.

Each of the times is displayed.

TIME ZONES
Greenwich Mean Time (GMT): 14:51:44
Eastern Standard Time (EST): 09:51:44
Central Standard Time (CST): 08:51:44
Mountain Standard Time (MT): 07:51:44

2.   After a few seconds, press your web browser's *Refresh* button to refresh the page, then wait a few more seconds and refresh again.

You need to refresh the page twice to get the cached copy for the *POST* verb (see: *Lesson 8-10: Enable caching (sidebar)*).

Because this page is cached, the *EST, CST* and *MT* values do not update to the correct time. The *Substitution* control updates regardless of caching, so the correct GMT time is displayed every time the page is refreshed.

TIME ZONES
Greenwich Mean Time (GMT): 14:52:21
Eastern Standard Time (EST): 09:51:44
Central Standard Time (CST): 08:51:44
Mountain Standard Time (MT): 07:51:44

Session 8: Exercise

1 Open *Exercise8* from your sample files folder.

2 Open the ASP.NET Configuration utility and add a new application setting with the *Name*: **ApplicationName** and the *Value*: **Exercise8**

3 Close your browser and create a new *Web User Control* named: **ApplicationName.ascx**

4 Add a *Label* control to your new *Web User Control* with the *ID*: **LabelApplicationName**

5 Open the code-behind file of your *Web User Control* and add code to the *Page_Load* event handler to retrieve the *ApplicationName* application setting and display its value in the *LabelApplicationName* control.

To retrieve application settings, use the *Sytem.Configuration.ConfigurationManager* class.

6 Open *Default.aspx* in Design view and add your *Web User Control* to the page.

7 Add a new *skin* file to the project, named: **VioletGridViews.skin**

8 Add code to your new *skin* file to set the *BackColor* property of *GridView* controls to: **Violet**

9 Open *Sator.aspx* and apply the *VioletGridViews* theme to the page.

10 Open *LuckyNumber.aspx* and enable caching on the page with a duration of 3600 seconds.

11 Add a new HTTP Handler (also called an ASP.NET Handler) to the project, named: **FeaturesHandler.cs**

12 Add code to your HTTP Handler to look for the word *LuckyNumber* in the requested path using the *context.Request.Path.Contains()* method and redirect the user to *LuckyNumber.aspx* if it is found.

13 Add a *Web.config* file to the *Features* folder and add code to apply the *FeaturesHandler* HTTP handler to the folder.

14 Add a new HTTP Module (also called an ASP.NET Module) to the project, named: **UserLogModule.cs**

15 Create a new method in your HTTP Module with the following code:

```
public void LogUser(object sender, EventArgs args)
{
}
```

16 Add code to the *LogUser* method to retrieve the *HttpApplication* object from the *sender* argument.

17 Add code to the *LogUser* method to log the *HttpApplication.User.Identity.Name* property using the *System.Diagnostics.Debug.WriteLine* method.

18 Remove any existing code from the *Init* method and then add code to attach your *LogUser* method to the *context.AuthorizeRequest* event.

19 Add code to the project's main *Web.config* file to apply the HTTP Module to the project.

| Exercise8 - Start | Exercise8 - End | If you need help slide the page to the left |

Session 8: Exercise Answers

These are the four questions that students find the most difficult to answer:

Q 16, 17, 18	Q 13	Q 12	Q 5

1. Add the following code to the *LogUser* method:
 	
HttpApplication CurrentApplication = (HttpApplication)sender;
 	
2. Add the following code:
 	
System.Diagnostics.Debug .WriteLine (CurrentApplication.User. Identity.Name);
 	
3. Add the following code to the *Init* method:
 	
context.AuthorizeRequest += new EventHandler (LogUser);
 	
This was covered in: *Lesson 8-8: Create an HTTP Module.*
	Add the following code to the *\<configuration>* tag in your new *Web.config* file:
	
	\<system.webServer>
	  \<handlers>
	    \<add verb="*"
	    path="*"
	    type="Exercise8.
	    FeaturesHandler"
	    name=
	    "FeaturesHandler"
	    />
	  \</handlers>
	\</system.webServer>
	
	This was covered in: *Lesson 8-6: Apply an HTTP Handler to a folder.*
		There are a number of ways you could accomplish this, but this simple code will suffice:
		
		if (context.Request. Path.Contains ("LuckyNumber"))
		{
		    context.Response. Redirect ("~/ LuckyNumber.aspx ");
		}
		
		This was covered in: *Lesson 8-5: Create an HTTP Handler.*
			Use the following code:
			
			LabelApplicationName .Text = System.Configuration. ConfigurationManager .AppSettings ["ApplicationName"];
			
			This was covered in: *Lesson 8-1: Work with application settings.*

If you have difficulty with the other questions, here are the lessons that cover the relevant skills:

1 Refer to: Essential Skills Session 1.

2 Refer to: Lesson 8-1: Work with application settings.

3 Refer to: Lesson 8-4: Create a Web User Control.

4 Refer to: Lesson 8-4: Create a Web User Control.

6 Refer to: Lesson 8-4: Create a Web User Control.

7 Refer to: Lesson 8-2: Create a skin.

8 Refer to: Lesson 8-2: Create a skin.

9 Refer to: Lesson 8-2: Create a skin.

10 Refer to: Lesson 8-10: Enable caching.

11 Refer to: Lesson 8-5: Create an HTTP Handler.

14 Refer to: Lesson 8-8: Create an HTTP Module.

15 Refer to: Lesson 8-8: Create an HTTP Module.

19 Refer to: Lesson 8-9: Implement custom security with an HTTP Module.

Session Nine: Web services and AJAX

> As far as the customer is concerned, the interface is the product.
>
> *Jef Raskin, American computer interface expert (1943-2005)*

Standard ASP.NET pages require the user to post back the page before the page can be updated. This means that the page has to be 'refreshed' in the user's web browser in order for any C# code to run.

AJAX (Asynchronous JavaScript and XML) allows pages to be updated without needing to refresh them. This allows you to create user interfaces that are smoother, faster and easier to use.

Some of the most popular web sites make extensive use of AJAX, giving them a more professional feel than their competitors. Facebook and Google are good examples of streamlined interfaces produced using AJAX.

While many developers use AJAX controls, few really understand how AJAX works. By the end of this session you'll not only be completely confident using ASP.NET's AJAX controls, but will also fully understand the concepts and technology behind AJAX.

Session Objectives

By the end of this session you will be able to:

- Create a web service
- Use a Service Reference to connect to a web service
- Create ScriptManager and UpdatePanel controls
- Add triggers to an UpdatePanel control
- Use the Timer control for scheduled updates
- Create a web method
- Call a web method using JavaScript
- Call a web method that returns a value using JavaScript
- Understand JQuery
- Directly call a web method using JQuery and JSON
- Directly call a web method that returns a value using JQuery

Lesson 9-1: Create a web service

Web services are special components that make your C# methods available on the internet in a standardized way.

Because web services all work to the same standard they can be used by any program, even programs written in an entirely different programming language.

Web services are one of the key components of AJAX, as they allow the JavaScript code on your web pages to interact with the C# code on your web server.

1   Open *StableBase* from your sample files folder.

2   Add a new Web Service to the project, named: **NewsService.asmx**

   1.   Right-click *StableBase* in the *Solution Explorer* and click Add→New Item… from the shortcut menu.

   2.   Click *Web* in the left-hand pane.

   3.   Click *Web Service* in the central pane.

   4.   In the *Name* box, type: **NewsService.asmx**

   5.   Click *Add*.

   Your new *Web Service* is created and opened. A web service is simply a class that extends the *System.Web.Services.WebService* class.

```
public class NewsService : System.Web.Services.WebService
{

    [WebMethod]
    public string HelloWorld()
    {
        return "Hello World";
    }
}
```

   The web service already contains a method named *HelloWorld*.

3   Test your new web service.

   1.   Right-click *NewsService.asmx* in the *Solution Explorer* and click *View in Browser* from the shortcut menu.

   A page appears showing a summary of your web service.

   2.   Click the *HelloWorld* link at the top of the page.

   A summary of the *HelloWorld* method is displayed.

If you are not completing the course incrementally use the sample file: **Lesson 9-1** to begin this lesson.

Sample files with the starting point for each lesson are also provided for all of the other lessons in this session.

note

SOAP and JSON

Web services expose their interface and return information using the SOAP protocol. SOAP stands for Simple Object Access Protocol.

All web services use the SOAP standard, so every web service transmits information in the same way.

ASP.NET web services are also able to return information in both XML and JSON format. JSON stands for JavaScript Object Notation.

When using SOAP to implement AJAX, JSON is a better alternative to XML and has largely replaced it because it is simpler to use with JavaScript. You'll learn more about JSON later in this session.

JSON information is still transmitted using the SOAP protocol in exactly the same way as XML.

important

Web method arguments and return values

Because web methods need to be accessible to any programming language, they can't use any of ASP.NET's advanced classes as arguments or return values.

All major programming languages are compatible with basic variable types such as *int* and *string*, so these can be used freely.

Web methods are able to make use of arrays but not *List* objects or other advanced collection types.

These limitations only apply to the arguments and return values of web methods. You can still use any C# code within the method itself.

HelloWorld

Test

To test the operation using the HTTP POST protocol, click the 'Invoke' button.

[Invoke]

3. Click the *Invoke* button to run the *HelloWorld* method.

    A new browser tab is opened, showing the XML code that was generated by the web service.

    ```xml
    <?xml version="1.0" encoding="utf-8" ?>
    <string xmlns="http://tempuri.org/">Hello World</string>
    ```

    This XML code conforms to the *SOAP* standard (see sidebar).

    Any SOAP-compliant program that calls the *HelloWorld* web method will be able to read this XML code and determine that the method returned a *string* with the value: *Hello World*.

4. Close your web browser and return to Visual Studio.

4   Add a *GetNews* web method to the web service that will extract news items from the database.

Add a new method to the web service using the following code:

[WebMethod]
public string[] GetNews()
{
    using (StableBaseDataContext Data = new StableBaseDataContext())
    {
        return Data.News.Select(News => News.NewsText).ToArray();
    }
}

```csharp
[WebMethod]
public string[] GetNews()
{
    using (StableBaseDataContext Data = new StableBaseDataContext())
    {
        return Data.News.Select(News => News.NewsText).ToArray();
    }
}
```

This method retrieves all records from the *News* table in the project's database, allowing them to be accessed via the web service.

It's important to note that you must always prefix web service methods with *[WebMethod]* in order for them to be available as part of the web service.

5   Build the project.

You must build the project in order to use your web service in the next lesson.

You learned about building projects in: *Lesson 1-4: Build, Rebuild and Clean a project.*

Lesson 9-2: Use a Service Reference to connect to a web service

note

Web References

The Professional version of Visual Studio allows you to create Web References as well as Service References.

Web References are almost identical to Service References, but are slightly simplified.

With the skills covered in this lesson, you should have no problems using Web References.

ASP.NET web applications can connect to any web service over the internet. You can then call their web methods in exactly the same way as any C# method.

In this lesson you'll create a reference to a web service and call its methods. This is sometimes called 'consuming' a web service.

1   Open *StableBase* from your sample files folder.

2   Add a Service Reference linking to the *NewsService.asmx* Web Service.

    1.   Right-click *References* in the *Solution Explorer* and click *Add Service Reference…* from the shortcut menu.

       A dialog appears, prompting you to enter the address of a web service.

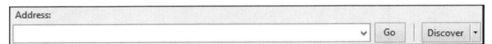

       You could connect to any web service anywhere on the internet by typing its address into the *Address* box and clicking *Go*.

       In this example, however, you're going to connect to a web service that is part of this project.

    2.   Click *Discover*.

       Your web service is discovered and appears in the *Services* box.

    3.   Expand *NewsService.asmx* by clicking the small arrow to the left of its name.

    4.   Expand *NewsService*.

    5.   Click *NewsServiceSoap*.

       The *GetNews* and *HelloWorld* methods are detected and displayed in the *Operations* box.

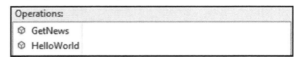

       You worked with these methods in: *Lesson 9-1: Create a web service.*

    6.   In the *Namespace* box, type: **NewsServiceReference**

```
Namespace:
NewsServiceReference
```

7. Click *OK*.

   The web service is now available to your application under the *NewsServiceReference* namespace.

3   Add code to call the *GetNews* method of the web service and display the returned information in the *LabelNews* control on the *Default.aspx* page.

   1. Open the code-behind file of *Default.aspx*.

   2. Add the following code to the *Page_Load* event handler:

      NewsServiceReference.
      NewsServiceSoapClient RemoteWebService = new
      NewsServiceReference.NewsServiceSoapClient();

      ```
      protected void Page_Load(object sender, EventArgs e)
      {
          NewsServiceReference.NewsServiceSoapClient RemoteWebService =
              new NewsServiceReference.NewsServiceSoapClient();
      }
      ```

      The *NewsServiceReference* namespace contains a class named *NewsServiceSoapClient*. This class can be used to call the methods of the web service.

   3. Add the following code on the next line:

      string[] NewsItems =
      RemoteWebService.GetNews().ToArray();

      ```
      NewsServiceReference.NewsServiceSoapClient RemoteWebService =
          new NewsServiceReference.NewsServiceSoapClient();
      string[] NewsItems = RemoteWebService.GetNews().ToArray();
      ```

      This code calls the *GetNews* method of the web service and retrieves its return value as a *string[]* array.

   4. Add the following code on the next line:

      foreach (string Item in NewsItems)
      {
      **   LabelNews.Text += Item + "<br />";**
      }

      ```
      string[] NewsItems = RemoteWebService.GetNews().ToArray();
      foreach (string Item in NewsItems)
      {
          LabelNews.Text += Item + "<br />";
      }
      ```

      This code iterates through the items in the *string[]* array and displays their values in the *LabelNews* control on the page.

4   View *Default.aspx* in your web browser.

   The two news items are retrieved from the web service and displayed on the page.

   ```
   NEWS
   Our horse "Sausage" wins a national competition!
   We welcome a new horse to our stables: "Toffee"
   ```

Lesson 9-3: Create ScriptManager and UpdatePanel controls

The *ScriptManager* and *UpdatePanel* controls enable you to add AJAX functionality to your pages automatically, without needing to write any JavaScript code.

1 Open *StableBase* from your sample files folder.

2 Open *Site.Master* in Design view.

You can see that a *ScriptManager* control is present at the top of the page.

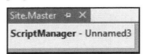

Because a *ScriptManager* control is present on this master page, it will be available on every page that uses this master page. This *ScriptManager* control is automatically included in the default master page for all new ASP.NET 4.5 Web Forms Application projects.

The *ScriptManager* control automatically generates JavaScript code to enable AJAX functionality. A *ScriptManager* control needs to be present on the page in order for the *UpdatePanel* control to work.

The *ScriptManager* control can be found in the *AJAX Extensions* category of the *Toolbox*. See sidebar for information on the other controls in the *AJAX Extensions* category.

3 Open *Default.aspx* in Design view.

This page contains a simple *Label* control that displays news items.

You made this page functional in: *Lesson 9-2: Use a Service Reference to connect to a web service.*

4 Add an *UpdatePanel* control to the page, just before the *LabelNews* control.

The *UpdatePanel* control can be found in the *AJAX Extensions* category of the *Toolbox*.

An *UpdatePanel* control creates an area of the page that can be updated using AJAX without refreshing the page.

5 Set the *ID* property of the new *UpdatePanel* control to: **UpdatePanelNews**

6 Move the *LabelNews* control inside the *UpdatePanel* control.

1. Click the *LabelNews* control to select it.

important

AJAX JavaScript

ASP.NET's AJAX controls use JavaScript code to enable a page to 'post back' without refreshing.

In previous versions of ASP.NET, the JavaScript code that is used for AJAX was automatically generated by the AJAX controls. The problem with this is that web browsers were unable to keep a cached copy of the AJAX JavaScript code, making pages slower to load.

In ASP.NET 4.5 the JavaScript code that is used for AJAX has been placed in separate files, allowing browsers to cache them. These files can be found in the /Scripts/WebForms folder of every new ASP.NET 4.5 Web Forms Application project.

The problem with this new functionality is that you must include these files in order for the AJAX controls to work properly. The AJAX files are automatically included in the *Site.Master* page that is included in every new project, but you may encounter problems if you are trying to upgrade older projects to ASP.NET 4.5.

If you are upgrading an older project, the best approach is probably to create a new project first and then copy the files from the older project into it. This will ensure that all of the new features are supported.

2. Click and drag the *LabelNews* control into the box marking the *UpdatePanel* control.

Now that the *LabelNews* control is inside the *UpdatePanel* control, it is possible for it to be updated without refreshing the page.

7   Add a *Button* control to the *UpdatePanel* control.

8   Set the *ID* property of the new *Button* control to:
ButtonUpdateNews

9   Set the *Text* property of the new *Button* control to:
Update News

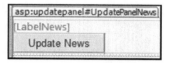

10   Add a *Click* event handler to the new *Button* control.

11   Add the following code to the new event handler:

```
using (StableBaseDataContext Data = new
StableBaseDataContext())
{
    var NewsItems = Data.News.Select(News=>News.NewsText);
    LabelNews.Text = "";
    foreach (string NewsItem in NewsItems)
    {
        LabelNews.Text += NewsItem + "<br />";
    }
}
```

```
protected void ButtonUpdateNews_Click(object sender, EventArgs e)
{
    using (StableBaseDataContext Data = new StableBaseDataContext())
    {
        var NewsItems = Data.News.Select(News=>News.NewsText);
        LabelNews.Text = "";
        foreach (string NewsItem in NewsItems)
        {
            LabelNews.Text += NewsItem + "<br />";
        }
    }
}
```

This code will retrieve the latest news items from the database and display them in the *LabelNews* control.

At present the page uses a web service to display the initial news items and then a post-back to update them when the button is clicked. While the page works correctly, it would be more streamlined if you used AJAX to update the news items without a post-back.

The *UpdatePanel* control can automatically implement AJAX, but it will not be able to do this until you set its *Triggers* property.

You'll add a trigger to your *UpdatePanel* control in the next lesson: *Lesson 9-4: Add triggers to an UpdatePanel control.*

Lesson 9-4: Add triggers to an UpdatePanel control

To refresh the contents of an *UpdatePanel* control, an update must be triggered. This is done by using the *Triggers* property of the *UpdatePanel* control.

1 Open *StableBase* from your sample files folder.

2 Open *Default.aspx* in Design view.

3 Set the *Triggers* property of the *UpdatePanel* control to trigger an update when the *Update News* button is clicked.

1. Select the *UpdatePanelNews* control.

   If you have difficulty doing this, select *UpdatePanelNews* from the drop-down menu in the *Properties* window.

2. Click the *Triggers* property and click its 'browse' button.

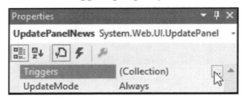

   The *UpdatePanelTrigger Collection Editor* dialog appears.

3. Click the *Add* button to add a new trigger.

4. Set the *ControlID* property of the new trigger to: **ButtonUpdateNews**

5. Set the *EventName* property of the new trigger to: **Click**

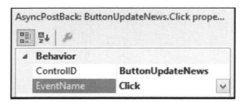

6. Click *OK*.

   Your *UpdatePanel* control is now complete.

   When the *Update News* button is clicked, the entire page will not be refreshed. Only the content inside the *UpdatePanel* control will be updated using AJAX.

4 Test the new AJAX functionality.

1. View *Default.aspx* in your web browser.

2. Open the *NewsAdmin.aspx* page in a new browser tab.

   To do this in Internet Explorer, first move your mouse cursor over *Admin* on the navigation bar. Then right-click *News* and click *Open in New Tab* from the shortcut menu.

---

note

Problems with UpdatePanel controls

In most situations, the *UpdatePanel* and *ScriptManager* controls are all that you will need to add AJAX functionality to your pages.

If your requirements are very complex, however, you may run into problems.

Complex C# code sometimes causes errors when used with the *UpdatePanel* and *ScriptManager* controls.

The code that is created by the *UpdatePanel* and *ScriptManager* controls is also very generic and unlikely to be very efficient.

If your requirements go beyond the limitations of the *UpdatePanel* control, you can write your own JavaScript code.

You'll learn how to do this later in this session.

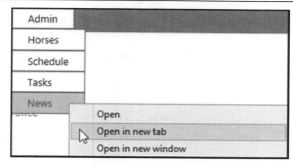

3. In the text box on the *Admin – News* page, type:
    Our news page now has AJAX functionality!

4. Click *Add News Item*.

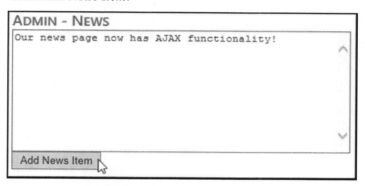

note

Why most programmers regard AJAX as a certain kind of magic

At the end of this lesson you may still have difficulty figuring out how the *ScriptManager, UpdatePanel, LabelNews* and *ButtonUpdateNews* controls work together to implement AJAX using SOAP-enabled methods.

It really is a very complex process and one that most professional programmers I have worked with couldn't even begin to explain to you!

In most situations, the *UpdatePanel* and *ScriptManager* controls are all that you will need to add AJAX functionality to your pages. For this reason, many programmers have given up on understanding the inner workings of AJAX with the justification that "it just works".

Later in this session you will further explore the inner workings of the JavaScript code that ASP.NET uses to implement AJAX. You will then be equipped to completely understand how Visual Studio has turned an incredibly complex coding task into a few clicks of the mouse.

5. Return to your original browser tab (the one containing *Default.aspx*).

6. Click *Update News*.

The news items are updated without refreshing the page!

To achieve this, the *UpdatePanel* and *ScriptManager* controls modified the *ButtonUpdateNews_Click* event handler to emulate a web service by returning SOAP-compliant XML. When the button was clicked, some JavaScript code called the *ButtonUpdateNews_Click* web method and received SOAP XML data. The returned values were then displayed inside the *UpdatePanel* control.

It's important to note that this functionality is completely unrelated to the web service that you created in: *Lesson 9-1: Create a web service*. The *UpdatePanel* and *ScriptManager* controls emulate the functionality of web services, but do not work with existing web services by default.

Later in this session you'll learn how to implement this functionality using your own JavaScript code.

Lesson 9-5: Use the Timer control for scheduled updates

Sometimes you may want part of your page to update itself automatically on a fixed schedule. This can be achieved by using the *Timer* control along with the *UpdatePanel* control.

1   Open *StableBase* from your sample files folder.

2   Open *Default.aspx* in Design view.

3   Delete the *ButtonUpdateNews* control.

   This *Button* control is no longer needed.

   Once the *Timer* control is in place, the news panel will be able to update itself automatically.

4   Add a *Timer* control to the page, inside the *UpdatePanel* control, next to the *LabelNews* control.

   You'll find it in the *AJAX Extensions* category of the *Toolbox*.

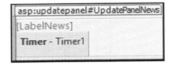

5   Set the *ID* property of the new *Timer* control to: **TimerNews**

6   Set the *Interval* property of the new *Timer* control to: **30000**

   Your *Timer* control will now 'tick' every 30 seconds (30,000 milliseconds).

7   Add a *Tick* event handler to the *Timer* control.

8   Copy all code from the *ButtonUpdateNews_Click* event handler.

   You wrote this code in: *Lesson 9-3: Create ScriptManager and UpdatePanel controls*

9   Paste the code into the *TimerNews_Tick* event handler.

```
protected void TimerNews_Tick(object sender, EventArgs e)
{
    using (StableBaseDataContext Data = new StableBaseDataContext())
    {
        var NewsItems = Data.News.Select(News => News.NewsText);
        LabelNews.Text = "";
        foreach (string NewsItem in NewsItems)
        {
            LabelNews.Text += NewsItem + "<br />";
        }
    }
}
```

Your *Timer* control will now refresh the news items from the database every time it 'ticks' (every 30 seconds).

10   Delete the *ButtonUpdateNews_Click* event handler.

11   Return to *Default.aspx* in Design view.

12 Set the *Triggers* property of the *UpdatePanel* control to use the new *Timer*.

1. Select the *UpdatePanelNews* control.

2. Click the 'browse' button next to the *Triggers* property.

3. Click *Remove* to remove the existing trigger.

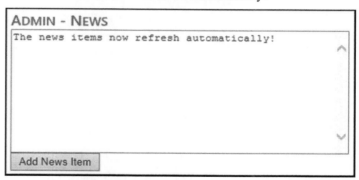

4. Click *Add* to add a new trigger.

5. Set the *ControlID* property of the new trigger to: **TimerNews**

6. Set the *EventName* property of the new trigger to: **Tick**

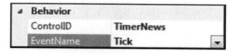

7. Click *OK*.

   Your *UpdatePanel* and *Timer* controls are now complete.

   Every 30 seconds, your *UpdatePanel* control will refresh the news items without refreshing the entire page.

13 Test your new AJAX functionality.

1. View *Default.aspx* in your web browser.

2. Open the Admin➔News page in a new browser tab.

   You did this previously in: *Lesson 9-4: Add triggers to an UpdatePanel control.*

3. In the text box, type:
   The news items now refresh automatically!

   ADMIN - NEWS

   The news items now refresh automatically!

   Add News Item

4. Click *Add News Item*.

5. Return to the browser tab containing *Default.aspx*.

6. Wait for 30 seconds.

   NEWS
   Our horse "Sausage" wins a national competition!
   We welcome a new horse to our stables: "Toffee"
   Our news page now has AJAX functionality!
   The news items now refresh automatically!

   The new item automatically appears without needing to refresh the entire page.

Lesson 9-6: Create a web method

The *UpdatePanel* control automatically changes event handlers into *web methods* that return SOAP-compliant XML. This enables the *ScriptManager* control to generate JavaScript code that uses this XML to display information on the page.

In this lesson you'll manually create a *web method*, which returns SOAP-compliant values. You'll then write JavaScript code to call this method in: *Lesson 9-7: Call a web method using JavaScript*.

1   Open *MegaChat* from your sample files folder.

This project is a chat site. It will use AJAX to display chat messages without needing to refresh the page.

This could be done more easily and simply by using the *UpdatePanel* and *ScriptManager* controls. For learning purposes you will implement this manually to better understand AJAX.

2   Open the code-behind file of *Default.aspx*.

3   Add a new web method using the following code:

```
[WebMethod]
public static void SendMessage(string MessageContent)
{
    using (MegaChatDataContext Data = new
    MegaChatDataContext())
    {
        Message NewMessage = new Message();
        NewMessage.MessageContent = MessageContent;
        NewMessage.MessageTime = DateTime.Now;
        NewMessage.MessageSessionID =
            HttpContext.Current.Session.SessionID;
        NewMessage.MessageUserName =
```

HttpContext.Current.Session["UserName"].ToString();
Data.Messages.InsertOnSubmit(NewMessage);
Data.SubmitChanges();
        }
    }

```
[WebMethod]
public static void SendMessage(string MessageContent)
{
    using (MegaChatDataContext Data = new MegaChatDataContext())
    {
        Message NewMessage = new Message();
        NewMessage.MessageContent = MessageContent;
        NewMessage.MessageTime = DateTime.Now;
        NewMessage.MessageSessionID = HttpContext.Current.Session.SessionID;
        NewMessage.MessageUserName = HttpContext.Current.Session["UserName"].ToString();
        Data.Messages.InsertOnSubmit(NewMessage);
        Data.SubmitChanges();
    }
}
```

This method adds a new chat message to the project's database.

The most important thing about this code is the *[WebMethod]* tag. This tells the method to return its values using the SOAP standard.

You learned about web services and SOAP in: *Lesson 9-1: Create a web service.*

note

Connecting to web services using the ScriptManager control

You can connect your *ScriptManager* control to a web service by setting its *Services* property.

The methods of the selected web service will then be made available in exactly the same way as the web method that you added in this lesson.

4   Open *Site.Master* in Design view.

5   Configure the *ScriptManager* control to enable page methods.

Set the *EnablePageMethods* property of the *ScriptManager* control to: **True**

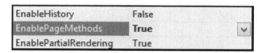

EnableHistory	False	
EnablePageMethods	**True**	⌄
EnablePartialRendering	True	

This tells your *ScriptManager* control to automatically create JavaScript code to enable access to any web methods in the page's code-behind file. This will make it easy to call a web method using your own JavaScript code.

You'll write the JavaScript code to call one of this page's web methods in the next lesson: *Lesson 9-7: Call a web method using JavaScript.*

Amongst other things, the *JQuery* library contains functions that enable advanced AJAX functionality. You'll learn more about *JQuery* in: *Lesson 9-9: Understand JQuery.*

Using the *JQuery* library, it's possible to call a web method without needing a *ScriptManager* control. You'll do this in: *Lesson 9-10: Directly call a web method using JQuery.*

Lesson 9-7: Call a web method using JavaScript

As this course focuses on C# code, your knowledge of JavaScript may be quite limited. JavaScript uses very similar logic and syntax to C# code, so you should be able to understand it with very little difficulty.

This course will not cover advanced JavaScript, but you will learn everything that you need to call web methods and enable AJAX features.

1   Open *MegaChat* from your sample files folder.

2   Open *Default.aspx* in Source view.

3   Add a new JavaScript *function* to the code, named: **SendMessage**

1.   Scroll down until you see the *<script type="text/javascript">* tag.

```
<script type="text/javascript">
    var MessageTimer;
    var ConnectionCount = 0;
    var UserName;
```

2.   Add the following code inside the *<script>* tag after: *var UserName;*

function SendMessage(message) { }

```
var UserName;

function SendMessage(message) {

}
```

This code defines a new JavaScript *function* named *SendMessage* with an argument named: *message*. JavaScript functions are almost identical to C# methods.

4   Add code to the *SendMessage* JavaScript function to call the *SendMessage* web method.

Add the following code to the *SendMessage* function:

PageMethods.SendMessage(message);

```
function SendMessage(message) {
    PageMethods.SendMessage(message);
}
```

This code is all that you need to call the *SendMessage* web method (which happens to have the same name as the JavaScript function) using JavaScript. This was possible because the *ScriptManager* control automatically generated JavaScript code for the *PageMethods* object (see sidebar).

The *SendMessage* web method writes a new row into the *MegaChat* project's database. You created the *SendMessage* web method in: *Lesson 9-6: Create a web method.*

5   Add code to the *SendMessage* JavaScript function to also display the message on the screen.

Add the following code on the next line of the function:

**DisplayMessage('<div style="color: blue"><b>'
+ UserName + '</b>: ' + message + '</div>');**

```
function SendMessage(message) {
    PageMethods.SendMessage(message);
    DisplayMessage('<div style="color: blue"><b>'
    + UserName + '</b>: ' + message + '</div>');
}
```

This calls this page's *DisplayMessage* JavaScript function, which displays the message inside the *<div>* tags with the *id*: *ChatBox*

6 Examine the JavaScript event handler that calls the *SendMessage* function.

Find the following code:

```
$('#TextAreaInput').keydown(function (event) {
    if (event.keyCode == 13 & !event.shiftKey) {
        SendMessage($('#TextAreaInput').val());
        $('#TextAreaInput').val("");
        event.preventDefault();
        return false;
    }
    else return true;
});
```

This code uses *JQuery* to call the *SendMessage* function when the user presses the **<Enter>** key in the HTML *TextArea* control called *TextAreaInput*. *TextAreaInput* is the area at the bottom of the page where the user will type in chat messages. See sidebar for a discussion of how this JavaScript code works.

7 Test your code.

1. Open the code-behind file of *Default.aspx*.

2. Set a breakpoint at the start of the *SendMessage* method.

```
public static void SendMessage(string MessageContent)
{
    using (MegaChatDataContext Data = new MegaChatData
    {
        Message NewMessage = new Message();
        NewMessage.MessageContent = MessageContent;
```

3. Click Debug→Start Debugging.

4. Enter a username and press **<Enter>**.

5. In the text box at the bottom of the screen, type:
Test message

6. Press **<Enter>**.

The breakpoint is encountered and you are returned to Visual Studio (switch back to Visual Studio manually if not).

7. Hover the mouse cursor over the *MessageContent* argument to check its value.

```
(string MessageContent)
    ⚙ MessageContent  🔍 ▾ "Test message" 🔄
```

The message was successfully passed from the JavaScript function (running in the user's browser) to your C# method (running on the web server) via AJAX without refreshing the page.

---

note

How the keydown JavaScript event handler code works

This code makes extensive use of the *JQuery* library.

Don't worry if you cannot completely understand the code at this stage because you'll learn more about JQuery in: *Lesson 9-9: Understand JQuery.*

Having said this, here's an overview of how the code works:

$('#TextAreaInput').keydown(function (event) {

This creates an event handler that will run whenever the user presses a key within the *TextAreaInput* control at the bottom of the page.

This event handler is only interested in the **<Enter>** key, so the next line checks which key the user pressed:

if (event.keyCode == 13 & !event.shiftKey) {

event.keyCode contains a code indicating which key was pressed. Key code number 13 indicates the **<Enter>** key. Notice also that this *if* statement checks to make sure that the **<Shift>** key is not held down.

If the **<Enter>** key is pressed, the contents of the *TextAreaInput* control are sent to your *SendMessage* function:

SendMessage($('#TextAreaInput').val());

The *val()* function retrieves the text that the user typed into *TextAreaInput*.

Next, the *val* function is used again to clear the contents of the *TextAreaInput* control:

$('#TextAreaInput').val("");

Ordinarily, the page posts back when the user presses the **<Enter>** key. To prevent this from happening, the following code is used:

event.preventDefault();

Lesson 9-8: Call a web method that returns a value using JavaScript

You learned how to use JavaScript to call a simple web method without a return value in the previous lesson: *Lesson 9-7: Call a web method using JavaScript*.

In order to call a web method that returns a value, you need to use a slightly different technique.

In this lesson you'll use JavaScript code to call the *GetMessages* web method (from the C# code-behind file of *Default.aspx*) and display its return value.

1　Open *MegaChat* from your sample files folder.

2　Open *Default.aspx* in Source view.

3　Examine the *GetMessages* JavaScript function.

    1.　Find the *GetMessages* function in the code.

```
function GetMessages() {

}
```

    This function does not yet contain any code.

    You're going to add code to this function to call the *GetMessages* web method.

    2.　Examine the *ConnectUser* function.

```
function ConnectUser(username) {
    PageMethods.Connect(username, function () {
        UserName = username;
        $('#ScreenMask').hide();
        $('#WelcomePanel').remove();
        ReceiveMessage("<div><b>Hi " + username + " and wel
        $(window).bind('beforeunload', function () { return
        MessageTimer = setInterval("GetMessages()", 1000);
    });
}
```

    At the bottom of this function, you can see the following code:

    MessageTimer = setInterval("GetMessages()", 1000);

    This JavaScript code creates a JavaScript timer that calls the *GetMessages* function every second (1000 milliseconds).

4　Add code to the *GetMessages* function to call the *GetMessages* web method.

    Add the following code to the *GetMessages* function:

    PageMethods.GetMessages(function (response) {

    });

note

JavaScript syntax when calling a web method that returns a value

In this lesson it appears as though you have added an argument when calling the *GetMessages* web method using JavaScript.

The *function* that you added isn't actually an argument. It is in fact a JavaScript function that will run when the *GetMessages* web method finishes and returns a value.

Without this function, your JavaScript code would have no way of knowing when the *GetMessages* web method was finished.

When a web method has both arguments and a return value, you need to specify the arguments before the function. You can see this done in the *ConnectUser* JavaScript function.

```
function GetMessages() {
    PageMethods.GetMessages(function (response) {

    });
}
```

After using C# you may initially find this syntax confusing. The code is very similar to the code that you created in: *Lesson 9-7: Call a web method using JavaScript*. The difference is that you have created a nested *function* within the arguments of the call to the *GetMessages* web method (see sidebar for a more detailed explanation).

This function will run when the *GetMessages* web method returns its value. The *response* object will retrieve the value that was returned by the method.

5 **Add code to display the returned data using the *DisplayMessage* function.**

Add the following code inside the nested function:

DisplayMessage(response);

```
function GetMessages() {
    PageMethods.GetMessages(function (response) {
        DisplayMessage(response);
    });
}
```

The *DisplayMessage* function displays the value that was returned from the *GetMessages* web method inside the *ChatBox* *<div>* tag.

6 **Test your code.**

1. View *Default.aspx* in your web browser and enter a user name.

2. Open another web browser window, copy the URL from the first window and enter a different user name when the application starts.

3. Position the browser windows side-by-side on your screen and chat between them:

Please enter a username:
Simon

Hi Mike and welcome to MegaChat!
Simon: Hello Mike, how are you today?
Mike: I'm fine, how are you Simon?

Hi Simon and welcome to MegaChat!
Mike: Mike signed in.
Simon: Hello Mike, how are you today?
Mike: I'm fine, how are you Simon?

The test messages are displayed by your JavaScript code without refreshing the page.

Lesson 9-9: Understand JQuery

JQuery is a library of JavaScript functions that massively simplifies many JavaScript techniques. *JQuery* is automatically included in all new ASP.NET Web Forms Application projects.

In this lesson you'll explore some commonly used features of *JQuery*.

1   Open *MegaChat* from your sample files folder.

2   Examine the JQuery files.

Expand the *Scripts* folder in the *Solution Explorer* window.

There are several copies of *JQuery* in this folder:

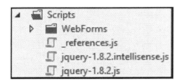

jquery-1.8.2.intellisense.js is a version of *JQuery* that has been commented to support Visual Studio IntelliSense. This is automatically used by Visual Studio to provide IntelliSense for *JQuery*.

jquery-1.8.2.js is the standard version of *JQuery*. This is the version that you will use for most purposes.

jquery-1.8.2.min.js is the same as the standard version but with all of the line breaks and comments removed. This makes the file smaller, but harder to work with when debugging.

The *jquery-1.8.2.js* file should be used for development purposes and the *jquery-1.8.2.min.js* file should be used for the final release.

3   Open *Site.Master* in Source view.

4   View the reference to *JQuery*.

Within the *ScriptManager* control, you can see a reference to *jquery*. The *ScriptManager* control attaches the JQuery files to the page using ASP.NET 4.5's new script bundling features. These are covered in Session 12 of the Essential Skills course in this series.

```
<asp:ScriptReference Name="MsAjaxBundle" />
<asp:ScriptReference Name="jquery" />
<asp:ScriptReference Name="jquery.ui.combined" />
```

This code is automatically included in all new ASP.NET 4.5 Web Forms Application projects, so JQuery is available on all pages that use the default master page.

If you don't want to use script bundling, you can include the JQuery files by using an ordinary *<script>* tag.

5   Add a JQuery function to *Default.aspx* that will run when the page loads.

1.   Open *Default.aspx* in *Source* view.

2.   Scroll down to the *<script type="text/javascript">* tag.

3.   Add the following code inside the *<script>* tag:

$(document).ready(function () {

});

note

jquery-ui-1.8.24.js

Along with the ordinary *jquery* files, you will see some files named *jquery-ui*.

JQuery UI is a library of JavaScript user interface improvements, and is separate from the 'standard' JQuery library.

JQuery UI is included with every new project, but isn't required for any of the techniques that you will learn in this course.

```
var UserName;

$(document).ready(function () {

});
```

All *JQuery* functions begin with a $ character.

This code uses the JQuery *ready* method to create a function that will run as soon as the page (*document*) has fully loaded.

This is extremely difficult to do without *JQuery* as each web browser requires different JavaScript code to accomplish this.

6   Use the *hide* and *fadeIn* methods of *JQuery* to make the *WelcomePanel* element fade in when the page loads.

1.   Add the following code inside the *$(document).ready* function:

$('#WelcomePanel').hide();

```
$(document).ready(function () {
    $('#WelcomePanel').hide();
});
```

This *JQuery* command will simply hide the *WelcomePanel* <div> tag pair from view.

```
<div id="WelcomePanel" style="padding: 10px; left: 50%; margin-left
    Please enter a username:
    <br />
    <input id="TextUserName" style="background: none repeat scroll
</div>
```

The *WelcomePanel* <div> tags contain the input control that asks the user to enter a username.

2.   Add the following code on the next line of the JQuery function:

$('#WelcomePanel').fadeIn(1000);

```
$(document).ready(function () {
    $('#WelcomePanel').hide();
    $('#WelcomePanel').fadeIn(1000);
});
```

The *fadeIn* JQuery method makes the hidden *WelcomePanel* <div> tag pair slowly fade into view.

The number *1000* indicates that the animation will last 1000 milliseconds (1 second). By changing this number you can alter the speed of the fade effect.

7   Test your code.

View *Default.aspx* in your web browser.

The *WelcomePanel* tag slowly fades into view rather than appearing instantly.

Lesson 9-10: Directly call a web method using JQuery and JSON

To be a complete AJAX expert, you should be capable of writing code to interface with web services and web methods without any of ASP.NET's AJAX controls.

In this lesson you'll use the *ajax* function of *JQuery* to call a web method directly, without any automation. It is, however, unlikely that you will ever want to do this when working in the Visual Studio environment.

The technique that you will learn in this lesson might be useful when working outside the Visual Studio environment, for example, when you need to work with PHP or JSP web applications.

This lesson also introduces JSON (JavaScript Object Notation). JSON syntax provides a way to define objects within JavaScript.

The *ajax* JQuery function demands an object for its argument which requires the use of JSON.

1 Open *MegaChat* from your sample files folder.

2 Open *Default.aspx* in Source view.

3 Add code to the *SendMessage* function to call the *SendMessage* web method directly.

> The *SendMessage* function currently calls the *SendMessage* web method by using the *PageMethods* object that is automatically generated by the *ScriptManager* control (see: *Lesson 9-7: Call a web method using JavaScript*).
>
> 1. Remove the following code from the *SendMessage* function:
>
> *PageMethods.SendMessage(message);*
>
> ```
> function SendMessage(message) {
>     DisplayMessage('<div style="color: blue"><b>'
>     + UserName + '</b>: ' + message + '</div>');
> }
> ```
>
> 2. Add the following code to the start of the *SendMessage* function:
>
> **$.ajax();**
>
> ```
> function SendMessage(message) {
>     $.ajax(
>
>     );
>     DisplayMessage('<div style="color: blue"><b>'
>     + UserName + '</b>: ' + message + '</div>');
> }
> ```
>
> 3. Add the following code inside the *$.ajax* function:
>
> **{ type: "POST",**
> **url: "Default.aspx/SendMessage",**
> **contentType: "application/json",**
> **dataType: "json", }**

```
$.ajax({
    type: "POST",
    url: "Default.aspx/SendMessage",
    contentType: "application/json",
    dataType: "json",
});
```

This is JSON code that creates an object with four properties.

The *url* property tells the *ajax* function to send a request to *Default.aspx/SendMessage*. This is the syntax that is needed to address a web method on a specific web page (the *SendMessage* web method on *Default.aspx*).

Because the request is sent using JavaScript, the page doesn't need to refresh in order to send the request. Instead, the request and response process will be handled by your JavaScript code using AJAX.

4. Add the following code on the next line (inside the curly brackets):

data: "{ MessageContent: '" + message + "'}"

```
$.ajax({
    type: "POST",
    url: "Default.aspx/SendMessage",
    contentType: "application/json",
    dataType: "json",
    data: "{ MessageContent: '" + message + "'}"
});
```

The *data* property uses JSON to create an object with a single *MessageContent* property (the argument that is required by the *SendMessage* web method).

The *data* property uses the JSON standard. Note that JSON properties are always named so they do not have to be specified in any particular order.

4 Test your code.

1. Click Debug→Start Debugging.

2. Enter a username and press **<Enter>**.

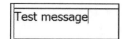

3. In the text box at the bottom of the screen, type:
Test message

Test message

4. Press **<Enter>**.

The breakpoint is encountered and you are returned to Visual Studio.

You added a breakpoint to the *SendMessage* web method in: *Lesson 9-7: Call a web method using JavaScript*.

5. Check the value of the *MessageContent* object.

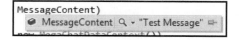

Your *JQuery* code sent the value to the web method correctly.

This code will work even without a *ScriptManager* control on the page.

You can use exactly the same technique to send a request to any web service or web method by simply changing the *url:* property.

Lesson 9-11: Directly call a web method that returns a value using JQuery

You learned how to use *JQuery* to call simple web services and web methods in: *Lesson 9-10: Directly call a web method using JQuery.*

You need to use a slightly different technique to call a web method that returns a value.

1   Open *MegaChat* from your sample files folder.

2   Open *Default.aspx* in Source view.

3   Remove all code from the *GetMessages* function.

```
function GetMessages() {

}
```

You're going to replace this code with a direct call to the *GetMessages* web method.

4   Add code to directly call the *GetMessages* web method.

Add the following code to the *GetMessages* function:

$.ajax({
   type: "POST",
   url: "Default.aspx/GetMessages",
   contentType: "application/json",
});

This is the same as the code that you used in: *Lesson 9-10: Directly call a web method using JQuery and JSON.*

This code will call the *GetMessages* web method, but you still need a way to retrieve the return value after the method has executed.

5   Add code to get the return value from the *GetMessages* method.

Add the following code inside the *$.ajax* function call (inside the curly brackets):

success: function(ValueReturned) {
   DisplayMessage(ValueReturned.d);
},

```
$.ajax({
    type: "POST",
    url: "Default.aspx/GetMessages",
    contentType: "application/json",
    success: function(ValueReturned) {
        DisplayMessage(ValueReturned.d);
    },
});
```

The *success* property defines a function that will run only if the method succeeds. ASP.NET web methods return an object with a single property called *d*, which contains the value returned.

You use this property to call the *DisplayMessage* JavaScript function, which displays the return value on the page.

6   Add code to handle errors.

Add the following code to the *$.ajax* function call:

error: function() {
   alert("An error occurred.");
   clearInterval(MessageTimer);
}

```
success: function (ValueReturned) {
   DisplayMessage(ValueReturned.d);
},
error: function () {
   alert("An error occurred.");
   clearInterval(MessageTimer);
}
```

The *error* property defines a function that will run if the web method returns an error.

This code simply displays an error message and stops the chat window from being updated.

The *clearInterval* JavaScript function stops the timer that checks for new chat messages.

7   Test your code.

1. View *Default.aspx* in your web browser and enter a user name.

2. Open a new web browser window, copy the URL from the first window and enter a different user name when the application starts.

3. Position the browser windows side-by-side on your screen and chat between them:

The test messages are displayed by your JavaScript code without refreshing the page.

You now have all of the skills that you need to implement AJAX features in your applications, either by using controls or JavaScript code.

Using AJAX, you can make your interfaces faster, more efficient and easier to use.

Session 9: Exercise

1   Open *Exercise9* from your sample files folder.

2   Add a new web service to the project, named: **TestService.asmx**

3   Build the project.

4   Add a new Service Reference to the project, connecting to *TestService.asmx*. Name it: **TestServiceReference**

5   Open *Time.aspx* in Design view.

6   Add an *UpdatePanel* control to the page and name it: **UpdatePanelTime**

7   Add a *Label* control inside the *UpdatePanel* control and name it: **LabelTime**

8   Add a *Timer* control inside the *UpdatePanel* control and name it: **TimerTime**

9   Set the *Interval* property of the new *Timer* control to: **1000**

10   Set the *Triggers* property of the *UpdatePanel* control to refresh when the *Tick* event of the *TimerTime* control is fired.

11   Add a *Tick* event handler to the new *Timer* control with the following code:

     LabelTime.Text = GetTime();

12   Open the code-behind file of *TimeManual.aspx* and make the *GetTime* method into a web method.

13   Open *Site.Master* in Design view and configure the *ScriptManager* control to enable Page Methods.

14   Open *TimeManual.aspx* in *Source* view and add code to the *GetTime* function to call the *GetTime* web method and display the resulting value in the *LabelTime* <div> tag.

     You can change the value in *LabelTime* by using the following code:

     $('#LabelTime').html(ValueToSet);

15   Modify your code to directly call the *GetTime* web method using the JQuery *$.ajax* function.

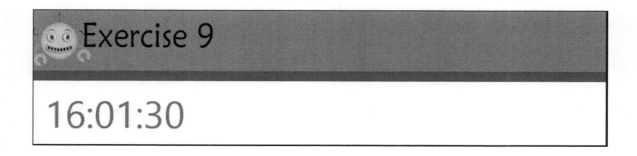

Exercise9 - Start   Exercise9 - End

If you need help slide the page to the left

Session 9: Exercise Answers

These are the four questions that students find the most difficult to answer:

Q 15	Q 14	Q 12	Q 4

Use the following code:
 	
``js
function GetTime() {
    $.ajax({
        type: "POST",
        url: "TimeManual.aspx/
GetTime",
        contentType:
"application/json",
        success: function(data) {
            $('#LabelTime').
            html(data.d);
        }
    });
}
``
 	
This was covered in: *Lesson 9-11: Directly call a web method that returns a value using JQuery.*
	Use the following code:
	
	``js
	function GetTime() {
	    PageMethods.
	    GetTime
	    (function (response) {
	        $('#LabelTime')
	        .html(response);
	    });
	}
	``
	
	This was covered in: *Lesson 9-8: Call a web method that returns a value using JavaScript.*
		Add the following code just above the *GetTime* method:
		
		[WebMethod]
		
		This was covered in: *Lesson 9-6: Create a web method.*
			1. Right-click *References* in the *Solution Explorer* and click *Add Service Reference...* from the shortcut menu.
			
			2. Click *Discover*.
			
			3. In the *Namespace* box, type:
			
			TestServiceReference
			
			4. Click *OK*.
			
			This was covered in: *Lesson 9-2: Use a Service Reference to connect to a web service.*

If you have difficulty with the other questions, here are the lessons that cover the relevant skills:

1   Refer to: Essential Skills Session 1.

2   Refer to: Lesson 9-1: Create a web service.

3   Refer to: Lesson 1-4: Build, Rebuild and Clean a project.

5   Refer to: Essential Skills Session 1.

6   Refer to: Lesson 9-3: Create ScriptManager and UpdatePanel controls.

7   Refer to: Lesson 9-3: Create ScriptManager and UpdatePanel controls.

8   Refer to: Lesson 9-5: Use the Timer control for scheduled updates.

9   Refer to: Lesson 9-5: Use the Timer control for scheduled updates.

10   Refer to: Lesson 9-5: Use the Timer control for scheduled updates.

11   Refer to: Lesson 9-5: Use the Timer control for scheduled updates.

13   Refer to: Lesson 9-6: Create a web method.

Session Ten: Advanced data access techniques

10

> Data is a precious thing and will last longer than the systems themselves.
>
> *Tim Berners-Lee, English computer scientist (born 1955)*

In this session you'll learn some of the more advanced techniques for accessing data from a database.

Some of the techniques that are covered in this session will be much easier to understand if you have an understanding of SQL (Structured Query Language).

As well as advanced database techniques, this session also teaches you how to read and write data from XML and CSV files.

Session Objectives

By the end of this session you will be able to:

- Use the Average LINQ method
- Use LINQ anonymous types
- Use the Sum and GroupBy LINQ methods
- Send SQL code through LINQ
- Connect to a database using the SqlClient namespace
- Run a SQL query using the SqlClient namespace
- Write data to a CSV file
- Read data from a CSV file
- Write data to an XML file
- Read data from an XML file
- Understand SQL injection attacks

Lesson 10-1: Use the Average LINQ method

The basics of accessing databases using LINQ are covered in Session 10 of the *Essential Skills* course.

In this lesson you'll learn how to use the *Average* LINQ method to carry out a complex database query.

1   Open *MarketTrader* from your sample files folder.

2   Open *MarketAverage.aspx* in Design view.

When complete, this page will allow the user to get the average value of a market across a range of dates.

To make this possible, you'll need to use the *Average* LINQ method.

3   Open the code-behind file of *MarketAverage.aspx*.

4   Add code to the *ButtonGetAverageValue_Click* event handler to retrieve records from the *Quote* table for the selected market and date range.

Use the following code:

```
using (MarketTraderDataContext Data =
new MarketTraderDataContext())
{
    int MarketID = Convert.ToInt32
     (DropDownListMarket.SelectedValue);
    DateTime StartDate = CalendarDateFrom.SelectedDate;
    DateTime FinishDate = CalendarDateTo.SelectedDate;
    var Result = Data.Quotes.Where(Quote =>
                Quote.MarketID == MarketID
            && Quote.QuoteDate >= StartDate
            && Quote.QuoteDate <= FinishDate);
}
```

If you are not completing the course incrementally use the sample file: **Lesson 10-1** to begin this lesson.

Sample files with the starting point for each lesson are also provided for all of the other lessons in this session.

```
protected void ButtonGetAverageValue_Click(object sender, EventArgs e)
{
    PanelParameters.Visible = false;
    PanelResults.Visible = true;
    using (MarketTraderDataContext Data = new MarketTraderDataContext())
    {
        int MarketID = Convert.ToInt32(DropDownListMarket.SelectedValue);
        DateTime StartDate = CalendarDateFrom.SelectedDate;
        DateTime FinishDate = CalendarDateTo.SelectedDate;
        var Result = Data.Quotes.Where(Quote =>
                            Quote.MarketID == MarketID
                        && Quote.QuoteDate >= StartDate
                        && Quote.QuoteDate <= FinishDate);
    }
}
```

note

Other LINQ aggregate methods

LINQ contains several other aggregate methods. These include:

Sum
Adds together the values of all records.

Count
Counts the number of records.

Max
Gets the highest value.

Min
Gets the lowest value.

First
Gets the first value.

If you're familiar with the SQL language, you'll recognize these as the counterparts to SQL functions.

note

An alternative technique

You could have calculated the average value using a C# *foreach* loop, but it is almost always better to have SQL Server perform the calculation for you.

There are two reasons why this is better:

1. SQL databases have all kinds of optimizations designed to speed up calculations.

2. If the calculation is done on a remote SQL server, the server only has to return a single record so network traffic is greatly reduced.

If you don't understand this code, refer to Session 10 of the *Essential Skills* course in this series.

5   Add code to retrieve the average value of the *QuoteValue* field from the *Quote* database table.

Add the following code on the next line:

**decimal AverageQuoteValue =
Result.Average(Quote => Quote.QuoteValue);**

```
                    && Quote.QuoteDate >= StartDate
                    && Quote.QuoteDate <= FinishDate);
decimal AverageQuoteValue = Result.Average(Quote => Quote.QuoteValue);
```

The *Average* LINQ method allows you to get a single average value from all of the records that were retrieved from the database.

The LINQ data context also contains some other useful aggregate methods (see sidebar). You'll learn more about some of these in: *Lesson 10-3: Use the Sum and GroupBy LINQ methods.*

You could be forgiven for thinking that the average value will be calculated after the results are returned by the database. In fact, the Visual Studio compiler is extremely intelligent and "looks ahead" in your code to send a single SQL query to the database that only returns the average value.

6   Add code to display the result on the page.

Add the following code on the next line (within the *using* statement):

LabelAverageValue.Text = AverageQuoteValue.ToString("0.00");

```
decimal AverageQuoteValue = Result.Average(Quote => Quote.QuoteValue);
LabelAverageValue.Text = AverageQuoteValue.ToString("0.00");
```

7   Test your code.

1. View *MarketAverage.aspx* in your web browser.

2. Click *Get Average Value*.

   The average value of the quotes for the selected period is displayed.

Lesson 10-2: Use LINQ anonymous types

All of the LINQ code that you've worked with so far has returned values in the form of objects that return all columns (also called fields) from each row in a database table.

Sometimes you don't need to return all of the columns for each record. By using *anonymous types*, you can create dynamic class structures that contain only the values you require.

In this lesson you'll use *anonymous types* to improve the efficiency of a LINQ query.

1   Open *SecFile* from your sample files folder.

2   Open *Files.aspx* in Design view.

> The *GridView* control on this page displays the names of each of the files stored in the *SecureFile* database table and allows them to be viewed when the user clicks *View File*.

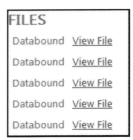

> The only values that this *GridView* control requires are the *SecureFileID* and *SecureFileName* from the *SecureFile* database table.

3   Examine the *SecureFile* database table.

1. Switch to the *Database Explorer* window in the right-hand pane.

2. Expand *SecFileConnectionString*.

3. Expand *Tables*.

4. Expand *SecureFile*.

> You can see that the *SecureFile* table contains three columns: *SecureFileID, SecureFileName* and *SecureFileBinary*.

5. Switch back to the *Solution Explorer* window.

4   Open the code-behind file of *Files.aspx*.

5   Examine the existing query in the *Page_Load* event handler.

```
using (SecFileDataContext Data = new SecFileDataContext())
{
    var Files = Data.SecureFiles;
    GridViewSecureFile.DataSource = Files;
    GridViewSecureFile.DataBind();
}
```

The existing code will return all of the values from the *SecureFile* table. This includes the binary data that is stored in the *SecureFileBinary* field.

The binary data isn't needed by the *GridView* control, so it's inefficient and wasteful to make the database retrieve it, especially since a large file could contain a huge amount of binary data.

6 Use an anonymous type to retrieve only the *SecureFileID* and *SecureFileName* columns.

Change the *var Files = Data.SecureFiles;* line to the following:

*var Files = Data.SecureFiles.***Select(SecureFile =>
new { SecureFile.SecureFileID, SecureFile.SecureFileName});**

```
using (SecFileDataContext Data = new SecFileDataContext())
{
    var Files = Data.SecureFiles.Select(SecureFile =>
        new { SecureFile.SecureFileID, SecureFile.SecureFileName});
    GridViewSecureFile.DataSource = Files;
    GridViewSecureFile.DataBind();
}
```

By calling the *Select* method and using the *new* keyword, you have created an *anonymous type*.

An *anonymous type* is a class that is created dynamically by LINQ. The class that is created by this code will contain two properties corresponding to the *SecureFileID* and *SecureFileName* database columns.

Anonymous types are similar to *Tuple* objects, as they create custom class structures without needing to define a class. You learned about *Tuples* in: *Lesson 2-1: Use the Tuple class.*

The *SecureFileBinary* field isn't just hidden. With this code it will never be retrieved from the database, saving valuable memory and processing power.

7 Test your code.

View *Files.aspx* in your web browser (log in with your Windows username and password if prompted).

FILES

MailModule.XML   View File

The *MailModule.XML* file name is retrieved from the database correctly. The page is still functional, but the database query is now more efficient.

Anonymous types allow you to do more than just specify the columns you need. By pairing them with LINQ aggregate methods you can use them to perform complex database queries.

You'll use an anonymous type with the *Sum* method in the next lesson: *Lesson 10-3: Use the Sum and GroupBy LINQ methods.*

---

important

Anonymous types and stored procedures

Although anonymous types add flexibility to LINQ queries, they also add complexity.

Very complex database queries should ideally be handled by stored procedures rather than LINQ code.

Stored procedures are covered in Session 10 of the *Essential Skills* course.

If you encounter a situation where anonymous types are used to implement complex queries, it is usually better to use a stored procedure instead of LINQ code.

---

note

Advanced LINQ code can confuse even expert programmers

The advanced LINQ syntax that is used in this lesson can be very confusing to work with.

Most programmers would avoid using LINQ to create advanced database queries because it makes their code harder to understand.

In circumstances where complex database queries are needed, it is usually better for a stored procedure to be created using the SQL language.

Most ASP.NET programmers do not have advanced SQL skills. Stored procedures are usually created by a specialized team member called a DBA (Database Administrator).

Lesson 10-3: Use the Sum and GroupBy LINQ methods

In this lesson you'll calculate the total balance of every account in the *Account* database table and group the results by currency. To do this, you'll use the *GroupBy* method, an *anonymous type* and the *Sum* method.

You learned about *anonymous types* in: *Lesson 10-2: Use LINQ anonymous types.*

1 Open *MarketTrader* from your sample files folder.

2 Open the code-behind file of *AccountBalance.aspx*.

3 Add code to the *Page_Load* event handler to retrieve all records from the *Account* database table.

Use the following code:

**using (MarketTraderDataContext Data =
new MarketTraderDataContext())
{
    var Result = Data.Accounts;
    GridViewAccountBalances.DataSource = Result;
    GridViewAccountBalances.DataBind();
}**

```
protected void Page_Load(object sender, EventArgs e)
{
    using (MarketTraderDataContext Data = new MarketTraderDataContext())
    {
        var Result = Data.Accounts;
        GridViewAccountBalances.DataSource = Result;
        GridViewAccountBalances.DataBind();
    }
}
```

This query will return every row in the *Accounts* table. If you view *AccountBalance.aspx* in your web browser you will see:

AccountID	CurrencyID	AccountBalance
1	1	250000.0000
2	1	900000.0000

4 Use the *GroupBy* LINQ method to group the results by currency.

Add the following code to the end of the LINQ query:

.GroupBy(Account => Account.Currency.CurrencyName);

```
var Result = Data.Accounts
    .GroupBy(Account => Account.Currency.CurrencyName);
GridViewAccountBalances.DataSource = Result;
GridViewAccountBalances.DataBind();
```

This code tells LINQ that you want to group the results by the *CurrencyName,* but it will not return any values. You will need to use an *anonymous type* in order to return any results.

5 Add an anonymous type to return the names of each group.

Add the following code to the end of the LINQ query:

.Select(Group => new { Group.Key });

```
var Result = Data.Accounts
    .GroupBy(Account => Account.Currency.CurrencyName)
    .Select(Group => new { Group.Key });
GridViewAccountBalances.DataSource = Result;
GridViewAccountBalances.DataBind();
```

This code is a little different to the code that you created in: *Lesson 10-2: Use LINQ anonymous types.*

The value that you specified in the *GroupBy* method is considered to be the *Key* value that the groups are organized into. For this reason, LINQ places the group names in the *Group.Key* property.

If you view *AccountBalance.aspx* in your web browser you will see:

6   Add an anonymous type to sum the values of each group.

Add the following code immediately after *Group.Key*:

**, TotalBalance =
Group.Sum(Account => Account.AccountBalance)**

```
.Select(Group =>
new { Group.Key,
    TotalBalance = Group.Sum(Account => Account.AccountBalance)
    });
```

The *Sum* method adds together the *AccountBalance* values for each group heading (each currency name).

When using aggregate functions (such as *Sum*) within an anonymous type, you must give a name to the resulting value.

You named the result of the *Sum* method by using the code: *TotalBalance =*

7   Test your code.

View *AccountBalance.aspx* in your web browser.

TOTAL ACCOUNT BALANCES BY CURRENCY	
Key	**TotalBalance**
Australian Dollar	315000.0000
Canadian Dollar	321000.0000
Great Britain Pound	1135000.0000
Japanese Yen	1299000000.0000
US Dollar	1150000.0000

Your database query is executed and the total account balances are displayed for each currency. Notice that the summed column is named *TotalBalance* as specified in your code.

As with a lot of LINQ code that requires *anonymous types*, it would be preferable (and easier) to do this using a stored procedure (see: *Lesson 10-2: Use LINQ anonymous types – sidebar*).

Lesson 10-4: Send SQL code through LINQ

As you know, the LINQ data context class automatically generates SQL code to retrieve information from the database.

Using the LINQ data context class, it's also possible to send SQL code directly to the database.

The SQL code that you'll use in this lesson is very simple and won't be difficult to understand. A SQL expert can extract absolutely any data from a database using SQL code.

1   Open *StableBase* from your sample files folder.

2   Open the code-behind file of *Default.aspx*.

3   Examine the LINQ query in the *TimerNews_Tick* event handler.

```
protected void TimerNews_Tick(object sender, EventArgs e)
{
    using (StableBaseDataContext Data = new StableBaseDataContext())
    {
        var NewsItems = Data.News.Select(News => News.NewsText);
        LabelNews.Text = "";
        foreach (string NewsItem in NewsItems)
        {
            LabelNews.Text += NewsItem + "<br />";
        }
    }
}
```

This event handler updates the news items on the page.

You wrote this code in: *Lesson 9-5: Use the Timer control for scheduled updates.*

In this lesson, you'll replace the LINQ query with manually written SQL code.

4   Replace the LINQ query with SQL code.

Replace the following line of code:

var NewsItems = Data.News.Select(News => News.NewsText);

…with:

**var NewsItems = Data.ExecuteQuery\<string\>(
"SELECT NewsText FROM News");**

```
using (StableBaseDataContext Data = new StableBaseDataContext())
{
    var NewsItems = Data.ExecuteQuery<string>("SELECT NewsText FROM News");
    LabelNews.Text = "";
    foreach (string NewsItem in NewsItems)
    {
        LabelNews.Text += NewsItem + "<br />";
    }
}
```

This code sends the following SQL query to the database:

SELECT NewsText FROM News

note

Sending SQL queries without results

In this example, you used the *ExecuteQuery* method to send SQL code to the database and retrieve the results.

If you want to send SQL code that doesn't return a result, such as an insert or update command, you can use the *ExecuteCommand* method of the LINQ data context.

note

Using ExecuteQuery with more complex record sets

In this lesson you used the *ExecuteQuery* method to run a SQL query that returned a collection of news items.

Each news item is a string value, so you specified <string> when calling the *ExecuteQuery* method.

SQL queries can return more complex record sets. For example, you might run a query that returns *CustomerForename* and *CustomerSurname* values.

In this instance, the query would return a collection of objects that have two *string* properties. You couldn't use *ExecuteQuery<string>* to extract this data.

The best solution in this situation would be to create a new *class* named *CustomerName* with *CustomerForename* and *CustomerSurname* properties.

You could then call *ExecuteQuery<CustomerName>* to return a collection of *CustomerName* objects containing the values you need.

A quicker but less professional approach would be to specify a *Tuple* when calling *ExecuteQuery*.

You learned about Tuples in: *Lesson 2-1: Use the Tuple class.*

This SQL code retrieves all of the *NewsText* values from the *News* database table. It will work identically to the LINQ query that it replaces.

Note that you must specify the data type that the SQL query will return for each record. In this case you have specified <string> because the *NewsText* field contains string data.

See sidebar for issues that will arise if your query returns more than one column

5   Test your code.

View *Default.aspx* in your web browser.

> ## WELCOME TO STABLEBASE!
>
> NEWS
> Our horse "Sausage" wins a national competition!
> We welcome a new horse to our stables: "Toffee"
> Our news page now has AJAX functionality!
> The news items now refresh automatically!

Your SQL query is executed successfully and the news items are returned.

Note that it is best practice to avoid this approach. All SQL code should ideally be stored within the database itself using stored procedures.

Placing SQL queries in your C# code makes it difficult to understand and maintain your data access code. It may also make your application vulnerable to SQL injection attacks.

You'll learn about SQL injection attacks in: *Lesson 10-11: Understand SQL injection attacks.*

Lesson 10-5: Connect to a database using the SqlClient namespace

Before the introduction of LINQ, databases were accessed using the classes in the *System.Data.SqlClient* namespace.

These older classes do not have the flexibility of LINQ, but you may see them being used in older projects.

1 Open MarketTrader from your sample files folder.

2 Open *DataAccess.cs*.

All of the methods in this class perform database queries.

3 Examine the *GetMarketQuotes* method.

```
public IEnumerable<Quote> GetMarketQuotes(int MarketID)
{
    return Data.Quotes
        .Where(Quote => Quote.MarketID == MarketID)
        .OrderBy(Quote => Quote.QuoteDate);
}
```

This method uses LINQ to return records from the *Quote* table.

You're going to replace this code using the classes from the *SqlClient* namespace.

4 Remove all existing code from the *GetMarketQuotes* method.

```
public IEnumerable<Quote> GetMarketQuotes(int MarketID)
{

}
```

5 Add *using* lines for **System.Data.SqlClient** and **System.Configuration**.

```
using System.Web;
using System.Data.SqlClient;
using System.Configuration;
```

6 Add code to the *GetMarketQuotes* method to retrieve the connection string from the *Web.config* file.

Use the following code:

string ConnectionString = ConfigurationManager.ConnectionStrings ["MarketTraderConnectionString"].ConnectionString;

```
public IEnumerable<Quote> GetMarketQuotes(int MarketID)
{
    string ConnectionString =
        ConfigurationManager.ConnectionStrings
        ["MarketTraderConnectionString"].ConnectionString;
}
```

A *connection string* contains the settings that are needed to connect to a database. Connection strings are stored in the *Web.config* file inside the *<connectionStrings>* tag.

The connection string was automatically added to the *Web.config* file by Visual Studio when the *MarketTrader* database was added to the project.

The *ConfigurationManager* class is part of the *System.Configuration* namespace.

7   **Add code to connect to your database.**

Add the following code on the next line:

using (SqlConnection Connection = new SqlConnection(ConnectionString))
{
   Connection.Open();
}

```
public IEnumerable<Quote> GetMarketQuotes(int MarketID)
{
    string ConnectionString = ConfigurationManager.ConnectionStrings
        ["MarketTraderConnectionString"].ConnectionString;
    using (SqlConnection Connection = new SqlConnection(ConnectionString))
    {
        Connection.Open();
    }
}
```

This code creates and opens a connection to the database.

Note that you have used a *using* statement to automatically dispose of the *Connection* object once you have finished working with it.

The *SqlConnection* class is part of the *System.Data.SqlClient* namespace.

8   **Create a *SqlCommand* object to send a command to the database.**

Add the following code on the next line within the *using* statement:

using (SqlCommand Command = Connection.CreateCommand())
{ }

```
using (SqlConnection Connection = new SqlConnection(ConnectionString))
{
    Connection.Open();
    using (SqlCommand Command = Connection.CreateCommand())
    {
    }
}
```

The *SqlCommand* class enables you to send SQL code to the database. It can also be used to execute stored procedures.

Once again you have enclosed the object in a *using* statement to automatically dispose of the *Command* object once you have finished working with it.

You'll use this object to execute a SQL query and retrieve the results in the next lesson: *Lesson 10-6: Run a SQL query using the SqlClient namespace.*

Lesson 10-6: Run a SQL query using the SqlClient namespace

You created code to connect to a database using the *SqlClient* namespace in: *Lesson 10-5: Connect to a database using the SqlClient namespace.*

In this lesson, you'll continue to use the *SqlClient* namespace to execute a SQL query and retrieve the results.

1   Open *MarketTrader* from your sample files folder.

2   Open *DataAccess.cs*.

3   Add code to the *GetMarketQuotes* method to specify a SQL query.

Add the following code inside the second *using* statement:

Command.CommandText =
"SELECT QuoteDate, QuoteValue FROM Quote
WHERE MarketID = " + MarketID +
" ORDER BY QuoteDate";

```
Connection.Open();
using (SqlCommand Command = Connection.CreateCommand())
{
    Command.CommandText =
        "SELECT QuoteDate, QuoteValue FROM Quote WHERE MarketID = "
        + MarketID + " ORDER BY QuoteDate";
}
```

This code provides a SQL query for the *SqlCommand* object.

The query will retrieve the *QuoteDate* and *QuoteValue* fields from the *Quote* table for records with the specified *MarketID*. The results will be sorted by *QuoteDate*.

Note that the SQL query will not be sent to the database until you call one of the *Execute* methods of the *SqlCommand* object.

4   Add code to execute the SQL query and retrieve the results.

Add the following code on the next line inside the *using* statement:

SqlDataReader Reader = Command.ExecuteReader();

```
Command.CommandText =
    "SELECT QuoteDate, QuoteValue FROM Quote WHERE MarketID = "
    + MarketID + " ORDER BY QuoteDate";
SqlDataReader Reader = Command.ExecuteReader();
```

This code sends the SQL query to the database and places the results in a new *SqlDataReader* object.

Note that the *SqlCommand* object has a few alternative methods to send different types of SQL code to a database (see sidebar).

5   Add code to extract the results from the *SqlDataReader* object and return them as a *List* collection of *Quote* objects.

1.   Add the following code on the first line of the method:

List<Quote> QuotesToReturn = new List<Quote>();

note

SqlCommand methods

The *SqlCommand* class has a number of methods that can be used to execute different types of SQL query:

ExecuteReader
Used for queries that return multiple results, as in this example.

ExecuteNonReader
Used for queries that do not return any results, such as update commands. Instead, this method returns the number of rows affected by the query.

ExecuteScalar
Used for queries that only return a single result. This method will discard all results after the first.

```
public IEnumerable<Quote> GetMarketQuotes(int MarketID)
{
    List<Quote> QuotesToReturn = new List<Quote>();
```

You'll extract the results into this collection. You placed this code on the first line of the event handler so that it will be available outside the *using* statements.

2. Add the following *while* loop on the next line inside the second *using* statement:

while (Reader.Read()) { }

```
SqlDataReader Reader = Command.ExecuteReader();
while (Reader.Read())
{
}
```

This *while* loop iterates through all of the database records that are contained in the *SqlDataReader* object. The *Read* method tells the *SqlDataReader* object to move to the next record. It returns *false* if there are no more records left.

3. Add the following code inside the *while* loop:

Quote NewQuote = new Quote();
NewQuote.QuoteDate = (DateTime)Reader["QuoteDate"];
NewQuote.QuoteValue = (decimal)Reader["QuoteValue"];
QuotesToReturn.Add(NewQuote);

```
while (Reader.Read())
{
    Quote NewQuote = new Quote();
    NewQuote.QuoteDate = (DateTime)Reader["QuoteDate"];
    NewQuote.QuoteValue = (decimal)Reader["QuoteValue"];
    QuotesToReturn.Add(NewQuote);
}
```

This code creates a new *Quote* object, populates it with the values from the *SqlDataReader* object and adds it to the *QuotesToReturn* collection.

4. Add the following code after the end of the second *using* statement:

Connection.Close();

This code closes the connection to the database.

5. Add the following code to the very end of the method:

return QuotesToReturn;

This code returns the list of quotes, completing your method.

6   Test your code.

1. View *MarketData.aspx* in your web browser.

2. Click *Get Data*.

The database records are displayed on the page.

As you have seen, the *SqlClient* classes require a huge amount of code compared to LINQ. My advice is to always use LINQ, but you may need this understanding to support legacy code that was written using an older version of ASP.NET.

---

important

Sending SQL code directly can be insecure

Sending SQL code directly to a database can make your application vulnerable to SQL injection attacks.

You'll learn more about SQL injection attacks in: *Lesson 10-11: Understand SQL injection attacks.*

It is possible to use the *SqlClient* classes in a secure way by using the *Parameters* property of the *SqlCommand* object, but it's better to use LINQ instead.

note

The Quote class was created by LINQ

The *Quote* class that you use in this lesson is part of the project's LINQ data classes (*MarketTrader.dbml*).

You could create your own custom class to store quote records instead of using the one that was generated by LINQ. You're only using the class that was automatically generated for the sake of convenience.

```
        QuotesToReturn.Add(NewQuote);
    }
}
Connection.Close();
```

```
        Connection.Close();
    }
    return QuotesToReturn;
}
```

Date	Value
01/01/2011	£12,880.91
01/02/2011	£12,808.21
01/03/2011	£12,769.85

Lesson 10-7: Write data to a CSV file

CSV files are a common format for the storage of data. CSV stands for *Comma Separated Values*.

CSV files are easy to work with and can be read by Microsoft Excel, making them an ideal way to output data from a web application.

Date	Value	
Databound	Databound	
Databound	Databound	
Databound	Databound	
Databound	Databound	
Databound	Databound	
Save as CSV	Save as XML	

1   Open *MarketTrader* from your sample files folder.

2   Open *MarketData.aspx* in Design view.

You're going to add code to make the *Save as CSV* button functional.

3   Add a *Click* event handler to the *ButtonSaveAsCSV* control.

4   Add code to retrieve records from the database.

Add the following code to the new event handler:

using (DataAccess DataClass = new DataAccess())
{
**   int MarketID =**
**   Convert.ToInt32(DropDownListMarket.SelectedValue);**
**   var Records = DataClass.GetMarketQuotes(MarketID);**
}

```
protected void ButtonSaveAsCSV_Click(object sender, EventArgs e)
{
    using (DataAccess DataClass = new DataAccess())
    {
        int MarketID = Convert.ToInt32(DropDownListMarket.SelectedValue);
        var Records = DataClass.GetMarketQuotes(MarketID);
    }
}
```

5   Add code to iterate through the database records.

Add the following code on the next line inside the *using* statement:

string CSVString = "";
foreach (Quote Record in Records)
{
}

```
var Records = DataClass.GetMarketQuotes(MarketID);
string CSVString = "";
foreach (Quote Record in Records)
{
}
```

The *CSVString* variable will be used to store the CSV data that you are going to create.

6   Add code to construct the CSV data.

Add the following code inside the *foreach* loop:

CSVString += Record.QuoteDate.ToShortDateString();
CSVString += ",";

note

Back-slashes in strings

The path used in this lesson uses two back-slash characters between each of the folder names.

This is because the back-slash is considered to be a 'special' character by C#, known as the 'escape' character.

A back-slash can be used before any 'special' character to allow it to be included in a string. It's also used to indicate special 'escape codes' such as \r and \n.

For example, if you wanted to include quote marks in a string, you would do so by using: \ "

Sometimes (as in this lesson) you really want to use a back-slash but need to work around C# recognizing it as an escape character. In this case, you can use a double back-slash to tell C# that you want a regular back-slash in your string.

If a *string* variable is marked with an error, it is often because it is trying to use special characters without first using a back-slash to 'escape' them.

CSVString += Record.QuoteValue.ToString("0.00");
CSVString += "\r\n";

```
foreach (Quote Record in Records)
{
    CSVString += Record.QuoteDate.ToShortDateString();
    CSVString += ",";
    CSVString += Record.QuoteValue.ToString("0.00");
    CSVString += "\r\n";
}
```

This code stores the values from the database in the *CSVString* variable, separating each value with a comma.

\r and \n are the 'escape codes' for a carriage return followed by a new line (see sidebar). New lines are used to separate records in CSV files.

7 Add code to save the CSV file onto the web server.

Add the following line of code after the *foreach* loop:

**System.IO.File.WriteAllText(
"C:\\Practice\\ASP.NET45 Expert\\MarketData.csv", CSVString);**

```
    CSVString += "\r\n";
}
System.IO.File.WriteAllText(
    "C:\\Practice\\ASP.NET45 Expert\\MarketData.csv", CSVString);
```

This code saves the CSV file to:
C:\Practice\ASP.NET45 Expert\MarketData.csv

See sidebar for the reason that you must use pairs of back-slashes in the path.

You've used the *File* class before in: *Lesson 7-3: Use the FileUpload control.*

8 Test your code.

1. View *MarketData.aspx* in your web browser.

2. Click *Get Data.*

3. Click *Save as CSV.*

4. Close your web browser.

5. Using Windows Explorer, navigate to:
   C:\Practice\ASP.NET45 Expert

6. Double-click *MarketData.csv.*

   If you have Microsoft Excel or another program that is capable of reading CSV files, the file will be opened in a familiar table layout.

   If you don't have a program that is capable of reading a CSV file, skip this step.

7. In Windows Explorer, right-click *MarketData.csv* and click: Open with→Notepad.

The CSV file is shown in its raw state.

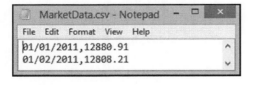

Lesson 10-8: Read data from a CSV file

You learned how to write data to a CSV file in the previous lesson: *Lesson 10-7: Write data to a CSV file.*

In this lesson you'll learn how to use C# code to read the data back from your CSV file.

1   Open *TextLand* from your sample files folder.

2   Open the code-behind file of *CSV.aspx.*

3   Examine the *ButtonReadFile_Click* event handler.

```
protected void ButtonReadFile_Click(object sender, EventArgs e)
{
    Stream CSVStream = FileUploadFileToRead.FileContent;
    StreamReader Reader = new StreamReader(CSVStream);
    while (!Reader.EndOfStream)
    {
        string TextFromFile = Reader.ReadLine();
        LiteralFileContent.Text += TextFromFile;
    }
}
```

This code allows the user to upload a file and display it on the page, but it isn't yet able to read CSV files properly.

You wrote this code in: *Lesson 2-3: Use the Stream class.*

4   Add a variable before the *while* loop to store the HTML result.

Use the following code before the *while* loop:

string HTMLResult = "<table>";

```
string HTMLResult = "<table>";
while (!Reader.EndOfStream)
{
    string TextFromFile = Reader.ReadLine();
```

You're going to display the contents of the CSV file in an *HTML* table, so the *HTMLResult* variable starts with a *<table>* tag.

5   Modify the *while* loop to split the CSV data into individual values.

1.   Remove the line:

LiteralFileContent.Text += TextFromFile;

```
while (!Reader.EndOfStream)
{
    string TextFromFile = Reader.ReadLine();

}
```

2.   Add the following line of code:

string[] CSVElements = TextFromFile.Split(',');

```
string TextFromFile = Reader.ReadLine();
string[] CSVElements = TextFromFile.Split(',');
```

The *Split* method changes the *TextFromFile* string into an array of strings.

It does this by splitting the text in the *TextFromFile* variable every time it finds a comma. Because you're reading a CSV file, this will split the data into its individual values.

6   Add code to convert the CSV values into HTML table cells.

1.   Add the following code on the next line:

HTMLResult += "<tr>";
foreach (string CSVElement in CSVElements)
{
    HTMLResult += "<td>" + CSVElement + "</td>";
}
HTMLResult += "</tr>";

```
string[] CSVElements = TextFromFile.Split(',');
HTMLResult += "<tr>";
foreach (string CSVElement in CSVElements)
{
    HTMLResult += "<td>" + CSVElement + "</td>";
}
HTMLResult += "</tr>";
```

This code adds *<tr>* and *<td>* tags to place the values in separate rows and columns in the HTML table that you are building from the CSV file.

2.   Add the following code after the *while* loop:

HTMLResult += "</table>";

```
    HTMLResult += "</tr>";
}
HTMLResult += "</table>";
```

This simply ends the HTML *<table>* tag after all of the values have been added to the table.

7   Add code to display the HTML table on the page.

Add the following code on the next line:

LiteralFileContent.Text = HTMLResult;

```
HTMLResult += "</table>";
LiteralFileContent.Text = HTMLResult;
```

8   Test your code.

1.   View *CSV.aspx* in your web browser.

2.   Click *Browse...* and navigate to: *C:\Practice\ASP.NET45 Expert*

3.   Click *MarketData.csv* and click *Open*.

You created *MarketData.csv* in: *Lesson 10-7: Write data to a CSV file*. If you haven't completed that lesson, you can obtain the file by downloading the sample files for this lesson from: *www.aspnetcentral.com*.

4.   Click *Read File*.

The CSV file is read and displayed on the page in a table.

01/01/2011	12880.91
01/02/2011	12808.21
01/03/2011	12769.85
01/04/2011	12684.88
01/05/2011	12778.19
01/06/2011	12861.72
01/07/2011	12928.29
01/08/2011	12853.85
01/09/2011	12948.36
01/10/2011	12857.88
01/11/2011	12773.71
01/12/2011	12807.02

Lesson 10-9: Write data to an XML file

1   Open *MarketTrader* from your sample files folder.

2   Open *MarketData.aspx* in Design view.

3   Add a *Click* event handler to the *ButtonSaveAsXML* control.

4   Add a *using* line for: **System.Xml**

```
using System.Web.UI.WebControls;
using System.Xml;
```

The *System.Xml* classes are used to read and write XML data.

5   Add the following code to the *ButtonSaveAsXML_Click* event handler to retrieve data from the database:

**DataAccess DataClass = new DataAccess();
int MarketID =
Convert.ToInt32(DropDownListMarket.SelectedValue);
var Quotes = DataClass.GetMarketQuotes(MarketID);**

```
protected void ButtonSaveAsXML_Click(object sender, EventArgs e)
{
    DataAccess DataClass = new DataAccess();
    int MarketID = Convert.ToInt32(DropDownListMarket.SelectedValue);
    var Quotes = DataClass.GetMarketQuotes(MarketID);
}
```

This code retrieves a collection of *Quote* objects from the database.

6   Add code to create a new XML document.

Add the following code on the next line:

XmlDocument Document = new XmlDocument();

```
var Quotes = DataClass.GetMarketQuotes(MarketID);
XmlDocument Document = new XmlDocument();
```

7   Add code to create a root element for the XML file.

Add the following code on the next line:

XmlElement RootElement = Document.CreateElement("Quotes");

```
XmlDocument Document = new XmlDocument();
XmlElement RootElement = Document.CreateElement("Quotes");
```

The *RootElement* object represents a *<Quotes>* tag that will be used as a 'root' tag to contain all of the other tags in the XML file.

8   Add code to create XML elements for each database record.

Add the following code on the next line:

**foreach (Quote QuoteRecord in Quotes)
{
   XmlElement QuoteElement =
   Document.CreateElement("Quote");
}**

```
XmlElement RootElement = Document.CreateElement("Quotes");
foreach (Quote QuoteRecord in Quotes)
{
    XmlElement QuoteElement = Document.CreateElement("Quote");
}
```

note

About XML

XML files offer a more powerful way to store data than CSV files.

You've seen XML data when viewing the *Web.config* file. HTML code is also a form of XML.

You'll write data into an XML file in this lesson.

For more about XML, see Session 3 of the *Essential Skills* course.

This code creates separate *<Quote>* tags for each of the *Quote* objects returned from the database.

9 Add code to set the attributes of each XML element.

Add the following code inside the *foreach* loop:

QuoteElement.SetAttribute("QuoteDate", QuoteRecord.QuoteDate.ToShortDateString());
QuoteElement.SetAttribute("QuoteValue", QuoteRecord.QuoteValue.ToString());

```
XmlElement QuoteElement = Document.CreateElement("Quote");
QuoteElement.SetAttribute("QuoteDate",
    QuoteRecord.QuoteDate.ToShortDateString());
QuoteElement.SetAttribute("QuoteValue",
    QuoteRecord.QuoteValue.ToString());
```

This code sets properties for each of the *<Quote>* tags.

10 Add code to attach the quote elements to the root node.

```
QuoteRecord.QuoteValue.ToString());
RootElement.AppendChild(QuoteElement);
```

Add the following code inside the *foreach* loop:

RootElement.AppendChild(QuoteElement);

This code will place each *<Quote>* tag inside the root *<Quotes>* tag.

11 Add code to attach the root node to the document.

```
        RootElement.AppendChild(QuoteElement);
}
Document.AppendChild(RootElement);
```

Add the following code after the end of the *foreach* loop:

Document.AppendChild(RootElement);

Finally, this code places the *<Quotes>* tag and all of its *<Quote>* tags into the XML document.

note

Alternative ways to write XML data

The *XMLDocument* class isn't the only way to write data to an XML file. The .NET framework also offers the *XMLTextWriter* class.

The *XmlTextWriter* class is similar to the *XmlDocument* class, but is only capable of writing XML data. The *XmlDocument* class is a better choice because it can be used for both reading and writing.

If you don't want to use either class, you can simply write XML data directly into a *string* variable.

12 Add code to save the XML document to the web server's hard drive.

Add the following code on the next line:

**Document.Save(
"C:\\Practice\\ASP.NET45 Expert\\MarketData.xml");**

```
Document.AppendChild(RootElement);
Document.Save("C:\\Practice\\ASP.NET45 Expert\\MarketData.xml");
```

If the double-backslashes are confusing you, refer to: *Lesson 10-7: Write data to a CSV file (sidebar).*

13 Test your code.

1. View *MarketData.aspx* in your web browser and click *Get Data.*

2. Click *Save as XML.*

3. Close your web browser and return to Visual Studio.

4. Click File→Open File…

5. Navigate to *C:\Practice\ASP.NET45 Expert* and open *MarketData.xml.*

```
<Quotes>
    <Quote QuoteDate="01/01/2011" QuoteValue="12880.9100" />
    <Quote QuoteDate="01/02/2011" QuoteValue="12808.2100" />
```

The data is displayed in XML format.

Lesson 10-10: Read data from an XML file

You wrote data to an XML file in: *Lesson 10-9: Write data to an XML file*.

In this lesson you'll learn how to use C# code to read the data back from your XML file.

1 Open *TextLand* from your sample files folder.

2 Open the code-behind file of *XML.aspx*.

3 Add a *using* line for: **System.Xml**

```
using System.Web.UI.WebControls;
using System.Xml;
```

4 Remove all code from the *if* statement in the *ButtonUploadXML_Click* event handler.

```
protected void ButtonUploadXML_Click(object sender, EventArgs e)
{
    if (FileUploadXML.HasFile)
    {

    }
}
```

5 Add code to the *if* statement to retrieve an *XMLDocument* object from the *FileUpload* control.

Add the following code inside the *if* statement:

XmlDocument Document = new XmlDocument();
Document.Load(FileUploadXML.FileContent);

```
if (FileUploadXML.HasFile)
{
    XmlDocument Document = new XmlDocument();
    Document.Load(FileUploadXML.FileContent);
}
```

6 Add code to extract *Quote* elements from the XML document.

Add the following code on the next line:

XmlNodeList Quotes =
Document.GetElementsByTagName("Quote");

```
XmlDocument Document = new XmlDocument();
Document.Load(FileUploadXML.FileContent);
XmlNodeList Quotes = Document.GetElementsByTagName("Quote");
```

This code extracts all of the *<Quote>* tags from the XML document and places them in the resulting *XmlNodeList* object.

You could also have extracted the *<Quote>* tags by using the XML document hierarchy (see sidebar).

7 Add code to iterate through the XML nodes.

Add the following code on the next line:

string HTMLResult = "<table>";
foreach (XmlNode Quote in Quotes)
{
}
HTMLResult += "</table>";

```
XmlNodeList Quotes = Document.GetElementsByTagName("Quote");
string HTMLResult = "<table>";
foreach (XmlNode Quote in Quotes)
{
}
HTMLResult += "</table>";
```

You're going to output the data into an HTML table in the same way as you did with a CSV file in: *Lesson 10-8: Read data from a CSV file*.

8   Add code to the *foreach* statement to extract the values from the XML nodes.

Add the following code to the *foreach* statement:

HTMLResult += "<tr><td>";
HTMLResult += Quote.Attributes["QuoteDate"].Value + "</td>";
HTMLResult += "<td>" + Quote.Attributes["QuoteValue"].Value;
HTMLResult += "</td></tr>";

```
foreach (XmlNode Quote in Quotes)
{
    HTMLResult += "<tr><td>";
    HTMLResult += Quote.Attributes["QuoteDate"].Value + "</td>";
    HTMLResult += "<td>" + Quote.Attributes["QuoteValue"].Value;
    HTMLResult += "</td></tr>";
}
```

This code extracts the *QuoteDate* and *QuoteValue* properties from the *XMLNode* objects and adds them to the HTML table.

9   Add code to display the table on the page.

Add the following code at the end of the *if* statement:

LabelResult.Text = HTMLResult;

```
}
HTMLResult += "</table>";
LabelResult.Text = HTMLResult;
```

10 Test your code.

1. View *XML.aspx* in your web browser.

2. Click *Browse...* and navigate to: *C:\Practice\ASP.NET45 Expert*

3. Click *MarketData.xml* and click *Open*.

   You created *MarketData.xml* in: *Lesson 10-9: Write data to an XML file*. If you haven't completed that lesson, you can obtain the file by downloading the sample files for this lesson from: *www.aspnetcentral.com*.

C:\Practice\ASP.NET45 E	Browse...	Upload XML

4. Click *Upload XML*.

   The XML file is read and displayed on the page in a table.

01/01/2011	12880.9100
01/02/2011	12808.2100
01/03/2011	12769.8500
01/04/2011	12684.8800
01/05/2011	12778.1900
01/06/2011	12861.7200
01/07/2011	12928.2900
01/08/2011	12853.8500
01/09/2011	12948.3600
01/10/2011	12857.8800
01/11/2011	12773.7100
01/12/2011	12807.0200

Lesson 10-11: Understand SQL injection attacks

Standard LINQ code offers an extremely secure way to access a database from a web page. LINQ will automatically ensure that users cannot gain unauthorized access to your database.

If you send SQL code directly to the database, either through LINQ or by using the *SqlClient* classes, you may be vulnerable to hackers using SQL injection attacks. You'll learn about SQL injection attacks and how to prevent them in this lesson.

1   Open *SecFile* from your sample files folder.

2   View *UserAdmin.aspx* in your web browser.

Log in with your Windows username and password if prompted.

3   Attempt a SQL injection attack.

In the above example, when the user *JeffK* is added to the database, LINQ will automatically generate the following SQL code:

INSERT INTO [dbo].[SecureUser]([SecureUserName])
*VALUES (***'JeffK'***)*

1.   In the text box, enter the following:

JeffK') DELETE FROM SecureUser SELECT ('

This is a typical SQL injection attack. If this page was insecure, the SQL code would be passed to your database, resulting in the following code being executed:

INSERT INTO [dbo].[SecureUser]([SecureUserName])
*VALUES (***'JeffK')***

DELETE FROM SecureUser

Select (')

If this code was sent to your database, it would delete the entire contents of the *SecureUsers* table! A malicious user could use this vulnerability to take complete control of your database.

2.   Click *Add User*.

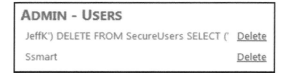

The SQL injection attack fails. Standard LINQ completely protects you from SQL injection attacks.

4 Introduce a SQL injection vulnerability.

1. Close your web browser and open the code-behind file of *UserAdmin.aspx*.

2. Remove all LINQ code from the *using* statement, but leave the call to the *GridViewSecureUsers.DataBind* method in place.

```
protected void ButtonAddUser_Click(object sender, EventArgs e)
{
    if (TextBoxNewUserName.Text.Length > 0)
    {
        using (SecFileDataContext Data = new SecFileDataContext())
        {
            GridViewSecureUsers.DataBind();
        }
    }
}
```

3. Add the following code at the start of the *using* statement:

Data.ExecuteCommand("INSERT INTO [dbo].[SecureUser]([SecureUserName]) VALUES ('" + TextBoxNewUserName.Text + "')");

```
using (SecFileDataContext Data = new SecFileDataContext())
{
    Data.ExecuteCommand(
        "INSERT INTO [dbo].[SecureUser]([SecureUserName]) VALUES ('"
        + TextBoxNewUserName.Text + "')");
    GridViewSecureUsers.DataBind();
}
```

This code sends the SQL code directly to the database without applying any of LINQ's security to it.

Your code is now vulnerable to a SQL injection attack.

5 Successfully carry out a SQL injection attack.

1. View *UserAdmin.aspx* in your web browser, logging in with your Windows username and password if prompted.

2. In the text box, enter the SQL injection code:

JeffK') DELETE FROM SecureUser SELECT ('

3. Click *Add User*.

The SQL injection attack succeeds and all of the users are deleted from the database.

Malicious users are constantly attempting SQL injection attacks on websites across the internet. You should always be careful to avoid code that could leave your site vulnerable.

The best way to prevent SQL injection attacks is to avoid sending SQL code directly to the database. If you always use standard LINQ or stored procedures you should never be vulnerable to SQL injection attacks.

Session 10: Exercise

1   Open *Exercise10* from your sample files folder.

2   Open the code-behind file of *TotalSales.aspx*.

3   Add code to the *Page_Load* event handler to extract the total of the *SaleValue* fields from the *Sale* database table using the LINQ *Sum* method. Display the result in the *LabelTotalSales* control.

TOTAL SALES
899280.14

4   Open the code-behind file of *Sales.aspx*.

5   Modify the *Page_Load* event handler to use an *anonymous type* which extracts the following fields:

Sale.SaleID
Sale.SaleQuantity
Sale.SaleValue
Sale.Customer.CustomerName
Sale.Product.ProductName

Customer	Product	Quantity	Value
Bill Washington	Expert Skills Book	289	8667.1100

6   Open the code-behind file of *SalesByProduct.aspx*.

7   Modify the *Page_Load* event handler to return the total of all sales values grouped by product name. To do this, use the *GroupBy* and *Sum* methods with an *anonymous type*.

Key	TotalSales
Essential Skills Book	312945.6500
Essential Skills Video	104755.0700

8   Open the code-behind file of *Customers.aspx*.

9   Add code to the *ButtonSaveAsCSV* event handler to save the data from the *Customers* collection into a CSV file.

Save the file to: **C:\Practice\ASP.NET45 Expert\Exercise10.csv**

10   Add code to the *ButtonSaveAsXML* event handler to save the data from the *Customers* collection into an XML file.

Save the file to: **C:\Practice\ASP.NET45 Expert\Exercise10.xml**

11   Open the code-behind file of *ReadDataFiles.aspx*.

12   Add code to the *ButtonReadCSV_Click* event handler to read the CSV file that you created and display it in the *LabelResult* control as an HTML table.

13   Add code to the *ButtonReadXML_Click* event handler to read the XML file that you created and display it in the *LabelResult* control as an HTML table.

Exercise10 - Start   Exercise10 - End

If you need help slide the page to the left

Session 10: Exercise Answers

These are the three questions that students find the most difficult to answer:

Q 13	Q 10	Q 7
Use the following code:	Use the following code:	Use the following code:

Q 13

Use the following code:

```
XmlDocument Document = new
XmlDocument();
Document.Load(
FileUploadDataFile.FileContent);
XmlNodeList CustomerNodes =
Document.
GetElementsByTagName
("Customer");
string HTMLOutput = "<table>";
foreach (XmlNode CustomerNode in
CustomerNodes)
{
   HTMLOutput += "<tr><td>" +
   CustomerNode.Attributes
     ["CustomerID"].Value + "</td>";
   HTMLOutput += "<td>" +
   CustomerNode.Attributes
     ["CustomerName"].Value + "</tr>";
}
HTMLOutput += "</table>";
LabelResult.Text = HTMLOutput;
```

This was covered in: *Lesson 10-10: Read data from an XML file.*

Q 10

Use the following code:

```
XmlDocument Document = new
XmlDocument();
XmlElement RootElement =
Document.CreateElement("Customers");
foreach (Customer CustomerToXML in
Customers)
{
   XmlElement CustomerElement =
   Document.CreateElement("Customer");
   CustomerElement.
   SetAttribute("CustomerID",
CustomerToXML.CustomerID.
   ToString());
   CustomerElement.
   SetAttribute("CustomerName",
   CustomerToXML.CustomerName);
   RootElement.
   AppendChild(CustomerElement);
}
Document.AppendChild(RootElement);
Document.Save("C:\\Practice\\ASP.NET45
Expert\\Exercise10.xml");
```

This was covered in: *Lesson 10-9: Write data to an XML file.*

Q 7

Use the following code:

```
var Result =
Data.Sales.
GroupBy(Sale =>
Sale.Product.
ProductName).
Select(Group =>
new {Group.Key,
TotalSales=
Group.Sum
(Sale =>
Sale.SaleValue)
});
```

This was covered in: *Lesson 10-3: Use the Sum and GroupBy LINQ methods.*

If you have difficulty with the other questions, here are the lessons that cover the relevant skills:

1   Refer to: Essential Skills Session 1.

2   Refer to: Essential Skills Session 1.

3   Refer to: Lesson 10-1: Use the Average LINQ method.

4   Refer to: Essential Skills Session 1.

5   Refer to: Lesson 10-2: Use LINQ anonymous types.

6   Refer to: Essential Skills Session 1.

8   Refer to: Essential Skills Session 1.

9   Refer to: Lesson 10-7: Write data to a CSV file.

11   Refer to: Essential Skills Session 1.

12   Refer to: Lesson 10-8: Read data from a CSV file.

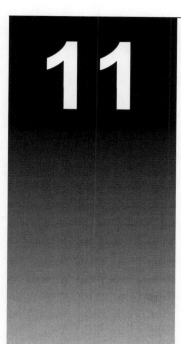

Session Eleven: Regular Expressions

> Some people, when confronted with a problem, think "I know, I'll use regular expressions." Now they have two problems.
>
> *Jamie Zawinski, American programmer (born 1968)*

Regular expressions offer a way to search and manipulate string data that goes beyond the capabilities of the *string* type.

Regular expressions are ideal for validation purposes. For example, they can be used to check whether a phone number or e-mail address is valid.

You'll also use the *RegularExpressionValidator* control in this session, which allows you to quickly add validation using regular expressions.

Session Objectives

By the end of this session you will be able to:

- Understand regular expressions
- Create a regular expression to extract words from text
- Create a regular expression for telephone numbers
- Create a regular expression for e-mail addresses
- Crate a regular expression for HTML links
- Use the RegularExpressionValidator control
- Work with regular expressions in C#
- Understand cross-site scripting attacks

Lesson 11-1: Understand regular expressions

Regular expressions can be complex but their basic principles are quite simple.

In this lesson you'll work with some basic regular expressions and gain an understanding of how they work.

1   Open *TextLand* from your sample files folder.

2   View *RegularExpressions.aspx* in your web browser.

This page allows you to test regular expressions.

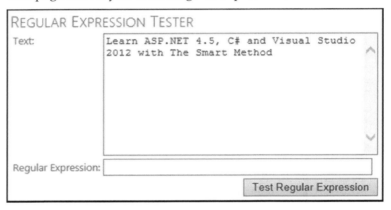

The regular expression entered in the *Regular Expression* box will be applied to the text in the *Text* box.

3   Find a word using a regular expression.

1. In the *Regular Expression* box, enter the word: **Learn**

Regular Expression:	Learn

2. Click *Test Regular Expression*.

The *Test Results* panel indicates that the regular expression found at least one match and the match is displayed.

TEST RESULTS

Does Expression Match? **YES**

Matched Text: Learn

This simple regular expression searches for any instances of the word *Learn*.

4   Test the regular expression: **asp.net**

1. Change the text in the *Regular Expression* box to: **asp.net**

Regular Expression:	asp.net

2. Click *Test Regular Expression*.

This time the regular expression doesn't match the text. This is because regular expressions are *case sensitive*.

If you are not completing the course incrementally use the sample file: **Lesson 11-1** to begin this lesson.

Sample files with the starting point for each lesson are also provided for all of the other lessons in this session.

3. Change the regular expression to: **ASP.NET**

Regular Expression: | ASP.NET

4. Click *Test Regular Expression*.

Does Expression Match? **YES**

Matched Text: | ASP.NET

This time the regular expression finds a match because it has the same capital letters as the word in the text.

5 **Create a regular expression to extract all numbers from the text.**

Test the following regular expression: **[0123456789]**

Does Expression Match? **YES**

Matched Text: | 4
5
2
0
1
2

This expression matches all of the numbers in the text. By placing characters in square brackets [], you can create a regular expression that matches any of those characters.

Note that square brackets are considered to be special characters in regular expressions. If you wanted to create a regular expression that searched for square brackets, you would need to *escape* the special characters (see sidebar).

6 **Modify the regular expression to match groups of numbers.**

Test the following regular expression: **[0123456789]+**

Does Expression Match? **YES**

Matched Text: | 4
5
2012

Instead of matching the numbers in *2012* individually, they are now returned as a single match.

The + special character searches for *1 or more* instances of the previous item in the regular expression (in this case the numbers in square brackets).

In this example the number *2012* is found because there are 4 consecutive instances of the numbers 0-9 in a row.

The numbers *4* and *5* are still found separately because they are broken up by a full stop.

7 **Shorten the regular expression.**

Test the following regular expression: **[0-9]+**

The results are exactly the same. By using a hyphen inside square brackets you can specify ranges of numbers or letters.

important

Escaping special characters

Complex regular expressions are created by using 'special' characters.

The following characters are considered 'special' by regular expressions:

^ $. | { } [ ] ( ) * + ? \

There may be occasions when you will want to create a regular expression that searches for one of these characters. You can do this by *escaping* the character using a back-slash.

The following regular expression will search for question marks:

\?

The following regular expression will search for either of the square brackets:

[\[\]]

Does Expression Match? **YES**

Matched Text: | 4
5
2012

Lesson 11-2: Create a regular expression to extract words from text

In this lesson you'll create a regular expression that extracts the individual words from a piece of text.

1 Open *TextLand* from your sample files folder.

2 View *RegularExpressions.aspx* in your web browser.

3 Create a regular expression that searches for any character *except* a space.

   1. In the *Regular Expression* box, enter the expression: **[^]**
      (Square Bracket, Caret, Space, Square Bracket).

   2. Click *Test Regular Expression.*

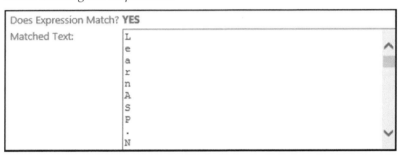

This regular expression matches every character except for a space.

[^] matches every character <u>except</u> for the characters that you specify in the square brackets. For example, the following expression would match any character that is <u>not</u> a number: *[^0123456789]*

4 Modify the regular expression to return words instead of individual characters.

   1. Modify the regular expression to the following: **[^]+**

   2. Click *Test Regular Expression.*

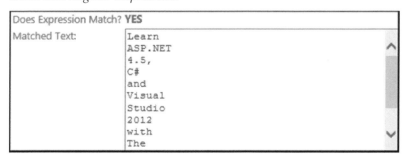

Now each individual word is matched.

You've used the + special character before, in: *Lesson 11-1: Understand regular expressions.*

The + character matches *one or more* consecutive instances of the preceding item (*[^]*) in the regular expression. In this case it will match *one or more* instances of characters that are *not* spaces.

5 Modify the regular expression to only return words that are 5 letters long.

1. Modify the regular expression to the following: **[^]{5}**

   By using a number in curly brackets, you can specify the number of characters that you want to match.

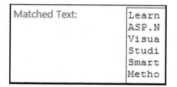

2. Click *Test Regular Expression*.

   This isn't quite what you wanted. The regular expression has found six instances where there are 5 non-space characters in a row, but you really only wanted it to find the words *Learn* and *Smart*.

   You might wonder why this expression didn't find, for example: *ASP.N, SP.NE* and *P.NET*. See sidebar for an explanation.

3. Change the regular expression to the following: **\b[^]{5}\b**

   Regular Expression: **\b[^]{5}\b**

   \b is a special code that matches 'word boundaries'. That is, the beginning or end of a word.

4. Click *Test Regular Expression*.

   Does Expression Match? **YES**
   Matched Text: `Learn`
   `Smart`

   The two 5-letter words are matched correctly.

6 Modify the regular expression to also match the word: **Method**

1. Change the regular expression to the following:

   (\b[^]{5}\b)|(Method)

   Regular Expression: **(\b[^]{5}\b)|(Method)**

   This expression would work equally well without the brackets, but they help to make the expression clearer.

   This regular expression will match anything that either matches the expression *\b[^]{5}\b* OR matches the expression *Method*.

   The vertical bar | is an OR operator, which allows you to create expressions that match more than one set of criteria. OR operators are covered in Session 7 of the *Essential Skills* course.

5. Click *Test Regular Expression*.

   As expected, *Method* is now matched by your regular expression along with the two 5-letter words.

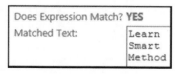

note

Avoid hugely complex regular expressions

In this lesson you will create a complex regular expression that is difficult to understand.

This is a good example of a situation where regular expressions may not be the best solution.

It might be theoretically possible to validate every possible world telephone number using a regular expression. In reality, a regular expression of such complexity would be virtually impossible to write and debug.

Instead, you could create a C# class to validate each country's telephone numbers separately. This would allow you to write clean, easily understood code that you could debug without difficulty.

Be cautious in your use of regular expressions. If they become too complex to easily understand, use a class instead.

Using the classes in the *System.Text.RegularExpressions* namespace, you can combine C# code and regular expressions. You'll learn how to do this in: *Lesson 11-7: Work with regular expressions in C#.*

Lesson 11-3: Create a regular expression for telephone numbers

1   Open *TextLand* from your sample files folder.

2   View *RegularExpressions.aspx* in your web browser.

3   In the *Text* box, enter the following phone number: **960459**

REGULAR EXPRESSION TESTER
Text: 960459

This is a simple 6-digit phone number.

4   Create a regular expression to match a 6-digit phone number.

Test the following expression: **[0-9]{6}**

Does Expression Match? **YES**

The expression matches correctly.

5   Add a hyphen to the phone number.

Change the phone number to: **960-459**

REGULAR EXPRESSION TESTER
Text: 960-459

Phone numbers are often written with hyphens or spaces splitting them into groups of three. Your regular expression should account for this.

6   Change the expression to account for hyphens or spaces.

Change the expression to: **(*[0-9]{6}*) | ([0-9]{3}[-][0-9]{3})**

Does Expression Match? **YES**

This regular expression is starting to get quite complex, so let's break it down to make it more readable.

([0-9]{6}   )
|
([0-9]{3}   [-]   [0-9]{3}   )

This matches the following:

(960459   )
OR
(960–459 OR 960 459   )

7   Add an area code to the phone number.

Change the phone number to: **(0)1632960-459**

REGULAR EXPRESSION TESTER
Text: (0)1632960-459

8   Modify your regular expression to account for the area code.

Change the expression to:
\(0\)[0-9]{4}(([0-9]{6})|([0-9]{3}[-][0-9]{3}))

Let's break this down again:

\(0\)   [0-9]{4}
(
  ([0-9]{6}   )
  |
  ([0-9]{3}   [-]   [0-9]{3}   )
)

The new code is all on the top line.

\(0\) will match (0). You need to use back-slashes before each of the brackets because they are special characters (see: *Lesson 11-1: Understand regular expressions – sidebar*).

[0-9]{4} will match a 4 digit number. This will match *1632*.

You've also added a new set of brackets to separate the six-digit phone number expression from the area code.

Does Expression Match? **YES**

---

note

Improving this expression

As mentioned above, phone number formats across the world are so different that creating a 'universal' regular expression would be almost impossible.

One potential solution is to simplify the regular expression so that it allows any combination of numbers, brackets, hyphens, dots and spaces, as well as the plus sign.

This regular expression would be:

[0-9 ().+\-]+

Although this regular expression could potentially match an invalid phone number, it wouldn't fail to match a valid phone number and would trap many common data entry errors.

Does Expression Match? **YES**

---

9   Modify your regular expression to make the area code optional.

Change the expression to:
(\(0\)[0-9]{4})?(([0-9]{6})|([0-9]{3}[-][0-9]{3}))

Breaking it down again:

(\(0\)   [0-9]{4}   )?
(
  ([0-9]{6}   )
  |
  ([0-9]{3}   [-]   [0-9]{3}   )
)

…matches:

((0)1632   ) - OPTIONAL
(
  (960459   )
  OR
  (960-459 OR 960 459   )
)

The area code expression is now in brackets followed by a question mark. The question mark character matches either 0 or 1 instances of the previous expression. The previous expression is:
(\(0\)[0-9]{4})

Because the regular expression will match if it finds either 0 or 1 instances of the area code, it will now work with or without an area code.

Even though this regular expression is very complex, it's still not a good solution. It relies on the user entering their phone number in a very specific way and isn't able to deal with country codes. See sidebar for ways to improve this regular expression.

Lesson 11-4: Create a regular expression for e-mail addresses

One of the most common uses for regular expressions is the validation of e-mail addresses. E-mail addresses are easier to match than phone numbers because they follow a more standardized format.

1 Open *TextLand* from your sample files folder.

2 View *RegularExpressions.aspx* in your web browser.

3 In the *Text* box, enter the following e-mail address: **info@ASPNETCentral.com**

4 Create a regular expression to match all text.

Test the following expression: **.+**

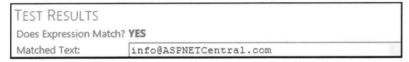

The full-stop character is used as a 'wildcard' by regular expressions. A full-stop will match any character.

By following the full-stop with a plus-sign, you have created a regular expression that matches 1 or more instances of any character. Of course, this will always match the entire text.

5 Modify the regular expression to force the e-mail address to include an @ sign.

1. Change the expression to: **.+@.+**

2. Test the regular expression.

The result appears to be the same.

3. Change the text in the *Text* box to: **infoASPNETCentral.com**

4. Test the regular expression.

The regular expression doesn't match as the e-mail address doesn't contain an @ sign, making it an invalid address.

6   Modify the regular expression to force the e-mail address to include an ending similar to *.com* or *.co.uk*.

All valid e-mail addresses end in a 'top level' such as *.com* or *.co.uk*.

This means that every valid e-mail address should contain at least one full-stop character after the @ character.

1.   Change the expression to: .+@.+\..+

Let's break down this regular expression a little:

.+   @ .+   \. .+
[Anything] @ [Anything] . [Anything]

For the full-stop to be recognized as an actual full-stop instead of being used as a special character, you must escape it with a back-slash.

You learned about escaping special characters in: *Lesson 11-1: Understand regular expressions (sidebar).*

2.   Change the text in the *Text* box to: **info@ASPNETCentral.com**

REGULAR EXPRESSION TESTER
Text: info@ASPNETCentral.com

3.   Test the regular expression.

TEST RESULTS
Does Expression Match? **YES**

4.   Change the text in the *Text* box to: **info@ASPNETCentral**

5.   Test the regular expression.

TEST RESULTS
Does Expression Match? **NO**

There's no full-stop character after the @ sign, so this e-mail address is invalid.

6.   Change the e-mail address to: **info@ASPNETCentral.co.uk**

TEST RESULTS
Does Expression Match? **YES**

7.   Test the regular expression.

Your regular expression matches *.co.uk* because it only requires there to be *at least* one full-stop after the @ sign. It will match no matter how many full-stops there are.

This is a good regular expression for e-mail addresses as it will never block a valid address. A determined user could still overcome this regular expression as it will allow multiple @ symbols or spaces within the e-mail address.

You could refine this regular expression further with the skills that you learned in: *Lesson 11-3: Create a regular expression for telephone numbers.*

You'll use this regular expression with the *RegularExpressionValidator* control in: *Lesson 11-6: Use the RegularExpressionValidator control.*

Lesson 11-5: Create a regular expression for HTML links

Internet search engines regularly scan or 'spider' pages on the internet. To do this, they search each HTML page for links and follow them to all of the pages that they link to. By repeating this process, a search engine can eventually locate every page on the internet.

Regular expressions offer an easy way to extract links from HTML code.

1   Open *TextLand* from your sample files folder.

2   View *RegularExpressions.aspx* in your web browser.

3   Enter some HTML code into the *Text* box.

Use the following code:

<html></html>

> REGULAR EXPRESSION TESTER
>
> Text: <html></html>

4   Create a regular expression to extract HTML tags.

1.   Test the following expression: **<.+?>**

> Server Error in '/' Application.
>
> *A potentially dangerous Request.Form value was detected*

An error occurs.

This error occurred because ASP.NET detected < and > characters inside the controls. ASP.NET automatically rejects these characters to prevent malicious users from attacking your site with a 'cross-site scripting attack'.

You'll learn more about this in: *Lesson 11-8: Understand cross-site scripting attacks*.

2.   Close your web browser and return to Visual Studio.

5   Disable validation on the *RegularExpressions.aspx* page.

1.   Open *RegularExpressions.aspx* in *Source* view.

2.   Add the following property to the *<%@ Page>* tag:

ValidateRequest="false"

This instructs ASP.NET to disable its security validation for the *RegularExpressions.aspx* page. This is all that you need to do in order to disable security on pages in ASP.NET 4.5.

If you were using ASP.NET 4.0, you would also need to add some code to *Web.config* before security would be disabled.

If you need to do this, you can find an ASP.NET 4.0 version of this lesson on our website at: www.aspnetcentral.com

important

Disabling validation is a security risk

ASP.NET's automatic security validation features protect your sites from being exploited by malicious users.

If you disable validation, you may be leaving your site vulnerable to attack.

In this lesson, you only disable validation for the *RegularExpressions.aspx* page.

As long as you are aware of the risks when writing your C# code, you can still ensure that this page is secure.

You'll learn more about the potential security risks in: *Lesson 11-8: Understand cross-site scripting attacks*.

note

.+ and .+?

When you use a regular expression using the **.+** syntax, the search is done using *permissive* matching.

This means that the regular expression will not stop searching when it finds a match. Instead it will continue searching the entire text.

For example, using the following HTML code:

Learn ASP.NET

…if you applied the regular expression **<.+>** to this HTML code, the expression would match the entire text:

Learn ASP.NET

This is because the search would not stop after finding the first > character. Instead the search continues until it finds the last > character.

If you use **.+?** instead of **.+**, the search uses *restrictive* matching. This means that it will stop searching as soon as a match is found.

The **<.+?>** regular expression would match only:

**
**

6   View *RegularExpressions.aspx* in your web browser.

7   Enter some HTML code into the *Text* box.

Use the following code:

<html><h1>My test HTML code</h1><a href="http://www.ASPNETCentral.com">Learn ASP.NET Web Site</a></html>

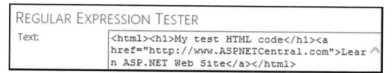

8   Create a regular expression to extract HTML tags.

Test the following expression: **<.+?>**

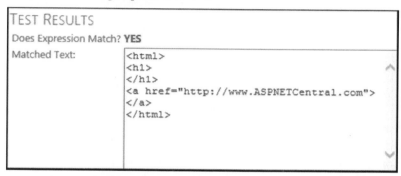

Each of the HTML tags is extracted. See sidebar for an explanation of why you used the ? special character in your regular expression.

9   Change the regular expression to only detect <a> tags.

Change the expression to the following: **<a.+?>**

TEST RESULTS
Does Expression Match? **YES**
Matched Text: `<a href="http://www.ASPNETCentral.com">`

This time only the <a> tag is extracted from the HTML code.

Using this regular expression, you could create your own 'web spider' program similar to those that are used by search engines.

Lesson 11-6: Use the RegularExpressionValidator control

The *RegularExpressionValidator* control allows you to easily add validation to controls on your pages using regular expressions.

The other validation controls are covered in Session 4 of the *Essential Skills* course.

1 Open *JoesBarWebApplication.sln* from your sample files folder.

2 Open *MailControl.ascx* in Design view.

This is the Web User Control that you created in: *Lesson 8-4: Create a Web User Control.*

3 Add a *RegularExpressionValidator* control to the right of the *ButtonSignUp* control.

You'll find this control in the *Validation* category of the *Toolbox*.

4 Set the *ID* property of the new control to:
RegularExpressionValidatorEmail

5 Configure the new control to validate the contents of the *TextBoxEmailAddress* control.

  1. Set the *ControlToValidate* property of the new control to:
  TextBoxEmailAddress

  2. Set the *ErrorMessage* property of the new control to:
  Invalid e-mail address

6 Set the regular expression for the control.

Set the *ValidationExpression* property of the *RegularExpressionValidator* control to:

.+@.+\..+

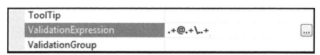

This is the regular expression that you created in: *Lesson 11-4: Create a regular expression for e-mail addresses.*

This *RegularExpressionValidator* control will only permit the user to enter text into the *TextBoxEmailAddress* control if it matches this regular expression.

7 Add server-side confirmation of your validation.

  1. Open the code-behind file of *MailControl.ascx.*

tip

Built-in regular expressions

Visual Studio contains a number of built-in regular expressions. You can access these by clicking the 'browse' icon next to the *ValidationExpression* property.

The built-in expressions include phone numbers for various countries, e-mail addresses and several others.

The built-in expressions are more complex than those that you've used in this session, but you should be able to understand them with the skills that you've learned.

2. Surround the contents of the *ButtonSignUp_Click* event handler with the following *if* statement:

    if (Page.IsValid)

    { }

```
if (Page.IsValid)
{
    System.Net.Mail.SmtpClient Client = new System.Net.Mail.SmtpClient();
    string AddressToSignUp = TextBoxEmailAddress.Text;
    Client.Send("Simon.Smart@ASPNETCentral.com", "Info@ASPNETCentral.com",
        "Discount Sign-Up", "Sign up " + AddressToSignUp);
    TextBoxEmailAddress.Text = "Thanks for signing up!";
    ButtonSignUp.Enabled = false;
    TextBoxEmailAddress.Enabled = false;
}
```

This code prevents users from bypassing the validation by disabling JavaScript on their browsers. This technique is covered in Session 4 of the *Essential Skills* course.

8   Test the validation.

1. View *Default.aspx* in your web browser.

2. In the last text box, enter: **info@ASPNETCentral**

This address is invalid because it is missing the *.com* at the end.

3. Click *Sign Up*.

Your *ErrorMessage* property is displayed and the invalid address is not sent to the server. The address is detected as invalid because it does not match the regular expression.

4. Change the e-mail address to: **infoASPNETCentral.com**

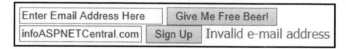

5. Click *Sign Up*.

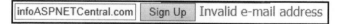

Once again, the address does not match the regular expression so it is not sent to the server. This time the address is invalid because it does not contain an @ symbol.

6. Change the e-mail address to: **info@ASPNETCentral.com**

7. Click *Sign Up*.

This time the address is sent to the server. This may cause an error if there is no mail server available.

8. Stop debugging and close Visual Studio.

Lesson 11-7: Work with regular expressions in C#

You can work with regular expressions in your C# code using the *System.Text.RegularExpressions* namespace.

In this lesson you'll use C# code to validate phone numbers using the regular expression that you created in: *Lesson 11-3: Create a regular expression for telephone numbers.*

1   Open *ForestWalks* from your sample files folder.

2   Open *Contact.aspx* in Design view.

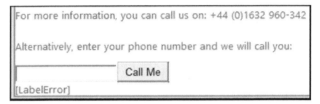

This page allows the user to submit a phone number.

You could validate the phone number using the *RegularExpressionValidator* control, but this time you'll use C# code instead.

3   Add a *Click* event handler to the *ButtonCallMe* control.

4   Add a *using* line for: **System.Text.RegularExpressions**

```
using System.Web.UI.WebControls;
using System.Text.RegularExpressions;
```

5   Add code to test the contents of *TextBoxPhoneNumber* against a regular expression.

1.   Add the following code to the *ButtonCallMe_Click* event handler:

string TextToTest = TextBoxPhoneNumber.Text;

```
protected void ButtonCallMe_Click(object sender, EventArgs e)
{
    string TextToTest = TextBoxPhoneNumber.Text;
}
```

This code simply retrieves the text from the *TextBoxPhoneNumber* control.

2.   Add the following code on the next line:

string RegularExpression =
@"(\([0-9]\)[0-9]{4})?(([0-9]{6})|([0-9]{3}[-][0-9]{3}))";

```
string TextToTest = TextBoxPhoneNumber.Text;
string RegularExpression =
    @"(\([0-9]\)[0-9]{4})?(([0-9]{6})|([0-9]{3}[ -][0-9]{3}))";
```

You created this regular expression in: *Lesson 11-3: Create a regular expression for telephone numbers.*

Notice that you preceded the *string* value with an @ symbol. See sidebar for an explanation.

important

Escaping special characters in C#

Just like regular expressions, C# has a number of characters that it considers 'special'. You must escape these if you wish to use them.

In this lesson, you're using the back-slash character in a *string*. The back-slash is considered 'special', so you must escape it.

C# offers a quick way to automatically escape special characters by adding an @ symbol before the *string*.

Using the @ symbol as you do in this lesson automatically escapes all special characters in a *string*.

Note that you can also escape special characters by using the back-slash character in the same way as you do in regular expressions.

Here's how the code would look if you escaped the special characters using back-slashes:

string RegularExpression =
"(\ \([0-9]\ \)[0-9]{4})?(([0-9]{6})|([0-9]{3}[-][0-9]{3}))";

3. Add the following code on the next line:

bool IsMatch =
Regex.IsMatch(TextToTest, RegularExpression);

```
string TextToTest = TextBoxPhoneNumber.Text;
string RegularExpression =
    @"(\([0-9]\)[0-9]{4})?(([0-9]{6})|([0-9]{3}[ -][0-9]{3}))";
bool IsMatch = Regex.IsMatch(TextToTest, RegularExpression);
```

The *Regex.IsMatch* method allows you to easily test whether a *string* matches a regular expression.

4. Add the following code on the next line:

MatchCollection Matches =
Regex.Matches(TextToTest, RegularExpression);

```
bool IsMatch = Regex.IsMatch(TextToTest, RegularExpression);
MatchCollection Matches = Regex.Matches(TextToTest, RegularExpression);
```

The *Regex.Matches* method returns a collection containing all of the matches that were found in the *TextToTest* string.

As this is a phone number, the regular expression shouldn't find more than one match.

5. Add the following code on the next line:

if (!IsMatch || Matches.Count > 1)
{
    LabelError.Text = "Invalid phone number";
}

```
MatchCollection Matches = Regex.Matches(TextToTest, RegularExpression);
if (!IsMatch || Matches.Count > 1)
{
    LabelError.Text = "Invalid phone number";
}
```

This code displays an error message if the regular expression doesn't match or if more than one match is found.

6   Test your code.

1. View *Contact.aspx* in your web browser.

2. In the text box, enter: **960-342**

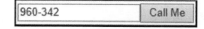

3. Click *Call Me*.

No error message is displayed. The phone number was detected as valid.

4. Enter the phone number: **960-34**

5. Click *Call Me*.

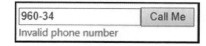

This phone number only has 5 digits so it does not match your regular expression and the error message is displayed by your C# code.

Lesson 11-8: Understand cross-site scripting attacks

Cross-site scripting attacks are similar to SQL injection attacks. You learned about SQL injection attacks in: *Lesson 10-11: Understand SQL injection attacks*.

Rather than trying to send SQL code to your database, cross-site scripting attacks try to manipulate the HTML code on your web pages. In this lesson you'll learn about cross-site scripting attacks and how to prevent them.

ASP.NET is highly secure against cross-site scripting attacks, but you should always be aware of the ways that malicious users might attempt to attack your sites.

1   Open *StableBase* from your sample files folder.

2   View *TaskAdmin.aspx* in your web browser.

This page displays a list of tasks and allows new tasks to be added.

3   Examine the HTML code of the *GridView* control.

1.   View the page's HTML code.

To do this in Internet Explorer, right-click on the page and click *View Source* from the shortcut menu.

2.   Examine the HTML code generated by the *GridView* control.

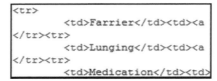

As you can see, each item is placed inside a *<td>* tag in an HTML table.

3.   Close the source code window.

4   Attempt a cross-site scripting attack.

1.   In the text box, enter the following:

**JeffK</td></tr></table><script>
alert('Hacked by JeffK');</script>**

This is a typical cross-site scripting attack.

If the attack is successful, the HTML code generated by the *GridView* control will appear as follows:

<tr>
    *<td>***JeffK</td>**
</tr>
</table>

```
<script>
    alert('Hacked by JeffK');
</script>
```

If the attack succeeded a *<script>* tag would be added to the page, allowing the malicious user to insert JavaScript code.

2. Click *Add Task*.

Server Error in '/' Application.

A potentially dangerous Request.Form value was detected

An error appears. By default, ASP.NET automatically blocks any attempts at cross-site scripting attacks.

You may recall seeing this error before, in: *Lesson 11-5: Create a regular expression for HTML links*.

3. Close your web browser and return to Visual Studio.

5   Make the site vulnerable to cross-site scripting attacks.

1. Open *TaskAdmin.aspx* in *Source* view.

2. Add the following property to the *<%@ Page>* tag: **ValidateRequest="false"**

TaskAdmin.aspx
`<%@ Page ValidateRequest="false"`

The *TaskAdmin.aspx* page is now potentially vulnerable to cross-site scripting attacks.

6   Attempt to carry out a cross-site scripting attack.

1. View *TaskAdmin.aspx* in your web browser.

2. In the text box, enter the following:

    JeffK</td></tr></table><script>
    alert('Hacked by JeffK');</script>

JeffK</td></tr></table><s   Add Task

3. Click *Add Task*.

Amazingly, the cross-site scripting attack still fails!

| Farrier | Edit |
| JeffK</td></tr></table><script> | Edit |

The *GridView* control automatically encodes its contents to prevent cross-site scripting attacks. Although the *GridView* control protects you, some controls (such as the *Literal* control) may now be vulnerable to attacks.

As long as you don't disable ASP.NET's built-in security, you should never need to worry about cross-site scripting attacks.

---

note

ASP.NET offers far more protection than other languages

In this course you have learned that ASP.NET automatically protects you from Cross Site Scripting and SQL Injection attacks, but this isn't true of all languages.

In other languages (such as PHP), you must be very careful to avoid writing code that is vulnerable to attack.

ASP.NET offers so much automated protection that it is easy to forget that it is possible for your web applications to be vulnerable.

It's very important to understand these vulnerabilities if you write code that steps outside ASP.NET's protected environment.

Session 11: Exercise

1   Open *Exercise11* from your sample files folder.

2   View *EmailRegex.aspx* in your web browser.

3   Enter a regular expression for e-mail addresses in the *Regular Expression* box and click *Test Expression*.

The correct regular expression should match the two valid e-mail addresses but not match the two invalid e-mail addresses.

4   Close your web browser, return to Visual Studio and open *EmailForm.aspx* in Design view.

5   Add a *RegularExpressionValidator* control to the page that will ensure that the *TextBoxEmailAddress* control contains a valid e-mail address.

6   Open the code-behind file of *EmailForm.aspx* and add C# code to confirm your *RegularExpressionValidator* control's validation even if the user has disabled JavaScript.

7   Open the code-behind file of *CustomerNumber.aspx*.

8   Add C# code to the *ButtonConfirm_Click* event handler to confirm that the *CustomerNumber* variable contains a valid 6-digit number.

9   Open *LinkExtractor.aspx* in Source view and disable security validation on the page.

10   View *LinkExtractor.aspx* in your web browser.

11   In the *Regular Expression* box, enter a regular expression that will extract HTML links.

12   Click *Extract Links*.

If you need help slide the page to the left ➡

Session 11: Exercise Answers

These are the four questions that students find the most difficult to answer:

Q 11	Q 9	Q 8	Q 3
Use the following regular expression: **<a.+>** This was covered in: *Lesson 11-5: Create a regular expression for HTML links.*	Add the following property to the *<%@ Page>* tag: **ValidateRequest="false"** This was covered in: *Lesson 11-5: Create a regular expression for HTML links.*	1. Add the following *using* line: **using System.Text. RegularExpressions;** 2. Add the following code: **bool IsValid = Regex. IsMatch(CustomerNumber, "[0-9]{6}");** 3. Enclose the remaining code in the following *if* statement: **if (IsValid) { }** This was covered in: *Lesson 11-7: Work with regular expressions in C#.*	Use the following regular expression: .+@.+\..+ This was covered in: *Lesson 11-4: Create a regular expression for e-mail addresses.*

If you have difficulty with the other questions, here are the lessons that cover the relevant skills:

1   Refer to: Essential Skills Session 1.

2   Refer to: Essential Skills Session 1.

4   Refer to: Essential Skills Session 1.

5   Refer to: Lesson 11-6: Use the RegularExpressionValidator control.

6   Refer to: Lesson 11-6: Use the RegularExpressionValidator control.

7   Refer to: Essential Skills Session 1.

10   Refer to: Essential Skills Session 1.

12

Session Twelve: Expert techniques

> The beginnings and endings of all human undertakings are untidy.
>
> *John Galsworthy, English author (1867-1933)*

At this stage you have expert-level knowledge of ASP.NET, C# and Visual Studio. With the skills that you've learned in this course, you will be able to use ASP.NET to its full potential.

Although all of the skills are in your possession, the .NET framework has much more to offer. There are over 33,000 classes in the .NET framework and it would take an enormous book to cover all of them.

In this session you'll learn some advanced techniques using some of the more useful classes that you haven't seen before.

Session Objectives

By the end of this session you will be able to:

- Store a file in a database
- Output a file to the user's web browser
- Run an external program
- Create a scheduled event using a Timer object
- Serialize an object to an XML file
- Deserialize an XML file back into an object
- Compress a file
- Decompress a file
- Use the System.Drawing classes to manipulate images
- Create a Captcha image system
- Create a page that can upload multiple files
- Extract multiple files from a request

Lesson 12-1: Store a file in a database

Enabling a web application to store files is a common requirement that requires an understanding of databases and binary data.

In this lesson you'll store files in a database as binary data.

1 Open *DotNetExpert* from your sample files folder.

2 Examine the project's database.

1. Switch to the *Database Explorer* window and expand *DotNetExpertConnectionString*.

2. Expand *Tables*.

3. Right-click *UploadedFile* and click *Open Table Definition* from the shortcut menu.

   The definition of the table's structure appears in the main Visual Studio window.

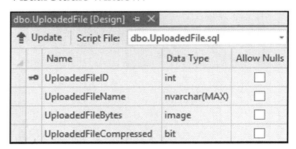

   Notice that the *UploadedFileBytes* column has a *Data Type* of: *image*. The *image* data type is designed to store any sort of binary data (not only images). You learned about binary data in: *Lesson 2-4: Use the Byte class.*

4. Switch back to the *Solution Explorer* window.

3 Open *Files.aspx* in Design view.

This page allows users to upload and download files.

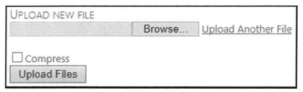

When it is finished, this page will enable the user to upload multiple files and compress them if required.

In this lesson, you'll simply enable the page to upload a single file.

4 Add a *Click* event handler to the *Upload Files* button.

5 Add code to upload a file to the database.

1. Add the following code to the new event handler:

   if (FileUploadNewFile.HasFile)
   {
       using (DotNetExpertDataContext Data = new

If you are not completing the course incrementally use the sample file: **Lesson 12-1** to begin this lesson.

Sample files with the starting point for each lesson are also provided for all of the other lessons in this session.

I have seen many systems implemented where the database stores a filename and the physical file is stored outside the database.

Files can be saved onto the web server by using the *System.IO.File* class.

This approach dates back to the days when databases could not handle large amounts of binary data but this reason is no longer valid.

I recommend saving files into a database for several reasons:

1. For security reasons, a web application may not be allowed access to the web server's hard drive. This would make the saving of physical files impossible.

2. Even if security policy allows, enabling a web application to save files to the web server's hard drive can require a lot of additional configuration.

3. Users are less likely to accidentally delete a database record than a physical file.

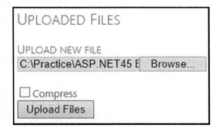

```
DotNetExpertDataContext())
{
    UploadedFile NewFile = new UploadedFile();
    NewFile.UploadedFileName =
        FileUploadNewFile.FileName;
}
}
```

```
protected void ButtonUploadFile_Click(object sender, EventArgs e)
{
    if (FileUploadNewFile.HasFile)
    {
        using (DotNetExpertDataContext Data =
            new DotNetExpertDataContext())
        {
            UploadedFile NewFile = new UploadedFile();
            NewFile.UploadedFileName =
                FileUploadNewFile.FileName;
        }
    }
}
```

This code checks whether the *FileUploadNewFile* control has a file ready for upload. If so, it creates a new *UploadedFile* LINQ object ready to be sent to the database.

2. Add the following code to the end of the *using* statement:

NewFile.UploadedFileBytes = FileUploadNewFile.FileBytes;

```
NewFile.UploadedFileName =
    FileUploadNewFile.FileName;
NewFile.UploadedFileBytes = FileUploadNewFile.FileBytes;
```

This code places the array of *byte* variables from the *FileUpload* control into the *UploadedFileBytes* database column.

Because the database column has a data type of *image*, it's able to accept a *byte* array without any problems.

3. Add the following code to the end of the *using* statement:

Data.UploadedFiles.InsertOnSubmit(NewFile);
Data.SubmitChanges();
GridViewUploadedFile.DataBind();

```
NewFile.UploadedFileBytes = FileUploadNewFile.FileBytes;
Data.UploadedFiles.InsertOnSubmit(NewFile);
Data.SubmitChanges();
GridViewUploadedFile.DataBind();
```

This code commits the new record to the database and refreshes the *GridView* control.

6 Test your code.

1. View *Files.aspx* in your web browser.

2. Click *Browse…* and navigate to your sample files folder.

3. Click *MarketData.csv* and click *Open*.

4. Click *Upload Files*.

The file is uploaded and saved into the database.

You'll learn how to retrieve the file and display it to the user in: *Lesson 12-2: Output a file to the user's web browser.*

Lesson 12-2: Output a file to the user's web browser

You saved a file into a database in the previous lesson: *Lesson 12-1: Store a file in a database.*

In this lesson, you'll learn how to retrieve the file from the database and send it to the user through their web browser.

1 Open *DotNetExpert* from your sample files folder.

2 Open *Files.aspx* in Design view.

```
UPLOADED FILES

LinqDataSource - LinqDataSourceUploadedFile

Databound    View File

Databound    View File
```

The file should be displayed when the user clicks one of the *View File* links in the *GridView* control.

3 Add a *RowCommand* event handler to the *GridViewUploadedFile* control.

4 Add code to retrieve the selected file from the database.

Add the following code to the new event handler:

```
int RowClicked = Convert.ToInt32(e.CommandArgument);
int UploadedFileID = Convert.ToInt32
(GridViewUploadedFile.DataKeys[RowClicked].Value);
using (DotNetExpertDataContext Data = new
DotNetExpertDataContext())
{
    UploadedFile FileToDisplay =
    Data.UploadedFiles.Single(UploadedFile =>
    UploadedFile.UploadedFileID == UploadedFileID);
}
```

```
protected void GridViewUploadedFile_RowCommand(object sender, GridViewCommar
{
    int RowClicked = Convert.ToInt32(e.CommandArgument);
    int UploadedFileID = Convert.ToInt32(GridViewUploadedFile.
        DataKeys[RowClicked].Value);
    using (DotNetExpertDataContext Data = new DotNetExpertDataContext())
    {
        UploadedFile FileToDisplay =
            Data.UploadedFiles.Single(
            UploadedFile => UploadedFile.UploadedFileID == UploadedFileID);
    }
}
```

This code retrieves the database record that corresponds to the entry that the user clicked. This technique is covered in Session 12 of the Essential Skills course in this series.

5 Add code to send the file to the user's web browser.

1. Add the following code at the end of the *using* statement:

Page.Response.AddHeader(
"content-disposition", "attachment;filename=" +
FileToDisplay.UploadedFileName);

```
UploadedFile FileToDisplay = Data.UploadedFiles.Single(Upload
Page.Response.AddHeader("content-disposition",
    "attachment;filename=" + FileToDisplay.UploadedFileName);
}
```

This code adds a new *header* to the web server's response. This header tells the user's web browser that the server is sending a file as an *attachment*, along with the name of the file.

By specifying *attachment* as the *content-disposition*, you are telling the web browser to download the file instead of trying to display it in the browser (see sidebar on facing page).

2. Add the following code on the next line:

byte[] FileBytes =
FileToDisplay.UploadedFileBytes.ToArray();

```
Response.AddHeader("content-disposition",
    "attachment;filename=" + FileToDisplay.UploadedFileName);
byte[] FileBytes = FileToDisplay.UploadedFileBytes.ToArray();
```

This code retrieves the file's binary data from the database and converts it back into a *byte* array.

3. Add the following code on the next line:

Response.BinaryWrite(FileBytes);
Response.End();

```
byte[] FileBytes = FileToDisplay.UploadedFileBytes.ToArray();
Response.BinaryWrite(FileBytes);
Response.End();
```

This code writes the file's binary data into the web server's response and ends the response.

Ending the response stops any more information from being added to the web server's response to the web browser. This means that ASP.NET will not add the page's HTML code to the response.

Because the file is being sent as an attachment, the web browser will keep the last copy of the web page visible instead of refreshing the page.

6   Test your code.

1. View *Files.aspx* in your web browser.

2. Click *View File* next to *MarketData.csv*.

UPLOADED FILES

MarketData.csv   View File

Do you want to open or save **MarketData.csv** from **localhost**?   [Open] [Save ▼] [Cancel]   ✕

You are prompted to open or save the file, just like any other file you might download from the internet.

3. Click *Cancel*.

---

note

Alternatives ways to send files to the user

In this lesson, you use the *Response.BinaryWrite* method to send binary data to the user's web browser, but there are two alternative methods that allow you to send files.

Both of these methods require a physical file to be present, so they cannot transmit a *byte[]* array from a database. To send files from a database, you will always need to use *BinaryWrite*.

Response.WriteFile

This method allows you to send a physical file to the web browser by specifying the path to the file.

For example:

Response.
WriteFile("C:\video.mp4");

Response.TransmitFile

TransmitFile is almost identical to *WriteFile,* but optimized for larger files.

In general, *TransmitFile* is the best choice as it works well with both large and small files.

Lesson 12-3: Run an external program

Sometimes you will want your web applications to run other programs on the web server. For example, you might want to run a PDF conversion program or a backup utility.

In this lesson you'll learn how to run external programs from your ASP.NET web applications.

1　Open *DotNetExpert* from your sample files folder.

2　Open *Backup.aspx* in Design view.

When complete, this page will backup and restore the application's database. You'll use an external program to do this.

3　Add a *Click* event handler to the *ButtonBackupNow* control.

4　Add a *using* line for: **System.Diagnostics**

```
using System.Web.UI.WebControls;
using System.Diagnostics;
```

The classes that are used to run external programs are held in the *System.Diagnostics* namespace.

Specifically, you'll use the *System.Diagnostics.Process* class.

5　Add code to the new event handler to run the *BackupDatabase.bat* program.

1.　Add the following code to the new event handler:

**string ProgramPath =
Server.MapPath("~/BackupDatabase.bat");**

```
protected void ButtonBackupNow_Click(object sender, EventArgs e)
{
    string ProgramPath = Server.MapPath("~/BackupDatabase.bat");
}
```

This code extracts the path to the program and places it in the *ProgramPath* variable.

Server.MapPath converts paths from internal paths (*~/BackupDatabase.bat*) into actual locations on the web server. In this case, the final path will be:

*C:\Practice\ASP.NET45 Expert\DotNetExpert\
DotNetExpert\BackupDatabase.bat*

2.　Add the following code on the next line:

Process.Start(ProgramPath);

```
string ProgramPath = Server.MapPath("~/BackupDatabase.bat");
Process.Start(ProgramPath);
```

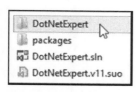

This simple code will run *BackupDatabase.bat* when the button is clicked.

This will work with any kind of program, not just *.bat* files (see sidebar).

6   Return to *Backup.aspx* in Design view.

7   Add a *Click* event handler to the *ButtonRestoreNow* control.

8   Add code to the new event handler to run the *RestoreDatabase.bat* program.

Add the following code to the new event handler:

string ProgramPath = Server.MapPath("~/RestoreDatabase.bat");
Process.Start(ProgramPath);

```
protected void ButtonRestoreNow_Click(object sender, EventArgs e)
{
    string ProgramPath = Server.MapPath("~/RestoreDatabase.bat");
    Process.Start(ProgramPath);
}
```

9   Test your code.

1.   View *Backup.aspx* in your web browser.

2.   Click *Backup Database Now*.

     BackupDatabase.bat is executed and appears on your screen.

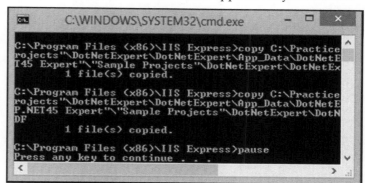

Note that you are seeing this because your own computer is acting as the web server. This wouldn't appear to users browsing the site over the internet.

3.   Press any key to close *BackupDatabase.bat*.

4.   Using Windows Explorer, navigate to the *DotNetExpert* folder in your sample files folder.

5.   Open the second *DotNetExpert* folder.

6.   Open the *Backups* folder.

     A copy of the database has been placed in this folder by the *BackupDatabase.bat* program. See sidebar if the folder is empty.

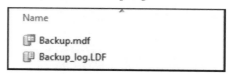

The *RestoreDatabase.bat* program simply copies the backup back into its original location.

Lesson 12-4: Create a scheduled event using a Timer object

Sometimes you will want code to run on a scheduled basis. For example, you might want to run a backup program daily.

Ideally, this should be done with a separate program on the web server, but this won't always be an option when using shared web hosting.

In this lesson you'll create a scheduled event by using the *Timer* class.

1 Open *DotNetExpert* from your sample files folder.

2 Open *Global.asax*.

Global.asax acts as a built-in HTTP module. You learned about HTTP modules in: *Lesson 8-8: Create an HTTP Module*.

```
public class Global : System.Web.HttpApplication
{

    void Application_Start(object sender, EventArgs e)
    {
```

Any code placed in the *Application_Start* event handler will run whenever the application is started by the web server.

3 Add a *using* line for: **System.Threading**

You'll use the *System.Threading.Timer* class to create your scheduled event.

Note that this is <u>not</u> the same as the *Timer* control that you worked with in: *Lesson 9-5: Use the Timer control for scheduled updates*.

```
using System.Web.SessionState;
using System.Threading;
using System.Diagnostics;
```

4 Add a *using* line for: **System.Diagnostics**

You'll need this namespace to run the backup utility using the *System.Diagnostics.Process* class.

5 Add a new static method to run the backup utility.

Add the following method to *Global.asax*:

static void RunBackup(object sender)
{
    string ProgramPath = ((HttpContext)sender).
    Server.MapPath("~/BackupDatabase.bat");
    Process.Start(ProgramPath);
}

```
static void RunBackup(object sender)
{
    string ProgramPath = ((HttpContext)sender).
        Server.MapPath("~/BackupDatabase.bat");
    Process.Start(ProgramPath);
}
```

This code is almost identical to the code that you wrote in: *Lesson 12-3: Run an external program*. When it is called, this method will run *BackupDatabase.bat*.

Note that this method uses the *object sender* argument because it is going to be used as a delegate method by the *Timer* class. You learned about delegate methods in: *Lesson 4-10: Understand delegate methods.*

6   Add a new static *Timer* object.

Add the following code to *Global.asax,* outside any event handlers:

static Timer BackupTimer;

```
public class Global : System.Web.HttpApplication
{
    static Timer BackupTimer;
```

7   Add code to start the timer in the *Application_Start* event handler.

Add the following code to the *Application_Start* event handler:

BackupTimer = new Timer(new TimerCallback(RunBackup), HttpContext.Current, 0, 86400000);

```
void Application_Start(object sender, EventArgs e)
{
    BackupTimer = new Timer(
        new TimerCallback(RunBackup),
        HttpContext.Current, 0, 86400000);
```

This code creates and starts your new *Timer*. This *Timer* object will call the *RunBackup* method every 24 hours (86,400,000 milliseconds).

The *Timer* class is very similar to the *Thread* class that you worked with in: *Lesson 3-6: Implement multi-threading using the Thread class.*

8   Test your code.

1. For testing purposes, change the interval of your *Timer* object from *86400000* to: **60000**

```
new TimerCallback(RunBackup),
HttpContext.Current, 0, 60000);
```

This will run the backup utility every minute instead of every 24 hours.

2. Click Debug→Start Debugging.

BackupDatabase.bat is executed and appears on the screen.

3. Press any key to close *BackupDatabase.bat.*

4. Wait for 1 minute.

BackupDatabase.bat appears again. This will continue every minute until the application stops.

5. Stop debugging and return to Visual Studio.

6. Change the timer interval back to: **86400000**

```
BackupTimer = new Timer(new TimerCallback(RunBackup),
    HttpContext.Current, 0, 86400000);
```

note

This is not an ideal solution

While you shouldn't have any problems using the *System.Threading.Timer* class, it isn't an ideal way to schedule tasks on your web server.

If you have direct access to the web server, you can use the Scheduled Tasks feature of Windows instead. This is a better solution as it is easy to see which tasks are scheduled.

With the *System.Threading.Timer* class, it's impossible to tell that a task is scheduled without looking at the source code of the application.

Lesson 12-5: Serialize an object to an XML file

You learned how to write information into an XML file in: *Lesson 10-9: Write data to an XML file*, but there's a much easier way to do this.

Using the *XmlSerializer* class, you can save any C# object into an XML file and easily convert these XML files back into objects.

1 Open *DotNetExpert* from your sample files folder.

2 Open *ObjectToXML.aspx* in Design view.

XML SERIALIZATION	
First Name:	Simon
Last Name:	Smart
Address 1:	The Smart Method Ltd, Burleigh Manor
Address 2:	Peel Road
Town:	Douglas, IOM
Country:	Great Britain
Post Code:	IM1 5EP
Serialize to XML file	Deserialize from XML file

Once complete, this page will enable you to save the name and address details into an XML file and retrieve them again.

3 Open the code-behind file of *ObjectToXML.aspx*.

4 Add a *using* line for: **System.Xml.Serialization**

```
using System.Web.UI.WebControls;
using System.Xml.Serialization;
using System.IO;
```

This namespace contains the *XMLSerializer* class.

5 Add a *using* line for: **System.IO**

This namespace contains the *StreamWriter* class. You'll need this to write the XML data to a file.

You learned about streams in: *Lesson 2-3: Use the Stream class*.

6 Examine the *ButtonSerializeToXMLFile_Click* event handler.

```
protected void ButtonSerializeToXMLFile_Click(object sender,
{
    Customer CustomerToSerialize = new Customer();
    CustomerToSerialize.FirstName = TextBoxFirstName.Text;
    CustomerToSerialize.LastName = TextBoxLastName.Text;
    CustomerToSerialize.Address1 = TextBoxAddress1.Text;
    CustomerToSerialize.Address2 = TextBoxAddress2.Text;
    CustomerToSerialize.Town = TextBoxTown.Text;
    CustomerToSerialize.Country = TextBoxCountry.Text;
    CustomerToSerialize.PostCode = TextBoxPostCode.Text;
```

This event handler creates an instance of the *Customer* class and populates its properties with the values entered by the user.

7 Add code to the *ButtonSerializeToXMLFile_Click* event handler to serialize the *CustomerToSerialize* object into an XML file.

1. Add the following code to the end of the event handler:

XmlSerializer Serializer = new XmlSerializer(typeof(Customer));

```
//Add code to serialize here
XmlSerializer Serializer = new XmlSerializer(typeof(Customer));
```

This code creates an *XmlSerializer* object that can convert (or 'serialize') *Customer* objects into XML files.

Note that the *typeof* keyword is needed to specify the type of object that the *XmlSerializer* will serialize.

2. Add the following code on the next line:

StreamWriter Writer = new StreamWriter(Server.MapPath("~/Customer.xml"));

```
XmlSerializer Serializer = new XmlSerializer(typeof(Customer));
StreamWriter Writer =
    new StreamWriter(Server.MapPath("~/Customer.xml"));
```

This code creates a *StreamWriter* object that will be used to write the XML file into the web application's root folder.

3. Add the following code on the next line:

Serializer.Serialize(Writer, CustomerToSerialize); Writer.Close();

```
    new StreamWriter(Server.MapPath("~/Customer.xml"));
Serializer.Serialize(Writer, CustomerToSerialize);
Writer.Close();
```

This code saves the XML file and closes the *StreamWriter* object.

This is all the code you need to save an object as an XML file.

8   Test your code.

1. View *ObjectToXML.aspx* in your web browser.

2. Change some values in the text boxes on the page.

3. Click *Serialize to XML file*.

```
Post Code:  TSM
 Serialize to XML file    Deserialize from XML file
```

4. Close your web browser and return to Visual Studio.

5. Click File➔Open File…

6. If you're not already in the *DotNetExpert* folder, navigate to: *C:\Practice\ASP.NET45 Expert\DotNetExpert\DotNetExpert*

7. Click *Customer.xml* and click *Open*.

The XML file that was generated is opened in Visual Studio.

```
<Customer xmlns:xsi="http://www.w3.org/2001/XMLSchema-insta
   <FirstName>Simon</FirstName>
   <LastName>Smart</LastName>
   <Address1>The Smart Method Ltd, Burleigh Manor</Address1>
   <Address2>Peel Road</Address2>
   <Town>Douglas, IOM</Town>
   <Country>Great Britain</Country>
   <PostCode>TSM</PostCode>
</Customer>
```

note

Serializing to binary files

As well as serializing objects to XML files, you can serialize them to standard binary files.

This is done using the classes in the *System.Runtime.Serialization* namespace.

Serializing objects to binary is a more involved process than serializing to XML, but it has exactly the same purpose.

The advantage of binary serialization is that the resulting files will be smaller than the XML files created through XML serialization.

The advantage of XML serialization is that the files it creates can be easily read by other XML-aware applications such as Microsoft Excel.

Binary serialization might seem useful if you want to serialize large amounts of information to a file, but a database is usually a better choice when you need to store large files.

Lesson 12-6: Deserialize an XML file back into an object

You converted a C# object into an XML file in: *Lesson 12-5: Serialize an object to an XML file.*

In this lesson, you'll deserialize the XML file, converting it back into a C# object.

1 Open *DotNetExpert* from your sample files folder.

2 Open the code-behind file of *ObjectToXML.aspx*.

3 Examine the *ButtonDeserializeFromXMLFile_Click* event handler.

```
protected void ButtonDeserializeFromXMLFile_Click(object sen
{
    Customer DeserializedCustomer = new Customer();

    //Add code to deserialize here

    TextBoxFirstName.Text = DeserializedCustomer.FirstName;
    TextBoxLastName.Text = DeserializedCustomer.LastName;
    TextBoxAddress1.Text = DeserializedCustomer.Address1;
    TextBoxAddress2.Text = DeserializedCustomer.Address2;
    TextBoxTown.Text = DeserializedCustomer.Town;
    TextBoxCountry.Text = DeserializedCustomer.Country;
    TextBoxPostCode.Text = DeserializedCustomer.PostCode;
}
```

This code creates an instance of the *Customer* class and places the values of its properties into the text boxes on the page.

You will need to add some code to populate the *DeserializedCustomer* object's properties with the values from the XML file.

4 Add code to deserialize the XML file.

1. Add the following code in the marked area:

   XmlSerializer Deserializer = new XmlSerializer(typeof(Customer));

   ```
   //Add code to deserialize here
   XmlSerializer Deserializer = new XmlSerializer(typeof(Customer));
   ```

   This is exactly the same class that you used to create the XML file in: *Lesson 12-5: Serialize an object to an XML file.*

   The *XmlSerializer* class is capable of both serializing and deserializing objects.

2. Add the following code on the next line:

   StreamReader Reader = new StreamReader(Server.MapPath("~/Customer.xml"));

   ```
   XmlSerializer Deserializer = new XmlSerializer(typeof(Customer));
   StreamReader Reader =
       new StreamReader(Server.MapPath("~/Customer.xml"));
   ```

This is similar to the code that you used in the previous lesson, but this time you are using a *StreamReader* object instead of a *StreamWriter*.

This is because you will be reading from the *Customer.xml* file instead of writing to it.

3. Add the following code on the next line:

**DeserializedCustomer =
(Customer)Deserializer.Deserialize(Reader);
Reader.Close();**

```
StreamReader Reader =
    new StreamReader(Server.MapPath("~/Customer.xml"));
DeserializedCustomer =
    (Customer)Deserializer.Deserialize(Reader);
Reader.Close();
```

This code converts the XML file back into a *Customer* object and closes the *StreamReader*.

Notice that you have to *cast* the result from the *Deserialize* method back to the *Customer* type.

5   Test your code.

1. View *ObjectToXML.aspx* in your web browser.

2. Clear the contents of all of the text boxes.

XML SERIALIZATION

First Name:	
Last Name:	
Address 1:	
Address 2:	
Town:	
Country:	
Post Code:	

Serialize to XML file   Deserialize from XML file

3. Click *Deserialize from XML file*.

XML SERIALIZATION

First Name:	Simon
Last Name:	Smart
Address 1:	The Smart Method Ltd, Burleigh Manor
Address 2:	Peel Road
Town:	Douglas, IOM
Country:	Great Britain
Post Code:	TSM

Serialize to XML file   Deserialize from XML file

The information is retrieved from the XML file and displayed in the boxes.

Serialization offers a really easy way to save objects to files and then to later load the file back into an object of the same type.

Lesson 12-7: Compress a file

When working with large amounts of binary data, you may want to compress it to save disk space.

The .NET framework includes classes that enable you to compress binary data using the GZIP algorithm.

1   Open *DotNetExpert* from your sample files folder.

2   Open *Files.aspx* in Design view.

You're going to add code to this page that will compress the uploaded file before saving it if the user ticks the *Compress* box.

3   Open the code-behind file of *Files.aspx*.

4   Add a *using* line for: **System.IO**

```
using System.Web.UI.WebControls;
using System.IO;
using System.IO.Compression;
```

You're going to need to use *Stream* objects for compression and decompression, so this namespace is useful.

You learned about streams in: *Lesson 2-3: Use the Stream class.*

5   Add a *using* line for: **System.IO.Compression**

The *GZipStream* class that you'll be using to compress the files is found in the *System.IO.Compression* namespace.

6   Add code to the *ButtonUploadFile_Click* event handler to compress the uploaded files.

1.   Replace the line:

NewFile.UploadedFileBytes = FileUploadNewFile.FileBytes;

…with:

if (!CheckBoxCompress.Checked)
{
    NewFile.UploadedFileBytes = FileUploadNewFile.FileBytes;
}
else { }

```
    FileUploadNewFile.FileName;
if (!CheckBoxCompress.Checked)
{
    NewFile.UploadedFileBytes = FileUploadNewFile.FileBytes;
}
else
{
}
Data.UploadedFiles.InsertOnSubmit(NewFile);
```

2.   Add the following code inside the new *else* statement:

MemoryStream CompressedStream = new MemoryStream();
GZipStream Compressor = new
GZipStream(CompressedStream,
CompressionMode.Compress);

note

ASP.NET also supports Deflate

As well as the *GZIP* algorithm, ASP.NET is also able to compress files using the *Deflate* algorithm.

Deflate generally takes longer but results in smaller files, although this is likely to vary depending on the file.

To compress using Deflate, use the *DeflateStream* class from the *System.IO.Compression* namespace.

The *DeflateStream* class works identically to the *GZipStream* class.

note

Compression is not guaranteed

Compressing a file won't always result in a smaller file size. Very small files are likely to be larger after compression because of the additional information that is added when compressing.

Some files already have compression of their own, such as JPEG images. Because JPEG files are already compressed they are unlikely to reduce in size if you attempt to compress them.

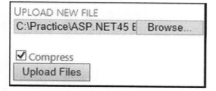

```
else
{
    MemoryStream CompressedStream = new MemoryStream();
    GZipStream Compressor = new GZipStream
        (CompressedStream, CompressionMode.Compress);
}
```

The *GZipStream* object will be used to compress the file.

The *CompressedStream* object will receive the compressed binary data.

3. Add the following code on the next line:

Compressor.Write(FileUploadNewFile.FileBytes, 0, FileUploadNewFile.FileBytes.Length);

```
    (CompressedStream, CompressionMode.Compress);
Compressor.Write(FileUploadNewFile.FileBytes, 0,
    FileUploadNewFile.FileBytes.Length);
```

This code tells the *GZipStream* object to compress the binary data from the *FileUploadNewFile* control and save it into the *CompressedStream* object.

You learned about the *FileUpload* control in: *Lesson 7-3: Use the FileUpload control.*

4. Add the following code on the next line:

Compressor.Close();

```
    FileUploadNewFile.FileBytes.Length);
Compressor.Close();
```

It's very important to call the *Close* method <u>before</u> attempting to extract the compressed data from the *MemoryStream* object.

If you do not call the *Close* method, the *GZipStream* will not finish compressing the data properly.

5. Add the following code on the next line:

NewFile.UploadedFileBytes = CompressedStream.ToArray();
NewFile.UploadedFileCompressed = true;

```
Compressor.Close();
NewFile.UploadedFileBytes = CompressedStream.ToArray();
NewFile.UploadedFileCompressed = true;
```

This code places the compressed data into the LINQ database object and marks it as compressed.

You learned about saving binary data into databases in: *Lesson 12-1: Store a file in a database.*

7 Test your code.

1. View *Files.aspx* in your web browser.

2. Click *Browse…* and browse to your sample files folder.

3. Click *MailModule.XML* and click *Open.*

4. Tick the *Compress* box.

5. Click *Upload Files.*

The file is compressed and uploaded. You'll learn how to decompress it again in: *Lesson 12-8: Decompress a file.*

Lesson 12-8: Decompress a file

You compressed a file and saved it into a database in: *Lesson 12-7: Compress a file*. In this lesson, you'll write code to decompress and display the file.

1   Open *DotNetExpert* from your sample files folder.

2   View *Files.aspx* in your web browser.

UPLOADED FILES

MailModule.XML   View File

MarketData.csv   View File

MailModule.XML is the compressed file that you uploaded in the previous lesson.

3   Attempt to view *MailModule.XML*.

The XML page cannot be displayed

   1.   Click *View File* next to *MailModule.XML*.

   2.   When prompted, click *Open*.

        You will be unable to open the XML file (it may appear blank). You will need to decompress it before it will be readable.

   3.   Close your web browser and return to Visual Studio.

4   Open the code-behind file of *Files.aspx*.

5   Add code to the *GridViewUploadedFile_RowCommand* event handler to decompress any compressed files.

   1.   Replace the following line of code:

        Response.BinaryWrite(FileBytes);

        …with:

        if (!FileToDisplay.UploadedFileCompressed)
        {
            Response.BinaryWrite(FileBytes);
        }
        else { }

```
byte[] FileBytes = FileToDisplay.UploadedFileBytes.ToArray();
if (!FileToDisplay.UploadedFileCompressed)
{
    Response.BinaryWrite(FileBytes);
}
else
{
}
Response.End();
```

   2.   Add the following code inside the new *else* statement:

        GZipStream Decompressor = new GZipStream(new MemoryStream(FileBytes), CompressionMode.Decompress);

```
else
{
    GZipStream Decompressor = new GZipStream
        (new MemoryStream(FileBytes), CompressionMode.Decompress);
}
```

        This *GZipStream* object will be used to decompress the data.

   3.   Add the following code on the next line:

MemoryStream DecompressedStream =
new MemoryStream();
byte[] DecompressionBuffer = new byte[4096];

```
(new MemoryStream(FileBytes), CompressionMode.Decompress);
MemoryStream DecompressedStream = new MemoryStream();
byte[] DecompressionBuffer = new byte[4096];
```

This code creates a new *MemoryStream* object to store the decompressed data.

The *DecompressionBuffer* byte array will be used to read the file in 'chunks' of 4096 bytes. It's necessary to do this because you cannot predict how large the file will be once it has been decompressed.

4. Add the following code on the next line:

int ByteCounter =
Decompressor.Read(DecompressionBuffer, 0, 4096);

```
byte[] DecompressionBuffer = new byte[4096];
int ByteCounter = Decompressor.Read(DecompressionBuffer, 0, 4096);
```

This code reads the first 'chunk' of decompressed data into the *DecompressionBuffer* array. The actual number of bytes that were returned is placed in the *ByteCounter* variable.

5. Add the following code on the next line:

while (ByteCounter > 0)
{
　　DecompressedStream.Write
　　(DecompressionBuffer, 0, ByteCounter);
　　ByteCounter = Decompressor.Read
　　(DecompressionBuffer, 0, 4096);
}

```
int ByteCounter = Decompressor.Read(DecompressionBuffer, 0, 4096);
while (ByteCounter > 0)
{
    DecompressedStream.Write(DecompressionBuffer, 0, ByteCounter);
    ByteCounter = Decompressor.Read(DecompressionBuffer, 0, 4096);
}
```

This *while* loop iterates through all of the decompressed data in the *Decompressor* object and writes it into the *DecompressedStream* object.

6. Add the following code after the end of the *while* loop:

Response.BinaryWrite(DecompressedStream.ToArray());

```
}
Response.BinaryWrite(DecompressedStream.ToArray());
```

This code writes the decompressed data into the web server's response. You learned about this in: *Lesson 12-2: Output a file to the user's web browser.*

6 Test your code.

```
- <assembly>
    <name>MailModule</name>
  </assembly>
```

View *Files.aspx* in your web browser and click *View File* next to *MailModule.XML*. Click *Open* when prompted.

This time the XML file is decompressed by your C# code and is readable.

Lesson 12-9: Use the System.Drawing classes to manipulate images

Spam is a huge problem on the internet, even for web applications. Spammers will often create automated systems to send unwanted messages through forms on your pages. To prevent this, many websites use "Captcha" images. These are images that contain text that a human can read, but that can't be easily read by an automated system.

In the following lessons you'll create a Captcha image using the classes in the *System.Drawing* namespace.

1   Open *DotNetExpert* from your sample files folder.

2   Open *Captcha.aspx* in Design view.

Once complete, this page will contain a working Captcha system.

3   Switch to Source view and examine the *<img>* tag.

```
<br />
<img src="CaptchaImage/Captcha.jpg"
<br />
```

The Captcha image does not yet exist but will be created by your code and retrieved from the *CaptchaImage* folder.

4   Open *CaptchaHandler.cs* from the *CaptchaImage* folder.

This is an HTTP Handler. You learned about these in: *Lesson 8-5: Create an HTTP Handler*.

This HTTP Handler will output the *Captcha.jpg* image that is requested by the *Captcha.aspx* page.

5   Add a *using* line for: **System.Drawing**

You'll use the *System.Drawing* classes to draw your Captcha image.

```
using System.Web;
using System.Drawing;
using System.Drawing.Imaging;
```

6   Add a *using* line for: **System.Drawing.Imaging**

This namespace contains the image formats that you'll need when saving your image as a *.jpg* file.

7   Expand the *IHttpHandler Members* region and examine the *ProcessRequest* method.

```
public void ProcessRequest(HttpContext context)
{
    string CaptchaText = GetCaptchaText(8);
    context.Session["Captcha"] = CaptchaText;
}
```

The method retrieves some random text from the *GetCaptchaText* method and saves it into the user's *Session*.

8   Add code to the *ProcessRequest* method to create your Captcha image.

1. Add the following code to the end of the method:

   Bitmap CaptchaImage = new Bitmap(120, 25);

   ```
   context.Session["Captcha"] = CaptchaText;
   Bitmap CaptchaImage = new Bitmap(120, 25);
   ```

   This code creates a new image that is 120 pixels wide and 25 pixels high.

2. Add the following code on the next line:

   Graphics GraphicsObject = Graphics.FromImage(CaptchaImage);

   ```
   Bitmap CaptchaImage = new Bitmap(120, 25);
   Graphics GraphicsObject = Graphics.FromImage(CaptchaImage);
   ```

   The *Graphics* class is used to manipulate images.

3. Add the following code on the next line:

   GraphicsObject.FillRectangle (Brushes.White, new Rectangle(0, 0, 120, 25));

   ```
   Graphics GraphicsObject = Graphics.FromImage(CaptchaImage);
   GraphicsObject.FillRectangle
       (Brushes.White, new Rectangle(0, 0, 120, 25));
   ```

   This code fills the entire image with white. Images are filled with black by default.

4. Add the following code on the next line:

   Font CaptchaFont = new Font("Arial", 16);

   ```
       (Brushes.White, new Rectangle(0, 0, 120, 25));
   Font CaptchaFont = new Font("Arial", 16);
   ```

   This *Font* object will be used to draw text onto your image. You've selected the *Arial* font at size 16.

5. Add the following code on the next line:

   GraphicsObject.DrawString(CaptchaText, CaptchaFont, Brushes.Black, new PointF(0,0));

   ```
   Font CaptchaFont = new Font("Arial", 16);
   GraphicsObject.DrawString
       (CaptchaText, CaptchaFont, Brushes.Black, new PointF(0, 0));
   ```

   This code draws the text from the *CaptchaText* variable onto your image using the font that you selected in your *CaptchaFont* object.

   Brushes.Black writes the text in black. You could select a different color by using a different *Brush* object.

   PointF(0, 0) tells the method to draw the text starting in the top-left corner of the image (at coordinates 0,0).

Your Captcha image will now contain the random text, but it is still relatively easy for a spammer to extract the text from the image using OCR technology.

You'll add code to make the image harder to read and then display the image on the page in: *Lesson 12-10: Create a Captcha image system.*

```
    120, Randomizer.Next(0, 25));
GraphicsObject.DrawLine(LinePen,
    0, Randomizer.Next(0, 25),
    120, Randomizer.Next(0, 25));
```

Lesson 12-10: Create a Captcha image system

You used the classes in the *System.Drawing* namespace to create a basic Captcha image in: *Lesson 12-9: Use the System.Drawing classes to manipulate images*. In this lesson, you'll add code to make the image harder for an automated system to read. You'll then display it on a page and test its functionality.

1   Open *DotNetExpert* from your sample files folder.

2   Open *CaptchaHandler.cs* from the *CaptchaImage* folder.

This is the HTTP handler that will create and display the Captcha image.

At the moment, the code simply draws some random text onto the image. This Captcha image would be better if it were harder to read.

3   Add code to draw random lines over the text.

1. Add the following code to the end of the *ProcessRequest* event handler:

Pen LinePen = new Pen(Brushes.Black, 2);

```
    (CaptchaText, CaptchaFont, Brushes.Black, new PointF(0, 0));
Pen LinePen = new Pen(Brushes.Black, 2);
```

This *Pen* object will be used to draw the lines onto your image. You've selected a *Black* color and a thickness of 2 pixels.

Pen objects are used to draw lines while *Brush* objects are used to fill areas with color.

2. Add the following code on the next line:

GraphicsObject.DrawLine(LinePen,
0, Randomizer.Next(0, 25),
120, Randomizer.Next(0, 25));

```
Pen LinePen = new Pen(Brushes.Black, 2);
GraphicsObject.DrawLine(LinePen,
    0, Randomizer.Next(0, 25),
    120, Randomizer.Next(0, 25));
```

This code uses your *Pen* object to draw a line from a random point on the left side of the image to a random point on the right side of the image.

3. Add the same line of code again to draw a second line.

Two random lines will now be drawn over the top of your Captcha image, making it significantly harder for an automated system to read.

4   Add code to output the image.

1. Add the following code on the next line:

CaptchaImage.Save(context.Response.OutputStream,
ImageFormat.Jpeg);

```
     120, Randomizer.Next(0, 25));
CaptchaImage.Save
    (context.Response.OutputStream, ImageFormat.Jpeg);
```

This code saves the image into the web server's response.

ImageFormat.Jpeg comes from the *System.Drawing.Imaging* namespace. This will save the image in JPEG format.

2. Add the following code on the next line:

context.Response.End();

```
CaptchaImage.Save
    (context.Response.OutputStream, ImageFormat.Jpeg);
context.Response.End();
```

Now that the image has been saved into the web server's response, it's good practice to end the response so that nothing else can be added to it. You've done this previously in: *Lesson 12-2: Output a file to the user's web browser.*

5 View *Captcha.aspx* in your web browser.

The image appears, but you still need to add code to the *Confirm* button to check whether the user has entered the correct code.

6 Add code to check whether the correct code was entered.

You may recall that the Captcha image's text is saved into the *Session* object when it is generated by the *CaptchaHandler* class.

1. Close your web browser and return to Visual Studio.

2. Open *Captcha.aspx* in Design view.

3. Add a *Click* event handler to the *ButtonConfirm* control.

4. Add the following code to the new event handler:

**if (TextBoxCaptchaAnswer.Text ==
Session["Captcha"].ToString())
{
    LabelResult.Text = "Correct!";
}
else LabelResult.Text = "Incorrect!";**

```
protected void ButtonConfirm_Click(object sender, EventArgs e)
{
    if (TextBoxCaptchaAnswer.Text == Session["Captcha"].ToString())
    {
        LabelResult.Text = "Correct!";
    }
    else LabelResult.Text = "Incorrect!";
}
```

7 Test your code.

1. View *Captcha.aspx* in your web browser.

2. Enter the correct code in the text box.

3. Click *Confirm*.

If you entered the correct code, *Correct!* is displayed.

note

Google's reCAPTCHA control

Google offer their own captcha control called *reCAPTCHA*. It is likely that you have seen this while using the internet.

Google offer an ASP.NET Web User Control that allows you to very easily integrate *reCAPTCHA* into your web sites.

If you don't want to go to the effort of creating your own captcha system, *reCAPTCHA* is an excellent alternative.

note

The Graphics class is capable of much more

The *Graphics* class isn't limited to simply drawing lines and text.

Using the advanced features of the *Graphics* class, you can manipulate images in any way imaginable.

Lesson 12-11: Create a page that can upload multiple files

You already know how to upload a single file using the *FileUpload* control, but uploading multiple files can be more difficult.

You could simply use multiple *FileUpload* controls, but that isn't an ideal solution. In this lesson you'll learn how to enable your users to upload as many files as they need.

1   Open *DotNetExpert* from your sample files folder.

2   Open *Files.aspx* in Design view.

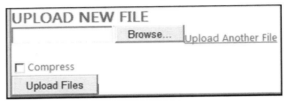

When the user clicks *Upload Another File*, another upload control should appear, enabling them to upload as many files as are needed.

You'll make this happen by using JavaScript and *JQuery*. You learned about *JQuery* in: *Lesson 9-9: Understand JQuery*.

3   Switch to Source view.

4   Examine the existing code.

```
<asp:FileUpload ID="FileUploadNewFile" runat="server" /
<span id="FileUploads"></span>
<a onclick="AddFileUpload(); return false;" style="text-
<br />
```

When the *Upload Another File* link is clicked, the *AddFileUpload* JavaScript function is called.

Notice that there is an empty *<span>* tag named *FileUploads*. This is where the JavaScript function will place the new upload controls.

5   Add code to the *AddFileUpload* JavaScript function to add a new upload control to the page.

Add the following code to the *AddFileUpload* JavaScript function:

**$("#FileUploads").append
('
<input type="file" runat="server" />');**

```
<script type="text/javascript">
    function AddFileUpload() {
        $("#FileUploads").append
        ('<br /><input type="file" runat="server" />');
    }
</script>
```

This *JQuery* code will add the following HTML code to the *<span>* tag that you noticed earlier:

*
<input type="file" runat="server" />*

<input type="file" /> is the HTML tag that ASP.NET generates from the *FileUpload* control.

Note that the *<input>* tag must have *runat="server"* in order for ASP.NET to extract the file when it is sent to the server.

6   Test your code.

1. View *Files.aspx* in your web browser.

2. Click *Browse* and browse to your sample files folder.

3. Click *AdvancedMath.XML* and click *Open*.

4. Click *Upload Another File*.

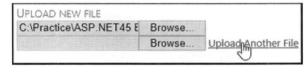

A second upload control appears on the page. You can click *Upload Another File* as many times as you like, enabling you to upload as many files as you need.

5. Click *Browse* on the new upload control and browse to your sample files folder.

6. Click *AdvancedMath.dll* and click *Open*.

7. Click *Upload Files*.

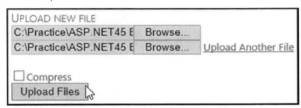

AdvancedMath.XML is uploaded, but *AdvancedMath.dll* is not.

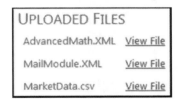

This page's C# code is not yet capable of handling multiple uploads.

You'll add code to extract every uploaded file from the *Request* object in the next lesson: *Lesson 12-12: Extract multiple files from a request*.

Lesson 12-12: Extract multiple files from a request

You learned how to create a page that can upload an unlimited number of files in: *Lesson 12-11: Create a page that can upload multiple files.*

In this lesson you'll add C# code that will extract the uploaded files and save them into the database.

1   Open *DotNetExpert* from your sample files folder.

2   Open the code-behind file of *Files.aspx*.

3   Remove all code from the *ButtonUploadFile_Click* event handler.

4   Add code to handle multiple files.

1.   Add the following code to the *ButtonUploadFile_Click* event handler:

HttpFileCollection UploadedFiles = Request.Files;

```
protected void ButtonUploadFile_Click(object sender,
{
    HttpFileCollection UploadedFiles = Request.Files;
```

This code retrieves the uploaded files from every control on the page, placing them in the *UploadedFiles* collection.

2.   On the next line, add the following *using* statement:

using (DotNetExpertDataContext Data = new DotNetExpertDataContext()) { }

```
HttpFileCollection UploadedFiles = Request.Files;
using (DotNetExpertDataContext Data =
    new DotNetExpertDataContext())
{
}
```

3.   Add the following *for* loop inside the *using* statement:

for (int Counter = 0; Counter < UploadedFiles.Count; Counter++) { }

```
    new DotNetExpertDataContext())
{
    for (int Counter = 0; Counter < UploadedFiles.Count; Counter++)
    {
    }
```

This *for* loop iterates through each file that was uploaded.

4.   Add the following code inside the *for* statement:

HttpPostedFile UploadedFile = UploadedFiles[Counter];

```
for (int Counter = 0; Counter < UploadedFiles.Count; Counter++)
{
    HttpPostedFile UploadedFile = UploadedFiles[Counter];
}
```

This code retrieves each file from the *UploadedFiles* collection and places them into the *UploadedFile* object.

5.   Add the following *if* statement on the next line:

if (UploadedFile.ContentLength > 0) { }

```
HttpPostedFile UploadedFile = UploadedFiles[Counter];
if (UploadedFile.ContentLength > 0)
{

}
```

This *if* statement confirms that the file is not empty.

6. Add the following code inside the *if* statement:

byte[] UploadedBytes = new byte[UploadedFile.ContentLength]; UploadedFile.InputStream.Read (UploadedBytes, 0, UploadedFile.ContentLength);

```
if (UploadedFile.ContentLength > 0) {
    byte[] UploadedBytes = new byte[UploadedFile.ContentLength];
    UploadedFile.InputStream.Read
        (UploadedBytes, 0, UploadedFile.ContentLength);
}
```

This code reads the binary data from each file and stores it in the *UploadedBytes* array.

7. Add the following code to send the files to the database:

UploadedFile NewFile = new UploadedFile(); NewFile.UploadedFileName = Path.GetFileName(UploadedFile.FileName); NewFile.UploadedFileBytes = UploadedBytes; Data.UploadedFiles.InsertOnSubmit(NewFile);

```
        UploadedFile.ContentLength);
UploadedFile NewFile = new UploadedFile();
NewFile.UploadedFileName = Path.GetFileName(UploadedFile.FileName);
NewFile.UploadedFileBytes = UploadedBytes;
Data.UploadedFiles.InsertOnSubmit(NewFile);
```

8. Add the following code after the end of the *for* loop:

Data.SubmitChanges(); GridViewUploadedFile.DataBind();

```
            Data.UploadedFiles.InsertOnSubmit(NewFile);
        }
    }
Data.SubmitChanges();
GridViewUploadedFile.DataBind();
```

This code commits the records to the database and refreshes the *GridView* control on the page.

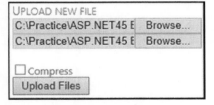

5   Test your code.

1. View *Files.aspx* in your web browser.

2. Click *Browse* and browse to your sample files folder.

3. Click *AdvancedMath.dll* and click *Open*.

4. Click *Upload Another File*.

5. Click *Browse* in the new upload control, select *MailModule.dll* and click *Open*.

6. Click *Upload Files*.

This time both files are uploaded to the system.

Session 12: Exercise

1   Open *Exercise12* from your sample files folder.

2   Open *CompressFile.aspx* in Design view and add a *Click* event handler to the *ButtonCompress* control.

3   Add code to the new event handler to compress the file from the *FileUploadCompress* control.

4   Add code to output the compressed file to the user's web browser.

5   Open *Global.asax*.

6   Add a new static method to *Global.asax* that runs the *CleanUp.bat* program.

7   Add code to the *Application_Start* event handler that will run the new method every hour.

8   Open *MultiUpload.aspx* in Source view.

9   Add code to the *AddFile* JavaScript function to add a new upload control to the *Uploads <span>* tag.

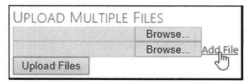

10   Open the code-behind file of *XMLConfiguration.aspx*.

11   Add code to the *ButtonLoadConfiguration_Click* event handler to deserialize the *Configuration.xml* file into the *LoadedConfiguration* object.

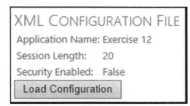

12   Open *BannerHandler.cs* from the *BannerImage* folder.

13   Add code to the *ProcessRequest* method to create and output an image.

        The image should be **700** pixels wide and **75** pixels high.

        The image should use the **Arial** font at size **60**

        The image should contain the text: **The Smart Method**

14   View *Banner.aspx* in your web browser to view the image.

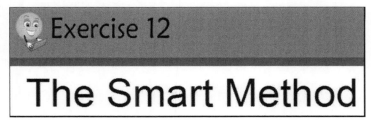

Exercise12 - Start   Exercise12 - End

If you need help slide the page to the left ➡

Session 12: Exercise Answers

These are the three questions that students find the most difficult to answer:

Q 13	Q 6, 7	Q 3, 4

Use the following code:
 	
Bitmap CaptchaImage = new Bitmap(700, 75);
Graphics GraphicsObject = Graphics.FromImage (CaptchaImage);
GraphicsObject.FillRectangle (Brushes.White,
new Rectangle(0, 0, 700, 75));
Font CaptchaFont = new Font("Arial", 60);
GraphicsObject.DrawString (BannerText, CaptchaFont,
Brushes.Black,
new PointF(0, 0));
CaptchaImage.Save (context.Response. OutputStream, ImageFormat.Jpeg);
context.Response.End();
 	
This was covered in: *Lesson 12-9: Use the System.Drawing classes to manipulate images and Lesson 12-10: Create a Captcha image system.*
	1. Create the method using the following code:
	
	static void RunCleanUp(object sender)
	{
	    Process CleanUp = Process.Start(
	    ((HttpContext)sender). Server.MapPath ("~/CleanUp.bat"));
	}
	
	2. Add the following code to the *Application_Start* event handler:
	
	Timer CleanUpTimer = new Timer(new TimerCallback (RunCleanUp), HttpContext.Current, 0, 3600000);
	
	This was covered in: *Lesson 12-3: Run an external program and Lesson 12-4: Create a scheduled event using a Timer object.*
		Use the following code:
		
		MemoryStream CompressedStream = new MemoryStream();
		GZipStream Compressor = new GZipStream(CompressedStream, CompressionMode.Compress);
		Compressor.Write(FileUploadFileToCompress. FileBytes, 0, FileUploadFileToCompress.FileBytes. Length);
		byte[] CompressedBytes = CompressedStream.ToArray();
		Response.AddHeader ("content-disposition", "attachment;filename=" + FileUploadFileToCompress. FileName);
		Response.BinaryWrite (CompressedBytes);
		Response.End();
		
		This was covered in: *Lesson 12-7: Compress a file and Lesson 12-2: Output a file to the user's web browser.*

If you have difficulty with the other questions, here are the lessons that cover the relevant skills:

1   Refer to: Essential Skills Session 1.

2   Refer to: Essential Skills Session 3.

5   Refer to: Essential Skills Session 12.

8   Refer to: Essential Skills Session 1.

9   Refer to: Lesson 12-11: Create a page that can upload multiple files.

10   Refer to: Essential Skills Session 1.

11   Refer to: Lesson 12-6: Deserialize an XML file back into an object.

12   Refer to: Essential Skills Session 1.

14   Refer to: Essential Skills Session 1.

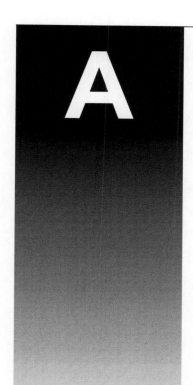

Appendix A: Skills Covered in the Essential Skills Course

You have to learn to crawl before you can walk.
You have to learn to walk before you can run.

Proverbs, unknown authors

In order to get the most out of this book you should already be very comfortable with the main features of ASP.NET, C# and Visual Studio. We also have an *Essential Skills* course for absolute beginners.

ISBN: 978-1-909253-04-9
380 pages.

ISBN: 978-1-909253-05-6
390 pages. (This book).

This (Expert Skills) book assumes that you have already mastered the skills taught in the *Essential Skills* book.

So how do you know if your skills are already advanced enough to tackle this book?

This appendix lists the objectives for each of the seven sessions in the *Essential Skills* course.

If you already have all (or at least most) of the skills taught in the *Essential Skills* course, you are ready to upgrade your skills to Expert level with this course.

Essential skills course outline

Session 1

- Install Visual Studio
- Check your Visual Studio and Windows version
- Set up the development environment and download the sample files
- Set up Windows for development
- Create an ASP.NET Web Forms Application project
- Create an ASP.NET Web Forms Site project
- Manage a project with the Solution Explorer
- Add and remove files from a project
- Run a project in debug mode
- View .aspx pages in Source and Design views
- Use automatic formatting
- Expand and collapse code regions
- Change properties in Design view
- Change properties in Source view
- Add controls to a page with the Toolbox
- Use the QuickTasks menu
- Get help

Session 2

- Understand HTML bold, italic and heading tags
- Understand HTML paragraph and break tags
- Understand the aspx page structure
- Use the title, meta, link and script tags
- Create an HTML table
- Navigate HTML with the tag navigator
- Display images and links on a page
- Work with CSS
- Use the CSS Properties window
- Use the div and span tags
- Work with JavaScript
- Work with HTML forms

Session 3

- Change properties with C#
- Add event handlers to controls
- Use Breakpoints
- Use Watches and Locals
- Understand the Exception object
- Understand the Page object
- Understand Request and Response
- Understand PostBack
- Work with ViewState
- Move between pages using C#
- Send data between pages
- Use Session
- Edit the Web.config file

Session 4

- Name controls correctly
- Use the Button control
- Use the Label and Literal controls
- Use the TextBox control
- Use the CheckBox control
- Use the RadioButton control
- Use the DropDownList control
- Use the RequiredFieldValidator control
- Use the RangeValidator and ValidationSummary controls
- Use common properties

Session 5

- Use IntelliSense
- Create a variable
- Use string variables properties and methods
- Use integer variables
- Use floating point variables
- Use Boolean variables
- Use DateTime variables
- Convert variables using Convert and Parse
- Convert variables using cast and ToString

- Perform basic mathematical operations
- Use the Math library for advanced mathematics
- Understand null
- Use object and var variables

Session 6

- Create a class
- Create an instance of a class
- Use the .NET framework
- Work with namespaces
- Create and use methods
- Create methods with arguments
- Create methods that return a value
- Create a private method
- Create a static method
- Create and dispose of instances
- Create a class constructor method

Session 7

- Use the if statement
- Use else and else if
- Use basic logical operators
- Use advanced logic
- Use get and set
- Use try and catch to handle errors
- Use comments
- Use summaries

Session 8

- Create an array
- Create a collection
- Iterate through a collection using foreach
- Iterate through a collection using a for loop
- Iterate through a collection using a while loop
- Use break and return

Session 9

- Use .NET's built-in security features
- Manage a site with ASP.NET Configuration
- Change authentication types
- Use the Login control
- Customize the Login control
- Use the CreateUserWizard control
- Use other login controls
- Add folder-level security
- Set up roles
- Use C# to limit access
- Use the security wizard

Session 10

- Work with SQL databases in Visual Studio
- Add LINQ data classes to a project
- Retrieve a single row of data using LINQ
- Retrieve multiple rows of data using LINQ
- Sort results and call stored procedures using LINQ
- Check whether a record exists using LINQ
- Update database records using LINQ
- Insert database records using LINQ
- Delete database records using LINQ
- Use LINQ with collections

Session 11

- Use the LinqDataSource control
- Attach a data source to a control
- Use the GridView control
- Add sorting and paging to a GridView
- Add editing features to a GridView
- Use the DetailsView control
- Use the SqlDataSource control
- Bind data to a control using C# code

Session 12

- Use master pages

- Handle errors with Global.asax
- Understand Web Optimization
- Understand FriendlyUrls
- Log errors to a database
- Create a Products page
- Create a Shopping Cart
- Create a Search page
- Add functionality to a Search page
- Create a Checkout page
- Create a Payment page
- Implement security
- Publish a site

Index

B

C

P

The Essential Skills book isn't only for beginners! Experts find it useful too.

Many purchasers of *Expert Skills* decide to also purchase the *Essential Skills* book (the first book in this series). *Essential Skills* isn't only for ASP.NET beginners. I often teach this course (as a classroom course) to professionals that have used ASP.NET for over ten years and they *always* gain some fantastically useful skills from the course.

While *Expert Skills* is aimed at users that are already comfortable with ASP.NET, *Essential Skills* assumes no previous exposure to ASP.NET, C# or Visual Studio and teaches all of the core skills. This is usually enough for a junior developer.

Turn back a few pages to *Appendix A* and you'll find a summary of all lessons taught in the *Essential Skills* book.

Search for it at **Amazon.com** or **Amazon.co.uk**.

You can also find links to book resellers stocking this title at the **ASPNETCentral.com** web site (click *Books* on the top menu bar).

ASPNETCentral.com

For many years I have dreamed of creating an online learning resource that would provide the same experience as my classroom courses.

My books cover the same material as my classroom courses, but it is clear that some learners need more than can be delivered via printed media. In 2013 we began the design of an ASP.NET Internet resource that aims to bring my classroom courses onto your desktop.

The site is available at: **www.ASPNETCentral.com**

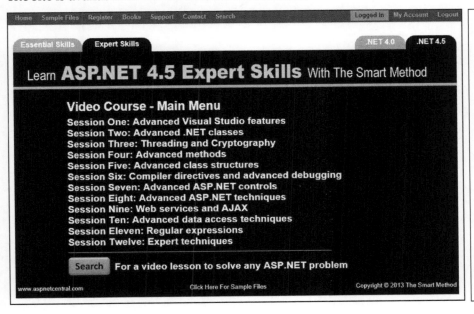

On the site I have recorded a video walk-through for each and every lesson in this book. The videos have also been indexed by keyword to provide a unique interactive ASP.NET reference resource.

Lessons can be viewed without cost by using our *FreeView* facility.

Enhanced features can also be unlocked for a small annual subscription

Printed in Great Britain
by Amazon.co.uk, Ltd.,
Marston Gate.